MW01599036

SPARTA AND WAR

SPARTA
&
WAR

Editors

Stephen Hodkinson

and

Anton Powell

Contributors

Jacqueline Christien, Jean Ducat, Thomas J. Figueira,
Stephen Hodkinson, Noreen Humble, Polly Low,
Marcello Lupi, Ellen Millender, Anton Powell,
Françoise Ruzé

The Classical Press of Wales

First published in 2006 by
The Classical Press of Wales
15 Rosehill Terrace, Swansea SA1 6JN
Tel: +44 (0)1792 458397
Fax: +44 (0)1792 464067
www.classicalpressofwales.co.uk

Distributor in the United States of America:
The David Brown Book Co.
PO Box 511, Oakville, CT 06779
Tel: +1 (860) 945–9329
Fax: +1 (860) 945–9468

ISBN 1-905125-11-9

A catalogue record for this book is available from the British Library

Typeset by Ernest Buckley, Clunton, Shropshire
Printed and bound in the UK by Gomer Press, Llandysul, Ceredigion, Wales

––––––––––––

*The Classical Press of Wales, an independent venture, was founded in 1993, initially to support the
work of classicists and ancient historians in Wales and their collaborators from further afield. More
recently it has published work initiated by scholars internationally. While retaining a special loyalty to
Wales and the Celtic countries, the Press welcomes scholarly contributions from all parts of the world.*

The symbol of the Press is the Red Kite. This bird, once widespread in Britain, was reduced by 1905 to some
five individuals confined to a small area known as 'The Desert of Wales' – the upper Tywi valley. Geneticists
report that the stock was saved from terminal inbreeding by the arrival of one stray female bird from Germany.
After much careful protection, the Red Kite now thrives – in Wales and beyond.

CONTENTS

Contents

INTRODUCTION

Stephen Hodkinson

The papers in this volume were originally given at the Fifth International Sparta Seminar held on 1st–4th September 2004 at the Université de Rennes II. The first two meetings of the Sparta Seminar took place in the form of specialized conferences in Cardiff in 1991 and Hay-on-Wye in 1997 (subsequently published as Powell and Hodkinson 1994; Hodkinson and Powell 1999). From the Third International Sparta Seminar onwards, our meetings have taken place as a panel within the recently-founded Celtic Conference in Classics: at Maynooth in 2000 (published as Powell and Hodkinson 2002), Glasgow in 2002 (Figueira 2004), and Rennes in 2004. The establishment of a long-term home for the Sparta Seminar within the framework of the Celtic Conferences provides for its future continuity through a regular series of biennial meetings. The Sixth International Sparta Seminar takes place around the time of publication of this volume, at the Fourth Celtic Conference at the University of Wales, Lampeter in late summer 2006; and initial plans are under way for our seventh Seminar, to be held at the Fifth Celtic Conference at the National University of Ireland, Cork, in summer 2008.

Placing the seminar within the Celtic Conferences also reflects our belief that the development of Spartan historical research is best served by interaction with scholars working in other fields of classical and ancient historical studies. Since the format of the Celtic Conferences gives participants in each panel the opportunity to attend sessions of other panels, the papers in this volume were given to, and have benefited from discussion by, audiences embracing both Spartan specialists and a range of experts in other fields. In addition, Anton Powell's paper was the opening general keynote address to the Rennes conference.

The first Sparta Seminar in 1991 (published as *The Shadow of Sparta*) took as its subject a specified subject: images of Sparta as reflected in the thought of other Greeks. At the following three seminars participants were given the freedom to select the subjects and themes they judged most pressing in Spartan research. For the Fifth International Sparta Seminar we decided to return to the original conception by choosing a particular theme: Sparta and War.

Behind this choice lay several academic reasons, personal and generic, immediate and longer-term. A long-term perspective of Powell's work – manifested in the sub-title of his first edited volume on Sparta, *Classical Sparta: Techniques behind her success* (Powell 1989) – has been an awareness of the unusual and effective procedures which enabled her to achieve such extraordinary success (considering her size) in the face of major enduring difficulties. Sparta's policy and practice in the field of war were undoubtedly among the most important 'techniques behind her success' – techniques not explored in the 1989 volume, but which he had recently begun to address in his contribution to the Fourth International Sparta Seminar on the subject of Spartan women and war (Powell 2004).

Military aspects of Spartan society have also been an occasional theme of my own previous research. My first published article on Sparta included discussion of the social implications of her military organization and the behaviour of her commanders abroad (Hodkinson 1983); and a subsequent article examined the impact of her prolonged engagement in foreign warfare during the late fifth and early fourth centuries on the growth of Sparta's internal social crisis (Hodkinson 1993). The decision to expand this occasional interest into a more concerted focus on the theme of 'Sparta and war' has been influenced by intellectual currents within the universities of Manchester and Nottingham. The theme for the present volume was initially conceived within the context of the creation, by the School of History and Classics at the University of Manchester, of a new Centre for the Cultural History of War.[1] (This is an appropriate point to acknowledge the academic and financial support that the International Sparta Seminars received from the University of Manchester during the first twelve years of their existence.) It has subsequently come to fruition following my move to the Department of Classics at the University of Nottingham: a department with a strong and longstanding expertise in Graeco-Roman warfare which had been jointly responsible for the volume from a seminar series on 'War and Society in the Ancient World', in which my 1993 article was published (Rich and Shipley 1993). The theme also fits well with the Department's current project on 'Sparta in Comparative Perspective, Ancient to Modern', in which the history and tradition of Sparta's military orientation, both real and imagined, are central issues.

Our choice of theme, we felt, was also highly appropriate for a conference to be held at the Université de Rennes II, the academic home for so many years of the distinguished social historian of ancient Greece, Yvon Garlan. Garlan's three books on ancient Greek warfare (*La Guerre dans l'antiquité*, *Recherches de poliorcétique grecque* and *Guerre et économie en Grèce ancienne*) – the first of which was published as early as 1972 – were ahead of their time in their focus, not so much on the details of equipment, technology and battle, as on war and military organization in their changing socio-economic, political and ideological contexts.[2]

Beyond these personal and contingent factors, however, our choice of 'Sparta and war' was influenced by our perception of a significant gap in recent Spartan historiography – a general paucity of studies exploring the interaction of war and society of the kind that Garlan provided a generation ago for Greece as a whole.

This gap in modern research is in some respects surprising, since the role of war has been a central theme in representations of Spartan society from antiquity to the present. The earliest literary evidence from archaic Sparta, the poetry of Tyrtaios, revolves around the military role of Spartan citizens and their duty to fight for the community. The alleged orientation of Spartan education and society towards war and empire is a significant theme in Plato's *Laws* and Aristotle's *Politics*. Images of fearsome Spartan mothers commanding their sons to return with their shields or on them, cheerfully burying their fallen menfolk or killing them on their cowardly return were a favourite topic of Hellenistic anecdotes and epigrams. Within the Roman Empire real or imagined Spartan military debates were prominent themes of rhetorical exercises, such as declamations and educational *progymnasmata* ('preparatory exercises'), from the first century AD to late antiquity. In Renaissance and early modern Europe Sparta's citizen militia formed an important model in the political thought of Machiavelli and classical republican theorists in England and France. Nineteenth-century liberal thought, in contrast, typecast Sparta's society as a warlike brotherhood; whilst theorists of social evolution such as Herbert Spencer categorized her as a classic case of the militant type of society in opposition to the modern industrial state. In the 1930s and 1940s Sparta was evoked by Nazi ideologists as a model of a military master race; and, conversely, German self-identification with Sparta was taken up eagerly by contemporary British intellectuals who portrayed both societies as reactionary militaristic land powers. Within U.S. Cold War defence analysis Sparta was frequently invoked as an ideal type for interpreting the Soviet Union as an economy and society in which military needs received first priority. Through all these periods the death of the 300 at Thermopylai has stood as a defining example of the character of Spartan society, embodying heroic military self-sacrifice in obedience to the law.

The role of war in Spartan society and policy was a central element in the two studies which inaugurated the modern era of Spartan historical research. Moses Finley's 1968 essay – which appeared in the edited volume, *Problèmes de la Guerre en Grèce Ancienne* – was a magisterial attempt to view the nature and significance of Sparta's military characteristics within the overall context of her social institutions. Ste Croix's 1972 book, *The Origins of the Peloponnesian War*, grounded a profound examination of Sparta's policy towards Athens in an interpretation of the military pressures deriving from her internal exploitation of the helots and the character of the Peloponnesian league. However, the resurgence of Spartan research stimulated by these seminal studies has, with certain exceptions, left the military aspects of Spartan society and policy to one side.

This was in part a consequence of Finley's and Ste Croix's own work. Finley argued that classical Sparta's military institutions were not in themselves the most distinctive or pivotal element of her citizen organization; and Ste Croix's study demonstrated that a proper investigation of her strategic policy required an understanding of its roots in her socio-economic and political structures. Prompted by these conclusions, the considerable outpouring of new research on Sparta since the 1970s has focused primarily upon issues of economy, society and culture. It has provided insights into a wider range of aspects of Spartan society than ever before: its alimentary customs, artistic and material culture, educational system, foreign connections, matrimonial and sexual practices, political organization, property system, religious cults, settlement patterns, subject populations – and much else besides. In place of older images of a narrow and limited society, these studies have given us a richer perception of the breadth, and sometimes even the diversity, of Spartan social life.

In contrast, classical Sparta's military institutions have been relatively neglected. Paul Cartledge's studies have shed important light on the development of those institutions in the archaic period;[3] and there have been several studies of the army's organization and military campaigns.[4] But, with certain exceptions, especially within French scholarship,[5] there has been little study of the impact of war on Spartan society or the interaction between her military and social organization and culture. As a consequence, whilst our comprehension of other aspects of Spartan society has been significantly renewed, and often revolutionized, over the course of the last generation, current understandings of Sparta's engagement in the sphere of war have remained largely unchanged.

This comparative neglect has not, of course, been confined to the history of Sparta. As recently as 1999, the editors of a volume on *War and Society in the Ancient and Medieval Worlds* could assert that 'scholars of antiquity had focused rarely and then only selectively on how the experience of war and the needs of military organization affected and were affected by their broader social milieux'.[6] As they noted, the paucity of studies on the relation between ancient Greek (and Roman) war and society was, in one sense, surprising because the interaction between military practices and institutions and their economic, social and cultural contexts has long been regarded as axiomatic by anthropologists, sociologists, and students of medieval and modern warfare. Even these fields, however, were affected by the tendency of historians in the second half of the twentieth century to treat 'military history' as a separate, traditional, elite-orientated, and somewhat inferior area of research in comparison with newer, vibrant fields such as social history and women's history – fields which aimed to view history 'from below' and (in their early years at least) largely shunned the sphere of war. This historiographical tendency – which influenced the direction of my own early research – took place against a broader contemporary backdrop of Western intellectual disenchantment with war and the 'military establishment', in the context of the Vietnam War, the escalating nuclear arms race, and the development of the Peace Movement.

In recent years, especially since the end of the Cold War, many of the barriers separating military and other branches of history have broken down. Military history, at least at the level of professional historiography, is undergoing a process of reinvention (Black 2004); and the experience of war, both 'from below' and 'from above', is a frequent theme in historical curricula and research. At the time when we were planning the Rennes seminar in winter 2002/03, we were aware that in ancient Greek history too the previous paucity of studies of the wider context of war was in process of being remedied by the recent or prospective publication of a number of pertinent edited volumes or monographs.[7] The time, we judged, was therefore ripe for a thematic seminar which would give historians of classical Sparta the opportunity to reassess the nature and role of her military institutions, practice and policy in the light of the revised understandings of the character of Spartan society that have developed over the last thirty years.

The enthusiastic response to our chosen theme, both from Spartan specialists and from scholars coming to the subject from other areas of expertise, reassured us of the accuracy of our judgement. In this volume we publish articles developed from ten of the papers given at Rennes. But the seminar also profited from five other papers (by Pamela de Condappa, Edmond Lévy, Nicolas Richer, Stefan Stanke, and Hans van Wees) which enriched our understanding of further aspects of our theme: warrior bodies and the creation of Spartan identity; Sparta in Plato; the Gymnopaidiai; representations of Spartan generals in Xenophon's *Hellenika*; and myths and realities of the Spartan army. One notable aspect of the profile of participants, apart from the Sparta Seminars' customary international representation, is its gender balance: on a theme traditionally thought more appealing to men, forty per cent of the papers at Rennes and half the articles in this volume are the work of women. Interestingly, despite this academic gender balance, the papers both here and at Rennes focus overwhelmingly on the practice and experience of war by Spartiate men.

The articles in the volume fall into three broad, though overlapping, sub-themes: war and society; military and civic geography; military practice and policy.

War and society. The four articles in this section deal with various aspects of the question of how Sparta's military practices in the sphere of war impinged upon and were moulded by the character of her civic society. The opening couple of papers discuss two distinct groups of citizens whose military performance earned them contrasting lifestyles and social opportunities. JEAN DUCAT discusses the group of citizens known to modern scholarship as the *tresantes* ('tremblers'), men judged guilty of cowardice in the face of battle. Despite (or perhaps because of) the apparent normative standing of Damaratos' famous pronouncement in Herodotus' *Histories* that Spartan warriors were commanded by law either to conquer or to die, there has been no previous detailed study of the range of evidence for the treatment and status of those men who failed to live up to this standard. Their treatment by the polis, Ducat shows, was by no means consistent, nor was their status as clear-cut as the sources' accounts would lead us to expect: so much so that Ducat expresses his doubt whether the *tresantes* ever existed as a general status. Useful as an ideological tool and as exemplary punishment for the errant behaviour of prominent individuals, the practicality of the harsh penalties claimed in general statements by ancient writers diminished when the behaviour of larger numbers of soldiers was concerned, especially in the face of Sparta's growing manpower shortage. In practice, Sparta's treatment of cowards in his day may not have differed as sharply from Athenian practice as Xenophon asserts.

THOMAS FIGUEIRA discusses a very different group of citizens (mainly young men in their 20s) whose achievements in the upbringing and army had gained them the conspicuous honour of selection for the corps of the 300 *hippeis*, which formed the lifeguard of Spartan kings. Despite their title, the *hippeis* of the classical period were no longer cavalry like their earlier pred-ecessors, but hoplite foot-soldiers: a change that probably took place as part of the broader re-organization of Spartan society in the later archaic period which entailed the harmonization of elite lifestyles and behaviours with those of the mass of citizens. From this point onwards the *hippeis* no longer came exclusively from wealthy families, but were chosen on merit in an annual process of selection in which three commanders known as the *hippagretai* each chose a personal contingent of 100 men. As Figueira's analysis indicates, the *hippeis* embody a close integration of the military and civic spheres. They acted as a military unit, either independently or as the king's lifeguard within the larger Spartan army; but they also served other public functions. They appear as an internal police force and are credited by one source as playing a counter-balancing political role within Sparta's mixed constitution. The process of their selection was a civic event, in which the reasons given for selection or rejection no doubt covered their performance in both military and non-military spheres. As with the *tresantes*, the institution's significance was weakened by the decline of Spartiate numbers, compelling their military integration with the standard citizen regiments at the same time as selection became less significant as a mark of social prestige owing to the reduced numbers of eligible citizens.

The categories of persons discussed by Ducat and Figueira were both distinctively Spartan. In contrast, the category of persons analysed in POLLY LOW's article, the war-dead, was clearly common to all Greek poleis. Yet, she argues, Sparta's modes of commemorating her war-dead fit into her political landscape in distinctive ways. Focusing on the period before the region's first external invasion in 370/69 BC (a period in which all Sparta's wars were fought outside, or at worst on the margins of, Lakonian territory), she notes an interesting differentiation between internal and external commemorations. The bodies of fallen warriors were given official burial away from Sparta, in collective tombs on the site of the battlefield or in nearby allied states. These tombs served public purposes: marking the borders of Spartan territory or the sites of Spartan victories and, even in the case of defeats, cementing alliances through a visible reminder to allied states that Spartans had died in defence of their lands. With the burial of the war-dead and its associated public ceremonial reserved for external contexts, commemoration inside Lakonia took on a different form, one unique to the region. This form was characterized by modestly sized, plainly decorated and sparsely inscribed memorial stones commemorating individual soldiers, some set up in Sparta itself, but others dispersed around Lakonia. These stones were probably private memorials put up by the kin of the deceased, which acted as sites of mourning and personal commemoration in the absence of a body, and also as modest tokens of family prestige at their kinsman's noble death. Though operating within the constraints imposed by the polis, they constitute a 'bottom-up' commemoration of military death which contrasts with the way that such commemorations were conducted in Athens and in many other poleis.

The papers of Ducat, Figueira and Low share at least two points of similarity. In method, each conducts its initial arguments through careful exposition and close interrogation of the relevant texts – whether literary or epigraphic – before proceeding to an examination of broader synthetic issues. In substance, each paper raises interesting and important questions about the interrelationship between the aspects of their subject that pertain specifically to the conduct of war (for example, the *hippeis'* roles on campaign, or the military factors behind the treatment of cowards and the war-dead) and those aspects that pertain to peacetime civic functions or to private concerns (the *hippeis'* policing and political roles and their members' prestige as an internal elite; the civic sanctions on cowards and their personal disgrace; the limits on family commemoration of their fallen kin). Similar methodological procedures and substantive issues characterize my own paper, which addresses the consistent tendency in twentieth-century historical scholarship and political ideology to view classical Sparta as a militaristic society, a polis which differed from other Greek states in its predominant concentration on military concerns. Tracing the development of contemporary representations of Spartan society from Tyrtaios to Aristotle, I argue that the earlier ancient sources viewed Sparta's military characteristics in primarily civic terms; and that perceptions of the overwhelmingly military orientation of her society emerged only later, in the politicized contexts of the Peloponnesian war and Sparta's early-fourth-century empire; and that even then such perceptions were not unqualified or unchallenged. In a subsequent synthetic analysis of the Spartiates' preparations for war and other facets of their society, I suggest that the military elements in Spartan life were significant, but not dominant over other aspects of their civic arrangements. A Spartiate's role as a warrior was only part, albeit an important part, of a wider range of citizen activities and duties: to borrow the succinct formulation of Jean Ducat (1999, 36), he was not so much a professional warrior as a professional citizen.

Military and civic geography. The articles in this section both address, though in very different ways, important spatial aspects of the interaction between Sparta's civic and military arrangements. JACQUELINE CHRISTIEN's paper distils the fruits of many years of first-hand topographical research in the Lakonian countryside and brings together a mass of disparate evidence scattered across diverse archaeological publications into a global survey of Sparta's fortifications and frontiers in the fourth century BC. The study of Sparta's historical geography offers, she believes, one means of unblocking the obstacles to our understanding created by the mirage rooted in most of the literary texts: especially in the late classical period, when the undermining of Sparta's hegemony made the defence of her extensive territory a pressing concern and archaeological evidence for the region's fortifications first appears in significant quantity. Retracing the development of her earlier studies, she records how she became aware that in Sparta's different border regions the configuration of fortified places created various lines of defence linked to the presence of key routes stretching towards and beyond the confines of Spartan territory: routes identifiable through a combination of traces on the ground and descriptions of military movements in ancient texts. Some of these lines of defence were created by the Spartans themselves during the period from the Peloponnesian war onwards. Others were the creations of neighbouring poleis, Argos and especially newly-liberated Messene, aimed at preventing Spartan incursions. The attribution of yet others remains unclear, especially in the complex, changing geo-political circumstances of north-western Lakonia and southern Arkadia following the foundation of Megalopolis. These geo-political changes, Christien argues, also stimulated institutional changes within Spartan society. It is no accident, for example, that in the period before the liberation of Messenia in 369 BC ancient discussions of Sparta's youngest military age grades focus on the *hippeis*, but that after Messenia's liberation the *krypteia* makes its first appearance, in Plato's *Laws*. The *krypteia*, she innovatively proposes, was an institution newly-designed for contemporary mid-fourth-century conditions, for the purpose of guerrilla-style campaigns against Sparta's former helots in Messenia: the model, according to a forthcoming article by Vincent Azoulay, for the novel argument in Isokrates' *Archidamos* that the Spartans should abandon their polis and form themselves into an army on the move.

In contrast, MARCELLO LUPI examines a longstanding ancient and modern controversy arising from the literary evidence: a controversy that originated in the fifth century BC regarding the existence and identity of a military unit called the 'Pitanate *lochos*', which Herodotus mentions in his account of the preliminaries to the battle of Plataia in 479 BC. Pitane is mentioned elsewhere by Herodotus as a village inhabited by Spartan citizens. In modern scholarship Herodotus' text has been combined with evidence from Roman times that Pitane was one of five Spartan villages (*ōbai*), in support of an influential thesis that the Spartan army in the late archaic and early classical periods was organized according to its villages (often described as the 'obal army'). Examining the problematic evidence regarding the status of the 'Pitanate *lochos*' and its commander Amompharetos, along with the traditions regarding their military role at Plataia, Lupi concludes that the unit should be identified with one of the three groups of 100 young citizens which together formed the 300 *hippeis,* with Amompharetos their commander being one of the three *hippagretai*. (This conclusion concurs with Figueira's study of the *hippeis*, which also argues for the separate identity of each of the three groups of 100 under its *hippagretēs*.) This identification means that Amompharetos' unit can no longer be viewed as deriving from one of five putative villages. Lupi suggests, instead, that it was based on one of Sparta's three civic tribes (Figueira, too, sees the tribes as the basis for the three groups of *hippeis*). But the question remains: why did Herodotus associate such a tribal unit with the village of Pitane? The answer, Lupi argues, lies in a radical reinterpretation of Sparta's citizen settlement pattern, which earlier scholars have misleadingly reconstructed on the very different Roman situation when the city was enclosed by a fortification wall. The citizen villages of unwalled classical Sparta, he suggests, were located over a much more extensive area of the Eurotas valley than that enclosed by the later wall. The village of Pitane covered the entire central area of the polis and, containing the joint residence of the two kings and the burial ground of at least one of the royal houses, was identified with the tribe of the Hylleis, named after Hyllos son of Herakles, from which the royal houses claimed descent. Hence Herodotus could describe the tribal unit loosely as the 'Pitanate *lochos*'. Lupi's paper offers a fascinating insight into how the link between the meritocratic-military units of the *hippeis* and the civic tribal divisions was also integrated with the geographical residence patterns of Spartan citizens; and how new interpretations of their military arrangements can lead to broader revisions in our understanding of the civic and spatial organization of the Spartan polis.

Military practice and policy. The papers in this section consider the Spartan army in action and the external policies which directed its practice of war. Here too there are important connections with the nature of Sparta's internal society. Noreen Humble's paper takes as its starting-point an apparently difficult passage in Xenophon's *Polity of the Lakedaimonians* regarding the Spartiates' unique capacity for continuing to fight with whoever is next to them, even when their formation is in disorder. She interprets the passage as a development of Xenophon's critique of the Spartan *politeia* earlier in the work, especially his emphasis on how the Spartiate training and lifestyle developed unquestioning obedience to orders, and on how such obedience rested less on internalized self-discipline than on fear of the dishonour attendant upon cowardice which made death seem preferable. Xenophon's remarks evoke numerous incidents in which Spartiate commanders had fought to the death in losing causes; but they also remind the reader of certain recent battles (such as Lechaion in 390 BC) when the Spartans were in disorder but had fought neither well nor to the death. Furthermore, Xenophon's indication that other soldiers lacked this capacity highlights the weaknesses involved in the polis' increasing reliance on non-Spartiate troops in the context of citizen manpower shortage, again evoking recent occasions when such troops had fled, leaving their Spartiate commanders to meet their deaths. His commentary thus offers an interesting contemporary analysis of the underlying causes of the deficiencies of Spartan campaigning and the increasing number of her military defeats in the early fourth century.

Ellen Millender's essay on 'The politics of Spartan mercenary service' investigates one particular category of the non-Spartiate troops indirectly signalled by Xenophon. As already noted, in the writings of Machiavelli and other Renaissance and early modern political theorists Sparta was frequently invoked alongside ancient Rome and certain contemporary republics as an example of a state whose freedom was grounded in its citizen militia, in contrast to other states, both ancient and modern, whose dependence upon mercenary leaders or troops had led to the loss of their liberty.[8] From this perspective, it is understandable that what Ellen Millender calls Sparta's 'contribution to the development of mercenary warfare' has not previously received much attention; and her examination of the important role that mercenaries played in Spartan statecraft may come as some surprise. Although rank-and-file Spartiate citizens did not engage in mercenary service, during the late fifth and early fourth centuries the Spartans not only exploited the growing supply of professional soldiers (with leading Spartiates acting as commanders of and advisers to Peloponnesian mercenary forces sent abroad), but even turned the Peloponnese itself into a sizeable mercenary market. Sparta's creation of her overseas empire would have been impossible without these developments. However, they also played a critical role in undermining her position. The availability of mercenary forces distracted the Spartan authorities from dealing with their declining citizen numbers and loosened the bonds between Sparta and her allies in the Peloponnesian league, thus undermining the twin sources of hoplite manpower that had underpinned her position as a leading power over the previous century and more.

The article by FRANÇOISE RUZÉ explores another important feature of Spartan power-building: her exploitation of treachery on the part of dissident elements within hostile states as an adjunct to her military campaigns. As she notes, Aeneas Tacticus' work *How to Survive under Siege* shows that such treachery was the primary means by which Greek cities were captured by besieging armies. There were specifically military reasons why the Spartans had particular need of such tactics: their well-known lack of expertise at siege warfare, deriving from the character of their citizen hoplite armies, combined with the paucity of their financial resources. The campaign in the Chalkidike in the late 420s is a case in point. The Spartan forces lacked the military might to take any of the Chalkidian cities by force, but both Torone and Mende were secured by the action of a few fifth-columnists. The exploitation of internal treachery, however, was not always sufficient: despite the presence of pro-Spartan dissidents at Akanthos and Amphipolis, both cities were only acquired after decision by the majority of citizens following persuasive speeches by Brasidas. In other contexts the exploitation of ties with known dissidents can be seen to affect the course of military campaigns, as in the campaigns against Argos in 418. King Agis first concluded a truce with two leading Argives rather than engage in combat. Then, during the subsequent battle of Mantineia, the 1000 select Argive troops were allowed to escape with minimal losses. It was probably the very same 1000 troops who subsequently assisted the Spartans to introduce oligarchies in Sikyon and in their own polis. However, the Spartans' overall military policy was not always dictated by such ties: they subsequently declined to give further military assistance to their oligarchic associates in Argos, acquiescing in the restoration of democratic rule when it became clear that the oligarchs were unable to establish an enduring regime.

In discussing the Spartans' decision in Argos, Ruzé compares it to their resolution regarding Athens in 403 to abandon support for the tyranny of the Thirty and permit the restoration of democracy. It is appropriate, therefore, that the volume concludes with ANTON POWELL's examination of the nexus of political, military and economic factors which led to that resolution, 'perhaps the most important decision that Sparta would ever make': in fact, a double decision, both on Athens' initial capture in 404 and during Sparta's subsequent interventions in 403, to allow her to survive in the face of powerful demands for her utter annihilation. The original contribution of Powell's essay is to locate the reasons for that decision less in terms of the foreign policy considerations frequently advanced in modern scholarship (the use of Athens as a counter-balance to the rising threat of Thebes) than in the potential impact on Spartan society of the spoils of war. The capture of the cities in Athens' empire had already given the Spartan polis and her leading commanders access to mobile wealth far beyond the resources of Lakonia and Messenia. Some prominent commanders had succumbed to the lure of private peculation. In their fright at the huge sums of coined money being sent back home by Lysander, the Spartans had debated whether they should ban it entirely and had eventually agreed to admit it only for public, not for private, possession. The prospect of what might happen to the dispersed distribution of power within the Spartan political system, should the immense private resources of the wealthiest city in Greece fall into the hands of individual Spartans (especially the ambitious Lysander, the commander on the spot in Athens both in 404 and 403), provides ample explanation for why Athens was allowed to survive with its wealth intact.

For Machiavelli and most other classical republican theorists, the one important difference between the citizen-militia republics of Sparta and Rome was that Rome was designed for expansion, but at the ultimate cost of her internal liberty at the hands of powerful military commanders; whereas Sparta, in contrast, was a republic designed not for expansion but for the preservation of its existing power and its internal freedom.[9] On Powell's thesis, Sparta's policy towards Athens suggests that Machiavelli's perception of the connection between her external restraint and internal liberty contains an essential element of truth. In 404 and 403 the Spartans eschewed taking full advantage of the potential for imperial power precisely because of its attendant threat to their liberty at home. Moreover, linking Powell's conclusions to Millender's study of mercenaries, we can suggest that Machiavelli's perception was correct (in principle, if not in detail) in another sense too. For him, as for other republican thinkers, the prime danger to the liberty of republics was the power of military leaders in command of mercenary troops with no loyalty to the republics they served. In the light of Millender's revelation of the scale of Sparta's dependence on foreign mercenaries – a phenomenon of which Machiavelli shows no awareness[10] – the fear that Lysander or another military leader with personal access to the resources of Athens might gain overweening power through command of an unprecedented mercenary army may have been a most potent consideration for other Spartans. At all events, it is clear that the Spartans applied the lessons of the danger of booty in their subsequent military practices. As Powell notes, in their foreign campaigns in the 390s booty captured by the main army was taken out of the control of army commanders and put into the hands of official booty-sellers, who conducted its sale and ensured that the receipts were used for public purposes. In this way Sparta successfully cut the Machiavellian knot which tied dependence on mercenaries to internal autocracy: indeed, her most frequent commander of mercenaries in the following generation was Agesilaos II, one of her legitimate kings.[11]

It remains to thank our hosts at the Université de Rennes II for providing the excellent facilities and hospitable environment in which we were able to conduct our discussions: our conference organizer Pierre Brulé and the Centre de Recherche et d'Étude des Sociétés et Cultures antiques de la Méditérranée; and the conference secretariat from the Maison de la Recherche en Sciences Sociales, especially Sébastien Bruneau and Marie-France Monnerais. Particular thanks are due to P.-J. Shaw for her expeditious translation into English of the article by Jean Ducat.

Notes

[1] One project of the new Centre, in which I was also involved as member of the editorial board of the *European Review of History /Revue Européenne d'Histoire*, was a conference on the theme of 'War, Culture and Humanity' in Manchester in April 2004. Several of the papers from the conference have appeared in the *ERH/REH* from issue 12.1 (2005) onwards.

[2] Garlan 1972; 1974; 1989.

[3] Cartledge 1977; 2001.

[4] Lazenby 1985; Sekunda 1998. The longstanding and vexed debate about the hierarchy of Spartan military units has continued unabated.

[5] e.g. Loraux 1977; Ducat 1999.

[6] Raaflaub and Rosenstein 1999, 1; though, oddly, they ignore the work of Garlan.

[7] e.g. Brun 1999; Corvisier 1999; Prost 1999; Amouretti et al. 2000; Van Wees 2000; Bekker-Nielsen 2001; Chaniotis and Ducrey 2002; Van Wees 2004; Chaniotis 2005. Some of the earliest works in this list were advanced textbooks for French students preparing for the *agrégation* (the competitive civil service entrance examination for those aiming to teach at the higher level of secondary education). The choice of nominated subject in ancient Greek history, 'Wars and societies in the ancient Greek worlds, 490 to 322 BC', testifies to the upsurge in French academic interest in the theme.

[8] Niccolo Machiavelli, *The Prince* ch. 12; *Discourses on Livy* 1.5; 1.6; 2.10.

[9] *Discourses* 1.5.

[10] For Machiavelli, the failure of Spartan imperialism in the mid-fourth century was the outcome of her empire becoming too extensive for the limited size of her citizen militia (*Discourses* 2.3).

[11] Cartledge 1987, 314–30.

Bibliography

Amouretti, M.-C., Christien, J., Ruzé, F. and Sineux, P.
  2000   *Le regard des Grecs sur la guerre: mythes et réalités*, Paris,.
Bekker-Nielsen, T. and Hannestad, L. (eds.)
  2001   *War as a Cultural and Social Force: Essays on warfare in antiquity*, Copen-
          hagen.
Black, J.
  2004   *Rethinking Military History*, London and New York.
Brun, P. (ed.)
  1999   *Questions d'histoire: guerres et sociétés dans les mondes grecs (490–322)*,
          Nantes.
Cartledge, P.A.
  1977   'Hoplites and heroes: Sparta's contribution to the technique of ancient
          warfare', *JHS* 97, 11–27.
  1987   *Agesilaos and the Crisis of Sparta*, London.
  2001   'The birth of the hoplite: Sparta's contribution to early Greek military organi-
          zation', in his *Spartan Reflections*, London 2001, 153–166.
Chaniotis, A.
  2005   *War in the Hellenistic World*, Malden, MA, Oxford and Victoria.
Chaniotis, A. and Ducrey, P. (eds.)
  2002   *Army and Power in the Ancient World*, Stuttgart.
Corvisier, J.N.
  1999   *Guerre et société dans les mondes grecs (490–322 av. J.-C)*, Paris.
Ducat, J.
  1999   'La société spartiate et la guerre', in F. Prost (ed.) *Armées et Sociétés*, 35–50.
Figueira, T.J. (ed.)
  2004   *Spartan Society*, Swansea.
Finley, M.I.
  1968   'Sparta', in J.-P. Vernant (ed.) *Problèmes de la guerre en Grèce ancienne*, Paris,
          143–60 = *The Use and Abuse of History*, 2nd edn., London 1986, 161–78

= *Economy and Society in Ancient Greece*, B.D. Shaw and R.P. Saller (eds.), London 1981, 24–40.

Garlan, Y.
1972 *La guerre dans l'Antiquité*, Paris; English translation, *War in the Ancient World: a social history*, London 1975.
1974 *Recherches de poliorcétique grecque*, Athens.
1989 *Guerre et économie en Grèce ancienne*, Paris.

Hodkinson, S.
1983 'Social order and the conflict of values in classical Sparta', *Chiron* 13, 239–81.
1993 'Warfare, wealth and the crisis of Spartiate society', in Rich and Shipley (eds.) *War and Society*, 146–76.

Hodkinson, S. and Powell, A. (eds.)
1999 *Sparta: New perspectives*, London.

Lazenby, J.F.
1985 *The Spartan Army*, Warminster.

Loraux, N.
1977 'La belle mort spartiate', *Ktema* 2, 105–120; reprinted as 'The Spartans' "Beautiful Death"', in her *The Experiences of Tiresias: The feminine and the Greek man*, Princeton 1995, 77–91.

Powell, A.
2004 'The women of Sparta – and of other Greek cities – at war', in Figueira (ed.) *Spartan Society*, 137–50.

Powell, A. (ed.)
1989 *Classical Sparta: Techniques behind her success*, London and Norman, Okla.

Powell, A. and Hodkinson, S. (eds.)
1994 *The Shadow of Sparta*, London and New York.
2002 *Sparta: Beyond the Mirage*, London.

Prost, F. (ed.)
1999 *Armées et sociétés de la Grèce classique: aspects sociaux et politiques de la guerre aux Ve et IVe s. av. J.-C*, Paris.

Rich, J. and Shipley, G. (eds.)
1994 *War and Society in the Greek World*, London and New York

Ste. Croix, G.E.M. de
1972 *The Origins of the Peloponnesian War*, London.

Sekunda, N.V.
1998 *The Spartans*, Oxford.

Van Wees, H.
2004 *Greek Warfare: Myths and realities*, London.

Van Wees, H. (ed.)
2000 *War and Violence in Ancient Greece*, London.

1

THE SPARTAN 'TREMBLERS'

Jean Ducat

In theory, the Spartans' military conduct was governed by a single, simple principle, the strict application of which, so it was said, was what gave their army its strength. In Herodotus (7.104), this is how Demaratus explains it to Xerxes:

> (the law) always requires the same thing of them: it forbids them to flee from battle however great the force confronting them; remaining at their post, they must overcome or perish.

An episode in Book 9 (53 and 55) provides an example of conformity with this principle that is so strict as to make it an absurdity: this is the story of a Spartan *lochagos*, Amompharetos, who, just before the battle of Plataea, stubbornly refuses, in the face of the enemy, to execute a manoeuvre ordered by his superiors, because it entails a slight withdrawal. Similarly, Thucydides comments thus (4.40.1) on the capitulation of 292 Lacedaemonian hoplites on Sphacteria (425):

> In Greek eyes, this was the most unexpected event of the war; because the general view of the Lacedaemonians was that nothing, neither hunger nor any other extremity, would make them surrender their weapons, but that they would keep them to the end, fighting as best they could even to the death.

That the Spartans should, in this situation, have been unfaithful to their principles was a palpable shock to the rest of the Greeks (and, as it turns out, to the Spartans themselves); this shows how the image of itself that Sparta had aimed to project was accepted without question by everyone.

Those who did not honour these principles laid themselves open to a sanction. This sanction appears to be well known, as much for its different modes as for the question of the circumstances in which it might be applied. Those who were deemed to have shown cowardice in battle suffered a form of disgrace which is described in several texts; these texts, if taken as complementing each other, enable us to conjure a picture of this penalty that appears coherent and complete. They were called the 'tremblers', *tresantes*, and the existence of this condition seems to be attested in texts ranging from the end of the seventh century (text 1) to 331 (the battle of Megalopolis; text 6). Amongst the Spartan institutions of the archaic and classical eras, that of the 'tremblers' would thus be one of the most permanent and best-known. After 331, we hear no more of it, which is hardly surprising: this is a period when – we can reasonably guess – many traditional Spartan practices fell into disuse; apparently, even the reformer kings did not attempt to revive it, unless it is to be subsumed within the vague and general expression 'Spartan discipline'.

It is doubtless because the 'tremblers' appear as a simple and unproblematic reality that there exists no actual monograph on the subject. The closest we have to such a thing is the article *Tresantes* in the *Real-Encyclopädie* by V. Ehrenberg (Ehrenberg 1937). It is, no doubt, the quality of this study that explains why no one has re-visited the subject. It is arranged chronologically: Ehrenberg conducts a successive study of all those historical episodes in which the 'tremblers' make an appearance, so the picture of this institution gradually develops of its own accord. Not once does he yield to the temptation of simplifying matters; he is plainly aware of the difficulties and uncertainties with regard to detail, and particularly of the fact that the sanction might be variable. But the genre of 'encyclopaedia article' has strict limits, if only from the point of view of dimension, and this did not allow Ehrenberg to examine the texts with as much detailed attention as would have been desirable.

Since this inaugural, and truly pioneering, study, there has to my knowledge been no overall treatment of this punishment other than that embarked upon by N. Loraux in her well-known article on the Spartan 'noble death' (Loraux 1977, 108–9 and 111–13); alongside the 'noble death' it was natural to evoke its complete opposite, the disgraced life, of which the coward's is the very image. Loraux offers an interesting critique of Ehrenberg's study. His principal fault, in her opinion, is that he aimed 'à une reconstitution de l'institution dominée par le présupposé éminemment idéologique de la décadence continue de Sparte à partir des guerres médiques' (p. 111). As far as the subject of decadence is concerned, this criticism is too harsh: Ehrenberg does not make use of the concept; he wishes only to observe that the Spartans applied this sanction less and less and, therefore, that they showed less and less respect for the rules they had established. On the other hand, I would perhaps be more radical than Loraux in identifying Ehrenberg's weakness chiefly as that of having aspired to write a linear history of the institution, and perhaps even of having thought it possible to write a history of it at all.[1]

Since the 'tremblers' are one of the most famous of Spartan realities, they are mentioned in all studies of any size devoted to Sparta, and are met with in many detailed enquiries. Even if some of these works offer interesting comments on matters of detail, there would be little advantage in searching them out and compiling a complete list; such a bibliography would bring nothing to the study of the subject. I will make one exception, for the sake of two books on Spartan law (or on the problem of discerning whether one can speak of any such law), and which necessarily come up against one problem, to which I shall also return: that of knowing how far the rule regarding the 'tremblers' is a legal reality, and how far a purely social sanction. While D. MacDowell (MacDowell 1986, 42–6) thinks he detects in it certain legal features, S. Link (Link 1994, 22–3 and 84–5) maintains that it is exclusively a social sanction, and that the only thing relating to law in this affair is the taking of the decision itself.

I. The principal texts

1. Tyrtaeus, fr. 11 West (8 Prato), 14–16.

> τρεσάντων δ' ἀνδρῶν πᾶσ' ἀπόλωλ' ἀρέτη.
> οὐδεὶς ἄν ποτε ταῦτα λέγων ἀνύσειεν ἔκαστα
> ὅσσ', ἢν αἰσχρὰ μάθῃ, γίνεται ἀνδρὶ κακά,

as for those who have trembled, they have lost all their worth.[2] No speech could enumerate all the evils that afflict the man who has formed this shameful thought.

V. 16, μάθῃ West, πάθῃ codd. The correction adopted by West seems to me to be demanded by the parallels he cites.

2. Herodotus 7.231–2.

> 231. ἀπονοστήσας δὲ ἐς Λακεδαίμονα ὁ Ἀριστόδημος ὄνειδός τε εἶχε καὶ ἀτιμίην· πάσχων δὲ τοιάδε ἠτίμωτο· οὔτε οἱ πῦρ οὐδεὶς ἔναυε Σπαρτιητέων οὔτε διελέγετο, ὄνειδός τε εἶχε ὁ τρέσας Ἀριστόδημος καλεόμενος. ἀλλ' ὁ μὲν ἐν τῇ ἐν Πλαταιῇσι μάχῃ ἀνέλαβε πᾶσαν τὴν ἐπενειχθεῖσαν αἰτίην. 232. λέγεται δὲ καὶ ἄλλον ἀποπεμφθέντα ἄγγελον ἐς Θεσσαλίην τῶν τριηκοσίων τούτων περιγενέσθαι, τῷ οὔνομα εἶναι Παντίτην· νοστήσαντα δὲ τοῦτον ἐς Σπάρτην, ὡς ἠτίμωτο, ἀπάγξασθαι.

231. When he returned to Lacedaemon, Aristodemos found he was disgraced and dishonoured. This dishonour consisted of the following things: no Spartan would kindle fire for him; no one addressed a word to him, and he had the mortification of being called Aristodemos the Trembler. But at the Battle of Plataea he completely wiped out the blame that hung over him. 232. They say another of the three hundred also survived, having been sent as a messenger to Thessaly; his name was Pantites. Because, on returning to Sparta, he was disgraced, he hanged himself.

Cf. 9.71 (Aristodemos at Plataea). On the fortunes of Aristodemos, see Ducat 2005.

3

3. Thucydides 5.34.2.

τοὺς δὲ ἐκ τῆς νήσου ληφθέντας σφῶν καὶ τὰ ὅπλα παραδόντας, δείσαντες μή τι διὰ τὴν ξυμφορὰν νομίσαντες ἐλασσωθήσεσθαι καὶ ὄντες ἐπίτιμοι νεωτερίσωσιν, ἤδη καὶ ἀρχάς τινας ἔχοντας ἀτίμους ἐποίησαν, ἀτιμίαν δὲ τοιάνδε ὥστε μήτε ἄρχειν μήτε πριαμένους τι ἢ πωλοῦντας κυρίους εἶναι. ὕστερον δὲ αὖθις χρόνῳ ἐπίτιμοι ἐγένοντο,

regarding those of them who had been taken prisoner on the island and who had laid down their weapons, it was feared that, impelled by the dread of being reduced to an inferior condition because of what had happened, they would, as long as they retained their full rights (or: although they still possessed full rights), start thinking up some plan of revolution. For this reason they were pronounced *atimoi*, even though some of them by now held magistracies. The effect of this *atimia* was such that they could not hold office, nor were they allowed to buy or sell. After a certain period, their full rights were restored to them.

4. Xenophon, *Lak. Pol.* 9.

4. ἐν μὲν γὰρ ταῖς ἄλλαις πόλεσιν, ὁπόταν τις κακὸς γένηται, ἐπίκλησιν μόνον ἔχει κακὸς εἶναι, ἀγοράζει δὲ ἐν τῷ αὐτῷ ὁ κακὸς τἀγαθῷ καὶ κάθηται καὶ γυμνάζεται, ἐὰν βούληται· ἐν δὲ τῇ Λακεδαίμονι πᾶς μὲν ἄν τις αἰσχυνθείη τὸν κακὸν σύσκηνον παραλαβεῖν, πᾶς δ᾽ ἂν ἐν παλαίσματι συγγυμναστήν. 5. πολλάκις δ᾽ ὁ τοιοῦτος καὶ διαιρουμένων τοὺς ἀντισφαιριοῦντας ἀχώριστος περιγίγνεται, καὶ ἐν χοροῖς δ᾽ εἰς τὰς ἐπονειδίστους χώρας ἀπελαύνεται, καὶ μὴν ἐν ὁδοῖς παραχωρητέον αὐτῷ καὶ ἐν θάκοις καὶ τοῖς νεωτέροις ὑπαναστατέον, καὶ τὰς μὲν προσηκούσας κόρας οἴκοι θρεπτέον, καὶ ταύταις τῆς ἀνανδρίας αἰτίαν ὑφεκτέον, γυναικὸς δὲ κενὴν ἑστίαν οὖσαν περιοπτέον καὶ ἅμα τούτου ζημίαν ἀποτειστέον, λιπαρὸν δὲ οὐ πλανητέον οὐδὲ μιμητέον τοὺς ἀνεγκλήτους, ἢ πληγὰς ὑπὸ τῶν ἀμεινόνων ληπτέον. 6. ἐγὼ μὲν δὴ τοιαύτης τοῖς κακοῖς ἀτιμίας ἐπικειμένης οὐδὲν θαυμάζω τὸ προαιρεῖσθαι ἐκεῖ θάνατον ἀντὶ τοῦ οὕτως ἀτίμου τε καὶ ἐπονειδίστου βίου,

4. In other cities, when someone displays cowardice, the only thing he suffers is to be called a coward; he frequents the same *agora* as the brave man, if he wants to, he sits next to him, and trains with him in the gymnasium. In Lacedaemon, on the other hand, any man would be ashamed to receive him as a mess-mate, and would blush to exercise with him in the gymnasium. 5. Often, when teams are being picked for a ball game, you see him left out, not chosen for any of them; when there is dancing, he is relegated to the demeaning positions. In the streets he has to give way to everyone, and if he has a seat, he must surrender it even to his juniors; at home he has to support his young female relatives, and bear in front of them the responsibility for their unmarried state; he must endure the sight of his own home with no wife in it, while also having to pay the fine for being unmarried; he may not walk around looking cheerful, nor may he try to imitate honourable men, on pain of being struck by his betters.

6. When *atimia* like this is imposed on cowards, I am not surprised that, there, they prefer death to a life so filled with dishonour and disgrace.

5. Isocrates
a. 8 (*On Peace*), 143.

ὑπὲρ ἐκείνων δ' οἱ μὴ τολμῶντες ἐν ταῖς μάχαις ἀποθνῄσκειν ἀτιμότεροι γίγνονται τῶν τὰς τάξεις λειπόντων καὶ τὰς ἀσπίδας ἀποβαλλόντων,

those who lack the courage to die for them (the kings) in battle are more *atimoi* than those who have abandoned their posts and thrown away their shields.

b. *Letter* 2 (*to Philip*), 6.

ἴδοις δ' ἂν καὶ Λακεδαιμονίους περὶ τῆς τῶν βασιλέων σωτηρίας πολλὴν ἐπιμελείαν ποιουμένους καὶ τοὺς ἐνδοξοτάτους τῶν πολιτῶν φύλακας αὐτῶν καθιστάντας, οἷς αἴσχιόν ἐστι ἐκείνους τελευτήσαντας περιιδεῖν ἢ τὰς ἀσπίδας ἀποβαλεῖν,

you can also see how the Lacedaemonians take great care to preserve the safety of their kings, and that they assign to them the most renowned of the citizens as their bodyguards, for whom the disgrace of allowing the king to be killed is worse even than that of having thrown away their shields.

6. Diodorus 19.70.

4. οἱ δὲ πεμφθέντες ὥς ποθ' ἧκον εἰς τὴν Λακωνικήν, εὗρον Ἀκρότατον τὸν Κλεομένους τοῦ βασιλέως υἱὸν προσκεκοφότα πολλοῖς τῶν νέων καὶ διὰ τοῦτο ξενικῶν πραγμάτων ὀρεγόμενον. 5. τῶν γὰρ Λακεδαιμονίων μετὰ τὴν πρὸς Ἀντίπατρον μάχην ἀπολυόντων τῆς ἀτιμίας τοὺς ἐκ τῆς ἥττης διασωθέντας μόνος ἐνέστη τῷ δόγματι. διόπερ αὐτὸν συνέβη καὶ τῶν ἄλλων οὐκ ὀλίγοις προσκόψαι, μάλιστα δ' οἷς ἦν τῶν νόμων τὰ πρόστιμα· οὗτοι γὰρ συστραφέντες πληγάς τε ἐνεφόρησαν αὐτῷ καὶ διετέλουν ἐπιβουλεύοντες,

on their arrival in Laconia, the envoys learnt that Akrotatos, son of King Cleomenes, had angered many of the young citizens, and, for this reason, was anxious to offer his services to a foreign country. While the Spartans, after the battle with Antipater, declared the survivors of the defeat to be free of *atimia*, he was the only one to oppose this decision. That is how he came to anger people so deeply, particularly those who fell under this stroke of the law. They were in league against him and beat him up, and were forever plotting against him.

7. Plutarch, *Lycurgus* 21.2 (where he deals with the songs taught to children).

ἔπαινοι γὰρ ἦσαν ὡς τὰ πολλὰ τῶν τεθνηκότων ὑπὲρ τῆς Σπάρτης εὐδαιμονιζομένων, καὶ ψόγοι τῶν τρεσάντων, ὡς ἀλγεινὸν καὶ κακοδαίμονα βιούντων βίον,

for the most part they were eulogies applauding the happy state of those who had died for Sparta, and songs censuring the tremblers, in which the pain and misery of their lives were depicted.

Cf. *Inst. Lac.* 14, *Mor.* 238a (identical).

8. Plutarch, *Agesilaus* 30.

2. ...τοῖς ἐν τῇ μάχῃ καταδειλιάσασιν, οὓς αὐτοὶ τρέσαντας ὀνομάζουσιν, ὀκνοῦντες τὰς ἐκ τῶν νόμων ἀτιμίας προσάγειν, πολλοῖς οὖσιν καὶ δυνατοῖς, φοβούμενοι νεωτερισμὸν ἀπ' αὐτῶν. 3. οὐ γὰρ μόνον ἀρχῆς ἀπείργονται πάσης, ἀλλὰ καὶ δοῦναί τινι τούτων γυναῖκα καὶ λαβεῖν ἄδοξον ἐστι· παίει δ' ὁ βουλόμενος αὐτοὺς τῶν ἐντυγχανόντων. 4. οἱ δὲ καρτεροῦσι περιιόντες αὐχμηροὶ καὶ ταπεινοί, τρίβωνάς τε προσερραμμένους χρώματος βαπτοῦ φοροῦσι καὶ ξυρῶνται μέρος τῆς ὑπήνης, μέρος δὲ τρέφουσι. 5. δεινὸν οὖν ἦν τοιούτους ἐν τῇ πόλει περιορᾶν πολλούς, οὐκ ὀλίγων δεομένη στρατιωτῶν. καὶ νομοθέτην αἱροῦνται τὸν Ἀγησίλαον. 6. ὁ δὲ μήτε προσθεὶς τι μήτ' ἀφέλων μήτε μεταγράψας, εἰσῆλθεν εἰς τὸ πλῆθος τῶν Λακεδαιμονίων· καὶ φήσας ὅτι τοὺς νόμους δεῖ σήμερον ἐᾶν καθεύδειν, ἐκ δὲ τῆς αὔριον ἡμέρας κυρίους εἶναι πρὸς τὸ λοιπόν, ἅμα τούς τε νόμους τῇ πόλει καὶ τοὺς ἄνδρας ἐπιτίμους ἐφύλαξε,

2. ...Thus, those who had shown themselves cowardly in battle, and whom they themselves call the tremblers, were both numerous and influential, and there was some hesitation about inflicting on them the *atimia* provided for by the laws, in case they should start a revolution. 3. In fact, not only are these people excluded from holding any office, but it is considered improper to give a spouse to one of them, or to receive one through him. Anyone who encounters them is free to strike them if he so chooses. 4. They have to resign themselves to going about in coarse and dirty clothing, to wearing patched and dull-coloured mantles, to shave only part of the beard, leaving the rest to grow. 5. It was dangerous, therefore, to allow so great a number of these characters into the city, and, moreover, there was a need for a large number of soldiers. Agesilaus was chosen as *nomothetēs*. 6. So he, without in any way adding to, or taking away from, or altering, the existing arrangements, presented himself to the Lacedaemonian people and told them that they must let the laws sleep today, so that, from tomorrow, they would be endowed with their full force for the rest of time. That is how, at a stroke, he preserved for the city its laws and citizens in full possession of their rights.

The anecdote is repeated in the *Comparison of Agesilaus and Pompey*; cf. *Reg. et Imp. Apophth.* 10, *Mor.* 191c, and *Apophth. Lac.* 73, *Mor.* 214a; Polyaenus 2.1.13.

These are the sources I propose to re-examine here. They fall into two categories: some recount specific episodes (texts 2, 3, 6, and 8 §§2 and 5–6); others give a general description of the punishment, presenting it in a particular perspective, namely a portrait of the 'trembler's' social condition (texts

4, 5, 7, and 8 §§3–4). That these two categories should exist is quite natural; what is more unexpected is that there should be a contradiction between the two, in that none of the features reflected in the general portraits appears in the descriptions of cases where the sanction has been meted out. This contradiction leaves some uncertainty hanging over the whole analysis, which is all the more awkward since the instances where the sanction was actually applied are reduced to two, both of which are, in addition, extreme cases: extreme harshness towards Aristodemos, extreme leniency towards the prisoners of Sphacteria.

II. Vocabulary

1. To the offence, or rather, to the offender, a term, ὁ τρέσας, οἱ τρέσαντες, is applied, which Plutarch (text 8 §2) presents as being typically Spartan, and of which he gives a definition, οἱ ἐν τῇ μάχῃ καταδειλιάσαντες, 'those who displayed cowardice in battle'. This term appears in Tyrtaeus (text 1), though whether it had already acquired its 'technical' meaning there, is something we shall have to ponder on; we find it next in Herodotus (text 2), as the vile name given to Aristodemos by the other Spartans. After that, it makes another appearance in Plutarch: in text 8, he is, in a way, putting it in inverted commas ('those whom they themselves call the tremblers'); in text 7 and in the apophthegm, *Mor.* 191c, he makes no comment on it. The fact that it is not found in Thucydides or Xenophon might cause surprise, but we know that these authors (with some qualifications in Xenophon's case) tend to avoid using local terminology. Thus, the only historical episodes in relation to which the term 'trembler' appears in a text are those of Thermopylae and Leuctra. The standard meaning of the word and its uses clearly demonstrate that it did not apply to the punishment, whatever that might have been, but to the man who had committed the offence of 'trembling' in battle.

To designate a person who is patently a 'trembler' (and even *the* 'trembler'), Xenophon (text 4 §§3, 4, 6) uses the most commonplace of terms, κακός, and, in the portrait (§ 5), he refers back to it by means of ὁ τοιοῦτος. As for δειλός, which one might expect, it only appears in the form of derivative verbs: Plutarch, text 8, τοῖς καταδειλιάσασι, and perhaps also Xenophon, *LP* 10.7, where the expression εἴ τις ἀποδειλιάσειε has, certainly, a more general application, but can and should include, and may even refer primarily to, the 'tremblers'.

2. There is no specific term that corresponds to the sanction itself; the authors use ἀτιμία. This term is not used by Tyrtaeus, but his phrase πᾶσ' ἀπόλωλ' ἀρετή carries the same meaning, if we read *atimia* in its strong sense. Herodotus, in each instance (text 2, and 9.71), pairs ὄνειδος and ἀτιμίη;

could this be to signify that the sanction had two aspects, one of them social (ὄνειδος), the other, judicial (ἀτιμίη)? The judicial aspect is absent, however, from his description. After this, the term appears commonly: in Thucydides, text 3, and in Diodorus' account echoing the same event, 12.76.1; in Xenophon, text 4 §6; in Diodorus, text 6; and lastly, in Plutarch, text 8 §2, and *Mor.* 214a, where the use of the plural, ἀτιμίαις, would perhaps suggest that the sanction is in fact multiple.

3. As is logical, the man who suffers the punishment is called ἄτιμος. The term appears in Thucydides, text 3, where it is contrasted with ἐπίτιμος (which he employs twice), which emphasizes the judicial aspect of the sanction; in Isocrates, text 5 (a comparative; there are, in fact, degrees in the condition of *atimia*); in Plutarch, *Mor.* 191c; and in Polyaenus 2.1.13 (a passage about Leuctra). The act whereby the Spartans declare *atimia* is designated in Thucydides, text 3 (cf. Plutarch, *Mor.* 191c), by the expression ἀτίμους ποιεῖν; the second apophthegm of Demaratus in Plutarch *Mor.* 222a expresses it as ἀτιμῶσι. The passive, ἠτίμωτο, occurs in Herodotus, text 2 (two instances).

This vocabulary is uniform. We may be tempted to conclude from this that, for other Greeks, it is the same sanction that has been taken or contemplated each time, whether after Thermopylae, Sphacteria, Leuctra, and Megalopolis. The notion that it proceeded from a fully fledged *nomos*, an actual rule, customary and invariable, does not emerge, however, before the time of Diodorus (text 6: τῶν νόμων τὰ πρόστιμα). We find it again more explicitly in Plutarch, who specifies that *atimia* resulted automatically from the application of the law (τὰς ἐκ τῶν νόμων ἀτιμίας, text 8 §2; cf. *Mor.* 191c, ἀτίμους εἶναι τοῦ νόμου κελεύοντος, and 214a, ἐκ τοῦ νόμου ἀτιμίας). The use of the term *atimia* to designate the sanction demonstrates that, in Greek eyes, the status of 'trembler' was not exclusively a Spartan entity; it could be thought of by reference to the same concept of 'deprivation of honour' as the penalty that was in use, under this name, in other Greek cities. This penalty, at least in Athens, could take widely varying forms. So it may be that, in the Spartan case, the word *atimia* could be employed, in certain cases, to designate a 'loss of rights' that stopped short of the extreme form described by Xenophon.

III. Origins: Tyrtaeus

Since the time of Ehrenberg, verse 14 of Tyrtaeus fragment 11 W (text 1) has been generally regarded as attesting that the condition of 'tremblers' was already in existence towards the end of the seventh century. That is in fact possible, but it is equally possible that this status did not yet exist; that Tyrtaeus may have deployed the word in its ordinary, rather than institutional, sense, to depict cowards by means of a powerful but quite natural image; and that it may be precisely this verse of Tyrtaeus' that is the origin of the Spartan usage for so describing them.[3] We know the position which these poems rapidly gained in Spartan culture,[4] and which they retained to the end of antiquity. This popularity would amply explain the term's having become the common usage. That is rather how I would see it. This interpretation seems to me to fit more closely with Tyrtaeus' mode of expression and the way his ideas are connected; one might also have doubts about whether the use of a technical term could be contemplated in the genre of poetry he was practising.

Does Plutarch's text (no. 7) associating the *tresantes* with poetry supply an argument one way or another? We should start by clarifying what this means: these poems that children were given to sing, were they in praise or censure of named people (as with the songs sung by young girls in *Lyc.* 14.6), or did the texts have a more general application? Our inclination would be to agree with the latter, because this corresponds with what is contained in the fragments of archaic lyric poetry that have come down to us.[5] What Plutarch says is particularly well suited to Tyrtaeus' poetry, and chiefly to the 'major fragments' 10, 11 and 12 W, extracts which constitute the essentials of what survived of his work, amongst a wide public, until the end of antiquity. To put it more precisely, the structure conveyed by Plutarch (which polarizes praise and censure) corresponds to that of fragments 10 and 11, where the praise of the *kaloi* alternates with censure of the *kakoi*. When Plutarch writes that, there is not the slightest doubt that it is Tyrtaeus he has chiefly in mind: consequently, his use of the term *tresantes* should be taken almost as a citation, referring, unquestionably, to the τρεσάντων δ' ἀνδρῶν of fr. 11; it therefore teaches us nothing new, even if Plutarch's acquaintance with the technical meaning which the word eventually acquired has an influence on the way he uses it: for him, the 'tremblers' are the opposite of those who have 'died for Sparta', which is not the case in fr. 11.

From the comparison, which is, in fact, a pertinent one, between the evils which Tyrtaeus says (fr. 11, v. 16) afflict 'those who trembled', and the picture of the wretched exile in fr. 10 (vv. 3–10), some have thought they could infer[6] that the coward, at this period, did not as yet suffer the sort of punishment described in the classical era, but, instead, suffered exile – an exile which, given that the person is reduced to begging, is combined with the confiscation or sequestration of his property – therefore, that there was as yet no such thing as a 'trembler' in the technical sense. However much I may like the conclusion, I could not approve the reasoning. The key to the interpretation is the participle προλιπόντα in verse 3: he has 'abandoned' his city and his lands. The Homeric uses of the verb (in the aorist participle, as in this case) demonstrate that it always applies to a *voluntary* departure, even if this voluntary character is, in general, highly formal. The best example is *Od.* 23.118–20, where Odysseus recalls the sort of a killer who 'abandons his parents and his native land' in order to escape either vengeance or judgement. The coward in fr. 10 has certainly not been *condemned* to exile; he has left so as to escape a sanction or a condemnation – which could be anything, starting with death... As for knowing whether a Spartan of the classical era wished (and was able) to go into exile to escape life as a 'trembler', this is a point I shall leave on one side for the moment (cf. below, p. 46).

It seems to me, then, that the presence in Tyrtaeus' verse of the word *tresantes* is no proof that this status existed at this period. When might it have appeared? It is possible that it was in the course of the sixth century, as a sort of conclusion drawn from reflections on the difficulties evident during the second Messenian war,[7] or during the period of the war with Tegea. But the turn of phrase used by Herodotus regarding Aristodemos (text 2), 'he suffered the disgrace of being called a trembler', may also suggest (though we should not insist on this interpretation) that it was the first time this epithet, taken from Tyrtaeus, was applied to a Spartan.

IV. The offence

Often this is barely characterized: the texts speak simply of 'cowardice', and in the vaguest terms. This is the case in Tyrtaeus, where it is only articulated through the use of the word 'tremblers', re-stated, further on, by means of ἢν αἰσχρὰ μάθῃ; these expressions are clarified a little by the fact that the 'tremblers' are contrasted (vv. 11–12) with 'those who have the courage to come to close quarters with the enemy, fighting in the front line'. This conception, at once negative (lack of courage) and maximalist, about cowardice goes far beyond the usual image of fleeing the field. Xenophon pays no attention at all to the misdeed committed and expresses himself almost as though a person became *kakos* by nature. In his account of Leuctra, Plutarch 'translates' *tresantes* by οἱ ἐν τῇ μάχῃ καταδειλιάσαντες; it is possible that this expression, which quite clearly relates to only a part of the fighting force, is directed at those who, at the end of the battle, gave themselves up to the 'save your own skin' attitude evoked by Diodorus (15.56.2–3). This vagueness is self-explanatory: it is not easy to arrive at an abstract definition of cowardice; it is an entirely relative notion and one that depends very largely on circumstances. It is this that made the application of a possible *nomos tōn tresantōn* so difficult; that, in turn, accounts for attempts to define the particular forms of behaviour likely to serve as objective criteria of cowardice. This is why, in Athens, there existed specific *graphai*: ἀστρατείας (defaulting), λιποταξίας (abandoning one's post), δειλίας (cowardice).

1. Flight is the most obvious of these criteria: it is easy enough, in principle, to distinguish from a tactical withdrawal, which is itself lawful if carried out under orders. The runaway stops fighting; he does not fall back, he turns his back; he does not remain in formation, it is every man for himself.

In the case of Leuctra, it is probably on account of the flight, which Diodorus (author of the fullest account of the battle) terms παντελὴς τροπή, 'an utter rout', 15.56.2,[8] and which occurred at the end of the battle (τὸ τελευταῖον), that a large number of Spartans should have deserved the sanction promised to 'tremblers'. Plutarch states this, not in *Agesilaus* 30, but in the apophthegm *Mor.* 214a: 'many of the Lacedaemonians had fled'; this indication is repeated, and with more detail, by Polyaenus 2.1.13, who speaks of shields being thrown away and posts abandoned.

At Megalopolis, it is perhaps because he reckoned they had fled that Akrotatos (text 6) regarded numerous Spartans as genuine 'tremblers'; but it emerges from the account of the battle (Diodorus 17.63.4) that this was a case of withdrawal executed on the orders of the king himself. If Akrotatos' accusation was based only on these grounds, it should be regarded as unjustified.

It would seem *a priori* entirely normal that the Spartans who really had fled in the face of the enemy should automatically be deemed 'tremblers'. Nevertheless there was one battle where it is patently clear that the Spartans fled without, apparently, being sanctioned for it: this is the battle of Lechaion (390). Xenophon's account (*Hell.* 4.5.17) does not hide the fact (even if he goes no further than to use the verb ἐγκλίνειν) that, at the end of the battle, 350 survivors (out of 600) found safety in flight, and even, seemingly, headlong flight: some even threw themselves into the sea, and it may be doubted whether, when they did so, they kept hold of their shields (among other things). Is it perhaps the desire to preserve Sparta's honour that explains the success of a hypothesis put forward by Grote, and reiterated by Ehrenberg and others:[9] Xenophon's remark concerning the wounded who, at the beginning of the battle, were evacuated to Lechaion, οὗτοι μόνοι τῆς μόρας τῇ ἀληθείᾳ ἐσώθησαν, 'they were the only ones of the *mora* actually to be saved', would be an allusion (a pretty obscure one!) to the fact that the other survivors were punished as 'tremblers'. Loraux quite rightly rejected this, saying that it was nothing more than an ethical judgement on Xenophon's part. On that last point, one might wonder: does an ethical notion of 'salvation' really have any place here? Is this really a judgement? I would see it rather as a strictly military observation, underlining the following paradox: only those who were wounded right at the beginning of the engagement, before it turned to tragedy for the Spartans, and who for that reason were carried to shelter, were out of the affair; the others, although apparently safe and sound, were not, if I may put it like that, out of the wood, and scarcely had more than a one-in-two chance of survival. This would amply explain Xenophon's remark, and there is nothing whatever to support our thinking that the fugitives of Lechaion had even suffered being accused on that score; Xenophon refers to nothing of this kind when reporting (4.5.10) the reactions to the defeat.

2. Throwing away the shield. In every city, this act is severely sanctioned as the one that most indubitably characterizes cowardice; that is certainly due to the symbolic worth of the shield in hoplite armies, but also, in practical terms, to the fact that, in order to flee, it is a matter of urgent necessity to get rid of this supremely cumbersome object;[10] that is what renders this action a reliable criterion of flight. So it is to be expected that, for the Spartans, jettisoning the shield qualifies the perpetrator, beyond discussion, as a 'trembler'. In fact this was certainly the case, but few texts say so, and not all of those are of the highest quality. First, there is the reference to this offence made by Isocrates (text 5 b), who treats it as a term comparable with the abandoning of the king. Then there is the apophthegm transmitted by Plutarch (Demaratus 2, *Mor.* 220a), who says that the Spartans 'inflict *atimia* (ἀτιμῶσι) on those who throw away their shield'. The offence is mentioned in the context of Leuctra, but only by Polyaenus (2.1.13), and one might ask whether, in that instance, it is not simply a commonplace expression for cowardice. Lastly, there are all the apophthegms, anecdotes and epigrams, which circulated in antiquity, on the theme of ἢ τὰν ἢ ἐπὶ τᾶς, 'With it or on it',[11] but these texts never describe the punishment meted out to the offender. The information Diodorus provides is different: after narrating the experience of Brasidas related by Thucydides (4.11), an experience in the course of which Brasidas, most unwillingly, lost his shield, Diodorus concludes (12.62.5): 'He had so surpassed all the others by his courage that if, according to Spartan custom, the loss of one's shield was punished by death, the very same event would confer glory on him.' And why not death? Should not Sparta be more severe than other cities? But the elaboration with which the sentence concludes is so patently rhetorical that it casts doubt on the authenticity of this information. On the whole, then, we may assume that to abandon one's shield did indeed entail the sanction we are studying.

3. Capitulation. To capitulate in open country was obviously not something the Spartans were used to doing, and Thucydides, when he records that of the hoplites on Sphacteria (4.40.1; I cited the text at the beginning of this chapter), is not slow to emphasize it. They were punished for it, and the manner in which this was done is something to which we shall have to return, and which Thucydides terms *atimia*. It is obvious that to surrender,

along with weapons and baggage, is to give a proof of cowardice equivalent to that of flight, and that it is difficult to do this without becoming separated from one's shield;[12] it is even worse, in that fugitives may be available for the rest of the war, whereas prisoners are an effective weapon in the hands of the enemy, and I believe that this, above all, is what the city held against those on Sphacteria.

4. The problem of *ataxia* and of *lipotaxia*. The term ἀταξία is not very precise. Most commonly it signifies disorder, lack of discipline; when this is a military offence, it perhaps refers to the disobeying of orders. When speaking of Derkylidas, Xenophon describes the punishment inflicted on those who were found guilty of this: 'He had been condemned to stand guard, holding his shield, which worthy Lacedaemonians regard as a dreadful disgrace: it is, in fact, the usual punishment for *ataxia*' (*Hell.* 3.1.9). This punishment would not, therefore, be the *atimia* imposed on 'tremblers'; but one might ask whether Xenophon is giving a full description of it here, or whether this 'standing in the pillory' was only one constituent of it. In any case, it has about it a touch of the spectacular which resembles certain aspects of the 'tremblers'' condition. To use, as an instrument of the punishment, the shield, symbol of hoplite steadfastness, links *ataxia* to the abandoning of the shield; but, by its nature, the offence is much more suggestive of *lipotaxia*, the deserting of one's post, which, in Sparta, should have figured among the offences committed by the 'tremblers', since Polyaenus (2.1.13) says that at Leuctra many of the Spartans had deserted their posts. In Athens, *lipotaxia* (rather than *ataxia*) was one of the offences liable to entail *atimia*.

5. The problem of wounds in the back. With his evocation of the fate of the 'tremblers' Tyrtaeus closely associates (by means of γάρ) that (vv. 17–20) of the warrior who sustains a spearthrust in the back. Here, the precise terminology is in itself important: an arrow or a javelin may hit the back of someone who is not, in fact, running away, but the same cannot be said of a spear. This leads, therefore, to the question of whether, in Sparta, those whose wounds were to the back were not, *ipso facto*, regarded as 'tremblers'. In fact, there exists a series of texts affirming that, there, the examination of wounds sustained was an actual practice. Some of these are undated and their documentary worth may be called into question: this is the case with the funerary epigram composed by Dioskorides (third century) for a certain Thrasyboulos 'who, when fighting the Argives, had received seven wounds, all to the front' (*Anth. Pal.* 7.229; Plutarch, *Ap. Lac.* 51, *Mor.* 234f–235a, vv. 2–3); even more is it the case for a text, in some respects a very odd one, of Aelian's (*VH* 12.21) on the role of mothers at the funerals of Spartan

warriors.[13] Texts dealing with actual battles inspire greater confidence: Diodorus says that at Leuctra, when the fighting began, 'those who resisted were killed or wounded; the blows were always dealt to the front' (15.55.4); and that, at Megalopolis, Agis the king was 'dealt numerous wounds, all of them to the front' (17.63.4). I believe that this is not simply a commonplace expression, and that an examination of wounds (unofficial, of course) was conducted. But it does not appear that this examination ever led to the imposing of punishment, and on two counts: when it is mentioned, the result is always positive, and it was only carried out on the dead (Leuctra is the sole case where the examination of the living wounded might be implied).

6. Surviving a defeat? Strict application of the principles explained to Xerxes by Demaratus, in Herodotus' account (7.104), would surely lead to a situation where anyone who had survived a defeat, however that may have come about, was regarded as a 'trembler'. Many modern scholars have thought that this was, in fact, the case.[14] It is true that there is a tendency in some texts to present the matter thus: Loraux noticed it in Plutarch's account of the aftermath of Leuctra,[15] and on the subject of Megalopolis, an expression of Diodorus' (text 6: '…they considered all the survivors of the defeat to be free of *atimia*') is in the same vein – even while other sentences in the same passage correct this impression. This simply shows that the belief we are discussing here was also widely held in antiquity, a fact which, given the times in which Diodorus and Plutarch were writing, is not at all surprising. In reality, if the survivors of Leuctra and Megalopolis were threatened with *atimia*, it is for another reason, and the only Spartan ever to have been punished for surviving a defeat is the unfortunate Aristodemos – to whom we may, if we like, add Pantites. Now, it is obvious that Thermopylae is not an ordinary defeat, and if Aristodemos was disgraced, it is, firstly, because he was the *only* survivor, but also, and chiefly, because, as Herodotus specifically states, Eurytos, who found himself in the same situation, *had* laid down his life. It is the epic of Thermopylae that has breathed life into the legend of the 'tremblers'; it is, likewise, that epic that was able to generate the belief that Sparta repudiated those of its warriors who survived a defeat.

7. Surviving one's King. In three of the four battles that make up this set of records, a king has met his death: Leonidas at Thermopylae, Cleombrotos at Leuctra, Agis at Megalopolis. Is this mere chance, or is surviving the king – which may be called 'letting him be killed' – a transgression that constitutes the offence of 'trembling'? Isocrates is quite categorical on the subject (text 5), although more so in *On the Peace* than in the *Letter*. In the former he seems to state that *all* the survivors of a defeat in which a king dies[16] are liable to

atimia in the same way as, or even more than, those guilty of deserting their posts or throwing away their shields. The second text corrects this assertion, the major part of which must be classed as rhetorical elaboration. The only ones concerned here are those whose battle station is around the person of the king and who act as his 'bodyguard' (φύλακες). Who exactly are they? The three hundred *hippeis* referred to by Thucydides in his account of the battle of Mantineia (5.72.4), as is generally thought? Or the one hundred 'chosen' (from among those three hundred?), mentioned by Herodotus (6.56)? This is not a question I intend to discuss here. Those accounts of battles that are available to us support the second of Isocrates' texts. At Leuctra, Xenophon (*Hell.* 6.4.13) and Diodorus (15.55.5 – 56.1) underline the extent to which those around the king fought fiercely, to the point either of being able to carry him, still living, from the field (Xenophon), or of retaining possession of his body (Diodorus); it is probably one of the elements that worked in favour of what, for brevity's sake, I shall term their acquittal. In the same way, when Diodorus is recounting the battle of Megalopolis, he firmly insists (17.63.4) on the fact that those who were fighting around Agis did not abandon him, but withdrew on his orders, leaving him on the field, in order to 'preserve themselves for the service of their homeland'. Now, in Book 19, 70, those affected by the proposed measure, to which Akrotatos was the only one opposed, were not all the survivors, as §5 might cause us to think; §4 states clearly that these were only 'young men' (πολλοὶ τῶν νέων). Thus he is dealing only with those who had fought around Agis, and the term 'young men' confirms that they were either the *hippeis* or a proportion of them. Surviving a king *can*, therefore, be punished as 'cowardice', but only in the case of those whose duty it was to surround him during a battle.

8. A form of *atimia* for 'civilian' offences? This is what is suggested by two passages in Xenophon's *LP*, the comparing of which brings the meaning into sharper focus. 10.7:

> εἰ δέ τις ἀποδειλιάσειε τοῦ τὰ νόμιμα διαπονεῖσθαι, τοῦτον ἐκεῖνος ἀπέδειξε μηδὲ νομίζεσθαι ἔτι τῶν ὁμοίων εἶναι,
>
> if someone, through cowardice, shrank from the hard effort required by the laws, he (Lycurgus) ordained that that man should no longer be reckoned a member of the *homoioi*.

Couched in very general terms, this formulation manifestly extends beyond the scope of purely military duties, something confirmed by the preceding sentence, which mentions 'every kind of virtue proper to the citizen'. But, one might say, the sanction described, that of being stripped of the quality of being 'Alike', is vague; is it certain that this means *atimia*? We need to look

15

at the other text. 3.3:

> ἐπιθεὶς δὲ καὶ εἴ τις ταῦτα φύγοι, μηδενὸς ἔτι τῶν καλῶν τυγχάνειν, ἐποίησε μὴ μόνον τοὺς ἐκ δημοσίου ἀλλὰ καὶ τοὺς κηδομένους ἑκάστων ἐπιμελεῖσθαι ὡς μὴ ἀποδειλιάσαντες ἀδόκιμοι παντάπασιν ἐν τῇ πόλει γένοιντο,

> by his ruling that if one of them (that is, the *paidiskoi*) dodged his obligations, he would forfeit his entitlement to the 'good things', he ensured that not only the representatives of the state, but also those responsible for each boy, should exercise the utmost vigilance to make sure that no shirking on his part could lead to the ruin of his reputation in the city.

What are the 'good things', *ta kala*, of which these unfortunate characters would henceforth be deprived? The expression, which seems typically Spartan, is usually translated 'honours'; but while honours, such as magistracies, are, in fact, included amongst them, the sense of the words is broader than that. They encompass everything that makes the life of the Spartan citizen a 'fine', that is to say noble, life, and one that is utterly free (μάλιστα ἐλεύθεροι, Critias). In the description, by that same Xenophon, of the 'trembler's' fate, we can read, by default, a list of these *kala*: communal dining, the gymnasium, games, dancing in chorus, the respect of one's juniors. It is clear that the destiny which, according to Xenophon, awaited those *paidiskoi* who fell short of Lycurgan discipline – a destiny evoked by the words ἀδόκιμοι παντάπασιν – resembles that of 'tremblers'. To be sure, they have not actually 'trembled', since that can only happen in the supreme test of battle, but the military metaphors underlying the vocabulary used in both passages (the verb ἀποδειλιάζω, which is common to both, contains the element δειλία, cowardice; διαπονεῖσθαι, in the first passage, contains πόνος, military 'exertion', which occurs in the sentence preceding the second passage, and to which ταῦτα refers) demonstrate the homology which unites, in the obligations of the citizen, both the civil and the military aspect. However, in all of that, we are dealing only with theory, or, to use a better term, ideology; official ideology, the image which Sparta presented to the outside world, and which Xenophon relays *ad lib*. One might be even more cautious faced with the 7th precept of the *Instituta Laconica* attributed to Plutarch (*Mor.* 237c), which relates that the *erastēs* convicted of having had physical relations with his *erōmenos* was punished with *atimia* for life. In reality, we know of not a single case where *atimia* was imposed on a Spartan for other than military reasons.

A certain number of specific actions, then, may be regarded as constituting or aggravating the crime of 'cowardice': flight, abandoning one's shield, capitulation, deserting one's post, abandoning the king. But none of these offences is strictly defined or codified, essentially because the procedure which follows it does not take the form of a trial as it does in Athens. There was nonetheless a hierarchy of misdemeanours, and hence of the sanction, if we believe Isocrates' statement (text 5 b), according to which abandoning the king was a greater dishonour than abandoning one's shield.

V. The sanction: social exclusion

For convenience in this study, we may divide the numerous constituents of the sanction into two categories – social measures (the conduct of shunning), and measures of a more legal and political aspect – while never losing sight of the fact that, for the Spartans themselves, such a distinction would have had little meaning.

Tyrtaeus describes the social sanction (text 1: ὅσσα … κακά), but in so vague a manner that, as we have seen, there is no certainty that this is already the same sanction that Xenophon described. The other texts describe a genuine distancing, termed 'boycott' by Ehrenberg [17] and 'social ostracism' by MacDowell;[18] but these terms only fit one feature of the reality, since the exclusion is not total.

1. Herodotus, in his account of Aristodemos, mentions only two sanctions, two that also present a peculiarity in that they do not appear in any other source:[19] no one offers fire to the 'trembler', and no one addresses a word to him. In order to explain the brevity of Herodotus' list, while still reconciling his description with those of other authors, it is naturally tempting to argue that it was not his intention to give a comprehensive account of Aristodemos' condition, but merely to give examples of some of its most stinging characteristics. His expression πάσχων τοιάδε, 'he suffered treatment of this kind', might appear to support this; but, in reality, τοιάδε does not necessarily imply that what follows should be only a selection of data.

The problem that immediately presents itself, then, is that of knowing whether we can legitimately combine Herodotus' account with those of Xenophon and Plutarch. It seems strange that this 'sending to Coventry',[20] this extreme form of boycott, which, in the end, makes the sanction discussed by Herodotus even more harsh than those discussed by the other authors, should not be mentioned by them. We might even wonder whether the sanctions are reconcilable: how conceivable is it that all the situations in which Xenophon, for example, places his 'trembler', could occur in absolute silence? We almost get the impression that the sanction we are dealing with here is not the same one: the *atimia* referred to by Herodotus constitutes exclusion from all social relations, which, as we shall see, is not the case with that of Xenophon and Plutarch. E. David seems to have been aware of this difference, but the interpretation he gives of it[21] creates some difficulty. For him, Aristodemos would not actually have been declared 'trembler', and the term, in his case, would only have been a kind of nickname. Actually, 'trembler' is 'a kind of nickname' *in every case*, the 'true' name being, as we know, *atimos*. In any case, what else does it mean to be a 'trembler' if not to be called by that term? [22]

2. The texts of Xenophon and Plutarch are of quite a different character: they offer a description of the 'trembler's' condition[23] which lists numerous features of it and is seemingly intended to be exhaustive; what they are presenting is a genuine *portrait* of it. We should start by reading Xenophon's account (text 4). The fact that he gives so much detail on the subject stems not (or not essentially) from a taste for the picturesque but from an ideological purpose, which is explained at §4. As in every part of his work on the laws of Sparta, he aims to contrast their rigour and efficacy with the laxity and illogicality found in other cities. This is why he takes the trouble to collect and explain to the last detail all the measures taken against the 'tremblers' to exclude them from the civic community. No doubt his information is excellent, but, when he speaks of 'other cities', his partiality leads him to distort things: it is not true, for example, that in Athens (the only case of which we have some small knowledge) the sole punishment faced by the coward was to be called a coward, and that he could continue to frequent the *agora* as though nothing had happened.[24] Certainly, Xenophon could say, by way of response, that it was not to the coward as such that entry to the Athenian *agora* could have been forbidden, but to someone on whom this form of *atimia* had been imposed after trial – but it would not be very convincing.

a. Exclusion from the *syssition*. One would have no hesitation in reading the word σύσκηνον as '*syssition* member': it is the usage constantly employed by the author of *LP*.[25] Still less would one have trouble thinking that 'any man would be ashamed to receive him' is tantamount, in practice, to exclusion, since the *syssition* only functions by means of mutual acceptance and unanimous consensus.

b. Exclusion from the gymnasium. Here, things are slightly different, and Xenophon's expression is to be taken literally. No one can *forbid* the 'trembler' to go into the gymnasium, but no one would be prepared to pursue a physical activity in his company, and thus such activities are rendered inaccessible to him. Given these conditions, it is hard to see what, other than pure masochism, could impel him to go to the gymnasium. On their own, these two forms of exclusion correspond, for a Spartan, to his being deprived of the very essence of those 'good things' offered by the city. After that, Xenophon moves on to measures that are more to do with the details of everyday life.

c. Another physical activity, the ball game. It may be surprising to find the adverb πολλάκις introducing both the ball game and dancing in chorus: does this signify that what is about to be described takes place no more than 'often', and thus that there are also times when the 'trembler' might participate in a game or have a regular place in a chorus? This seems scarcely probable, and it might be preferable to take the view that, with this adverb, Xenophon is indicating that these things, whilst not as rigidly regulated as communal messing and gymnastic activities, still take place often, and form part of the flow of life. All the same, one could also maintain the following argument: if the 'trembler' was invariably excluded from games, he would no longer even turn up there; whereas if it so happened, even just once in every ten games, that he was accepted, he would regularly try his luck, which would then give the others the fun of humiliating him. We might think this process too subtle to be attributable to the Spartans, but, when it comes to devising humiliations, the inventiveness of human societies knows no bounds, and it is in the nature of the overall exclusion imposed on the 'trembler' that it should not be complete, precisely in order to make it more distressing.

We only have any real knowledge of ball games in the Imperial era, when they officially formed part of the *ephēbeia* and even seem to constitute its crowning event.[26] For the hellenistic era we know nothing,[27] and, for the classical, our only source is this text.[28] At this period, the game must already have been a little like what certain texts enable us to reconstruct for the Roman era. The problem facing us is that of establishing whether the matches in question take place within the framework of an official competition, or whether these are spontaneous street games. Ollier[29] claims that there was a close relationship between the games to which Xenophon refers and those of the Roman era, which makes one think that for him they are official competitions. Kennell reckons that they are street games because the participants are adults; in fact, he thinks it inconceivable that competitions existed for any but the young. This does not seem to me an acceptable argument; there is no reason why there should not have been 'tremblers' among the *hēbōntes*, and competitions for those aged over thirty, as in the Gymnopaediae. The only thing that could perhaps settle the matter, then, is to examine in detail the wording of the text itself. The adverbial διαιρουμένων τοὺς ἀντισφαιριοῦντας, 'when teams are being picked for a ball game', seems at first to imply, through the opposition of genitive and accusative, the existence of an authority, independent of the teams, who does the selecting, which would mean that the setting is an official competition. But this is not necessarily the case. When one watches games being played in the street or on recreation grounds, one sees that the commonest procedure is as follows. A group arrives, close-knit and undifferentiated, of those who want a game.

19

From this group there immediately emerge, by a general, tacit consent, two leaders, who are regarded as the best players. It is they who alternately, and position by position, assemble the teams, in such a way that the least able are the last to be picked, some of them even failing to be picked at all, at the point when the teams are reckoned complete. Now, the words used by Xenophon, διαιρεῖσθαι and ἀχώριστος, seem to me perfectly suited to a process of this kind. So, like Kennell, I think that it is better to view this as a game organized spontaneously between youths and young men at some place or other in town. Our 'trembler' may approach, become interested in what is going on, and, tacitly, offer himself for a place in the team: a wasted effort, for, by unanimous agreement, he is almost invariably left on the side.

d. What he says about dancing in chorus, whilst certainly crystal clear to the readers of the time, is not obvious to us. As before, the first problem is to ascertain whether the dances in question are official, performed during festivals and before spectators, or dances improvised among friends, purely as a distraction, as is still (albeit less and less) the practice in Greece. The Spartans' passion for dance was proverbial, as is shown, for instance, by a phrase from a satirical poet of the beginning of the fifth century, Pratinas of Phleious, as cited by Athenaeus (14.632f; f. 2 Bergk), Λάκων ὁ τέττιξ εὔτυκος ἐς χόρον, 'the Laconian cicada, always ready for a dance'.[30] To see the Spartan being assimilated, on account of his inordinate love of dancing (inseparably linked with song), to the cicada, symbol of improvidence in Aesop's fable, may well surprise those who want to see only the Tyrtaean face of Sparta and forget that of Alcman; but that is how it is, which means that this dancing could very well be spontaneous. Nevertheless, in contrast to what happens in the ball game, the 'trembler' here is not left on one side; this suggests that the dancers are not at liberty to reject him, and thus that the dancing is organized by the state.[31] An examination of the second problem confirms this: what are these 'demeaning positions' to which the 'tremblers' are relegated? It would seem *a priori* inconceivable that certain positions in the choruses which sang and danced at religious festivals could have been deemed 'contemptible' or 'demeaning'.[32] Nevertheless, some texts demonstrate that this was indeed the case. Those in question are two apophthegms from the collection of *Apophthegmata Laconica*. In Agesilaus 6 (*Mor.* 208d), the future king, while still a child, finds himself assigned a place in the chorus of the Gymnopaediae that is 'almost out of sight', ἄσημος τόπος. The apophthegm of Damonidas (*Mor.* 219e) specifies that the humiliating position assigned to him by the chorus leader was in the back row;[33] in the other version of it (*Reg. et Imp.*, *Mor.* 191f) the word τελευταία is used.

e. With the following two sentences, which are closely linked, the author tackles the question of precedence. The idea is that, for the 'trembler', the normal rules governing precedence are suspended, and that in every situation he must give way. As all Greeks knew, the rule at Sparta required the youngest to observe the following marks of respect towards the oldest: to give them priority in the places where one usually walks, in the streets; and where one normally sits, to vacate, and offer them, one's seat. Herodotus states that the Spartans were the only Greeks to observe these customs,[34] the best known of which was that of yielding one's seat.[35] A Spartan inscription recently published,[36] and almost contemporaneous with Xenophon, shows that this really was what happened; it is carved on a marble seat dedicated to Alea, and ends with the words τὼς δὲ νέως τοῖς περγυτέροις ὑποχάδδην, 'that the young surrender their place to their elders'.

f. The next subject to be introduced concerns family life and, in particular, marriage. The discussion forms a firmly structured unit and combines, by opposition, τὰς μὲν κόρας | γυναικὸς δέ. The first part of the sentence poses serious problems of sense. The προσήκουσαι κόραι are young girls over whom the 'trembler' exercises *kyrieia*. At first glance one may think that they are his daughters, but for that to be possible they would need to have been born before his 'trembling', since we later learn that he cannot marry. It could also refer to his sisters, if the father is dead (this seems often to have been the case in Sparta, by the time children reach this age), or even to his more distant relations; in any case, the vagueness of the expression is surprising. Be that as it may, the natural interpretation seems to be that what is under discussion is their education, and thus that, if their *kyrios* had not been a 'trembler', this would have taken place outside the home. Where, though? Should we take this to mean the choruses, where some young girls received what might seem like a form of education? Only part of their time was spent on this, however, and it is obvious that the home is where girls were, in the main, brought up. Further, Lipka[37] is absolutely right to point out that, in the classical era, ἀνανδρία normally means 'cowardice'; as he sees it, the young girls, irked by being confined at home, are constantly upbraiding their *kyrios* for his cowardice. Nonetheless, it would be surprising if, in a sentence which, as I have said, forms a unit, and where the subject is (for the 'trembler') the absence of marriage, this word *anandria* should mean anything other than female celibacy. So, a better interpretation (it is, indeed, the most common) would be that τρέφειν has its literal meaning, 'to feed', and that what forces the young girls to remain at home is the impossibility of their *kyrios*'s marrying them off; that is why they belabour him with reproaches. This is clearly how Plutarch (text 8, §3) interprets Xenophon: δοῦναί τινι τούτων γυναῖκα sums up the second part of the sentence, and λαβεῖν the first.

21

As for the 'trembler' himself, in symmetrical fashion 'he sees his home devoid of a wife'. He cannot marry, then, but one is tempted to ask what happens if he is married already: it is eminently possible that, in this situation, the marriage would have been dissolved. Xenophon adds that the fact that marriage is impossible for him does not exempt him from paying a fine, ζημία. This fine is obviously one imposed on unmarried men. It is not one of the sanctions Plutarch describes when discussing this subject in his *Life of Lycurgus* (15.1–3), but, at the end of his *Life of Lysander*,[38] he does make an allusion to it, no doubt derived from a third-century author, Ariston of Ceos.[39] The unmarried man, therefore, did pay a fine. This should not be viewed as an annual tax, quasi fiscal in nature, but as a penalty, probably imposed by the ephors.[40]

We have still to establish the best way to view the 'trembler's' inability to contract a marriage, on his own account or on that of others. MacDowell[41] and Link,[42] for once in agreement, reckon that it existed only in fact and not in law, being solely the result of a social situation: it is because no other *kyrios* countenanced having any relations with the 'trembler' that he was unable to conclude a marriage. The principal argument for adopting this view is that the context, in Xenophon, is one of social exclusion, this again being a matter of fact rather than of law; that, moreover, is how Plutarch reads this clause, as we shall see. On the other hand, we cannot deny that the fine mentioned immediately afterwards by Xenophon is a legal reality. This clause may be compared with the passage in Thucydides (text 3) describing the *atimia* inflicted on the former prisoners of Sphacteria. These men lost another aspect of *kyrieia*: they are no longer 'their own masters' when it comes to concluding a sale or purchase. This comparison, which to me seems inescapable, leads me to conclude that the sanction reported by Xenophon was itself also legal in character; this would be only natural: marriage is a social action, but also, by virtue of its implications in matters of finance, economics, prestige and power, it is also undoubtedly, in the societies of Greek cities, one of the most legalistic actions that exists. That dimension cannot be lacking here.

g. To round off this portrait, Xenophon returns to the social life of the 'trembler', but on a very particular point: his appearance. It is an appropriate appearance for him, and one which he must strictly maintain. He is forbidden to walk through the town *liparos*. This adjective is difficult to translate;[43] it signifies the mark of prosperity, of that *eudaimonia* the meaning of which is nearer to material well-being than to happiness. Spartan citizens, it seems, had not only to be happy at being Spartan citizens, but to display this happiness as well; the 'trembler' had to adopt a bearing that would render him utterly distinct from them. This is what Xenophon says: he must not 'imitate' honourable men; his demeanour must constitute a kind of uniform enabling him to be recognized at once for what he is, which in turn would allow the forms of discrimination discussed earlier to be applied to him. The same went for the helots; they, too, says Myron of Priene, had a kind of uniform, in their case a garment, and their physical appearance itself had to reflect their inferior condition.[44] Like the helots, those 'tremblers' who failed to observe this rule were punished, though in a less severe manner; while the helot was put to death, the 'trembler' could only be struck by the person who caught him at it. I do not agree with Link, therefore, when he maintains[45] that this striking was not punitive, but merely an expression of the contempt of which the 'trembler' was the object. In the first place, we can see that, unlike the citizens (or: the other citizens), as MacDowell rightly pointed out,[46] he was not protected by the law from being struck; it follows that this striking, coming as it does straight after the comment about the 'offence in appearance', was indeed the punishment for it.

3. The passage from Plutarch (text 8, §§3–4) may be divided into two parts, which correspond only approximately to paragraphs. The first is made up of notices drawn from other authors. The exclusion from any of the magistracies is certainly taken from Thucydides (text 3); we shall come back to that. The rest are repeated from Xenophon, but Plutarch selects, summarizes, adapts, and sometimes modifies the data. Without one's being able to say why, he omits all the points which, in Xenophon's account, precede that of marriage. Of that subject he gives a summary which is highly satisfactory and, at the same time, shows how he interprets the text: the ban is, in principle, social, not legal (ἄδοξόν ἐστί). The information on striking he both summarizes and distorts: it is no longer a punishment against the 'offence in appearance' but a mark of contempt which the citizens might visit on the 'tremblers' as the fancy takes them. We may draw a lesson in method from this observation: as I have said when discussing education,[47] we can seek information on what happened in the classical era from Plutarch, but only on condition that we check it against Xenophon. In this case, too, we cannot base an argument solely on information as it appears in Plutarch, as Link has done; we must also refer to the 'original', and where there is a discrepancy, it is, of course, the 'original' that must be treated as authoritative.

The beginning of the following sentence (§4), 'they have to resign themselves to going about in coarse and dirty clothing', broadly constitutes a repetition of Xenophon's sentence concerning the 'trembler's' appearance, '(he) cannot walk about looking cheerful, nor may he try to imitate honourable men'. Thus, 'they have to resign themselves' (καρτεροῦσι) is a more banal transposition of the process employed by Xenophon, namely, a long string of verbal adjectives describing the obligation. But, if the analogy works for 'coarse' (ταπεινοί), which conveys very well the sense of Xenophon's statement, 'dirt' (αὐχμηροί) is a novel indication, perhaps a significant one (because this feature, unlike the others, implies the total collaboration of those being punished), but perhaps also a simple notice of what comes next. In fact, this no longer owes anything to the author of the *LP*, and that obviously raises the question of its source, together with the corollary, its value. These questions will be examined later on; for now, we shall consider in themselves the data transmitted by Plutarch. He adds two fresh details to the portrait of the 'trembler'. Firstly, his garment. The cloak, called a τρίβων, is well known: it is thick and robust, but rougher and devoid of elegance, the cloak of the peasant, and also of the philosopher, who, by wearing it, displays his contempt for luxury. From Plutarch's pen, the word has no pejorative connotation, rather the reverse: for him, the *tribōn* is one of the emblems of Spartan austerity and virtue;[48] being regarded, from the hellenistic era onwards (cf. Hodkinson 2000, 220), as the Spartan garment *par excellence*, it is not what signifies to Plutarch the contempt felt for the 'trembler'. It is the adjectives, therefore, that convey this sense. The word προσερραμμένος is used to describe one fabric sewn with another. This may mean 'patchwork', and it seems that by interpreting the next piece of information as meaning 'brightly coloured', commentators may sometimes have envisaged the kind of motley worn by Harlequin or by a clown,[49] which obviously would set the 'trembler' utterly apart. I believe it was nothing of the kind. Certainly, βαπτός only means 'stained', and the expression χρώματος βαπτοῦ – in the singular, hence there is *only one* colour, which would exclude Harlequin's motley – can just as well mean 'of a brilliant colour', applied to a wedding garment,[50] as 'of sombre hue', applied to a mourning garment;[51] but one could not say that the 'trembler' was 'in festive mode', and a shimmering garment would contradict the ταπεινοί which precedes it. It seems to me that the colour absolutely has to be a sombre one. This cloak, then, is patched and dun-coloured;[52] a poor and shabby garment, unquestionably, and, for that reason, shameful, but devoid of the clownish element that has sometimes been attributed to it.

The other detail added by Plutarch, that of the semi-shaven beard, has an entirely different meaning. I cannot quite see the point of the – by now almost traditional[53] – comparison with the ephors' annual proclamation ordering citizens to shave their moustaches;[54] neither of these two data sheds any light on the other. J.P. Vernant[55] has pondered on the proper way to view this semi-shave: is one cheek clean-shaven and the other not, or is the beard cut to half its usual length? Since Plutarch's text on this point is crystal-clear, his enquiry seems superfluous. The real question, then, is what this curious practice means. The answer is supplied by the passage of Herodotus (2.121*d*) where he tells how the thief of Rhampsinitus, having made the guards drunk so that he can recover his brother's body, shaves the right cheek of each one 'by way of insult' (ἐπὶ λύπῃ). One might object that, since the action happens in Egypt and not in Greece, this text is not conclusive,[56] but there is another which shows that in Greece, too, the semi-shave was a mark of derision: lines 226–7 of Aristophanes' *Thesmophoriazusae*. Euripides says to Mnesilochos, whom he has half shaved: 'Won't you be laughed at, with your face half shaved?' Are we looking here at an allusion to the 'tremblers', as N. Richer has suggested?[57] That would show that this aspect of the portrait of the Spartan *atimos* was well known to the Athenian public around 410; but the text is perfectly understandable without that. It appears that the practice of semi-shaving someone, to make fun of and humiliate him, was known throughout the ancient world: not only in Greece and Egypt, therefore, but also among the Hebrews and their neighbours. 2 Samuel, 10, 4: Hanun, king of the Ammonites, causes the ambassadors sent by David to be subjected to this treatment, as an insult; this is the origin of the first Ammonite war. Curiously, this practice is associated, as it is in Plutarch's text about the 'tremblers', with a peculiarity (although a different one) of dress: 'He ordered each to be shaved of half his beard, and his garment to be cut to half its length, from the level of the thigh.' One possible explanation for the universal nature of this practice is that it works in every case: it works as well for societies where the rule is to be clean-shaven as for those where it is to be bearded, and for those where there is no rule either way.

Concerning the information supplied by Plutarch, there remains the fundamental question: is it reliable?[58] There is no problem about the cloak, for Plutarch is only summarizing what Xenophon says, namely, that the 'trembler' may not go about *liparos*; shame and poverty are his companions. In the case of the semi-shave, the situation is very different. To Xenophon's description, which is focused on the process of exclusion, it adds a new and important note of insult and cruel humiliation.[59] This detail is not, in itself, improbable; it recalls the 'ritual' of humiliating helots in the *syssition*. What is difficult to credit, though, is that Xenophon should have had no knowledge of so striking a feature, or if he did know of it that he should not have taken account of it. We have to admit that it is a serious problem and ask ourselves who Plutarch's source could have been.

The 'trembler' seems, then, to be caught in a web both of demeaning obligations and of embargos. From this point of view, his condition is somewhat like that of the Crypteian:[60] in a sense, the exclusion of the latter is more radical in that he may not have any contact with other people and is condemned to roam in the wilderness, but it remains a temporary condition and is almost akin to a game. In the case of the 'trembler', it is the others who, in their relations with him, have to effect the embargos: in the *syssition*, the gymnasium, ball games, in choruses, in matrimonial relations. So we may ask what sanction was imposed on a person who failed to respect the embargos, a person who, in any of life's domains, agreed to maintain true social relations with his old fellow citizen who had become 'taboo'. Was he, in his turn, assimilated to the 'tremblers'? There is no certainty that it was necessary to go that far; there was probably no sanction other than that of 'shame' (Xenophon: αἰσχυνθείη), which also works like an exclusion, albeit a less formal one than that of the 'trembler'. As regards the demeaning obligations, these are required of the 'trembler' himself: giving way in the street, giving up his seat, maintaining a demeanour and physical appearance in conformity with his condition. By virtue of these, he shows that he subscribes to the very standard that excludes him from society, and collaborates in administering his own punishment.

Taking the sanction as a whole, the social aspect was certainly the most distressing. Exile might perhaps have been preferable: we shall come back to this, when we look at the case of Aristokles and Hipponoidas. Death, too, might have been preferable. Herodotus (text 2, §232) records, in indirect style, the suicide of Pantites, who would have been a fellow of Aristodemos; but he gives the impression that he is not wholly convinced of the story. David has suggested[61] reading an allusion to suicide into the final sentence of that passage of Xenophon's (text 4), where the point at issue is that of 'preferring death to such *atimia*'. This is a tempting interpretation, but in my view it is belied by the fact that this sentence forms a 'circle' together with the first one in the chapter, ἄξιον δὲ τοῦ Λυκούργου καὶ τόδε ἀγασθῆναι, τὸ κατεργάσασθαι ἐν τῇ πόλει αἱρετώτερον εἶναι τὸν καλὸν θάνατον ἀντὶ τοῦ αἰσχροῦ βίου, ('Lycurgus must also be admired for creating a situation where, in the city, honourable death should have been preferable to dishonourable life'), a sentence in which suicide is absolutely excluded by the words καλὸς θάνατος.

These modes of exclusion are at once actual and symbolic. To some extent they are actual by virtue of being symbolic, since, when it comes to social relations, it is principally the symbols that count; but exclusions such as those from the *syssition*, and the gymnasium, and the inability to conclude a marriage, involve the very foundations of Spartan life. What could be more normal than to exclude the *kakos* (which, in the end, is perhaps a more precise and more correct term than *tresas*, in spite of appearances) from all *kala*? Alongside such serious measures, an irritation like being excluded from a ball game may seem trifling. A. Powell[62] has quite rightly made us aware that this element is somewhat unexpected in so tragic a context and would seem to be more at home where, say, one out of a group of children has been put in quarantine. Powell concludes from this that the society created by adult Spartans preserved some features of the child-society in which it began, during education. This is doubtless true, but we should not infer from it that Spartan society had anything of the puerile about it; it is simply that, in our eyes, there is a certain analogy between Spartan society and those of children, which is due to the fact that, there, the individual is fused into the community and only really exists by virtue of it.

The most remarkable feature of this exclusion is that it is not total. No one is saying that the 'trembler' should be excluded from his *syssition* or gymnasium; it is just that no one there wants his company. No one is saying that he must be excluded from the ball games; it is just that no one wants him in the team. He is not excluded from the chorus: he may join in, but only in an 'ignominious' position. His *kyrieia* within the family is not taken away from him and conferred on one of his male relatives: it is, in a sense, 'frozen' and cannot be exercised. He is not forbidden to walk in the streets, or to sit with others where one usually sits: but he must give way, and give up his seat, while his dress, his bearing, his expression, must conform to what is ordained by a code that applies to no one but him. He is allowed, therefore, to take some part in the social life of the city, provided he does no more than hang about on the edge of it. So he is not a radical outcast, like the helot; but it is, perhaps, the ambiguity of this situation that makes it worse than utterly miserable to endure. He may watch other people living their lives, he is always on the point of joining in, but each time remains left on the side. I do not think we need see in this a deliberate refinement of cruelty; this behaviour has no conscious aim, but constitutes a system of signs that expresses the imposition of a segregated position in the hierarchy of the city.

VI. THE SANCTION: INSTITUTIONAL FEATURES

The features of the 'tremblers'' condition that we have just studied belong in the most classic of sociologies and are conceivable in any traditional society that is firmly structured and based on a code of honour. They give a quite spectacular instance of what may be a 'shame-culture'. But the 'tremblers'' condition has another side to it, whose existence rests on the fact that Sparta is also a political society which functions according to the rule of law.

1. The 'trembler' and the rank of citizen. One of the citizen's chief prerogatives was his eligibility to hold magistracies; was the 'trembler' stripped of this? Thucydides (text 3) may appear explicitly to say so, but his statement refers only to the former prisoners of Sphacteria, and this does not obviously entitle us to apply it to 'tremblers' in general (if indeed there were 'tremblers in general'). Plutarch makes the same assertion, and this time in a sentence about all 'tremblers', but what he is indicating may only be extrapolated from

the lone record of Thucydides. So we might well have reservations about the sources; the fact remains that it is hard to imagine Spartans agreeing to obey men whom they have declared unworthy and to whom they mete out various forms of insulting treatment. This is more especially the case as the magistracies include appointments to military commands: how could those be entrusted to men who have been punished for cowardice? Plutarch specifies – when Thucydides does not – that 'tremblers' were excluded 'from every office'. To that we may add the Athenian parallel: exclusion from holding office is a feature, so to speak, of the very basis of Athenian *atimia*. Even so, care is needed when using this parallel: of course it would be a mistake not to draw a comparison with Athens (Ehrenberg, for instance, might be held to have made this mistake), but the comparison should be kept as such, and not turned into the basis of an argument. On the whole, we may reckon that exclusion from office is something almost obvious.

To admit that, however, does not entail regarding the 'trembler' as having been demoted from his rank as Spartan citizen; this point also needs discussion. In support of the existence of such a demotion, it may be stressed that Spartan citizens received the appellation – which has something of a title about it – 'peers', *homoioi*. It is obvious that one who suffers the 'trembler's' *atimia* ceases to be 'peer' with the others; in respect of the Spartans, he is neither peer nor even equal to them; he becomes their inferior. If one thinks that this argument presses language too far, one may also refer to Xenophon's sentence (*LP* 10.7), already cited (p. 15), 'if anyone shrinks from the effort required of him by the laws, he should no longer be reckoned one of the *homoioi*'. The civic virtues to which this text refers undoubtedly included military ones: Plato even reproaches the Spartans for having too far reduced virtue to the single military standard. So, it looks as though we can infer from this passage that, in Xenophon's time at least, the 'trembler' was demoted from his rank as Spartan citizen.

A doubt on this point could have been raised from an anecdote told by Aeschines.[63] Is the individual who, in this account, puts a proposal to the Spartan assembly, a 'trembler'? If he was, that would obviously prove that 'tremblers' retained this fundamental prerogative of the citizen. Aeschines' vocabulary is ambiguous: while, at the end, τῶν ἀποδεδειλιακότων... ἀνθρώπων might seem to echo Xenophon's text discussed above, the wording at the beginning, ἀνδρὸς βεβιωκότος αἰσχρῶς, which is more specifically applied to the 'anonyme indigne', as Richer has christened him, leads rather to the conclusion that it was on account of his private life that the 'righteous' looked askance on him. F. Ruzé considers it possible that the person in question is a 'trembler', but she formulates other hypotheses as well;[64] Richer alone seems to agree. Perhaps we do better to trust Plutarch:

the language he employs when he repeats the anecdote in the *Moralia*[65] demonstrates that he saw in this individual someone who was disqualified only in the moral sense. I even think it can be proved that for Aeschines the incident did not involve a 'trembler'. In fact, before he introduces the anecdote, the author holds up the Spartans to the Athenians as an example of severity when it came to eligibility to speak; yet this individual put a proposal to the Spartan assembly, whereas in Athens, according to Aeschines himself,[66] that was forbidden to *atimoi*.

I do not think, either, that one could, at this point, derive an argument from Thucydides' passage about the prisoners of Sphacteria (text 3), and the fact that it says only that they were rendered ineligible to hold magistracies, and does not mention a loss of citizen rank; because we have still to determine whether this text can be applied to 'tremblers' in general. In fact, there are solid arguments to support the notion that they retained their civic status. I do not regard those used by Link as being in this category;[67] but the fact is that the 'trembler' continues to participate – within certain limits and in a certain way – in the life of the city. What does Xenophon's description show? That he is an object of contempt and avoidance for the civic community. That does not prove that he was excluded from it (in a sense one might say that it demonstrates almost exactly the reverse): the case of the unmarried, whose membership of the citizen body is not called in question at all, clearly shows that in Sparta one could be a citizen and, at the same time, an object of contempt. And, in fact, the 'trembler' pays the fine imposed on the unmarried, just as do citizens in those circumstances. What, then, are we to make of Xenophon, *LP* 10.7? Should we conclude that, among the Spartan citizenry, only those with unblemished records deserved the 'title' of *homoioi*?[68]

For my part, I do not mean to claim either that the 'tremblers' lost their citizen rank, or that they retained it. For a start, it may be that matters varied with circumstances: thus, one could maintain that Aristodemos lost his citizenship, and that the prisoners of Sphacteria retained theirs. Above all, among the Greeks this rank comprised such a multiplicity of rights and prerogatives that it could have been restricted without being withdrawn altogether; the problem should not be couched in all-or-nothing terms. Take the case of the fourth-century Athenian in a state of *atimia*; in its full form it would forbid him to do the following:[69] hold a magistracy; be a judge; speak or make a proposal in, or even attend, the assembly; frequent the *agora* and the sanctuaries; bring, or testify in, a lawsuit. None of the really important rights remain to him, and yet no one would claim that he is not a citizen any more, even when he no longer meets the theoretical criteria laid down by Aristotle;[70] he is not registered as a metic. In this respect, the situation in

Sparta was possibly rather similar; there would have been citizens of reduced rank, who no longer had a right to the 'title' *homoioi*.

2. The 'trembler' and war. We might be tempted to think it a matter of course, at least in principle, that the 'trembler', having displayed his incapacity for fighting, lost – by virtue of the tacit rule 'once a trembler always a trembler' – another fundamental prerogative of the citizen, membership of the army; his presence there could deprive the phalanx of the cohesion that was indispensable to it. Nevertheless, we also know that, during the classical era, the Spartans had men fighting as hoplites who were not citizens – inferiors and even helots.

Records of the practice, as lawyers would say, appear contradictory as well. Besides, there are only two of them. The first is the case of Aristodemos, who, despite being deemed a 'trembler' after Thermopylae, still fought at the battle of Plataea (Herodotus 9.71). Tending the other way are the events which Plutarch records, several times, and with some minor differences, as having occurred in Sparta after Leuctra. According to him, one of the reasons that led the Spartans to refrain from declaring those who had fled that battle to be 'tremblers', was that in such circumstances the city could not afford to deprive itself of so many fighting men.[71] The matter is expressed like this, *en passant*, as if it were taken as read that 'tremblers' could no longer fight. The difference between the fate of Aristodemos and that hanging over the survivors of Leuctra is explained by Ehrenberg (col. 2296) in terms of a hardening of the city's attitude to 'cowards', which had developed in the interim; but the trend we observe goes, rather, in the opposite direction. Hence it is the case of Aristodemos which must have contravened the rule, and, in fact, everything in its context is exceptional: the nature of the 'defeat' at Thermopylae, the decisive character of the battle of Plataea, the fact that Aristodemos was the only one in his predicament,[72] the fact that he was absent from Thermopylae and so did not actually 'tremble'.

Despite the very limited number of known cases, it seems to me probable that the 'tremblers' were removed from the army for the duration of their punishment. I would even be inclined to think that this was the most fundamental form of exclusion, the one of which all the others were merely the consequence: what it actually meant was that the 'trembler' had lost his very *manliness* (is not one of the names for cowardice *anandria*?), and the entire catalogue of exclusions could be re-examined from that point of view (above all, *syssition*, gymnasium, precedence and *kyrieia*).

3. The 'trembler' and the law. Did the condition of 'tremblers' have specifically legal aspects? From the rules that concern them, MacDowell[73] picked

out three which to him seemed relevant to law: exclusion from magistracies and perhaps from all political activity; the fact that the law did not in every case protect them from physical violence; lastly, the clause reported by Thucydides and which we are about to examine. By contrast, Link[74] sees a legal character only in the actual decision to declare someone a 'trembler'; in his view, all the other measures are the province of social exclusion only. Not only would I side with MacDowell on this issue, but I am tempted to add a fourth measure to his list, the one concerning marriage (see above, p. 22). We still have to look at what Thucydides says, 5.34.2 (text 3): ...ἀτιμίαν δὲ τοιάνδε ὥστε μήτε ἄρχειν μήτε πριαμένους τι ἢ πωλοῦντας κυρίους εἶναι, 'the effect of this *atimia* was such that they could not hold office, nor had they the right to buy and sell.' What concerns us here is the clause on buying and selling: if this is not a legal matter, we might ask what else could be such. The key word is κυρίους; it expresses the inability to be a contractant with full rights in matters of buying and selling. The goods at which this is aimed are those for which the transfer is made by contract, such as property and slaves.[75] While this measure is severe, it should also be noted that it is limited in scope, as are those that bring about social exclusion: the 'trembler' retains the ownership and the management of his property, all he loses is the right to part with them, without this right's being transferred to anyone else (he keeps the *ius utendi* and loses the *ius abutendi*). I wonder whether the primary purpose of this partial removal of *kyrieia* was not to prevent the *atimoi* concerned from realizing their assets so that they could go into exile and thus escape the condition awaiting them. It seems logical, in any case, to relate this clause to the one concerning marriage, since in both cases we have to deal with the loss of *kyrieia*; that would affirm the entirely legal nature of the 'trembler's' inability to conclude a marriage on his own account or on that of others.

Are we justified, though, in combining Thucydides' and Xenophon's accounts? On the specific point of loss of *kyrieia*, I think the close relationship and the manifest complementarity of the two clauses make it legitimate to do so; but in the background a preliminary problem raises its head: how to interpret Thucydides? There are actually two ways of understanding this text. According to the first, the author is giving a partial description of a sanction which is, in terms of facts, the same as that analysed by Herodotus, Xenophon and Plutarch. His description would be a partial one, whether intentionally, because he would not have wanted to launch into a discussion of *atimia*, and restricted himself to a few illustrative examples; or because his own intellectual make-up would cause him to focus his attention on the political and legal aspects, while excluding anything that smacked of picturesque detail: no one expects from Thucydides the kind of description supplied by

31

Xenophon. The sanction concerned would always be the same in every case, and one would have to combine Herodotus, Thucydides, Xenophon and Plutarch, in order to create a complete picture of it. We could accept that, but what is very strange, even so, is that Thucydides reproduces nothing from Herodotus on this point, in the same way that Xenophon, in his turn, repeats nothing from either Herodotus or Thucydides; not until Plutarch do we find someone compiling the accounts of his predecessors, and that, as we have seen, only partially. Whereas the Greeks' *corpora* of knowledge have generally been built up by a process of accumulation and successive repetition (with occasional corrections), here everything proceeds as though each of the three historians from the classical era had been intent on presenting his own particular version of the condition of the 'trembler'.

It is doubtless preferable, then, to interpret the text in another way. The very formulation of Thucydides' account seems to preclude his having intended only a partial description. It is for that reason that one would agree with Link[76] in reckoning that the sanction against the prisoners of Sphacteria was strictly as Thucydides described it; which implies, among other things, that the *atimoi* could still attend the assembly and would not be the objects of any of the irksome measures enumerated by Herodotus, Xenophon and Plutarch. That could be explained in terms of how the institution evolved through the fifth century: around 420, the 'tremblers'' *atimia* would have been reduced to the level of what Thucydides describes; as for the picture painted by Xenophon and Plutarch, it would be totally unrealistic (despite the present tense used by Xenophon), harking back to an earlier time, perhaps even before the Persian wars. But this is a somewhat complicated solution, and it is certainly better to regard Spartan *atimia*, like that of Athens, as a sanction with a highly variable geometry (as Ehrenberg already thought). In an arsenal of possible sanctions, a list of which (whether or not complete) could be obtained by adding up all those which different authors report in their accounts of historical events which are always singular, the Spartans would have chosen, case by case and according to circumstances, internal as much as external, the ones that seemed to them appropriate. Thus they would have decided, for reasons to be analysed later, to impose on the prisoners of Sphacteria a peculiarly limited form of *atimia*, in which the inability to buy and sell by contract would have had as its main purpose the preventing of 120 citizens from leaving, at a stroke, for a foreign country. Comparison with the punishment inflicted, according to Herodotus, on Aristodemos, suggests that the number of *atimoi* and the severity of the sanction imposed on them were in inverse proportion. This is understandable: it was as easy for the city to inflict social exclusion on one or two as it was both practically difficult and politically dangerous to do so when the number of those guilty exceeded a hundred. And if there were several hundred, as was probably the case after Leuctra, the punishment became virtually impossible, as Plutarch also emphasizes (text 8, §5).

4. The limit of the sanction. Was the 'trembler's' *atimia* conceived as perpetual, or should we take the view that, occasionally, he could make amends, and thereby have it lifted? Link,[77] relying on the case of Aristodemos (cf. text 2), maintains that the sanction was unending. The way he fought at Plataea may actually be interpreted as an indication that there was no hope for him; he would court death willingly, and this would just be a more glorious variant of Pantites' suicide.[78] Herodotus, however, emphasizes in no uncertain terms that that was the interpretation of Aristodemos' adversaries, and he declares himself in total disagreement with it. We can side with him over this without reservation. The very fact that Aristodemos had been allowed to fight, when, as we have seen, the rule was most certainly that 'tremblers' were disqualified, could only give him reason to think that the Spartans intended to give him a chance to redeem himself, something that was already a major step towards granting a pardon. The way he conducted himself in battle can be explained by his urgent need to seize this opportunity, and also by the rage that possessed him if he reckoned he had been punished unjustly. The motive for his conduct, therefore, may just as well have been hope as despair. Indeed, the Spartans acknowledged that he had made amends, since, after the battle, they regarded him as a serious candidate for the 'prize for valour', though, as with his successful competitors for the prize, awarded posthumously. Had he survived, would he have recovered his rights? Is it his noble conduct or his death that gained him his pardon? No one can say, and it is probable that the Spartans never settled that question.

In the only other known case of Spartans on whom *atimia* was imposed for cowardice, those of Sphacteria, there was a term to the sanction. Thucydides (text 3) is laconic on the subject, but his wording, 'after a certain time, they recovered their full rights', suggests that the punishment was not of very long duration, and that the *atimoi* did not have to do anything special for the sanction to be lifted. Combined with the moderate nature of the penalty, the likelihood that it was brief heightens the impression one might have – and which Thucydides perhaps intended to convey – of a sanction that was pretty much a formality.

On the condition of the 'tremblers', the richest text in terms of what it teaches is still that of Xenophon, which we can render complete by referring, on one point, to Plutarch's, provided we regard that as trustworthy. It is the richest, because it provides a great deal of precise detail, and also because, here, the social aspect of the sanction is the most original and spectacular.

Unfortunately it is impossible to make out to which actual historical event this description belongs; it may therefore appear as no more than an idealized picture. Moreover, still on the subject of this social aspect of the punishment, we have also to take account of Herodotus' text, which seems to be describing a much harsher sanction. The other major text is that of Thucydides, which shows not only that the sanction had a political and legal aspect as well, but also, and chiefly, that, according to the circumstances, it could take a form that differed completely from that described by Xenophon.

VII. THE DECISION

We have still, now, to ponder on how the decision was taken to impose this punishment on such and such a citizen or group of citizens. Insofar as this is principally a social exclusion it seems conceivable that there may have been no formal and 'legal' decision, and that it might have been the entire community who, in a spontaneous reaction to a patent infraction of the military code of honour, turned its back on those guilty and adopted a manner towards them, the spontaneous nature of which did not preclude its being strongly codified, whereby they were segregated and their status diminished. But legal measures such as those described by Thucydides cannot be taken like this; these are decisions which concern the citizen body, gathered in assembly, and which imply some political discussion. In the abstract, we could imagine the decision as liable sometimes to be taken in one way (e.g. against Aristodemos), sometimes in another (e.g. against the men of Sphacteria). We could also think in terms of an evolution, proceeding from spontaneous sanction at the beginning of the fifth century to formal decision by the end of it. To settle this requires us to examine how things were carried out in each case. What such an examination will show is that there is always a debate: firstly, to determine whether the citizens on trial were or were not guilty of cowardice, and secondly, since the sanction is variable, to fix on the ways in which it should be applied.

A. Aristodemos

Herodotus almost certainly thought that Aristodemos was the sole survivor of Thermopylae. Indeed, while, after having told his story, he recalls, very briefly (7.232), the claim that there was another (Pantites), he seems to have only a very limited belief in it: that feeling is conveyed by this very brevity, by the guarded tone of his introductory phrase (λέγεται δὲ καί), by the fact that Pantites' fate is just a doublet of the second version of Aristodemos', and lastly, and perhaps chiefly, by the language describing Aristodemos at 9.71.[79] So we should take our cue from Herodotus, and speak of Aristodemos as 'the sole survivor of Thermopylae'.

The historian devotes two lengthy discussions to the fate of Aristodemos, presenting them in two episodes: the first, after Thermopylae, the second, posthumously, after Plataea. That, for a start, testifies to his interest in this character; but what is even more remarkable is the way in which, in the second episode, he becomes personally involved and takes an almost vehement stance. Perhaps this is because in this passage he is fulfilling the promise made in his *incipit*, to perpetuate the memory of the deeds accomplished during the war.

1. After Thermopylae: 7.228–9. These two paragraphs set out the two versions collected by the investigator of Aristodemos' conduct at the time of the battle. From its length, plainly the shorter, from its being placed second in the passage, and also from the tone of the account, it seems quite clear that Herodotus did not favour the second version. Perhaps this is because it is simplistic and allows Aristodemos no excuse, which raises the suspicion of partiality: despatched to take a message, he dawdled on the way so as to be sure of returning after the battle was over. The proof of his cowardice lay in the fact that his fellow-messenger, who accompanied him on the mission (perhaps Eurytos, as in the first version), himself returned in time to die with the others.

The first version gives a much more subtle image of Aristodemos' behaviour. Under the guise of a reported account ('the story they tell...') of his actions, it actually sets out the motives, almost the 'whereas clauses', for condemning him. This was not the automatic consequence of his having survived the battle. Herodotus presents, in the shape of a lengthy argument, the reasons for the Spartans' 'anger' towards Aristodemos. The opinion of the city is presented as a whole; but the fact that this 'anger' had to be justified shows that in reality there was a debate about it. Aristodemos had his defenders, who mounted a 'justification' of his conduct (the term πρόφασις appears twice, in §229 and §230). We might reconstruct their speech as follows. 1. Suffering from a disease of the eyes to the point where he could see nothing (as is proved by the way in which Eurytos, who was in the same situation, had to be guided onto the battlefield), he was in no condition *actually* to fight (look at the travesty of a fight in which Eurytos met his death). 2. It was Leonidas himself who had despatched him to the camp.

For the accusers, it is precisely the behaviour of Eurytos that strips of all its worth the excuse put forward in Aristodemos' defence, by proving that, even in those circumstances, it was possible to enter the fray and there meet a 'noble death'. The truth of the matter is that Aristodemos lacked courage (λιποψυχέοντα); it is not because of any justification that he did not take part in the fighting, but because of cowardice. In that part of the discussion where he expresses his personal opinion (δοκέειν ἐμοί), Herodotus, while very probably agreeing that Aristodemos was, actually, a coward, analyses what really motivated the accusers: it is a matter, not of the simple demand of justice, but of 'anger' (μῆνις, μηνῖσαι). Why did 'the Spartans' feel anger against Aristodemos? Ostensibly because, faced with the same choice as Eurytos, he lacked the courage to take the same decision, the only one worthy of a Spartan. But why 'anger'? I would say that it was basically because Aristodemos reduced the number of the heroes from 300 to 299, which is a much less satisfactory figure since it spoiled Sparta's claim to uniqueness: here, as elsewhere, the ideal of 'zero default' had not been attained. Aristodemos appeared in broad daylight – and not just to the Spartans, which was the most serious matter of all – as a *failure* of the Spartan system for creating citizens, with its double aspect of training and selection. There he was, someone who had surmounted all the tests, passed through all the filters, until he was accepted into this super-elite of 300; he does all that, only to behave, in the end, like a common coward. It called into question the whole system, and tarnished the city's image.[80] That is what his fellow citizens could not forgive in Aristodemos. One might also ask whether his conduct did not implicitly pose another question for the Spartans, one that was much more disturbing and which could not be voiced openly: that of knowing whether the strategic choice made by Leonidas was really the best one for the city and for the Greeks. From being the black sheep, Aristodemos would thus become the scapegoat.

There was, therefore, a discussion on the case of Aristodemos, even if his was already a lost cause; Herodotus himself, who was to make an impassioned plea for him in Book 9, plainly regarded his condemnation as normal. It is probably the fact that he had his defenders that explains why he was more or less given a second chance by being allowed to fight at Plataea.

2. After Plataea: 9.71. The discussion, when this kind of posthumous trial took place, was certainly much fiercer than the one following Thermopylae. It was not, we should take care to note, a process of rehabilitation: no one seems to have opposed the view that Aristodemos, by his heroic death, had wiped out his offence; Herodotus says so explicitly (7.231, text 2), and the very fact that he should have been admitted as a contender in the 'competition' for the prize of valour shows that he had been tacitly reintegrated into the society of the *homoioi*. The issue under discussion was to establish whether he should be counted, along with Poseidonios, Philokyon and Amompharetos, themselves also dead (apparently a condition that must be met in order to claim excellence), among the Spartan *aristoi* in battle. Although, as it is presented in Herodotus' text, the advancing of Aristo-

demos' candidacy seems to be on the historian's own initiative, Herodotus must have had some basis for it; Aristodemos must have had supporters at the time. For Herodotus to have known about it, there must have been some who had fought at Plataea who could testify to his exploits, and they could only do that within the setting of this debate. For his supporters, not only did Aristodemos belong with the *aristoi*, he was even at the top of the list. Herodotus shares this view (κατὰ γνώμας τὰς ἡμετέρας), and maintains it with exceptional vigour (ἄριστος μακρῷ). The declaration that Aristodemos had accomplished ἔργα μεγάλα is all the more powerful for the fact that it emanates even from his adversaries.

These also had a strong case. Firstly: perhaps Aristodemos did fight like a Diomedes or a Tydeus, but he did not fight as a hoplite should. He sought out individual actions, he lost control (λυσσῶντα), and even, in a character- istic misdemeanour, abandoned his post (ἐκλείποντα τὴν τάξιν) – not, indeed, to run away, quite the contrary, but it is no less a misdemeanour for that. One could say that he fought as the 300 fought in the final stage of Thermopylae,[81] but it was not the point at issue; he had been late for a battle.

The second argument: Aristodemos 'manifestly wanted to die', βουλόμενον φανερῶς ἀποθανεῖν, in order to escape his condition as 'trembler'. To contest his case more effectively, his adversaries chose, from among the recognized *aristoi*, a champion; this was Poseidonios, whose actions were the very opposite of Aristodemos': he did not court death (οὐ βουλόμενον ἀποθνῄσκειν), and he fought not like a maniac but like a true man of spirit (ἄνδρα γενέσθαι ἀγαθόν).

Neither Aristodemos' defenders, nor Herodotus, who powerfully echoes them, accept this indictment.[82] Herodotus reckons that the argument was made in bad faith: 'it may even be that they said this out of *phthonos*', ταῦτα καὶ φθόνῳ ἂν εἴποιεν. *Phthonos*, 'jealousy'? It is hard to see why the Spartans should have been jealous of Aristodemos. Rather, it is bad faith, bias; they interpret as a desire for death behaviour which finds a much more natural explanation in Aristodemos' need to accomplish individual exploits in order to redeem himself. They were unwilling to admit that someone condemned for cowardice should, in the end, when it came to the supreme test, show himself to be every bit as much a hero as those of Thermopylae; because this meant acknowledging that, by condemning Aristodemos, the Spartan system was once again revealed as defective. This, for Herodotus, is the real reason for the hostility of many Spartans towards Aristodemos after Plataea. This attitude is thus disqualified; none the less the fact remains that it carried the day, which is only logical, the Spartans being both judge and litigant in the affair.

3. The setting for the debates. The question of the prize for valour at Plataea was debated in what Herodotus terms a *leschē*, γενομένης λέσχης. The *leschē*, a meeting place, chiefly for the Elders, and also the meeting itself, is a well-known fact of Spartan life;[83] there, one of the favourite topics of conversation was, in fact, the behaviour of younger citizens.[84] But this is not the case here. This discussion was every Spartan's concern, and it was impossible to assemble all of them in a single *leschē*. Herodotus employs the term, then, in its non-technical sense: meeting, discussion, both together. The use of the word, however, is probably meant to signify that the setting of the debate was not really political, which, given its objective, is perfectly logical. The meeting most probably took place not at Sparta, but at Plataea; it was a soldier's assembly. Three citizens were finally honoured: would this have been one per tribe? If that was the case, perhaps Aristodemos and Poseidonios were competitors in the same tribe: this would be another explanation, possibly, of the prominence of Poseidonios in the discussion relating to Aristodemos; but we should admit that Herodotus seems to think it perfectly possible for four *aristoi* to be chosen.

After Thermopylae, the debate reflected in Herodotus' text could also have taken place, to some extent, in a non-political setting; Aristodemos' conduct was doubtless examined, over a period, in the *syssitia*, the *leschai*, and by groups of citizens in the gymnasia or the *agora*, but it is practically certain that 'demoting' a Spartan required a decision then to be taken by the assembly.

B. Sphacteria

1. Hesitation prior to the decision. The Spartans took their time before deciding to sanction the prisoners of Sphacteria restored to them by the Athenians under the terms of the peace. This hesitation is easily explained. Firstly, it was not obvious that they were culpable. They had fought courageously for as long as that had been possible. To their plea for instructions the authorities had responded ambiguously;[85] something like 'act for the best' (Thucydides 4.38.3); they would not have responded any differently if, without daring to spell it out, they had wanted the warriors to give priority to their own safety. To justify themselves, the prisoners could claim that this had not been a hoplite engagement, and that all the courage in the world was of no avail against a hail of arrows.[86] All of that the Spartans knew and understood; the days of Thermopylae were long past.

Next, their numbers ('about 120', Thucydides 4.38.5) posed a practically insoluble problem. To disqualify 120 warriors was difficult to contemplate for a city stricken with oliganthropy. It was one thing to impose social ostracism on one or two, but to do it to 120 was quite another matter; it was difficult to put into effect, and, as Thucydides emphasizes, it would have been to create a group dangerous in its very numbers.

But Thucydides dwells above all on their rank. Twice he says 'the men on the island' were not just anybody: he indicates at 5.15.1, that the Spartans among the prisoners 'were prominent men',[87] and at 5.34.2 (our text 3), that some of them held magistracies. While they were prisoners, the city always sought doggedly to recover them (4.15.2, 19.1, 41.3, 117.1–2; 5.15.1–2); it had them mentioned specifically in the peace treaty (5.18.7). What was the reason for this insistence? Loraux [88] considers two hypotheses, which, moreover, should not be thought of as mutually exclusive: 'récupérer le capital humain' and 'mettre à l'ombre des hommes qui font le déshonneur de la cité'. The second of these explanations is interesting, even if the phrase 'mettre à l'ombre' is perhaps to falsify matters a little: it would imply that the sole aim in recovering them was to punish them, something which was not actually done at once, far from it. Nevertheless, I think that, if formulated differently, this hypothesis is a fertile one. If we go back to the scenario of the *atrakton* apophthegm, at 4.40.2, there we see 'one of the Athenian allies' asking questions, with an irony that stung one of the prisoners, dwelling on the contradiction between the code of his city and the very fact of his being there, a prisoner. This is the picture it conjures. Those prisoners were not there in secret; on the contrary, the Athenians exhibited them, like exotic animals in a zoo, and people could mock them at their leisure. Imagine the grandsons of the heroes of Thermopylae being displayed as though they were in cages! Obviously it was unbearable for the Spartans, and they had to put a stop to it as quickly as possible. It was also a reason for them to be angry with those whose conduct had given the Athenians this opportunity for propaganda. Sparta smarted from it all the more for the fact that those involved were men of standing: now we understand why Thucydides dwelt on this point.

2. The chronology of the decision. Some time elapsed between the prisoners' return to Sparta and their being condemned, and it is the existence of this delay that shows the Spartans' hesitation. It would be nice if we could establish its precise duration. Lewis asserted that a year elapsed,[89] but that strikes me as excessive. Certainly, Thucydides sets the concluding of the peace in his tenth year (5.20.1), and the condemnation of the prisoners in his eleventh; but the peace was only definitively concluded 'once winter was over, when the spring came' (*ibid.*), and the prisoners only returned at the beginning of the summer of the eleventh year (5.24.2). The condemnation took place during this summer. It was part of the same set of measures as the emancipation of the Brasideioi: the last internal problems stemming from the war were being settled. So the delay could not have exceeded a few months.

Delay there was, however, as is demonstrated by the fact that some of those condemned held magistracies.[90] 5.34.2 (text 3): ...ἤδη καὶ ἀρχάς τινας ἔχοντας.[91] The present tense and the use of ἤδη (not 'already', but 'henceforth', 'from that moment'), excludes the possibility that these were magistracies held before their capture. There is no other way of understanding the wording than by concluding that they had been elected to these offices after their return, probably at the end of the summer, just before they were condemned. So, not only did the authorities delay in causing them to be sanctioned, but the Spartans had enough faith in them to elect them. This is a completely paradoxical situation. Not because they were elected: that just shows that apparently the Spartan community agreed to let bygones be bygones and to regard the former prisoners as citizens like the rest. The paradox lies in the fact that, after all that, they were condemned, and Thucydides understands perfectly well that this is what he has to explain.

3. Motives for the decision. Diodorus' version (12.76.1) is plain and simple: the Spartans imposed *atimia* on the former prisoners of Sphacteria 'for having tarnished Sparta's image', ὡς τὴν Σπάρτην ἀδοξοτέρον πεποιηκότας. We should take this account the more seriously because this part of Diodorus' sentence looks like a preamble to a decree,[92] and a motive of this kind fits perfectly with the feeling generated in Sparta by the Athenians' exhibiting of the prisoners.[93] This version is quite logical, therefore, but only so long as it is set, as it is by Diodorus, in the perspective of a punishment decided upon immediately after the prisoners' return, without a prior change of heart. Besides, preferring the more complex version given by Thucydides does not entail denying that there is any weight in the motive indicated by ὡς...πεποιηκότας: this form of words could actually figure in any case in the text of the decree, which constituted the 'official version' of the affair, and the motive it articulates retains its worth.

Thucydides cannot restrict himself to this official and simplifying phrase, because what he has to explain is the Spartans' complete change of heart. To do this he turns to psychology, one might even be tempted to call it in-depth psychology.[94] The issue is not the punishing of cowardice, nor is it the re-establishing of the city's image; the motive, on the Spartans' side just as on that of the former prisoners, is a fundamental feeling – fear.[95] Moreover, the term for this feeling is inexact, since this is less a case of dread-fear than it is of calculated fear, the anticipating of a negative outcome, the forecast of which makes it advisable to take counter-measures. This is the kind of fear that galvanizes one to action; it is one of the means of enabling reason to control, or at least try to control, the future. It governs the actions of the two parties, beginning with the Spartans: they are afraid that the former prisoners would be afraid … and probably they were indeed afraid of this, though they did not need to be.

What the Spartans dread is clearly stated: an act of rebellion on the part of the former prisoners. It is obvious that their number and their cohesion play a prominent part in this fear. Compared with what happens after a defeat – where the authorities can select, from among a large number of those who actually fled, a few, who are supposedly even more cowardly than the rest but who are actually punished as an example –, the case of Sphacteria was especially difficult, because all the men involved had been in exactly the same predicament: they had all capitulated, and, if the authorities elected to punish them, they had to punish all of them alike. So it was automatically a powerful group, by virtue of their numbers and rank, that would be created by this punishment. And if they were not punished? This, according to Thucydides, was the course the Spartans tried to follow, but it ended in failure.

The historian strives, then, to explain what the Spartans feared that the former prisoners feared. At first glance, as Ehrenberg has ably explained (col. 2295), the reasoning ascribed to them is illogical. The demotion feared by the former prisoners is none other than the 'tremblers'' *atimia*; now, they have been spared this, they may think, and it is only this fear which is going to make it, in the end, inevitable. On the other hand, the Spartans are dreading a disturbance; well, it is the punishment, and that alone, that can generate it.

Thucydides' reasoning takes place at a less stolidly rational level. As Loraux has suggested,[96] 'l'attitude des Spartiates pourrait s'expliquer par la force de l' αἰσχύνη dans la collectivité lacédémonienne… Mieux valait donc, peut-être, sanctionner une anomalie par des punitions tangibles que de laisser se déve-lopper remords et honte, ferments de dissolution du corps social'. In fact it is probable that after the return of the prisoners, when, since no one was saying anything, they realized that perhaps there was no intention to punish them, the authorities (the ephors) sensed a sultry unease setting in. Tormented by shame, the former prisoners gradually developed an almost Dostoievskian desire for punishment and redemption.

This is how Loraux saw the story. But Thucydides certainly did not; for him the feeling at work was not *aischynē*, but fear. As long as the former prisoners were not punished, they were expecting the punishment and afraid of it; that fear was what could urge them to plan a *coup d'état*. So punishing them was the only way to settle the situation. In any case, Thucydides' text can only be really be understood if we accept that what he meant to explain is less the fact that a sanction had been taken (since, in this case, it is difficult to circumvent Ehrenberg's criticism) than the belated, limited and temporary character of that same sanction. A limited sanction: here is what reinforces the impression that it consisted only of what was stated by Thucydides. A temporary sanction, almost a formality: something more like role-play. In this affair, the 'true' status of 'tremblers' is only there as an almost obsessional dimension of the former prisoners' psychology. The punishment actually inflicted on them was a long way from that thought proper for 'tremblers'.

C. Leuctra

1. Problems of historicity. Nowhere in Xenophon is there any question of a debate in Sparta on the punishment of possible 'tremblers' after Leuctra: in his account of the battle there is no actual rout either, but a succession of withdrawals. This absence is the more striking in that he reports (6.4.16) the reactions in the city the day after the defeat. Nor is there anything in Diodorus, where the account nevertheless ends with reference to a rout. Only in Plutarch (repeated in Polyaenus) does there appear a debate on the 'tremblers', of which there are three versions: *Agesilaus*, 30.2–6 (text 8), *Mor.* 191c, and *Mor.* 214a. We can see straightaway that this situation poses a serious problem of historicity. Assuming this anecdote were authentic, Xenophon could have omitted it as being scarcely a glorious matter for Sparta or for Agesilaus: because, while Plutarch admires the 'political astuteness' of the king in this situation,[97] this would not square very well with the image Xenophon is trying to give him, and would be an unfortunate reminder of chapter 14 of *Lak. Pol.* which shows the Spartans seeking by any means they can to circumvent the laws of Lycurgus. That is possible, but the problem remains.

If we knew who it was, Plutarch's source would be an important ingredient in our assessment. For the versions in the *Moralia*, we may assume that the sources are the collections of apophthegms on which Plutarch has drawn; but they themselves have sources. In the *Life of Agesilaus*, the account displays several minor differences compared with the apophthegms: in the motives for the absence of punishment, in the role of the ephors (absent from the *Agesilaus*), in the tenor of the king's speech. That does not necessarily mean that there Plutarch was using a source other than the apophthegms, and it may simply result from the way in which, in the *Lives*, he adapts these for use. Only *Agesilaus*, however, contains the phrase τοὺς νόμους δεῖ σήμερον ἐᾶν καθεύδειν which is so striking. We know Plutarch made extensive use of Theopompos in this *Life*, notably over the invasion of Laconia, and a phrase like that would fit perfectly with what we know of this historian's style.[98] Whatever we think of him, we would all agree that he is a source to be taken seriously. So it is possible and even probable that there was a discussion about the 'tremblers' after Leuctra; this does not mean, by the way, that Plutarch's account is truthful in every respect.

2. The Spartans' hesitation. In Plutarch's accounts, all the conditions seem to be mustered for numerous Spartans to be declared 'tremblers': on the one hand, the cowardice is presented as having been patent; on the other, everything happens as if 'the law' was formal and imperative, and entailed an invariable punishment, take it or leave it. Everyone seems to agree that it should not be inflicted. The reasons for this state of opinion are set out in different ways depending on the texts. Firstly, there is (in *Agesilaus* 30.5, and *Mor.* 214a) the observation that the city is more than ever in need of fighting men; this is presented in a more striking form in *Mor.* 191c and 214a: the ephors see the city 'empty of warriors'. Other reasons are the number of potential 'tremblers' (*Agesilaus*, 30.2 and 5; *Mor.* 214a; Polyaenus) and the fact that they are important men (δυνατοί, *Agesilaus*, 30.2). Finally, there is the fear that, if they are punished, they will plot some sort of revolution (νεωτερισμός). This line of argument is singularly lacking in originality. The importance of the guilty parties and the fear of revolution are certainly taken (perhaps already by Theopompus) from Thucydides. Fear about their numbers is an obvious motive. As for the lack of warriors, this is an argument used (but in the converse sense, by the enemy) on several occasions in Xenophon's account of the invasion of Laconia.[99] Perhaps one could suggest drawing a distinction between those arguments which although obvious are none the less likely, and others which are purely and simply borrowed, and only figure here in order to give the effect of an accumulation.

3. The discussion. Its objective is narrowly restricted: since everyone was convinced of the necessity not to inflict punishment, all they had to do was to find an expedient enabling them not to apply 'the law'. Who led this discussion? Not Agesilaus; in the *Life*, it is 'the Spartans' (unspecified plurals at §2 and §5), and, in the *Moralia*, the ephors. All the versions come back into agreement over the designating of Agesilaus as *nomothetēs*; in fact, it appeared to the Spartans that it was going to be necessary to abrogate or modify 'the law'. Even if this *nomothetēs* has no power of decision, but only of proposition, this designation, which the text presents as natural, is in reality very strange. We never hear tell of anything like this in Sparta, and this measure implies a surprising attachment to the letter of the law. The final debate takes place in the assembly (Agesilaus puts forward his proposal εἰς τὸ πλῆθος τῶν Λακεδαιμονίων, *Agesilaus*, 30.6; εἰς τὸ μέσον, an archaic-looking phrase, *Mor.* 191c; εἰς τὸ δημόσιον, *Mor.* 214a), and it is they who decide – not to decide anything.

All in all, then, we can accept that there was a debate in the assembly on the case of the runaways from Leuctra, and that Agesilaus took the side of those who were unwilling to take any sanction against them; a side which carried the day, no doubt very easily. Everything else is more than uncertain, especially as regards 'the law'.

D. Megalopolis

Diodorus (19.70.5, our text 6) reports a discussion about the 'tremblers' after the battle of Megalopolis, of 331: τῶν μὲν Λακεδαιμονίων μετὰ τὴν πρὸς Ἀντίπατρον μάχην ἀπολυόντων τῆς ἀτιμίας τοὺς ἐκ τῆς ἥττης διασωθέντας μόνος (Ἀκρότατος) ἐνέστη τῷ δόγματι. This was no doubt, as after Leuctra, a debate in the assembly; the term δόγμα may apply to a decree, but also to any type of decision. This presentation of events calls for two comments.

1. Chronologically speaking, this is the first text in which the idea of a *'nomos about tremblers'* appears (later in the text: οἷς ἦν τῶν νόμων τὰ πρόστιμα).[100] The sentence cited above might lead one to think that it was aimed at all the survivors; but what follows, connected with the account of the battle (17.63.4), clearly shows that it concerned only the *neoi*, only those, therefore, who made up Agis's bodyguard.[101]

2. It is a little strange that a decree (to which only Akrotatos would be opposed) should be proposed with the aim of *not* deciding on punishment. This is doubtless why Link[102] assumes that *atimia* had previously been decided on, and that the decree in question was one of amnesty (ἀπολύειν τῆς ἀτιμίας). But it is difficult to make sense of the text in this way (it is a question of 'considering them free' of the *atimia* provided for by 'the law'), and, after Leuctra, the decision not to punish was taken directly. So, δόγμα would be better interpreted as 'a decision' rather than as 'a decree' in due form.

As with the case of Leuctra, there arises a problem of historicity. If we admit it for Leuctra, we may admit it for Megalopolis: in 331 there was no longer any need for the hypocritical words attributed to Agesilaus. In favour of the veracity of Diodorus' account (whatever his source) we may plead the very particular form in which the young men's hatred is directed at Akrotatos: it results in a kind of ostracism which assails him as if it were he who was the 'trembler'; like the 'trembler', he is struck, and by those who really were 'tremblers'. So cruel a persecution of someone who is, even so, the 'heir apparent', is most surprising, and this, paradoxically, reinforces its probability.

In all the known cases, then, the decision to inflict or not to inflict 'tremblers'' *atimia* was the result of a public discussion among the assembled citizens; whether the men in question took part in it, we do not know. The whole sanction, including the most purely social of its aspects, thereby takes on a political hue.

VIII. CONCLUSION

Having reached the end of this journey, it seems to me necessary to look back over it, in order to recapitulate the problems that remain unsolved. These are numerous, and some of them lie at the very heart of the matter.

The structure of the tradition about the 'tremblers' is extremely odd. None of the authors of the classical era repeats what his predecessor has said on the subject; thus they give the impression that each of them is describing a different reality. One is naturally tempted to explain this situation as Ehrenberg has done, in terms of a gradual transformation of the institution, each historian describing it at a precise moment in its evolution, either, for Herodotus and Thucydides, at that point in the history where the episode in which it occurs takes place, or, for Xenophon, in his own time. If one considers the sequence, Aristodemos – Sphacteria – Leuctra, the following explanation seems to be inescapable: the transition would have been made from a very severe sanction to a very lenient one, ending with no sanction at all. The Spartans would have been less and less capable of respecting the norm which they themselves had decreed.

We would be well advised, in my view, to guard against being seduced by the obviousness of this interpretation. Firstly, we should note that any evolutionary model which is based on a mere three cases can only be regarded as hypothetical. Next, and particularly, we should only compare what is comparable. The case of Aristodemos, whether we consider his offence or his punishment, is not truly comparable with any other. Not having taken part in the fighting, and on the very orders of Leonidas to boot, it cannot be said that he actually 'trembled', and we could perfectly well imagine that, had circumstances obliged him to fight, he would have behaved just as well as the others; it was his misfortune to return alive from a heroes' fight, in which all the others, being clearly unable to gain the victory, had perished. His punishment was exceptionally harsh, however, not only by comparison with other known cases, but also by comparison with the norm conveyed in the portrait drawn by Xenophon (see above, p. 17). His offence and his punishment only make sense in the context of Thermopylae, where the logic is that of the heroic world, not the real. Aristodemos is for evermore the negative model paired with the positive one offered by the other 299.

It seems to me that it is by its nature, then, that the 'tremblers'' *atimia* was a variable sanction. It was not a penalty fixed once for all, but an 'arsenal' of measures from among which the city (personified by the citizens' assembly) chose on each occasion. A 'trembler' of the kind described by Xenophon may appear (and manifestly did appear to this author, who insists a great deal on this point) as a strange reality, at all events peculiar to Sparta; but that only holds good for this extreme and, in a sense, ideal form. The fact that the punishment took, according to circumstances, very variable forms, dispels much of this strangeness, and enables it to be closely compared with the Athenian *atimia* of the fourth century. The offences punished in this way were, as is natural, almost the same, apart from the 'abandoning of the king', for which there can be no Attic equivalent. As for the sanction, in both cities it included both an element of social exclusion and a political element; it is the proportions which differ. In Athens, the social element is only represented by exclusion from the *agora*, the hub of masculine social activity, and, occasionally, from sanctuaries, whereas in Sparta – though we should remember that this means the Sparta of Xenophon's portrait, not the real one as in the case of Sphacteria – it entailed a multiplicity of exclusions. Conversely, the legal and political element is more extensive in Athens.[103] Finally, the most profound difference lay, on the whole, in the taking of the decision: in Sparta, a vote by the assembly, in Athens, a lawsuit, where, certainly, the number of those who decided was generally smaller, but where the rights of defence were guaranteed.

To complete this comparison, we must also take account of the fact that in Sparta there seem to have existed, for offences of the same category, punishments of a more commonplace kind. Diodorus (12.62.5) asserts that throwing away one's shield was punishable by death; but we might question that information.[104] Likewise, Lycurgus (*Against Leocrates*, 129) cites a Spartan law which 'formally prescribes death for all those who do not agree to risk their lives for their homeland'; here too we may doubt, since the offence so punished tallies with one of those covered by the 'tremblers'' *atimia*. Lastly, according to Thucydides (5.72.1), after the battle of Mantinea in 418, two polemarchs, Aristokles and Hipponoidas, were banished from Sparta for having refused, in battle, to carry out an order which they judged unreasonable; but, while no one has questioned this information, it has been interpreted in different ways. Lewis[105] accepted the matter as Thucydides states it. MacDowell[106] assumes that the punishment was in reality a heavy fine, and that the polemarchs would prefer to go into exile. Link[107] thinks that they were punished with 'tremblers'' *atimia* but that they chose to go into exile. This hypothesis should be discarded if, as I tend to think, the withdrawal of *kyrieia* in matters of selling property was normally a constituent of this *atimia*: in fact, in order to set off for a foreign country in a reasonable state, one has to be able first to realize one's assets. Besides, it assumes as if it were obvious the fact that, given the choice between *atimia* and exile, Spartans normally chose exile. No doubt that was what happened in Athens; but the mentalities of the two cities are very different, to the extent that this problem, which we have already encountered on several occasions,[108] would be better left open. MacDowell's thesis, which relies on the fact that, for offences that are almost (but not strictly) alike, the punishment was actually a fine, is thus more robust than Link's; but we might regard as better still that of Lewis, who confines himself strictly to what Thucydides says. All in all, I judge it highly probable that, for military offences, there were other punishments besides 'tremblers'' *atimia*; the *real* importance of this sanction is thereby singularly diminished.

One of the most striking features of this *atimia* is the *very scanty extent of its historical reality*. Without actually being a myth, it is manifestly something more talked of than practised. In the fourth century, talking about it is all that happens, and when it *is* talked about, it is essentially to work out how best to set about *not* applying it; it is one more skeleton in the Spartan cupboard. In the fifth century, its application is only attested in two cases, each of which is, in its own way, extreme, and neither of which fits the portrait given by Xenophon. This dearth of cases based in reality poses a serious problem. It is tempting to circumvent it by assuming that there were numerous cases of which we know nothing. That is, in fact, likely; but it is equally possible to embark on another, less perilous, route, by considering the beginnings, and the end, of 'tremblers'' *atimia*.

As we have seen, it is not certain that this form of *atimia* already existed in the era of Tyrtaeus. His text shows only that, in his time, and, surely, for a long time before that, 'cowardice' incurred unanimous reprobation. The manner in which Herodotus expresses himself on the subject of Aristodemos may be regarded as an indication that that was the first time the term *tresas*, repeated from Tyrtaeus' verse, was applied to a Spartan; so it would be both the first and the last known example of a 'trembler' in the entire history of Sparta. The last: in actual fact, one could not say that the former prisoners of Sphacteria were genuinely treated as 'tremblers' (and besides, Thucydides does not use this term). The acknowledged renunciation of this sanction, which proved definitive, only occurred in 371 (or perhaps as early as 390, since, as far as we know, the runaways of Lechaion were not punished); but it is plain that it was moribund from 421 onwards. That makes for a pretty short history, which does not leave much room for numerous cases of it.

How are we to explain this rapid disappearance? The obvious answer is that Spartan society was experiencing a deep crisis. Suffering more and more severely from oliganthropy, Sparta no longer had enough citizens to be able to afford the luxury of disqualifying a significant number of them (this is exactly what Plutarch says, text 8, §§2 and 5). Thucydides (text 3) has analysed, with acuteness, another aspect of this crisis. The practice of an *atimia* such as this was only possible in a society which was strongly cohesive and sure of its own stability. At the time of the Peloponnesian war, and, with even greater reason, in the fourth century, Spartan society could not have coped with the tensions which the presence of an important number of *atimoi* in its midst would have engendered.

I think we have to go further. Even if the number of Spartans had not fallen dramatically, even if their community had retained its full cohesion, they would still have found it very difficult to apply the kind of *atimia* described by Herodotus or Xenophon to the cases of Sphacteria, or Lechaion, or Leuctra. The real problem, when it comes to the applicability of 'tremblers'' *atimia*, is a permanent problem because it is, as we have seen, an arithmetical one. How could one even imagine more than a hundred demoted Spartans living in the city under the conditions described by Xenophon? This is a punishment which by its nature can only be applied to a few people at a time. The drama lies in the fact that the number of those who would have deserved this sanction only grew larger. At Thermopylae, 299 (or 298!) Spartans out of 300 agreed to die to preserve the image of Sparta; at Sphacteria, which was, as Thucydides says (4.40.1), the turning point in the affair, the 120 survivors refused to do this, and the city, being in no position to inflict the full sanction on them, had to confine itself, with craven relief, to a mitigated and temporary punishment. Here we meet again the idea of crisis: in future, the majority of citizens, with excellent justification, will put their lives before the code of the city, and the city has to consent to it. So it is not just as a result of circumstances that Aristodemos was the only 'true' 'trembler'. The truth is that, for the rigorous application of this *atimia*, he was the ideal case, as the one and only survivor of a battle fought by heroes. Thus, the burden of the arithmetical problem is this: the severity of the sanction, while it existed, was not proportional to the gravity of the offence, but inversely proportional to the number of those guilty.

This has brought us, quite naturally, to the last significant problem: to what historical reality may Xenophon's portrait actually refer? Of the two known cases where the sanction was applied, the one to which it comes closest is obviously that of Aristodemos, but between them there exists one difference in character: while Xenophon's 'trembler' participates in the life of the community even while remaining forever at its margins, Aristodemos was radically excluded from it by a wall of silence. From the peculiarly lively and concrete character of Xenophon's description it is tempting to conclude that it must refer to a contemporary reality and one which he was able to observe: but on what occasion? The fact that he uses the present tense does not prove that what he is describing existed in his own time: he does the same throughout his treatise, while he notes in chapter 14 that at least some of these customs are no longer observed by the Spartans; this is the eternal Sparta, the Sparta of Lycurgus. The *atimia* he depicts may have existed in the fifth century, and even – if one does not accept that Aristodemos was the first 'trembler' – in the sixth. It may have been inflicted on individuals or small groups, following military engagements that were of too little importance for the sources to have preserved their memory, and I am convinced that it is this way of looking at it that most of my colleagues will consider the best. We should note, however, that these are only hypotheses, and are as indefinite as they are gratuitous. More important still, the very possibility that a portrait of the 'trembler in general' might be truthful seems to be denied by the historical evidence, which shows this *atimia* as essentially variable.

In these circumstances, we might seriously contemplate another possibility: that, here, we are face to face with another element of the Spartan myth. This portrait of the 'trembler', which Xenophon's Spartan informants presented to him as truthful, could be no more than an ideal construct, produced after the episode, in no respect very glorious, of Sphacteria: a sort of ideological screen, designed to mask the fact, patently obvious from now on, that the city was no longer capable of making its citizens respect the code which, in Herodotus' account, Demaratus explained to Xerxes.

Notes

[1] Other criticisms formulated by Loraux: Ehrenberg underestimated the importance, in Sparta, of αἰδώς and of αἰσχύνη (p. 109, n. 29; 112 and n. 56), words denoting the interiorization of the norm; he was wrong in repeating Grote's hypothesis on the 'tremblers' at Lechaion (p. 111). Some information on the 'tremblers' may also be found in Velho 2002.

[2] Note the use of tenses: in someone who has trembled (once in the past = aorist), every kind of value has been destroyed (forever = perfect).

[3] It seems to me that this is what Cairns means, 1993, 162, n. 53: '" tremblers", 11, 14, came to denote a class of dishonoured Spartiates'.

[4] See, for example, Plato, *Laws* 1.629b (Megillos 'glutted', διακορής, with Tyrtaeus).

[5] Cf., to the same effect, Nafissi 1991, 307, n. 130: 'non si tratta di elogi *ad personam*'.

[6] Cairns 1993, 162.

[7] Ehrenberg 1937 (col. 2292) thinks that an episode (on the historicity of which, moreover, he has some just reservations) in the 'second Messenian war', related by Pausanias 4.7.7, may be connected with Tyrtaeus' mention of the 'tremblers'. But: (1) this episode belongs to the first war; (2) the charge levelled at the Spartan warriors is not that of having 'trembled' but that of having broken the oath set out at 4.5.8; (3) they are not condemned to suffer a sanction resembling in any way the fate of the 'tremblers', but are simply reprimanded by the Elders.

[8] On the *tropē*, cf. Hanson 1990, 229.

[9] Ehrenberg 1937, cols. 2295–6; Cawkwell 1983, 397.

[10] Cf. Hanson 1990, 101 and 232.

[11] On this subject, see, in particular, Hammond 1979/80, and Nafissi 1991, 296–300.

[12] We know that the Athenians displayed in the Stoa Poikile some at least of the 292 Lacedaemonian shields captured on this occasion; Pausanias 1.15.4. One of them has been recovered: *The Athenian Agora* 14, 92–3, fig. 26 and pl. 48d.

[13] Cf. Ducat 1999a, 163–4.

[14] Thus, Cawkwell 1983, 397; David 1989a, 9; Link 1994, 22 and 84.

[15] Loraux 1977, 111, n. 47.

[16] Certainly that might happen even when they were victorious, but no examples of it exist. In fact, as long as the situation was normal, the king was well protected.

[17] Ehrenberg 1937, col. 2293.

[18] MacDowell 1986, 44.

[19] Is this simply because, once Herodotus had mentioned them, neither Xenophon nor Plutarch thought it would serve any purpose to repeat them? This is not what normally happens; besides, Plutarch repeats certain details which Xenophon had mentioned before him.

[20] Cf. David 1999, 124 and n. 45.

[21] David 1989b, 15 and n. 80.

[22] Herodotus puts it very well: he suffered the disgrace of being called Aristodemos the Trembler, ὄνειδος εἶχε ὁ τρέσας Ἀριστόδημος καλεόμενος.

[23] In Xenophon's account the word 'trembler' does not appear (he calls him κακός, then ὁ τοιοῦτος). For all that, one could not doubt for a moment (be it only on account of Plutarch's text) that it was the 'trembler' he had in mind.

[24] On Athenian *atimia*, see the very full discussion by Hansen 1976, 54–98; on the ban against going to the *agora*, p. 62: Hansen thinks that this ban was total, and that it was the place itself that was closed to the *atimos*, and not just the activities conducted there.

[25] The verb συσκηνεῖν: 5.4; 13.1. Συσκήνια: 5.2. Σύσκηνος: 7.4; 13.7; 15.5. On the origin of these usages, see Nafissi 1991, 320–1.

[26] Fully discussed in Kennell 1995, 39–40.

[27] Kennell 1995, 110–11.

[28] Kennell 1995, 131.

[29] Ollier 1934, 49.

[30] On this text, see Constantinou 1998, 26–8.

[31] This is the opinion expressed by Ollier 1934, 49, though he does not supply an argument for it.

[32] Ollier (loc. cit.) has perceived this difficulty clearly.

[33] Lipka (2002, 178) deduced from Ephorus 70 F 149 (*ap.* Strabo 10.4.21) that in Crete, also, there were more and less honourable positions in the choruses; but in the text, χοροῖς is only a conjecture, admittedly a plausible one, instead of the traditional θρόνοις.

[34] 2.80, where he assembles, as does Xenophon, the forms of behaviour to be observed in the streets and in places were one would sit.

[35] Numerous examples are collected by David 1991, 64–5, and by Richer 1998, 392, n. 19. To these may be added *Clouds*, l. 993, where, even if it does not openly refer to Sparta, the allusion seems transparent.

[36] Kourinou-Pikoula 1998; cf. *REG* 1999, *Bull. Epigr.*, no. 241. Cassio 2000 is concerned with quite another aspect of the text.

[37] Lipka 2002, 178. Cf. Cartledge 2001, 121 and n. 93 (*kyrieia* in Sparta) and 94 (the

meaning of *anandria*).

[38] *Lysander*, 30.7: ...καὶ ἀγαμίου δίκη καὶ ὀψιγαμίου καὶ κακογαμίου.

[39] The text and references are in Richer 1998, 458, n. 21. Ariston uses the term ζημία, 'fine', which is more specific than Plutarch's δίκη (here meaning 'punishment'); ζημία is also what Xenophon uses. Lipka (2002, 179) has doubts about the historical reality of fines for both late and bad marriages.

[40] It is they who would have sanctioned Archidamos for having married a woman who was too small (Plutarch, *Agesilaus* 2.6) or ugly but rich (Athenaeus 13.566a–b): a case, apparently, of a 'bad marriage'. Cf. Richer 1998, 425.

[41] MacDowell 1986, 45.

[42] Link 1994, 22, n. 161.

[43] Lipka (2002, 180) gives it its primary meaning, which is 'greasy', 'smeared with oil', but this results in a more-than-bizarre translation. Its figurative sense, which is just as common, is infinitely more appropriate.

[44] Ducat 1990, 107 (text), 111–15 (uniform), 119–20 (physical appearance).

[45] Link 1994, 22, n. 162. On the reason for this error, cf. below, this page.

[46] MacDowell 1986, 45.

[47] Ducat 1999b, 44. The difference is that here the possible gaps between Xenophon and Plutarch could not reflect an evolution of the institution, since we hear no more of it after 331.

[48] *Lycurgus* 30, 2; cf. David 1989a, 11.

[49] David 1989a, 9–10, reflects this opinion.

[50] Aristophanes, *Ploutos*, l. 530.

[51] Hegesippos the Comic, cited by Athenaeus, 7.290c.

[52] In the same vein, Ehrenberg 1937, col. 2293.

[53] MacDowell 1986, 155; David 1989a, 10, and 1989b, 15; Richer 1998, 254, n. 56.

[54] Richer 1998, 251–5.

[55] Vernant 1989, 193–4.

[56] Although Egyptian guards must normally have been clean-shaven; to accept this detail as forming part of the original story, one would have to assume, as does Legrand, that these guards were foreign mercenaries.

[57] Richer 1998, 254, n. 56.

[58] This problem arises in relation to the whole of Plutarch's account (our text 8): cf. below, p. 42.

[59] This is firmly emphasized by David 1989a, 10, ('miserable clowns'); 1989b, 15, ('buffoons', 'miserable clowns'). He points out, judiciously, that while they make others laugh, they themselves are not entitled to be cheerful – always assuming they want to be.

[60] Ducat 1997.

[61] David 1991, 92; 2004, 33.

[62] Powell 1998, 234; 2001, 238.

[63] *Against Timarchos*, 180–1. This text has been studied by Richer 1998, 357–60.

[64] Ruzé 1997, 160, n. 8: 'weakness' during the *agōgē*, celibacy. None of these hypotheses is really convincing.

[65] 41b; 233f; 801b. On these texts, cf. Richer 1998, 358, n. 197.

[66] *Against Timarchos*, 29.

[67] Link 1994, 23: that the 'trembler' could 'legally' contract a marriage; that to give

Aristodemos the prize for valour at Plataea could have been contemplated (cf. below, p. 36).

[68] This idea was common at one time; see for example, Forrest 1968, 131–2. We find both Toynbee and Huxley making the same distinction between 'Spartiates' and 'Spartans'.

[69] Hansen 1976, 61–3.

[70] *Politics* 3.1275a23: τὸ μετέχειν κρίσεως καὶ ἀρχῆς (whatever those terms might mean).

[71] *Agesilaus* 30.5 (text 8), where this line of reasoning is put forward anonymously, as though it was the author's own; *Mor.* 191c and (a more complete version) 214a, where it is used by the ephors.

[72] Pantites, if he existed, committed suicide.

[73] MacDowell 1986, 45.

[74] Link 1994, 22 and n. 162; 84 and n. 39.

[75] We know from Ephorus (fr. 117) that only the sale of helots for export was forbidden. S. Hodkinson (2000, 84–5) has pondered on how the ban on buying and selling should be understood. After having explored the 'explanatory power' (his wording) of Fustel de Coulanges' interpretation, which I had followed in an article of 1983 and which I repeat here, his final conclusion is to a different effect: this would be a ban on the buying and selling of merchandise in the market. The reason for this choice lies in the parallel he has established between the sanctions reported by Thucydides and two of the restrictions affecting the *hēbōntes*. It is correct that one of them is common to both cases: the impossibility of holding a magistracy. The other would be the one, mentioned by Plutarch (*Lycurgus* 25.1), forbidding the *hēbōntes* to go to the *agora*-market. But, as is clearly demonstrated by the Athenian example (Aristophanes, *Knights*, l. 1373; Isocrates, *Panathenaicus*, 48), this is by no means a disabling measure; on the contrary, it is one designed to protect the young against the *agora*'s corrupting influence. So, on this point, the parallel put forward by Hodkinson has no validity, and I maintain my position (albeit I agree with discarding the reference to Roman law). Moreover, I do not see how, in Sparta, the ban on engaging in commercial activity in the *agora* could constitute a sanction, when, as we know, an activity of that kind was not considered very honourable for an *homoios*.

[76] Link 1994, 22–3.

[77] Link 1994, 23.

[78] This is also what Ehrenberg thought, 1937, cols. 2293–4. M. Clarke (2002, 75) judiciously points out that suicide by hanging was, for the Greeks, typically female: the story of Pantites is manifestly an edifying tale, centred on the idea of manliness.

[79] 'The only one of the Three Hundred to have returned from Thermopylae safe and sound'. This expression could also be explained by the hypothesis that §232 of Book 7 may have been added after the redaction of the whole work, or by the fact that, in the end, Pantites committed suicide. But, even in these cases, it remains obvious that Herodotus had scant interest in this character.

[80] Cf. the motive, according to Diodorus, for condemning the prisoners of Sphacteria: 'having tarnished Sparta's image' (see below, p. 40).

[81] On the *atē* of Thermopylae (Herodotus 7.223: παραχρεώμενοί τε καὶ ἀτέοντες), cf. Loraux 1977, 116–17, who makes this comparison with Aristodemos' conduct at Plataea, and Clarke 2002, 75.

[82] Link 1994 believes in Aristodemos' death-wish; he would have wanted to die both because the sanction was imposed in perpetuity (p. 23) and because it was unbearable (pp. 84–5). This is not what Herodotus thinks. The reaction of some when confronted with Aristodemos' exploits might be compared with the reaction – an ambiguous one – of the ephors in the face of the extraordinary, not to say extravagant, conduct of Isadas, son of Phoibidas, during the Theban attack on Sparta (Plutarch, *Agesilaus* 34.11).

[83] David 1991, 97–100; Nafissi 1991, 318–27.

[84] David 1991, 99.

[85] An ambiguity stressed by Loraux 1977, 122 and n. 54, and by Lewis 1977, 31.

[86] This is the meaning of the *atrakton* apophthegm, recorded at 4.40.2: those who died in the fighting were no braver than those who surrendered, it was just a matter of chance.

[87] A difficulty is created, at the end of the sentence, by what is probably a corruption (ὁμοίως), and for which no satisfactory remedy has been found; but, according to the commentators (*HCT* 4 and Hornblower 2, ad loc.), the general meaning is clear.

[88] Loraux 1977, 112, n. 55.

[89] Lewis 1977, 31: 'for a year'. MacDowell 1986 is more cautious: 'for some time' (p. 46).

[90] The problem has been noticed by Lewis and MacDowell.

[91] In grammatical terms, it is natural to associate τινας with ἀρχάς: this is what J. de Romilly does ('ils occupaient déjà certaines fonctions publiques'). But τινας may also be related to τοὺς ληφθέντας, which fits better with what is, in any case, the meaning of this sentence.

[92] For an example of a decision concerning *atimia*, see the consequences of Megalopolis, below, p. 44.

[93] See above, p. 39.

[94] On the part played by psychological explanation in Thucydides, cf. Huart 1968.

[95] Cf. Loraux 1977, 112, n. 56: 'La peur est pour Thucydide un motif essentiel des actions humaines'. The historian often ascribes this feeling to the Spartans in their relations with their 'minority groups', notably the helots: cf. Ducat 1990, 139–40.

[96] Loraux 1977, 112, n. 56.

[97] *Comparison of Agesilaus with Pompey*, 2.3: οὐ γέγονε ἄλλο σόφισμα πολιτικώτερον.

[98] Cf. *Treatise on the Sublime*, 31.1.

[99] *Hell.* 6.5.23 (the Arcadians) and 25 (the men of Karyai).

[100] Cf. above, p. 8.

[101] Cf. above, p. 15.

[102] Link 1994, 162, n. 106.

[103] As we can observe, from this example, Sparta is certainly a society of shame, but also, and at the same time, a society of guilt; a society founded on custom, but also on legal rules; a society that is both traditional and political. In the form in which Xenophon describes it, the social exclusion suffered by the 'trembler' illustrates this ambivalence. Some of its aspects, such as the eviction from ball-games, the positioning in choruses, the prescribed dress and behaviour, and (in Plutarch) the half-shaven face, would certainly be quite at home in one of the traditional societies studied by ethnologists. But we should not forget that forms of behaviour which segregate and humiliate, and which are quite comparable in their principles, were also in use, concurrently with

physical annihilation, in societies as highly political as the various totalitarian systems of the 20th century (I think, for example, of the way in which, in Soviet society, the spouses, parents and relatives of those who had been executed or sent to the camps were humiliated, marginalized and excluded).

[104] See above, p. 12.
[105] Lewis 1977, 31.
[106] MacDowell 1986, 148.
[107] Link 1994, 84 and n. 40, 146.
[108] See above, pp. 10 and 26.

Bibliography

Cairns, D.L.
1993   *Aidos. The psychology and ethics of honour and shame in ancient Greek literature*, Oxford.
Cartledge, P.
2001   *Spartan Reflections*, London.
Cassio, A.C.
2000   'Un' epigramma votivo spartano per Atene Alea', *RFIC* 128, 129–34.
Cawkwell, G.L.
1983   'The decline of Sparta', *CQ* 33, 385–400.
Clarke, M.
2002   'Spartan *ate* at Thermopylai?', in A. Powell and S. Hodkinson (eds.) *Sparta: Beyond the mirage*, Swansea and London, 63–84.
Constantinou, S.
1998   'Dionysiac elements in Spartan cult dances', *Phoenix* 52, 15–30.
David, E.
1989a   'Dress in Spartan society', *The Ancient World* 19, 3–13.
1989b   'Laughter in Spartan society', in A. Powell (ed.) *Classical Sparta: Techniques behind her success*, London and New York, 1–25.
1991   *Old Age in Sparta*, Amsterdam.
1999   'Sparta's kosmos of silence', in A. Powell and S. Hodkinson (eds.) *Sparta: New perspectives*, Swansea and London, 117–46.
2004   'Suicide in Spartan society', in T.J. Figueira (ed.) *Spartan Society*, Swansea, 25–46.
Ducat, J.
1990   *Les Hilotes*, BCH Suppl. 20, Paris.
1997   'La cryptie en question', in *Esclavage, guerre, économie; hommages à Y. Garlan*, Rennes, 43–74.
1999a   'La femme de Sparte et la guerre', *Pallas* 51, 159–71.
1999b   'Perspectives on Spartan education', in A. Powell and S. Hodkinson (eds.) *Sparta: New perspectives*, Swansea and London, 43–66.
2005   'Aristodémos le trembleur', *Ktéma* 30, 205–16.
Ehrenberg, V.
1937   Article *tresantes* in *RE* VI A 2, col. 2292–7.
Forrest, W.G.
1968   *A History of Sparta 950–192 BC*, London.

Hammond, M.
1979/80   'A famous exemplum of Spartan toughness', *CJ* 75, 97–109.

Hansen, M.H.
1976   Apagoge, Endeixis *and* Aphegesis *against* Kakourgoi, Atimoi *and* Pheugontes, Odense.

Hanson, V.D.
1990   *Le modèle occidental de la guerre*, Paris. Trans. of *The Western Way Of War*, New York, 1989.

Hodkinson, S.
2000   *Property and Wealth in Classical Sparta*, Swansea and London.

Huart, P.
1968   *Le vocabulaire de l'analyse psychologique dans l'oeuvre de Thucydide*, Paris.

Kennell, N.
1995   *The Gymnasium of Virtue*, Chapel Hill and London.

Kourinou-Pikoula, H.
1998   'Μνᾶμα γεροντίας', *Horos* 10–12, 259–76.

Lewis, D.M.
1977   *Sparta and Persia*, Leiden.

Link, S.
1994   *Der Kosmos Sparta*, Darmstadt.

Lipka, M.
2002   Xenophon's Spartan Constitution. *Introduction, text, commentary*, Berlin and New York.

Loraux, N.
1977   'La belle mort spartiate', *Ktéma* 2, 105–20.

MacDowell, D.M.
1986   *Spartan Law*, Edinburgh.

Nafissi, M.
1991   *La nascità del kosmos. Studi sulla storia e la società di Sparta*, Perugia.

Ollier, F.
1934   *Xénophon*. La République des Lacédémoniens, Paris and Lyon.

Powell, A.
1988   *Athens and Sparta*, London. 2nd edn 2001.

Richer, N.
1998   *Les Ephores*, Paris.

Ruzé, F.
1997   *Délibération et pouvoir dans la cité grecque*, Paris.

Velho, G.
2002   'Les déserteurs des armées civiques en Grèce ancienne ou la négation du modèle du citoyen-soldat', *Et. Class.* 70, 239–56.

Vernant, J.P.
1989   'Entre la honte et la gloire: l'identité du jeune Spartiate', in *L'individu, la mort, l'amour*, Paris, 173–209 (= *Métis* 2, 1987, 269–300).

2

THE SPARTAN *HIPPEIS*

Thomas Figueira

My subject is the body of elite Spartan troops who were denominated *hippeis* ('horsemen').[1] They numbered 300,[2] and paradoxically, despite their nomenclature, served as infantrymen. Thucydides was sensitive to this irony, speaking of the 'so-called *hippeis*' (Thuc. 5.72.4: οἱ τριακόσιοι ἱππῆς καλούμενοι).[3] His context is their utilization at Mantineia (418), which demonstrates that they were hoplites, not horsemen. Ephorus, transmitted through Strabo, confirms their status as infantry, contrasting them with their Cretan counterparts.[4] As often with Spartan institutions, much of our unambiguous evidence derives from the classical period, when the *hippeis* had long existed, and when military exigencies facing Sparta were already forcing significant adaptations.

Ancient evidence

Herodotus supplies our first important evidence. Some of this material is transparently pertinent; for other attestations, a case for relevance must be made. We shall return to the latter after the remaining evidence is introduced. One clearly relevant passage is 8.124.3. Among high honors accorded Themistokles for service against Xerxes in 480 was an escort to the Spartan border with Tegea by the *hippeis*,[5] an unparalleled distinction at the time of Herodotus' writing. Among the Spartans who bestowed attention on such ritual, this gesture constituted a symbolic elevation, if only within a limited context, to parity with Sparta's Heraclid kings, whom the *hippeis* customarily accompanied. Herodotus also describes them as λογάδες ('picked troops').[6] This qualifier is not only confirmed by their manner of conscription, as described by Xenophon (*LP* 4.4), but also supported by a gloss of Hesychius implying they were ἐπίλεκτοι ('picked men').[7]

Another Herodotean reference presents some interpretative challenges. Recounting a sixth-century Spartan conflict with Tegea, Herodotus refers to the *hippeis*.[8] Victory turned on possession of the bones of Orestes, which a Spartiate called Likhas acquired. Likhas was one of the ἀγαθοεργοί ('benefactors'), a term sufficiently obscure that the qualifier 'so-called' is also affixed to it. The ἀγαθοεργοί were the eldest who left the *hippeis*, five each year, individuals charged with serving the community the next year. Lexical glosses confirm that selection depended on ἀνδραγαθία ('manly excellence'), and the *Suda* has the choice handled by the ephors.[9] This anecdote attests to the early existence of the *hippeis*, certainly in the mid-fifth century when Herodotus was questioning informants, and, arguably, at its dramatic date, 570–60.

While our story is pervaded with folk motifs and may not be literally factual, let alone provide a true causation for the treaty between Sparta and Tegea, background details, such as Likhas' status as ἀγαθοεργός and what that implied, were hardly sheer fabrications. The ἀγαθοεργοί were tasked with public duties of an occasional nature.[10] They were clearly magistrates, as their public service and annual term indicate. Lexical notices confirm this.[11] Photius uses the phrase 'agents of the magistrates'. The lexica cite Didymus that this 'benefaction' included control of Spartiate conduct, since the ἀγαθοεργοί possessed authority 'regarding those acting unlawfully at home and abroad' (*Lex. Seguer.*; Photius) or 'devoted themselves to the cognizance of good *mores* among the other Spartans' (ΣAel. Arist.). Like the ἀγαθοεργοί, the *hippeis* themselves and their commanders, the *hippagretai*, had official status. Strabo, following Ephorus, describes the *hippeis* as constituting an ἀρχή ('magistracy').[12] Hesychius specifically calls the *hippagretai* an ἀρχή.[13]

In the classical period, some or all of the *hippeis* were arrayed on the battlefield with the king or (probably) anyone substituting for him. Thucydides' narrative of Mantineia (418) exhibits this deployment (5.72.4).[14] At Mantineia and elsewhere, at least during the fifth century when Spartan manpower was still relatively high, the *hippeis* served as what were called 'lifeguards' in early modern armies, i.e., picked troops tasked with accompanying and providing security for the force commander. At Mantineia, Agis led them in the decisive attack, falling on older Argives, the Argive *pente lokhoi*, allies from Kleonai and Orneai, and the Athenians. A similar disposition may have occurred at Leuktra, at least if an emendation of Xenophon is allowed.[15] In the received text of *HG* 6.4.14, the *hippoi* ('horsemen'), aides of the polemarch, and others on the right yielded before the massed Theban left. As the Spartan cavalry had already been turned (6.4.13), it is preferable to follow the majority of editors in reading οἱ μὲν ἱππεῖς instead of οἱ μὲν ἵπποι. The *mora* ('regiment') to which an important component of the *hippeis* was attached had been overwhelmed.

Viewing the *hippeis* as lifeguards is consistent with the treatment by Herodotus of honors accorded Spartan kings. He notes 100 picked men (ἄνδρας λογάδας) who guard a king on campaign (6.56).[16] At any single time, one third of the *hippeis*, with their commander, a *hippagretas*, may have undertaken this duty. This usage therefore apparently existed before *c.* 491, when both kings could campaign together and might need protection simultaneously. In that case, the integrity of the three units of 100, forming the *hippeis*, could only be preserved by assigning one unit of 100 to each king. About the royal bodyguards, Isocrates speaks more generally of τοὺς ἐνδοξοτάτους τῶν πολιτῶν ('the most distinguished of the citizens') (*Ad Philipp.* 6). Dionysius states οἱ γενναιότατοι τῶν νέων τριακόσιοι ('three hundred most noble [or most excellent] of the young men') were guards of the kings (*AR* 2.13.4).

Xenophon states that a group of *hippeis* were assigned scouting duty (οἱ προερευνώμενοι ἱππεῖς), when the Spartan army was on normal march with enemy troops absent (*LP* 13.6).[17] These *hippeis* were probably true cavalrymen, acting as advance scouts. Regardless of this determination, a parallel query emerges. What was the ἄγημα of the first *mora* that Xenophon mentions accompanying the king if the enemy appeared? The ἄγημα also appears in a list of the standard maneuvers of the phalanx (*LP* 11.9).[18] Since the elite *hippeis* act as royal protectors elsewhere, the ἄγημα has been considered an embodiment in some fashion of that corps,[19] a conclusion supported by use of the term for elite units of Alexander's army. Arrian associates one ἄγημα with the *hypaspists*, out of whom they were an even more elite unit,[20] and also mentions the ἄγημα of the Companion cavalry.[21] An equation of the ἄγημα with the *hippeis* naturally raises the issue how this elite unit was incorporated into the Spartan tactical structure. That exploration, however, is best postponed until our investigation of the *hippeis* in light of Spartan demography.

As elite troops, the *hippeis* were also important instruments of the state in facing internal danger.[22] Treating the suppression of the conspiracy of Kinadon *c.* 400,[23] Xenophon notes the role of some of the *hippeis* (*HG* 3.3.9).[24] The authorities took pains to isolate Kinadon from his fellow conspirators and to surround him with trustworthy persons for arresting him. Consequently, the ephors bade Kinadon go to the eldest of the *hippagretai* (a term meaning 'marshals of the *hippeis*') and request six or seven of those attendant on him. A sensible extrapolation is that these were *hippeis* under command of the *hippagretas* in question. So it appears that some of his unit of 100 were available at discretion of each *hippagretas* throughout the day. Although Kinadon thought the *hippeis* were to help him arresting others, the *hippagretas* and the *hippeis* in question were informed in advance of their mission to arrest Kinadon himself.

Besides Xenophon's explicit statement that Kinadon had undertaken similar missions previously, the entirely matter-of-fact way in which this enterprise was handled indicates that the *hippeis* were regular state agents in maintaining order in Lakōnikē. The ephors gave Kinadon a σκυτάλη ('message baton') with names of those to be arrested. His mission was not a contrived pretext. He was to bring from perioikic Aulon certain Aulonites and helots, and a particularly beautiful local woman who seemed to be 'ruining' the Spartans going there, young and old (*HG* 3.3.8). The verb is λυμαίνομαι, which commonly connotes active molestation, revealing a remarkable example of gender inversion.[25] This characterization nicely dramatizes Spartan fears of outside contamination; even perioikic Aulon in Lakōnikē itself could embody such a threat. Concomitantly, the choice of this 'police' detail suggests the young *hippeis* were expected to be superior to the risk of tainting. Xenophon equates Kinadon himself with the *hippeis* assisting him, since he was to go on his ostensible mission σὺν ἄλλοις τῶν νεωτέρων ('with others of the younger men'). It is tempting to speculate that his suitability for such tasks might have derived from his own service as a *hippeus* before he lost Spartiate rank.

The function of the *hippeis* as an emergency force can perhaps also be inferred from another incident. Unfortunately, the name of the unit in question is not specified, and this is one of the episodes in Herodotus that only arguably involves the *hippeis*. At Plataia (479), the Persian Mardonios was killed by a Spartan named Aeimnestos (according to the Herodotean manuscripts) or perhaps Arimnestos (9.64.2).[26] Herodotus says discursively that he fell with his 300 men in the Stenyklaros plain during the war against 'all the Messenians'.[27] Here Herodotus accepts an Athenian or rebel perspective on the helot revolt (from 465) as in fact a Messenian war against the Spartans. Thus, the anecdote may have a non-Spartan provenance. The emphasis on the presence of 'all the Messenians' portrays a lopsided battle as well. Arimnestos, described as an ἀνὴρ λόγιμος ('notable person'), is a likely candidate for a senior *hippagretas*. This incident preceded the victory, at which the seer Teisamenos presided, that drove the rebels from the Stenyklaros plain onto Mt. Ithome.[28] Arimnestos may have commanded the *hippeis* who were rushed into Messenia after the earthquake to head off a concentration of dissidents in a stratagem that underestimated the impetus of the rebellion. The main Spartan force was needed to drive the rebels from the open field. If this interpretation is correct, the *hippeis* are again seen as an elite strike force.

Herodotus also reports a Spartan tradition on the deployment of another elite force of 300 fighters at the Battle of the Champions (1.82.3).[29] This engagement occurred *c.* 546 when the Spartans occupied the Thyreatis. The Spartan 300 are again *logades* ('picked men') just like the *hippeis*. Indeed, it would be incongruous for the Spartans to choose another elite group of the same size, inasmuch as the *hippeis* probably already existed, if we believe the anecdote about Likhas. If these men were truly the *hippeis*, the Battle of Champions would provide an excellent instance of their deployment as the first military recourse of the state.[30] The heroism of the Champions had strong psychological resonance for Spartan society, encoded not only in ritual behavior[31] but also in social gesture. Herodotus reports that Spartiates wore their hair long after the victory (1.82.8), as though the triumph of these exemplary young men had rejuvenated the whole community, and could continue to do so through ritual repetition.[32] The fallen champions were accorded heroic honors on the site.[33]

A final contingent of 300 Spartans who might represent the *hippeis* appears during the first Theban invasion of the Peloponnesus (370).[34] Xenophon reports an ambush in the precinct of the Tyndaridai during the attack on Sparta that was mounted by a force of about 300 younger hoplites, backed up by a small contingent of cavalry (*HG* 6.5.31). The operation was successful in forcing the enemy to retreat. Our analysis of the episode is hampered by the presence on the scene of other *hippeis* who undoubtedly were cavalrymen.

In a sense, the *hippeis* of archaic and classical Sparta were already a group standing in surrogacy to an original body of aristocratic Spartan cavalry. It is unsurprising then that another body of picked troops could relate to them in the same spirit of institutional metonymy, such as the 300 who stood with Leonidas at Thermopylai.[35] The campaign of Leonidas in 480 was probably shaped by compromises between those preferring a forward defensive strategy against Xerxes and others reluctant to send any troops at all beyond the Isthmus. Herodotus did not pierce the shroud of secrecy veiling Spartan decision-making, and does not investigate any basis in factional politics for the composition of Leonidas' force.[36] Yet, the identity of the famous 300 Spartans of Thermopylai was sufficiently enigmatic to warrant just such a deeper scrutiny of Spartan traditions and contemporary intentions.

Basing oneself on the Herodotean account of the Spartan royal bodyguard, one would reasonably expect the *hippeis*, or, at least, a unit of 100 of them under a *hippagretas*, to have accompanied Leonidas. Yet, comparative evidence also implies that the *hippagretai* and their *hippeis* were deployed at the order of the ephors (as seen in the Kinadon affair), just as the ephors certainly mobilized the army.[37] *Hippeis* were not sent with Leonidas, probably because the ephors were unwilling. Thus, Leonidas seems to have decided to muster a royal unit of 300 elite troops in their place (Hdt. 7.205.2). The participle ἐπιλεξάμενος to describe the process of mustering indicates their status as 'picked troops', comparable to the *hippeis*. These men are described as ἄνδρας τε τοὺς κατεστεῶτας τριηκοσίους καὶ τοῖσι ἐτύγχανον παῖδες ἐόντες in the main manuscript tradition. The condition that these men must have sons may correlate with Leonidas' departure at the time of the Karneia.[38] He was leaving each household represented by a male at the festival. Since there were only 300 with Leonidas, the king had not brought along the *hippeis* and an indeterminate number of men with children. Nor can the *hippeis* and the men with children merely be the same people.[39] The existence of sons for all the enrolled indicates they were mainly men over thirty, while the *hippeis* were probably mainly under thirty.[40]

Scholars disagree how to construe the participle κατεστεώτας with the criterion of possessing sons in the relative clause. Powell prefers 'customary', How and Wells opt for 'assigned by law', and Liddell-Scott interprets as 'regular'.[41] Yet, these men seem most assuredly not to have been the customary (or the like) *hippeis*. Grote is representative of nineteenth-century scholarship in suggesting 'of mature age', which is hard to parallel in Herodotus and otiose in light of the provision for possessing sons.[42] All these interpretations still leave, however, a clumsiness of phrase with the following clause. Legrand emends ἄνδρας τε τῶν κατεστεώτων Τριηκοσίων.[43] This is attractive, especially if Τριηκοσίων is understood as an alternative name for the *hippeis* themselves and not merely a number, and the participle can mean 'those appointed' or 'those who had become'.[44] Denied the *hippeis*, Leonidas enrolled an equivalent force from former *hippeis* who had children. Paradoxically, their heroic deaths, although the 300 were not serving *hippeis*, may have served to enhance the glory of that corps still further through their previous connection.[45]

The selection of the *hippeis*

In his *Constitution of the Lacedaimonians* (*LP* 4.3–4), Xenophon describes the selection of the *hippeis*, a process attributed to Lykourgos.[46] The ephors select three *hippagretai*, who were men in young adulthood.[47] Each *hippagretas* chose 100 *hippeis*. The second element of their title is derived from ἀγρέω ('take'), an equivalent of Attic αἱρέω. *Hippagretai* could be equated with Hipparchs.[48] These officers clearly commanded their contingent of 100, as already seen from the participation of the senior *hippagretas* in the arrest of Kinadon. As there was a new body of ephors annually, there would be a new board of *hippagretai* each year.

Xenophon establishes the existence of this magistracy *c.* 400, but Thucydides may vouch for it even earlier. The second-in-command over the Spartans trapped on Sphakteria (425) was named Hippagretas (4.38.1).[49] He was undoubtedly a middle-aged senior officer, being the second-in-command of a unit the size of a *lochos* ('battalion'), and was probably born before 465. Some antecedent of Hippagretas made his tenure of that office sufficiently notable to justify his descendant receiving the name.[50] The three-fold organization of the *hippeis* (cf. thirty *gerontes*) may reflect the three aboriginal Dorian tribes, so that the three divisions of *hippeis* could derive from an early Spartan tribal army. The respect for the authority of the eldest *hippagretas* seen in the Kinadon affair (Xen. *HG* 3.3.9) may also descend from this earliest developmental stage. In contrast, the five ἀγαθοεργοί parallel the number of ephors and remind us of the five-regiment army (reflecting perhaps four *obes* of Sparta with Amyklai).[51]

The process of selection was marked by a populist spirit imbued with a performative aspect. The *hippagretas* had to make manifest (διασαφηνίζων) his reasons for inclusion and rejection. The honor of selection could be referenced in shorthand as τὰ καλά ('the fair things').[52] The verb for rejection is ἀποδοκιμάζω. This same term is used for the rejection by the Attic *Boulē* and Dikasteric Courts of candidates allotted for office, which included judging *hippeis* ineligible.[53] Accordingly, selecting the *hippeis* probably occurred before the assembly, where all Spartans could observe the *hippagretai* stating rationales for specific inclusions and exclusions.[54] We should probably not imagine a selection procedure as formalized as an Attic *apodokimasia*, but an occasion at which candidates for inclusion, their kinsmen, and partisans shouted out names and reacted vocally with approval and disapprobation to choices and explanations (see below on Pedaritos).

On practical grounds, an individual *hippagretas* could not pick his whole contingent at one go, since that would permit his monopolizing the best candidates. Presumably, each *hippagretas* took a turn choosing one of 100, perhaps with the eldest going first. By same processes that balance teams in informal competition (like picking sides in sandlot sports in America, and cf. Ducat, this volume, pp. 19–20), the *hippagretai* would create roughly equivalent rosters. A *hippagretas* who did not select the most qualified was subjected to public disapproval. If selection rotated, a biased *hippagretas* would cede to his colleagues a relatively better candidate. The public character of the selection enacted for the community the values that it held most significant for achieving social prestige.[55]

This dramatization of civic excellence and legitimized *eris* provided the context for an exemplary anecdote about the Spartiate Pedaritos told by Plutarch,[56] for whom the story was something of a favorite.[57] Pedaritos departed the selection of the *hippeis* with bright and smiling countenance, although not chosen. This deportment presumably contrasted with the usual angry demeanors and vocal objections observed in others passed over. And he then made an explicit point of his pleasure that Sparta had 300 better men than himself. This riposte is, to be sure, marvelously two-edged, for it congratulates the state for the excellence of its corps of *hippeis*, while inviting the hearer to conclude as well that Pedaritos' manifest *aretē* made his exclusion an indefensible aberration.[58] An injustice was committed, but Pedaritos was so confident in his embodiment of Spartan ideals that he did not need to protest it.[59] Harpocration and the *Suda* describe him as one of the *kaloi*, recalling τὰ καλὰ of Xen. *LP* 3.3, 4.4, and implying he was chosen on another occasion.[60] Strikingly, in the most elaborate retelling (*Mor.* 231b),[61] Pedaritos makes his characterization to the ephors themselves, who asked why he was laughing. Their question could then be answered by Pedaritos as though it implied that the ephors themselves thought that he had a just cause for disappointment, regardless of their actual intent.[62]

This anecdote offers our only direct evidence on an individual selection (or non-selection, should we say). It is indeed possible that victors in the panhellenic games had a presumptive claim to be selected *hippeis* – for the next year or until the next iteration of the festival in question? – since Plutarch also attests to *Olympionikoi* having the privilege of fighting near the kings.[63]

Returning to Xenophon in his *LP*, the sentences just preceding his comments on the *hippagretai* reveal that he thought the purpose of this institution was to create an ἔρις ('competition') over ἀρετή ('excellence') in order to instill as much ἀνδραγαθία ('manliness') as possible (4.1–2). By implication then, the *hippagretai* chose from the ἡβῶντες ('young men').[64] By context we can determine that eligibility continued to at least thirty, because Xenophon introduces the next phase of Lykourgan law-giving by discussing those who, having passed the ἡβητικὴν ἡλικίαν ('early manhood'), were eligible for important offices.[65] Concordantly, Plutarch describes the escorts of Themistokles as *neoi*; Dionysius uses the same term for the royal bodyguards.[66] Aristophanes of Byzantium describes the status of Hippeus as standing in a sequence of maturational stages: first *meirakion,* then *meirax, neaniskos,* and *neanias* (...μειράκιον· εἶτα μεῖράξ τε καὶ νεανίσκος καὶ νεανίας, ὁ αὐτός).[67] Of the last stage, he adds Λακεδαιμόνιοι [Eustath. Λάκωνες] δὲ τούτους ἱππεῖς ἐκάλουν, καὶ τοὺς προεστηκότας [Eustath. προεστῶτας] αὐτῶν ἱππαγρέτας (The Lacedaimonians [Laconians] used to call these *hippeis* and the ones presiding over them *hippagretai*). By implication, this stage was followed by the age of marriage, i.e., around thirty. Aristophanes was well informed, since he also describes the role of the *hippagretai*. The predictability of entering the *hippeis* was affected by the level of Spartiate population. A significant proportion of all males 20–30 would have served when Spartan population had declined to its fourth-century levels.

The sequel to selection by the *hippagretai* illustrates how this ἔρις played out (Xen. *LP* 4.5–6). Not only did those excluded monitor those chosen to detect behavioral deviation, but they also continually challenged their qualifications for inclusion. Challenges took the demonstrative form of fist fighting. This fighting was treated in a spirit of relaxation from adult norms of deportment. Like the various acts of theft in which boys in the *agōgē* indulged, acts that were encouraged but punished on detection, any

Spartiate could part the combatants. Any fighter refusing to co-operate faced intervention by the *paidonomos*, the official supervising the *agōgē*, and subsequent punishment by the ephors.[68] These impromptu boxing matches acted as rehearsals for next year's selection of new *hippeis*, inasmuch as they established the worthiness of their victors to be chosen then.[69]

Here was a mechanism for instilling aggressiveness through continual stimulation of confrontation that presents a superficially primitive mode of male socialization. The mustering of the *hippeis* was a means for encoding (i.e., converting concepts into procedural acts) and representing a particular ethos of masculinity. By their embodiment of specifically Laconian social norms, the *hippeis* manifested to the community superior male ἀρετή. By their vulnerability to challenge, they symbolized the fragility of the attainment of exemplary status, and the need for external monitoring to maintain worthiness. The ἔρις over selection of the *hippeis* continued the agonistic processes embodied in the *agōgē*, serving as a psychological consolidation for young adults.[70] For them, admission to the messes and the status of a soldier and citizen could mark a certain relaxation of the earlier close supervision against deviation. The confrontations involving the *hippeis* counteracted backsliding. Nonetheless, the impact of the challenges was reduced markedly when exclusivity of the *hippeis* decreased with the decline of Spartiate numbers.

Yet, as so often for Sparta, the archaic is revealed as archaizing, since the mechanism for generation and suppression of this ἔρις and interpersonal friction served to maintain a military unit within a disciplined army of interchangeable citizen actors. And this unit was trained to fight under strict tactical control and was organized under a hierarchy of command.[71] The impression is a striking one: it is as if we were to combine in the same social order the behavioral conditioning of the fierce Yanomami of the Amazonia and the military administration of the conquistadors.[72]

The selection mechanism outlined by Xenophon is reconcilable with the institution of the ἀγαθοεργοί attested by Herodotus.[73] Our sources mention no age limit for membership in the *hippeis*, and there may have been none in principle or law. Combat-related deaths, incidental mortality, and the wear and tear of service winnowed out older *hippeis*. Older men endured competitive pressure from younger men every year at the moment of selection. Relatively older *hippeis* would have been passed over and weeded out annually. Therefore, the five oldest men at the end of the year of service would have been especially qualified, because they had survived ordinary physical and selective challenge from younger men. These five 'graduated' or 'retired' to the rank of the ἀγαθοεργοί without undergoing the discomfiture of failing to be selected at some later date.[74] With men 20–30 comprising the main strength of the *hippeis*, men over thirty were few in any eventuality.

The reconstruction just offered has the advantage of conforming to the most direct reading of the sources.[75] Other hypotheses on the formation of the corps require rejecting one or more important testimonia. To believe *hippeis* had indefinite tenure until superannuated is incompatible with the tradition of fighting between those selected and excluded.[76] Such confrontations would then become pointless as demonstrations of worthiness. The idea of older Spartiates tussling with younger men on a permanent basis appears a bit bizarre especially when one recalls the respect expected from the young toward their elders (e.g., Plut. *Lyc.* 15.2).

The related idea of service from selection until thirty copes with the problem of older *hippeis*, but still makes the fistfights hard to countenance.[77] Equally unacceptable is the hypothesis that the five 'graduating' ἀγαθοεργοί were balanced by an equivalent intake.[78] Since five twenty-year-old recruits per year would not staff a corps of 300, even using all 45 year-classes, some *ad hoc* assumptions or adjustments become necessary, such as supposing each *hippagretas* chose five twenty-year-olds and the service period was twenty years. Naturally, even twenty classes are insufficient, as the older year-classes were reduced through mortality. Moreover, quite a few middle-aged *hippeis* would still serve. Finally, any method of choice that does not require the whole corps chosen annually weakens the thrust of the anecdote about Pedaritos. Surely, this story makes best sense if 300 supposedly better men had just been chosen in preference to him.[79]

The populist spirit that imbued procedures for enrolment of the *hippeis* was appreciated in antiquity. The significance of the *hippagretai* for maintaining the civic order was revealed through a striking analysis of the Spartan constitution that has survived under the name of Archytas. He was the fifth-century Pythagorean philosopher from Taras, the Spartan colony in southern Italy, a statesman famous for his friendship with and influence on Plato.[80] His analysis[81] derives from *On Law and Justice* and is excerpted extensively by Stobaeus.[82] The dialect is a mixture of Doric and Ionic that may well reflect classical west Greek Pythagorean diction. The attribution to Archytas is controversial,[83] although some recent authorities accept his authorship unconditionally.[84] At a minimum, this treatise was a pastiche of genuine material from Archytas and other early Pythagoreans recast by a later compiler.[85] The reflection here of the classical Spartan polity and social conditions implies an inclusion of late fifth-/early fourth-century material.

'Archytas' attributes the success of Sparta to its mixed constitution in a sense differing from other observers.[86] The Spartan πολιτεία was compounded from δαμοκρατία, ὀλιγαρχία, βασίλεια, and ἀριστοκρατία.[87] The representative elements are the kings for μοναρχία, *gerontes* for ἀριστοκρατία, ephors for ὀλιγαρχία, and *hippagretai* and *ko(u)roi* for δημοκρατία. Contrasted to other analyses, a fourfold rather than threefold *schema* explains the polity, and the *hippagretai* and *kouroi* have substituted for the ephors as the democratic component.[88] The *ko(u)roi* equaling the *hippeis* here may be genuine recollection of Spartan usage.[89] Our author appreciates that νόμος ('law') has to be ἀγαθός and κάλος, as well as κάρρων ('predominant') (Doric for κρείσσων). He adds an understanding of what we call 'checks and balances' by insisting that the μέρη ('constitutional elements') must be in reciprocal balance or proportion (ἀντιπεπονθέναι).[90] He clarifies 'reciprocal balance' by observing its occurrence when the same ἀρχή controls and is controlled. The verb ἀντιπάσχω is common in mathematical works in this connotation.[91] An attestation from the *Nicomachean Ethics* demonstrates that it was considered to belong to Pythagorean diction (*EN* 1132b21–6). For 'Archytas', the ephors balance the kings, and *gerontes* balance the ephors.

The *hippagretai* and the *hippeis* are described as μέσοι ('mediate') among the other ἀρχαί.[92] They are set against other authorities insofar as they ῥέψωντι ('counterbalance') any of the ἄρχοντες ('office-holders') who are aggrandizing. It is important to emphasize that this function belonged to a period when the civic body was still so large that one could speak of 300 men as differentiated from the remaining citizens. It is doubtful whether Archytas or anyone else would bother distinguishing, for example, 300 *hippeis* from the total citizenship of 1,000 in mid-fourth-century Sparta. In fourth-century Sparta, the distinction between the *hippeis* and the remaining Spartiates was merely that existing between *neoi* and older men.

Recalling their meritocratic selection and the populist means by which the choice was portrayed and justified, one can envisage the psychological influence that the *hippeis* could bring to bear through vociferation and gesture, whenever they were assembled. It is then open to ask further whether the function of the *hippeis* as a separate, 'peer' governmental branch had further institutional grounding. A candidate for such a mechanism would be the mysterious 'so-called small assembly' (τὴν μικρὰν καλουμένην ἐκκλησίαν) that Xenophon mentions in passing during the conspiracy of Kinadon (*HG* 3.3.7).[93] Under the conditions of ongoing overseas campaigning and garrison duties in late fifth- and fourth-century Sparta, the *hippeis* were possibly convoked as a representative body for conducting affairs when the majority of the army was not mobilized. In that case, were the rules of procedure of this body more populist than those governing the entire assembly? Determining the identity of the 'small assembly', however, is probably impossible, given the present state of the evidence.

The evolution of the *hippeis*

The ultimate origin of the *hippeis* lay in the early archaic cavalry of Sparta.[94]

Comparative evidence indicates that the proto-*hippeis* would have derived from the aristocracy.[95] We need not take a position on the nature of this force by deciding whether they were true cavalrymen or mounted hoplites.[96] Our sources do not reveal terminology encoding such distinctions. There was no archaic cavalry 'revolution', a transformation that paralleled the 'hoplite revolution'. The creation of structured cavalry units with uniform equipment and an ability to fight cohesively awaited the classical period and culminated in the Macedonian army. Early archaic elite horsemen utilized a variety of weapons and fighting techniques. The proto-*hippeis* probably shifted between using horses as fighting platforms and fighting on foot as circumstances dictated. They were assisted in so doing by dependents or young fighters who were themselves often mounted. Nafissi has collected the evidence on Laconian pottery for such young 'squires'.[97]

The strength of such an archaic mounted force lay not in its ability to perform complex maneuvers and launch co-ordinated attacks. Massed attacks using shock tactics were in any event particularly difficult. Few early adversaries of Sparta could offer the organized resistance that elicited such counteraction. Rather, when they in operated in Laconia and Messenia, the proto-*hippeis* enjoyed some of the advantages initially possessed by European invaders when faced with Amerindian adversaries. European and native fighters operated in distinct universes of space and time. A mounted force could undertake sudden incursions, closing with its targets too quickly for opponents to react or mass their forces. It could break off attacks easily or shake off contact with adversaries. It could utilize a superior awareness of its environs to weigh the value of its targets and to assess threats to its safety. It could exploit victory more effectively. During the earliest campaigns in Messenia, one priority might have been to drive off the horses of their victims, leaving them at a permanent disadvantage.

These proto-*hippeis* were subsumed in the seventh-century transformation that redistributed land and access to dependent labor and homogenized political rights and social behavior. These changes ended an early archaic cavalry of aristocrats. Its continuance would have challenged the application of a single *agōgē*, for young riders required extensive equestrian instruction. The possession of horses and accoutrements of service were a conspicuous expression of elite status; thus cavalry service involved implicit claims to political leadership. Such ostentation in civic δίαιτα ('lifestyle') had to be excluded in emergent 'Lycurgan' Sparta. Instead of the previous corps, based on birth and wealth, a new elite body was created whose membership was determined by public recognition of ἀρετή in its Spartan connotations. The empanelment of the new *hippeis* embodied a particularly Spartan mode of meritocracy, one in which confirmation of agonistic 'excellence' radiated down from older exemplars.

Because this late-archaic social order was a brilliant institutionalization of the possibilities of hoplite warfare, it was perhaps inevitable that the elite corps must become hoplites themselves. It was unclear whether it would have been practical to support a cavalry *corps d'élite* of 300 by state levies for horses, feed, and equipment in an early *polis* administration such as 'Lycurgan' Sparta. Whatever judgment is made, however, on the general issue of public subsidization of cavalry in archaic *poleis*, to subsidize a corps (like the *hippeis*) with a shifting membership that was annually reconstituted seems beyond feasibility. Moreover, if the Spartans had opted for a utilitarian, publicly-subsidized cavalry troop, all the educative, behavioral, and symbolic benefits afforded by the classical *hippeis* in acting as exemplars of the Spartiate archetype, could not exist. Making them hoplites instead interwove the *hippeis* into the broader ideological texture of Spartan existence.

Furthermore, the representations of mounted attendants on Laconian pottery demonstrate that the original aristocratic *hippeis* were accompanied on campaign by armed youths, presumably dependent on them. Consequently, the transition to the late-archaic, 'Lycurgan' corps of *hippeis* was not only a populist, egalitarian metamorphosis, but also a generational homogenization to incorporate the same young men who had merely assisted before. Hence, as seen from 'Archytas', another name for the *hippeis* could justifiably be the *ko(u)roi*. Tyrtaean exhortations toward the νέοι were perhaps intended to surmount a 'generation gap' of differential commitment for suppressing the Messenians.[98] Membership in the 'Lycurgan' *hippeis* offered a more palpable incentive.

Dionysius of Halicarnassus uses the term *paraspistai* for the *hippeis*, which he construed to denote soldiers who were both cavalrymen and infantrymen (*AR* 2.13.4). This interpretation is an oddity, because παρασπιστής customarily means 'shield-bearer' or 'auxiliary comrade'.[99] On the strength of the parallel attestations, the Spartan *paraspistai* ought to be the young auxiliaries of the *hippeis*, who might join them as fighters, possibly, but not necessarily on foot.

Dionysius' connection of the *hippeis* with the early Roman *Celeres* might justify his interpretation, as his discussion implies (2.13.3–4, cf. 64.3). The *Celeres* were equated contradictorily with both the bodyguard of Romulus and the early Roman cavalry.[100] Yet, that might still fail to account fully for his παρασπιστής as dual purpose soldier. That connotation does not appear in other Greek accounts of the *Celeres,* and no Roman source links *Celeres* and *hippeis*. Dionysius' utilization of παρασπιστής may therefore be an aberration. If so, nothing further needs saying. Nonetheless, the option deserves to be canvassed that he found the word in his source and misunderstood its meaning under the influence of the irreconcilable traditions on the Roman

Celeres. The survival of several versions of a sadly abbreviated gloss hints that a debate existed regarding application of παρασπιστής to infantry and/or cavalry: παρασπιστής· παρεστώς [':' or ';'] ὁπλίτης.[101] Thus, Dionysius may have found preserved in a *Lakōnika*, a Hellenistic treatise on Sparta, the word παρασπιστής as an alternative term for Hippeus. Sosibius (*FGH* 595) is one possibility, because his works lie behind many lexical glosses on Sparta.[102] Alternatively, a Roman-era Spartan 'constitutionalist' may have made the connection between the *Celeres* of Romulus and the Spartan *hippeis*.

In that case, the equation of a Hippeus with a παρασπιστής could illuminate the transition from early archaic cavalry to late archaic and classical *hippeis*. One stage was the elevation of young *paraspistai* to parity with proto-*hippeis* and their selection from the whole body of the *homoioi*. The prerogatives of the proto-*hippeis* then eroded under the pressure of the homogenizing and meritocratic trends of 'Lycurgan' Sparta. The proto-*hippeis* disappeared, save for the *hippagretai*, leaving only the young *paraspistai* as the corps of *hippeis*.

Concomitantly, the term ἀγαθοεργός seems to be a Laconian variant for εὐεργέτης, the cross-cultural denomination for public benefactor.[103] In practical terms, public recognition as a 'benefactor' in seventh-century *poleis* was limited to aristocrats who served the community conspicuously as warriors, poets, donors, envoys, athletes, and authorities in sacred activities. The implications of the title of ἀγαθοεργός are that these routes to recognition as 'benefactor' were closed at Sparta. The conjunction of successful service in the *hippeis* and tenure as an ἀγαθοεργός, while amenable to Spartan social logic, was not a necessary development. This deliberate act of integration is another function of the overall movement toward homogenization and toward the nullification of elite self-representation. Spartan society recognized as ἀγαθοεργοί only those who emerged from a long sequence of tests as embodiments of its socio-cultural values. In this light, the office of the ἀγαθοεργοί was a remarkably populist feature.

The demography of the *hippeis*

A corps of 300 representing the armed might of the entire Spartan elite was not a very impressive force. We may compare unfavorably the 1,500 cavalry that Aristotle stated Lakōnikē could support during the mid-fourth century, alongside 30,000 hoplites (*Pol.* 1270a29–31.). If we applied the same proportion of 20% to relate the *hippeis* to Aristotle's potential, his 30,000 hoplites reduce to 6,000. That would include both *homoioi* and *perioikoi*, and represent an outside limit. Even if one discounts Aristotle's main point that a more conventional Spartan economic system would yield more soldiers, clearly the infantry associated with 300 cavalry numbered far below the highest attested levels of Spartiates.[104] Indeed, the number of Spartan citizens *c.* 650 is likely to have been closer to the 2,000 Isocrates says constituted the Dorian invaders of Laconia than the 8,000–10,000 peak population (12.255). By comparison, a stele in the sanctuary of Artemis Amarynthia at Eretria records an array of an archaic Eretrian army containing 600 cavalry and 3000 hoplites (Strabo 10.1.10 C448). Applying the ratio implied by Eretria (cavalry = a sixth of troops) would yield 1,500 hoplites to accompany the *hippeis*. Thus, the complement of *hippeis* might preserve evidence on the size of the Spartiate class in seventh-century Laconia.

However, the constant size of the corps obscures its changing significance in the evolving demography of Sparta.[105] During the sixth century, the *hippeis* became an ever more elite force. In the army at Plataia, they constituted only 3% of 10,000 hoplites and 6% of 5,000 Spartiate hoplites aged 20–49; they would have been less than 4% of Spartiate adult males. If the Spartiates ever reached 10,000, the *hippeis* were only 3%. At any one time during the period from 480 to 465, the serving *hippeis* would have been a small minority of men 20–30, comprising 15%, if drawn exclusively from that age bracket. Consequently, competition would have been especially keen over selection to such an elite group, with a strong impetus toward choosing the young, athletic, and aggressive. While more than 300 20–30-year-olds served over their prime years, as many as two hundred new 20-year-olds joined the pool of possible *hippeis* annually.

This elite body fought the Battle of Champions and perhaps confronted the Messenian rebels (465). If my hypothesis is correct, men who demobilized from these *hippeis* were enlisted by Leonidas for Thermopylai. Demographic confidence made the Spartans willing to risk the complete loss of this elite unit, a disaster they apparently suffered on at least two occasions. The whole corps was indeed not irreplaceable.

Nonetheless, the demography of the *hippeis* parallels the decline of the Spartiate class. Around 450, the *hippeis* were, hypothetically, about 4% of Spartans aged 20–49 (*c.* 8200), but now 10% of Spartiates of that age range (*c.* 3055). Of Spartiates 20–30 (*c.* 1173), the *hippeis* were already less elite, admitting one in four (26%) in any one cohort. The anecdote of Pedaritos probably belongs to this period of many alternative candidates. The proportions are similar for Pylos (425): *hippeis*, 11% of Spartiates of prime military age (*c.* 2755) and 28% of Spartiates 20–30 (*c.* 1058) in each year. Thereafter the velocity of decline accelerated. At Mantineia (418), the *hippeis* were possibly 14% of Spartiates 20–49 (*c.* 2251), but an annual cohort was 37% of those 20–30 (*c.* 864). At the Nemea River (394), they were, at least, 16% of Spartiates 20–49 (*c.* 1833) and 43% of those 20–30 (*c.* 704). Among the Spartiates 20–49 (*c.* 938) at time of Leuktra (371), *hippeis* amounted to 30%.

Before Leuktra, a remarkable 84% of young men aged 20–30 (*c.* 360) could be selected *hippeis* in any one cycle. This demographic decline affected the *hippeis* in several ways.

In the first instance, the *hippeis* became progressively a much less elite body, as those with some service became incrementally a larger proportion of citizens. Young men had at least ten opportunities to be selected. From some point early in the fourth century, almost all Spartiates 20–30 had an excellent chance to serve. Many superior warriors over thirty may well have continued to be selected.

Several incidents dramatize the practical battlefield impact of the manpower decline. At Sphakteria (425), Spartan population decline rendered the capture of the garrison (including 120 Spartiates) a catastrophe and the turning point in the Archidamian War. But why did the Spartans opt for supplying the force on Sphakteria by allotting *ad hoc* garrisons from all the *morai* ('regiments')?[106] Such a posting seems a natural mission for the *hippeis*; the island could only accommodate a limited force. The sequence of allotted garrisons indicates not only determination to buffer ordinary Spartiates from mortal risk or capture by spreading the danger broadly, but also betrays reluctance to risk the lives of the *hippeis*, paradoxically the community's ultimate risk-takers.

In 420, after an armistice had expired, Argos offered Sparta an agreement preserving for each party an opportunity to settle ownership of the disputed Thyreatis by another duel between 'champions' (Thuc. 5.41.2). The Spartans now viewed this option as foolishness, but, reluctant to provoke hostilities, were prepared to accept. The cost of sacrificing 300 picked men was no longer a prospect to be faced serenely. They may also have judged that their *hippeis* might not fare well against the best 300 from an Argive elite unit of 1,000 (training at public expense).[107] The Argive *logades* excelled at Mantineia (418), where they were superior to the Spartans man for man.[108] The decline of the *hippeis* is finally traced in the ability of another elite corps, the Theban Sacred Band, to maul the Spartans at Leuktra (371) and Mantineia (362).[109] At Leuktra, at least some *hippeis* directly faced the Sacred Band in the battle line.

Secondly, the Spartiate decline probably affected tactical deployment of the *hippeis*. As inheritors of the pre-eminence of an early archaic mounted aristocracy, originally the *hippeis* had perhaps been brigaded separately, outside the system of *morai* and *lokhoi*, i.e., distinguished from the hoplite formations either built from social units (like messes) or from territorial divisions. As the Spartiates diminished, it become increasingly imprudent to concentrate so many at one place within the phalanx on every occasion. That concentration thinned the Spartiates out along the front of the rest of the battle line. The first reflection of a progression toward treating *hippeis* as ordinary soldiers may be found in the army as reorganized after the Great Earthquake. It contained only forty-eight *pentēkostyes* ('fiftieths') of *c.* 150 in six *morai* (twelve *lokhoi*). The *hippeis* probably comprised the missing two *pentēkostyes*; thus they no longer stood totally outside the army structure.[110]

We lack evidence to determine whether the *hippeis* actually operated as a 'maneuver formation' before the Peloponnesian War. After 431, our source material stands against tactical autonomy. The *hippeis* are not enumerated separately by Thucydides in his description of Spartan forces at Mantineia (418).[111] Nonetheless, there were enough *hippeis* near the king to make noting their presence important. Their place must thus be found in other Spartan units that Thucydides does enumerate. As Xenophon implies, the *hippeis* were the ἄγημα of the first *mora*. How large was this unit? One possibility is an *enōmotia*, the smallest tactical unit.[112] A single *enōmotia* of 32–35, however, will certainly not account for the *hippeis* around the king at Mantineia and probably at Leuktra. At Mantineia (418), the *hippeis* could replace as many men as two *pentēkostyes* of eight *enōmotiai*, if all stood by the king.[113] Rather than outside the structure of the *morai* in two supernumerary *pentēkostyes,* the two *pentēkostyes* of *hippeis* were now integrated within the first *mora*.

After Mantineia in 418, the Spartans seem to have reorganized their forces yet again by halving the *enōmotiai*, which had become too small.[114] Thus, the maximum size of the ἄγημα was now two *pentēkostyes*, in total four *enōmotiai*. It may be this force that Aristophanes supposedly invoked in his *Lysistrata*, when he speaks of an attack by four *lokhoi*. The scholia note that the four *lokhoi* were Spartan and used by the king.[115] These so-called *lokhoi* would have to be *enōmotiai*.[116]

However, concentrating all the *hippeis* in one spot made the Spartiates of the other *morai* across the front of the phalanx dangerously shallow. Therefore at Mantineia and afterward, the size of the ἄγημα may have varied above a minimum of one *enōmotia*. Some important engagements probably required the largest commitments. Spartans may have transferred *hippeis* into the rightmost *mora* as the size of the army and the tactical situation required, building up to the eight or four *enōmotiai* just conjectured. This explanation presupposes that individual *hippeis* had now assumed dual military identities as members of *enōmotiai* of regular *morai* and as members of the *hippeis*. By Leuktra, a full-scale engagement at which there were only seven hundred Spartiates in all, most *hippeis* must have served in the *morai*.[117] If the *hippeis* had been brigaded separately at Leuktra, only 100 Spartiates would be left for each of the four *morai* present (*c.* 576 men each). In contrast, if 100 *hippeis* stood with the king, the others could have stood across the front line of a phalanx whose first row needed *c.* 192 men.

Greater dependence on the *hippeis* in regular units may have meant that they were supplemented or deployed differently in their role as body-guards.[118] At Koroneia (394), fifty *neoi*, sent out as volunteers from Sparta, guarded Agesilaos, and were decisive.[119] This selection of those 'most in their masculine prime and strongest' probably drew from *hippeis* to whom a significant proportion of young men now belonged. When the *mora* from Lekhaion was routed by Iphikrates (390), Agesilaos, who was on the Peiraion peninsula, was accompanied by unspecified *doryphoroi* ('spear-bearers') (Xen. *HG* 4.5.8).[120] These may no longer have been *hippeis*, but could have included ordinary *homoioi*, *hypomeiones*, and *perioikoi*.

Thirdly, by the late fifth century, during the Attic raids on Lakōnikē, genuine Spartan cavalry lay so far in the past that Spartans had to scramble to create a mobile force of 400 cavalry and bowmen to counter Athenian pillaging.[121] Later cavalry *morai* were established to match infantry *morai*.[122] The independent activity of such paired units became regular,[123] perhaps being a precondition for individual use of an infantry *mora* abroad.[124] These genuine horsemen, however, were of low quality.[125] The wealthy provided horses and equipment, but the troopers themselves came from other classes.[126]

Conclusion

Scrutiny of the institutional order of an archaic *polis* should never ignore the strongly aesthetic component of legislation. Nowhere is this observation more important than for 'Lycurgan' Sparta. When one examines the *hippeis*, a secondary detail of social engineering emerges that elegantly complements other structures. Along with the messes, the *hippeis* blended the *agōgē*, for which the corps served as culmination, with the adult *diaita*.[127] As a markedly agonistic institution, the *hippeis* symbolized a more intense embodiment of the struggle to live in accordance with 'Lycurgan' norms. The *hippeis* provided a powerful military tool against external adversaries and a device, as the case of Kinadon suggests, against internal enemies. If the analysis attributed to Archytas may be credited, the *hippeis* wielded a subtle dampening effect on the oligarchic tendencies of the rest of the state authorities. The social rami-fications of the corps of *hippeis* were expressed through these interactions. Concomitantly, the interplay and tight integration of social structures meant that the Spartan polity, as a mechanism rather than as an ideological system, was blighted systematically over time. The institution of the *hippeis* was so profoundly integrated that it may have lacked autonomous vitality, and could not activate itself to redress other weaknesses. The decline of the *hippeis* as a military force was perhaps merely the overt sign of their loss of social and political significance.

Acknowledgements

My gratitude is owed to Anton Powell and Stephen Hodkinson for their friendship and collegiality over the years in including me in the International Sparta Seminars and their publications. Thanks are also deserved by Professor Pierre Brulé and his colleagues at Rennes who made our Sparta sessions there so congenial and stimulating. I should like to thank Andrey Eremin of Samara State University and University of Nottingham for generously translating the fine Russian article of Y.A. Andreyev.

Notes

[1] For general discussion: Busolt-Swoboda 1926, 2.704, 706; Andreyev 1969; Cozzoli 1979, 84–97; Lazenby 1985, 10–12; Richer 1998, 470–2; Lipka 2002, 143–5; also Lammert 1913a; 1913b, 1689. Tigerstedt 1965/74, 1.178 and Andreyev 1969, 27 (n. 10) suggest the *hippeis* were the models for the Persian ephebes in Xenophon's *Cyropaedia* (1.2.9–12; cf. 1.2.3).

[2] Hdt. 8.124.3; Thuc. 5.72.4.

[3] Herodotus (8.124.3) also felt specification was necessary: οὗτοι οἵ περ Ἱππέες καλέονται. Note Andreyev 1969, 25.

[4] Strabo 10.4.18 C481 ~ Ephorus *FGH* 70 F149. Dionysius of Halicarnassus alone has them as *paraspistai*, serving as both cavalry and foot soldiers (*AR* 2.13.4). Did they originally possess this dual role? Or did Dionysius misunderstand the rare term *paraspistēs* (below, pp. 69–70).

[5] Cf. Plut. *Them.* 17.1.

[6] Cf. Hdt. 1.36.2, 3, 43.1, 82.4 (Spartiates at the Battle of Champions); 6.15.1; 6.56 (Spartiates guarding the kings); 9.11.3 (perioikic hoplites mustered for Plataia), 21.3, 63.1. At 6.56, the manuscript variant is λογχάδας.

[7] Hescyh. s.v. ἱππαγρέτας, ι 776 Latte.

[8] Hdt. 1.67.5. Cf. ΣAel. Arist. *Tett.* 172.1.50–6; Phot. s.v. ἀγαθοεργοί, α 79 Th.

[9] Phot. s.v. ἀγαθοεργοί; *Suda* s.v. ἀγαθοεργοί, α 115 Latte.

[10] Hdt. 1.67.5: τοὺς...Σπαρτιητέων τῷ κοινῷ διαπεμπομένους μὴ ἐλινύειν ἄλλους ἄλλῃ.

[11] *Lex. Seguer.* ἀγαθοεργοί, *Anec. Gr.* Bekker 1.333.30–4; Phot. s.v.; on Didymus 3.1, cf. Schmidt 1854, 23; Σ *Tett.* 172.1.55–6. Didymus derived from Sosibios or another author of a Hellenistic *Lakōnika*.

[12] Strabo 10.4.18 C481 ~ Ephorus *FGH* 70 F149.

[13] Hesych. s.v. ἱππαγρέτας.

[14] *HCT* 4.112, 121.

[15] e.g. Lazenby 1985, 10–11, cf. 155–6, 160. Cf. Anderson 1970, 247. Caution is advised; note Figueira 1986, 180–1 (n. 38).

[16] Lipka 2002, 145. Andreyev 1969, 29 (n. 18) wonders whether the 300 provided those *hippees* who announced a king's death to all in Lakōnikē (Hdt. 6.58.1). That would solidify their special relationship to the kings.

[17] Spence 1993, 149.

[18] Lipka 2002, 200, 218, 268.

[19] Kahrstedt 1922, 302; Busolt-Swoboda 1926, 2.706 (n. 3); Cozzoli 1979, 87; Lipka 2002, 218. Cf. Anderson 1970, 248–9; Lazenby 1985, 11, 128, 155, 180 (n.7). However, the *hippeis* were not brigaded separately at Mantineia (418), and they could

not all have stood with king Kleombrotos at Leuktra (below p. 73).

[20] Arr. *Anab.* 1.1.11, 8.3–4; 2.8.3; 3.11.9; 5.2.5; 7.7.1, 29.4.

[21] Arr. *Anab.* 4.24.1; 5.12.2, 13.4, 22.6; 6.2.2, 21.3, 22.1; 7.6.4, 11.3, 29.4.

[22] Ollier 1934, 34; Richer 1998, 470–3, 514, 519, who also notes the soldiers who mounted guard over the temple of Athena Khalkioikos, when Pausanias fled there (Lyc. *Leoc.* 128).

[23] Cf. Cozzoli 1979, 95–7, against whom note Richer 1998, 469–70.

[24] See Andreyev 1969, 27; also Cartledge 2002, 236, who would, however, urge caution in generalizing from the episode.

[25] Compare Hdt. 5.33.3, 9.79.1; Eur. *Ba.* 353–4; Lys. 28.15; cf. Isoc. 4.175.

[26] The paleographical variant is Ἀμνήστου. Aristodemus *FGH* 104 F1.2.5 also has Aeimnestos. Plutarch *Arist.* 19.1 offers, however, Ἀρίμνηστος. See Poralla #31: 1985, 14.

[27] Cf. Lazenby 1985, 55.

[28] Hdt. 9.35.2; Paus. 3.11.8.

[29] See also the poem sometimes attributed to Simonides (*AP* 7.431 = fr. LXV Ca.); Paus. 2.38.5 (*epilektoi*); Strabo 8.6.17 C376; cf. Plut. *Mor.* 231e. In general: Brelich 1961, 22–34. See note 30 below.

[30] In support: Moretti 1948, 209–13; Detienne 1968, 135–6; Nafissi 1991, 157; Richer 1998, 471. Cf. Lazenby 1985, 54, 78; also Cozzoli 1979, 90–1, who doubts the initial duel of the picked men as an exaggeration from the later pitched battle in which the *hippeis* excelled (noting Isoc. *Archid.* 99 : ...καὶ τῶν τριακοσίων τῶν ἐν Θυρέαις ἅπαντας Ἀργείους μάχῃ νικησάντων...). This claim must be owed to a compression of causation based on the thought that the courage of the elite unit set in motion the events leading to a total Argive defeat. Paus. 10.9.12 is actually also evidence for a two-stage engagement.

[31] See Athen. 15.678B–C with Sosibius *FGH* 595 F5; *Suda* s.v. Γυμνοπαιδεία, γ 486; *Lex. Seguer.* s.v., *Anec. Gr.* Bekker 1.234.4–6; Hesych. s.v. Πάρπαρος, π 1003; *IG* V.1.213.53; Georg. Choeroboscus *GG* 4.1.297; also Pliny *NH* 4.5.17. See Brelich 1961, 30–4; 1969, 188–91; Nafissi 1991, 303–9.

[32] The three choruses (boys, men, and old men) performing at the Gymnopaidia might be associated with the victory in the Thyreatis (Sosibius *FGH* 595 F5). The phrase identifying the choruses is corrupt. Accepting the emendation ἀρίστων ἀνδρῶν, Nafissi (1991, 303–5) suggests the *hippeis* provided the men's chorus and their *erōmenoi* the boys' chorus. See also Jacoby 3b.646–7. Since another selection stage was needed to move from 300 *hippeis* to chorus members in any case, I should argue that cognate procedures were operative in choosing different, but overlapping groups .

[33] *SEG* 13.266; cf. Paus. 2.38.6. See Nafissi 1991, 303–8; also Figueira 1993, 306. It is tempting to associate the *hippeis* and specifically their service in the Thyreatis with the so-called 'Laconian Rider', a mounted ephebic figure found on mid-sixth-century Laconian pottery, who is accompanied by symbols of victory and heroization. See Nafissi 1991, 160, 304–5; also Stibbe 1974; Pipili 1987, 76.

[34] Lazenby 1985, 166; Figueira 1986, 208.

[35] Cf. Lazenby 1985, 54–5, who confuses his reconstruction by introducing year-classes of stable size.

[36] His failure can be paralleled both in the tangled account of Spartan factional disputes regarding policies toward Aigina and Athens *c.* 490 and in his understanding of

Spartan reactions to Datis' landing at Marathon. See Figueira 1993, 126–7, 136–7.

[37] Richer 1998, 324–36.

[38] Hdt. 7.206.1. See Grote 1888, 4.173 (n. 1); also Figueira 1986, 174–5.

[39] Cozzoli 1979, 92–3 suggests he brought the customary 100 guards from the *hippeis*, augmented to 300 with men with children.

[40] Macan 1908, n. 8–9 (1.307) would have them as the *hippeis* themselves, with Herodotus misunderstanding the term λογάδες. See also Moretti 1948, 210; Stein 1882, n. 10 (196–7).

[41] Powell 1938, 192; see also Stein 1882, 196; How and Wells 1912, 2.223; Liddell-Scott 855.

[42] Grote 1888, 4.173 with n. 3, and those noted in Macan 1908, n. 8 (1.307).

[43] Legrand 1951, 214, opting for men chosen from the Three Hundred and among those with children. See also Cartledge 2002, 176. Vaticanus 2369 offers τοῦ κατεστεῶτος Τριηκοσίων.

[44] Hdt. 4.166.1; cf. 1.59.6; 1.65.4; 1.94.2; 3.72.2; 3.89.3; 5.88.2 (passive); also 3.143.1; 6.59; 7.106.1.

[45] Another hypothetical appearance of the *hippeis* should, however, be rejected. The text of Hdt. 9.85.1–2 reads ἰρέας and ἰρέες in two *loci* for those buried in a Spartan tumulus at Plataia. A common emendation has been ἰρένας or ἰρένες (Valkenaer; cf. den Boer 1954, 288–98); an alternative has been ἱππέας or ἱππέες (Jeanmaire 1939, 545–7; Lazenby 1985, 181, n. 16; cf. den Boer 1954, 290). So the *hippeis* have been emended into the passage either directly (our latter alternative) or indirectly under the guise of the *eirenes*. See Kelly 1981; Nafissi 1991, 302–3. This hypothesis faces difficulties with the identity of Amompharetos, even if he was a *hippagretas* (a supposition lacking warrant in the text). See Figueira 1985, 301–2; 1986, 179 (n. 35). For persuasive defense of the manuscript readings: Richer 1994, 52–5; Brulé and Piolot 2004, 155–8.

[46] In general: Andreyev 1969, 26; Rebenich 1998, 106–7.

[47] Their age is not absolutely ascertainable. The ostensible antecedent for αὐτῶν…ἐκ τῶν ἀκμαζόντων τρεῖς ἄνδρας seems to be τοὺς ἡβῶντας (4.2). Cf. MacDowell 1986, 67. Yet, the ἀκμάζοντες ('those at peak manhood') are men over 30. Pettersson (1992, 86–7) believed they could be anywhere from 30 to 60. But note Aris. *Rhet.* 1390b9–11, with a physical acme 30–35, mental acme, 49. Xenophon states that Lykourgos mandated marrying ἐν ἀκμαῖς τῶν σωμάτων (in the prime of their manhood) or around thirty (*LP* 1.6). Therefore, αὐτῶν has an implied antecedent from the previous section (4.2) in those men who reached 'the highest level of manly excellence' (ἐπὶ πλεῖστον ἀφικνεῖσθαι ἀνδραγαθίας). The parallel office of Hipparch at Athens was also to be chosen ἐκ τῶν ἀκμαζόντων (Xen. *Hipparch.* 2.2), and Hipparchs were senior officers, each commanding 1,000 cavalry.

[48] Hesych. s.v. ἵππαρχος, ι 784 Latte.

[49] *HCT* 3.477–8.

[50] The alternative is to surmise that our passage became corrupt and was imperfectly repaired. The officers above (Epitadas) and below (Styphon) Hippagretas in the command hierarchy receive patronymics (albeit Epitadas in 4.8.9). Possibly, a name with patronymic was lost, one accompanied by the specification that the man himself was a *hippagretas*. Note Kahrstedt 1922, 302, 309. Some such conjecture is implied by Liddell-Scott under ἱππαγρέται (833).

[51] ΣArist. *Lys.* 453 (citing Thuc. 5.68.3); ΣThuc. 4.8.9; Hesych. s.v. ἐδωλός, ε 549

Latte; Phot. s.v. λόχοι, λ 232 Th.; Aris. fr. 546 Gigon. See Figueira 1986, 179–81.

⁵² Xen. *LP* 4.4; cf. 3.3 for a broader category of honors. See n. 55 below.

⁵³ Ἀποδοκιμάζω: [Aris.] *Ath. Pol.* 45.3, 55.2, 4; Attic *hippeis*: *Ath. Pol.* 49.1–2 (ἀδόκιμος: 49.1). See Bugh 1988, 15–19 on ceramic evidence for the cavalry *dokimasia*.

⁵⁴ Thus, reselection was hardly 'automatic'; cf. Anderson 1970, 248.

⁵⁵ The hypothesis that this review function implies that *hippagretai* had more general supervisory responsibility for young men is speculative. Cf. Hodkinson 1983, 247 (n. 20); also Singor 1999, 84 (n. 10). But compare Hesych. s.v. παιδαγρέται (codd.: παιλ-)· ἀρχή τις, ἐπὶ ἱππέων, π 88 Latte.

⁵⁶ This Pedaritos (name variants: Ducat 2002, 21–2) was probably the harmost on Chios (412–11) who engineered a narrow oligarchy and fell trying to break the Athenian *epiteikhismos* (Poralla 1985, 104, #599; Ducat 2002, 25–32). See Thuc. 8.28.5, 32.2–3, 33.3–4, 38.3–5, 39.2, 40.1, 55.2–3, 61.2; *Hell. Oxy.* 2.1; Isoc. *Archid.* 53; Harpocrat. s.v. Πεδάριτος, with Theopompus *FGH* 115 F8; *Suda* s.v. Παιδάριτος, π 848 Latte; Plut. *Mor.* 241d–e. His father Leon may have been the statesman of that name (Thuc. 3.92.5; 5.44.3; Xen. *HG* 2.3.10; Poralla #482) and his brother perhaps Antalkidas. See *HCT* 5.69; Cartledge 1987, 145, 288; Ducat 2002, 22–5.

⁵⁷ Plut. *Lyc.* 25.4; *Mor.* 191f (*Regum et imperatorum apophthegmata*); *Mor.* 231b (*Apophthegmata Laconica*).

⁵⁸ Its assertive quality ensures that this is not the defensive laughter of a loser, which is usually self-deprecating. Nor was defensive laughter surely objectionable at Sparta on the basis of this anecdote, since the point of the ephors' query may have been particular. Why was Pedaritos who had reason for disappointment acting contrarily? Cf. David 1989, 4–5.

⁵⁹ The anecdote does not explain whether his complaisance included refraining from physical challenges to those selected. Or would that mode of passivity constitute unacceptable deviance?

⁶⁰ *Suda* s.v. Παιδάριτος; Harpocrat. s.v. Πεδάριτος. Cf. Ducat 2002, 23–4.

⁶¹ I agree with Ducat 2002, 16–17 that the ephors' query probably belongs to the original narrative. While apophthegm connoted to Plutarch and presumably to its initial compiler the patriotic principle 'the city ahead of everything', unlike Ducat, I think that Pedaritos' encoded self-assertion may well derive from an underlying historical source.

⁶² Extrapolating on David 1989, 4–5, Ducat 2002, 15–16, raises, but rightly questions, the possibility of derisive laughter which the ephors had a right to treat as transgressive, the odium of which Pedaritos had to dissipate by a conforming remark.

⁶³ *Lyc.* 22.4. In the framing for the anecdote is the detail that Spartan kings were accompanied into battle by victors in the great games (also noted in *Mor.* 639e). Hence a contestant refused a bribe to persevere to victory. Answering his defeated adversary's query as to what he gained, he replied, 'stationed in front of the king, I shall fight the enemy' (πρὸ τοῦ βασιλέως τεταγμένος μαχοῦμαι τοῖς πολεμίοις). Xen. *HG* 2.4.33 mentions the Olympic victor Lakrates, who fell (with two polemarchs) when Pausanias fought Attic democrats before the Peiraieus (403). Conceivably, he was a Hippeus, fighting near the king. See Hodkinson 1999, 169–70; 2000, 259; Lipka 2002, 144.

⁶⁴ Cartledge 1987, 158, suggests interestingly that the excellence of Sphodrias as ἡβῶν (in Arkhidamos' appeal to his father Agesilaos: Xen. *HG* 5.4.32) encodes service as a Hippeus.

[65] Xen. *LP* 4.7. See Kennell 1995, 129–30.

[66] Plut. *Them.* 17.1; DH *AR* 2.13.4.

[67] Arist. Byz. *Nomina aetatum* (Miller 1868, 428–34) ~ Eustath. *Il.* 2.630.11–15 (*Ad Il.* 8.727).

[68] See Kennell 1995, 121.

[69] Cf. Andreyev 1969, 26, where the fight victors (improbably) replace the losers.

[70] Note Ducat 1999.55–7.

[71] See Powell 1998, 141.

[72] Note Chagnon 1983, 170–89.

[73] Cf. Kahrstedt 1922, 301.

[74] Cf. ΣAel. Arist. *Tett.* 172.1.53–54: ἀγαθοεργοὶ…οἵτινες ἐξῆρχοντο τοῦ βαθμοῦ, ('*agathoergoi*…the ones who office hold by reason of their grade'). Note Ollier 1934, 34.

[75] See Busolt 1905, 404; Kahrstedt 1922, 217; Ollier 1934, 34; Hodkinson 1983, 247–9 with n. 22 (p. 248).

[76] Cf. Cozzoli 1979, 88–9, where the introduction of the *neōteroi* of Thuc. 5.54.3, 75.1 is particularly maladroit. These were males 18–20 (Hodkinson 1983, 247 [n. 20]).

[77] Cf. Busolt 1905, 404; Cartledge 1987, 204–5; Anderson 1970, 248. This hypothesis can be combined with a system where thirty new members are chosen annually. See How and Wells 1919, 1.91; more recently, Singor 1999, 68–9, 84 (n. 10), a discussion marked by *ad hoc* formulations.

[78] Lazenby 1985, 53, 182 (n. 28).

[79] Ducat 2002, 33 reaches the same conclusion.

[80] See Guthrie 1962, 1.333–6.

[81] Cf. Aalders 1975, 33–5.

[82] Stobaeus *Flor.* 4.1.135–8; 4.5.61. See Jeanmaire 1939, 544–5; Andreyev 1969, 24–5; Guthrie 1987, 191–2 for translation.

[83] Guthrie 1962, 335 (n. 3); Huffman 2005, 509–602 tentatively declares the fragments spurious, but notes that both the use of the term *apatheia* and the affinity to Archytas fr. 2 speak in favor of authenticity.

[84] Cordano 1971; Mathieu 1987, n. 41 (p. 246). Cf. Tigerstedt 1965/74, 1.233, 518 (n. 46); Huffman 2005, 599–601 for the earlier bibliography.

[85] Delatte 1922, 71–124, esp. 109–14; Ollier 1933/43, 1.204–6; Wuilleumier 1939, 583–4 with n. 1 (584). This conclusion would address Huffman's concerns over the parallels of *On Law and Justice* with the pseudo-Pythagorean treatises of Dictogenes, Damippos, and Metopos.

[86] Cf. Plato *Laws* 691D–92A, 712D–E; Aris. *Pol.* 1265b33–66a4; 1294b18–41; Plut. *Mor.* 719a–c ~ Dicaearchus fr. 41 W; also Isoc. 3.24; Plut. *Lyc.* 29.6. See Richer 1998, 496–501.

[87] Stob. *Flor.* 4.1.138 (34.16–27 Thesleff).

[88] Aristotle (*Pol.* 1265b39–66a2) distinguishes two views on the ephors, as a democratic feature or as a tyrannical element, with the democratic influence in the *syssitia* and other aspects of the Spartan lifestyle (note 1270b7–17; Xen. *LP* 8.4). Our text belongs in the latter camp. Cf. 1272a31–42, 1294b18–40. See Lipka 2002, 173; Hodkinson 2005, esp. n. 23.

[89] A late-sixth-century funerary relief is a dedication of *koroi* in honor of Theokles (*IG* V.1.457). See Bourguet 1927, 35–6 (#1,). These *ko(u)roi* could, however, be a cult group. See also Kennell 1995, 139–40, who cites Wace 1937, 220.

[90] Compare fr. 42.20 Thesleff from [Archyt.] *Peri paideuseōs ēthikēs*: οὐ γὰρ ἀντιπαθέες

ἔντι ταὶ ἀρεταί.

[91] Some early examples: Apoll. Perg. *Conica* 2.20.61; Archim. *De sphaera et cylindro* 1.48, 50, 52, 104, 106, 109, 116; *De conoidibus et sphaeroidibus* 1.157; *De planorum aequilibriis* 2.87, 89, 101; *Quadratura parabolae* 2.171; *Ad Eratosthenem methodus* 3.87, 99, 101; Eudoxus fr. 289 Lasserre; Euclid *Elementa* (Stamatis) 6.14, 15, 16, 19, 30; 10.22; 11.34, 36; 12.9, 15.

[92] Ephorus also treated the *hippeis* as an ἀρχή (Ephorus *FGH* 70 F149).

[93] Jeanmaire 1939, 544–5; Detienne 1968, 135; Beattie 1975, 16–19, who introduces the governmental body of the Three Hundred at Gortyn. Cf. Andreyev 1969, 29 (n. 17); Nafissi 1991, 154.

[94] Greenhalgh 1973 for context.

[95] Moretti 1948, 209–10; Detienne 1968, 136–7; Nafissi 1991, 153–62; also Spence 1993, 2–4.

[96] Nafissi 1991, 82, 89–90, 153, 158, arguing strongly from artifactual evidence for mounted hoplites; also Chrimes 1949, 376–7.

[97] Nafissi 1991, 158–62. See (e.g.) Stibbe 1972, ##36–8 (with pp. 216–17), #219 for mounted hoplites and youths.

[98] Tyr. fr. 10.15–18, 27–30; 11.10–14; 12.13–14.

[99] Cf. Eur. *El.* 886; *Cyc.* 6; Posidonius *FGH* 87 F116 (DS 5.29.2); in the weaker sense of 'comrade' also Aes. *TGF* 3, fr. 303 (= fr. 605 Mette); Eur. *Ph.* 1165; Demades fr. 84 de Falco; Polyb. 11.18.2; DH 3.14.2; ΣAel. Arist. 3.292.15D.

[100] Bodyguard: Livy 1.15.8, cf. 1.13.8; DH 2.13.1–4 (with Valerius Antias fr. 2P), 29.1, 64.3; Plut. *Rom.* 26.2, cf. 10.2, 13.1, 20.1; *Numa* 7.4; Zonaras 7.4, 5, cf. 10 (from Dio Cassius); cf. DS 8.6.3. *Equites*: Festus 48.2–5L; Pliny *NH* 33.9.35; Servius *Aen.* 11.603; J. Lyd. *De mag.* 1.9, 14, 37; Pomponius *apud Dig.* 1.2.2.15. See Hill 1938; Ogilvie 1965, 83–4.

[101] Hesych. s.v. παρασπιστής, π 672 Latte; likewise *Suda* s.v., π 437 Adler; Photius s.v., π 390 Porson.

[102] Figueira 2003 [2005] offers a review of the possibly Sosibian glosses.

[103] The concepts of ἀγαθοεργία and εὐεργεσία are equivalent: Phot. s.v. ἀγαθοεργοί, α 79 Th.; Eustath. *Od.* 2.286.25–26; Damascius *VI* fr. 24 Z (*Suda* s.v. ἀγαθοεργία, α 114, citing Pythagoras), cf. fr. 324. Cf. Porphyr. *De abstin.* 2.40–41; ΣHom. *Od.* 3.36; ΣHes. *WD* 214ter, 297; ΣAes. *Septem* 702–4a, 703a–b, d. For χρηστουργία and ἀγαθοεργία: *Suda* s.v. χρηστουργία, χ 516. The largest proportion of the instances of this vocabulary derives from Christian writers, starting from Paul *Tim.* 1.6.18.

[104] Aris. *Pol.* 1270a37–8: 10,000; Hdt. 7.234.2: 8,000 (480).

[105] See Figueira 1986 for all data.

[106] Thuc. 4.8.9.

[107] Thuc. 5.67.2; DS 12.75.7 (*HCT* 4.105–6).

[108] They subsequently Laconized. See DS 12.79.4–7, 80.2–3; Aris. *Pol.* 1304a25–7; Plut. *Alcib.* 15.2; Thuc. 5.80.2, 81.2 , cf. 5.73.4.

[109] Plut. *Pelop.* 23.2–4, cf. 19.3–4; DS 15.55.2–4; 56.2; 86.4; cf. Xen. *HG* 6.4.14; 7.5.22–4.

[110] Figueira 1986, 179–80.

[111] Thuc. 5.67.1–68.3. See Busolt 1905, 403; Anderson 1970, 247; Figueira 1986, 180–1 (n. 38), cf. 187–92. Cf. Toynbee 1969, 399; Lazenby 1985, 41–3, 46; Cartledge 2002, 218.

[112] Cf. Lipka 2002, 200, 218.

[113] For this reconstruction: Figueira 1986, 180–1 (n. 38).

[114] Figueira 1986, 200–1 on Xen. *LP* 11.4.

[115] Arist. *Lys.* 453–4 with scholia. See also Hesych. s.v. ἐδωλός, ε 549 Latte; Phot. s.v. λόχοι, λ 232 Th.; Aris. fr. 546 Gigon.

[116] Lazenby 1985, 53, 182 (n. 28); Figueira 1986, 180–1 (n. 38).

[117] Cf. Toynbee 1969, 400–1; Lazenby 1985, 22; Cartledge 2002, 251.

[118] Anderson 1970, 245–8; Figueira 1986, 180–1 (n. 38).

[119] Plut. *Ages.* 17.2; 18.2–3.

[120] Xen. *HG* 4.5.8.

[121] Thuc. 4.55.2. See Lammert 1913b, 1699; Cozzoli 1979, 84–5.

[122] Their subunits, *oulamoi* of 50 combatants, were given a 'Lycurgan' pedigree (Philostephanus fr. 30, *FHG* 3.33; cited by Plut. *Lyc.* 23.1). *Oulamos* could be an archaism, as it is used in the *Iliad* for a throng of men (4.251, 273; 20.113, 379), but was also a Hellenistic technical term (e.g., Polyb. 6.28.3–4, 33.10, 35.2).

[123] Xen. *HG* 4.5.11–13, 16, cf. 4.2.16; 5.4.39; *LP* 11.4 (Rebenich 1998, 125–6).

[124] That the commander of each cavalry *mora* was a ἱππαρμοστής (Xen. *HG* 4.4.10, 5.12) – to be contrasted with a *hippagretas* – may reinforce this conclusion.

[125] Xen. *HG* 6.4.10–11.

[126] Foreign troopers (Xen. *Hipparch.* 9.4), and perhaps also *perioikoi*, *hypomeiones*, and *neodamōdeis*.

[127] Hence, Plato *Laws* 760A–763C blends the Spartan *krypteia* (in the youths' role as rural guardians) with the *hippeis* (in their selection, close supervision, and police functions) in the institution of the *agronomoi/phrourarkhoi* and *agronomoi/kryptoi*. Note also that the *hippeis* may have been the model for the Persian ephebes in Xenophon's *Cyropaedia* (1.2.9–12; cf. 1.2.3). See Tigerstedt 1965/74, 1.178; Andreyev 1969, 27 (n. 10).

Bibliography

Aalders, G.J.D.
  1975   *Political Thought in Hellenistic Times*, Amsterdam.
Anderson, J.K.
  1970   *Military Theory and Practice in the Age of Xenophon*, Berkeley.
Andreyev, Y.A.
  1969   'СПАРТАНСКИЕ "ВСАДНИКИ"' ['Spartan "Knights"'], *VDI* 4, 24–36.
Beattie, A.J.
  1975   'Some notes on the Spensitheos decree', *Kadmos* 14, 8–47.
Boer, W. den
  1954   *Laconian Studies*, Amsterdam.
Bourguet, E.
  1927   *Le dialecte laconien*, Paris.
Brelich, A.
  1961   *Guerre, agoni e culti nella Grecia arcaica*, Bonn.
  1969   *Paides e Parthenoi*, Rome.
Brulé, P. and Piolot, L.
  2004   'Women's way of death: fatal childbirth or *hierai*? Commemorative stones at Sparta and Plutarch, *Lycurgus*, 27.3', in T.J. Figueira (ed.) *Spartan Society*,

Swansea, 151–78.

Bugh, G.R.
  1988   *The Horsemen of Athens*, Princeton.
Busolt, G.
  1905   'Spartas Heer und Leuktra', *Hermes* 40, 387–449.
Busolt, G. and Swoboda, H.
  1920/26   *Griechische Staatskunde*, 2 vols., Munich.
Cartledge, P.
  1987   *Agesilaos and the Crisis of Sparta*, London.
  2002   *Sparta and Lakonia*², London. 1st edn 1979.
Chagnon, N.
  1983   *Yąnomamö: The fierce people*³, New York.
Chrimes, K.M.T.
  1949   *Ancient Sparta: A re-examination of the evidence*, Manchester.
Cordano, F.
  1971   'Sui frammenti politici attribuiti ad Archita in Stobeo', *PP* 26, 290–300.
Cozzoli, U.
  1979   *Proprietà fondiaria ed esercito nello stato spartano dell'età classica*, Rome.
David, E.
  1989   'Laughter in Spartan society', in A. Powell (ed.) *Classical Sparta: Techniques behind her success*, London and Norman, Okla., 1–25.
Delatte, A.
  1922   *Essai sur la politique pythagoricienne*, Liège.
Detienne, M.
  1968   'La phalange: problèmes et controverses', in J.-P. Vernant (ed.) *Problèmes de la guerre en Grèce ancienne*, Paris, 119–42.
Ducat, J.
  1999   'Perspectives on Spartan education in the classical period', in S. Hodkinson and A. Powell (eds.) *Sparta: New perspectives*, London, 43–66.
  2002   'Pédaritos ou le bon usage des apophtegmes', *Ktema* 27, 13–34.
Figueira, T.J.
  1985   'Chronological table: Archaic Megara, 800–500 BC', in T.J. Figueira and G. Nagy (eds.) *Theognis of Megara*, Baltimore, 261–303.
  1986   'Population patterns in late archaic and classical Sparta', *TAPA* 116, 165–213.
  1993   *Excursions in Epichoric History: Aiginetan essays*, Lanham.
  2003 [2005]   '*Politeia* and *Lakōnika* in Spartan historiography', *AJAH* 2.2.
Greenhalgh, P.A.L.
  1973   *Early Greek Warfare: Horsemen and chariots in the Homeric and archaic ages*, Cambridge.
Grote, G.
  1888   *A History of Greece*, London.
Guthrie, K.S.
  1987   *The Pythagorean Sourcebook and Library*, Grand Rapids.
Guthrie, W.K.C.
  1962   *A History of Greek Philosophy*, vol I: *The earlier Presocratics and the Pythagoreans*, Cambridge.

Hill, H.
   1938   'Equites and Celeres', *CP* 33, 283–90.

Hodkinson, S.
   1983   'Social order and the conflict of values in classical Sparta', *Chiron* 13, 239–81.
   1999   'An agonistic culture? Athletic competition in archaic and classical Spartan society', in S. Hodkinson and A. Powell (eds.) *Sparta: New perspectives*, Swansea, 147–87.
   2000   *Property and Wealth in Classical Sparta*, Swansea.
   2005   'The imaginary Spartan *Politeia*', in M.H. Hansen (ed.) *The Imaginary Polis*, Royal Danish Academy, Acts of the Copenhagen Polis Centre, Copenhagen, 222–81.

How, W.W. and Wells, J.
   1912   *A Commentary on Herodotus*, Oxford.

Huffman, C.A.
   2005   *Archytas of Tarentum: Pythagorean, philosopher and mathematician king*, Cambridge.

Jeanmaire, H.
   1939   *Couroi et Courètes*, Lille.

Kahrstedt, U.
   1922   *Griechisches Staatsrecht: Sparta und seine Symmachie*, Göttingen.

Kelly, D.H.
   1981   'Thucydides and Herodotus on the Pitanate *Lochos*', *GRBS* 22, 31–8.

Kennell, N.
   1995   *The Gymnasium of Virtue: Education and culture in ancient Sparta*, Chapel Hill.

Lammert, F.
   1913a   'ἱππαγρέται', *RE* 8.2, Stuttgart, 1651.
   1913b   'Ἱππεῖς', *RE* 8.2, Stuttgart, 1689–1700.

Lazenby, J.F.
   1985   *The Spartan Army*, Warminster.

Legrand, P.-E.
   1951   *Hérodote* Histoires *VII*, Paris.

Lipka, M.
   2002   *Xenophon's* Spartan Constitution, Berlin.

Macan, R.W.
   1908   *Herodotus, the seventh, eighth, and ninth books*, London.

MacDowell, D.M.
   1986   *Spartan Law*, Edinburgh.

Mathieu, B.
   1987   'Archytas de Tarante: Pythagorien et ami de Platon', *BAGB*, 239–55.

Miller, E.
   1868   *Mélanges de littérature grecque*, Paris.

Moretti, L.
   1948   'Sparta alla metà del VI secolo: II. La Guerra contro Argo per Tireatide', *RFIC* 26, 204–22.

Nafissi, M.
   1991   *La nascita del* Kosmos, Naples.

Ogilvie, R.M.
    1965   *A Commentary on Livy. Books 1–5*, Oxford.
Ollier, F.
    1933/43   *Le mirage spartiate*, Paris.
    1934   *La république des Lacédémoniens*, Paris.
Pettersson, M.
    1992   *Cults of Apollo at Sparta: The Hyakinthia, the Gymnopaidiai and the Karneia*, Stockholm.
Pipili, M.
    1987   *Laconian Iconography of the Sixth Century BC*, Oxford.
Poralla, P.
    1985   *A Prosopography of Lacedaimonians. From the earliest times to the death of Alexander the Great (X–323 BC)*², rev. A.S. Bradford, Chicago.
Powell, A.
    1998   'Sixth-century Lakonian vase-painting: continuities and discontinuities with the 'Lykourgan' ethos,' in N. Fisher and H. van Wees (eds.) *Archaic Greece: New approaches and new evidence*, Swansea, 119–46.
Powell, J.E.
    1938   *A Lexicon to Herodotus*, Cambridge.
Rebenich, S.
    1998   *Xenophon: Die Verfassung der Spartaner*, Darmstadt.
Richer, N.
    1994   'Aspects des funérailles à Sparte', *CCG* 5, 51–96.
    1998   *Les éphores: Études sur l'histoire et sur l'image de Sparte (VIIIᵉ–IIIᵉ siècles avant Jésus-Christ)*, Paris.
Schmidt, M.
    1854   *Didymi Chalcenteri grammatici Alexandrini fragmenta quae supersunt omnia*, Leipzig.
Singor, H.W.
    1999   'Admission to the *syssitia* in fifth-century Sparta', in S. Hodkinson and A. Powell (eds.) *Sparta: New perspectives*, Swansea, 67–89.
Spence, I.G.
    1993   *The Cavalry of Classical Greece*, Oxford.
Stein, H.
    1882   *Herodotos*⁴, 3, Berlin.
Stibbe, C.M.
    1972   *Lakonische Vasenmaler des sechsten Jahrhunderts v. Chr.*, Amsterdam.
    1974   'Il cavaliere laconico', *MNIR* 36, 19–37.
Tigerstedt, E.N.
    1965/74   *The Legend of Sparta in Classical Antiquity*, Uppsala.
Toynbee, A.
    1969   *Some Problems in Greek History*, Oxford.
Wace, A.J.B.
    1937   'A Spartan hero relief', *AE*, 217–20.
Wuilleumier, P.
    1939   *Tarente*, Paris.

3

COMMEMORATING THE SPARTAN WAR-DEAD

Polly Low

The overall theme of this chapter is not one which is uniquely relevant to Sparta, or even to the ancient world. Sparta, like other Greek city-states, was regularly involved in conflict, and, like other Greek city-states, had to face the problem of what to do with one of the regular by-products of ancient (and all) warfare: dead soldiers. But the particular way in which the Spartans of the classical period dealt with that problem, and the ways in which their practice compares with that of other Greek states, can be revealing not only of the roles played by soldiers and by war in Spartan society, but also of Spartan attitudes and approaches to broader questions of politics and diplomacy.

The immediate fate of the dead after a battle was (in theory, at least) governed by a series of panhellenic, even international, conventions. But once the dead had been collected from the battlefield, the *nomoi* regulating their subsequent treatment varied from *polis* to *polis*: some states repatriated their dead, others buried them at the site of the battle; some insisted on collective commemoration, others allowed for individual burial; some included elaborate civic rituals in their commemorative activities, others adopted a more low-key approach.[1] Perhaps the only thing which these various customs have in common is the wide range of functions which they can be seen to perform, from the practical through the religious and emotional to the political. I do not want to suggest that any one of these factors is more important than any other, but I do want to concentrate in what follows on the last of those functions: the political. I propose also to focus on one particular aspect of commemorative practice: the creation of physical monuments to the war-dead. I explore two ways in which the commemoration of the Spartan war-dead fits into the Spartan political landscape. First, and more broadly, what is political about these memorials? Second, and more literally, is it possible to say anything, on the basis of the monuments' physical locations, about the role they might have played in Sparta's political life?

This investigation falls into two main sections. The second part concentrates on monuments to the Spartan dead which are located outside

Spartan territory. The first section, however, stays closer to the Spartan homeland, in order to explore the nature and implications of what is perhaps the most distinctive variety of Spartan war memorial: the group of grave stelae known as the ἐν πολέμῳ ('in war') inscriptions.

These are first described by Plutarch, once in the *Life of Lycurgus* (27.2), and again in the *Instituta Laconica*:

τῶν δὲ τάφων ἀνεῖλε τὴν δεισιδαιμονίαν ἄπασαν ὁ Λυκοῦργος, ἐν τῇ πόλει θάπτειν τοὺς νεκροὺς καὶ πλησίον ἔχειν τὰ μνημεῖα τῶν ἱερῶν συγχωρήσας. περιεῖλε δὲ καὶ τοὺς μιασμούς, συνθάπτειν δ' οὐδὲν ἐπέτρεψεν, ἀλλ' ἐν φοινικίδι καὶ φύλλοις ἐλαίας θέντας τὸ σῶμα περιστέλλειν κατ' ἴσον ἅπαντας. ἀνεῖλε καὶ τὰς ἐπιγραφὰς τὰς ἐπὶ τῶν μνημείων, πλὴν τῶν ἐν πολέμῳ τελευτησάντων, καὶ τὰ πένθη καὶ τοὺς ὀδυρμούς.

Lycurgus did away with all superstitious fear connected with burials, granting the right to bury the dead within the city, and to have the tombs near the shrines. He also abolished the pollutions associated with death and burial. He permitted the people to bury nothing with their dead, but only to enfold the body in a red robe and olive leaves, and all to treat their dead alike. He also abolished inscriptions on memorials, except of those who had died in war, and also did away with mourning and lamentation.   (*Inst. Lac.* 18 = *Mor.* 238d)

Two important features of this account need to be emphasized: that it is only soldiers killed in war to whom inscribed commemoration is allowed; and that the form of commemoration under discussion is not, necessarily, burial, but μνημεῖα – memorials or monuments.[2]

The precise significance of that choice of vocabulary will be discussed further below. First, though, it is worth taking a closer look at the physical embodiment of this (alleged) Lycurgan injunction, because this is one of those rare, pleasing, moments when literary and material evidence seem to be providing the same story. So while it need not follow that the rule had anything to do with Lycurgus, we can at least be confident that what is being described is a genuine Spartan practice.

There are twenty-four known (and twenty published) examples of stelae commemorating a man who died ἐν πολέμῳ, 'in war'.[3] These inscriptions are generally treated as a single body of evidence, and they do display some striking similarities. Most obviously, they share a form of words: typically a simple name – no patronymic, no ethnic, and no other qualifying information apart from the phrase ἐν πολέμῳ. (There are three exceptions to that pattern, all of which will be mentioned below.) In general, all that can be known about these people, on the basis of these stones, is that they existed, they had a name, and they died in war. In terms of conveying information, these monuments might seem to occupy the minimalist end of the commemorative spectrum.

The same could be said of the overall impression conveyed by these stones: the most conspicuous thing about them is how deeply unimpressive they are (see *Fig.* 1). They are carved on various sorts of local Spartan stone (often a dull grey or reddish marble), and what the inscription lacks in beauty is not remotely compensated for by size: the largest monument is 90 cm high (and this is one which records two names: see *Fig.* 2);[4] the smallest 13.5 cm,[5] and the average height is around 36 cm. Only three – all later examples – have any sort of decoration.[6] In other words, this is the sort of monument which is more likely to cause a stubbed toe than an awed intake of breath.

But some things can be said in their defence. The individual monuments may be fairly underwhelming, but other features of the corpus are more impressive. First, it is worth noting that, although these inscriptions are usually lumped into a single group, they cover a remarkable chronological range: precise dating of this sort of text is not really possible, but even vague dating (based primarily on letter-forms) shows that the texts start to appear in the mid-fifth century, and continue through to the first century BC. This form of memorial continues in spite of being surrounded by changing fashions in other aspects of commemorative practice, not to mention changing political,

Fig. 1a. *IG* V.1 703 (SM 377): 'Ainesias, in war', Sparta acropolis, early 4th century. Photo courtesy the Sparta Museum.

Fig. 1b. *IG* V.1 1591 (SM 1000): 'Olbiadas, in war', Pellana, 4th century. Photo courtesy the Sparta Museum.

Fig. 2. *IG* V.1 708 (SM 509): memorial, possibly 3rd century, of 'Euryades, Olympic Victor, in war; [Taskos], in w[ar]'. Photo courtesy the Sparta Museum.

social and cultural circumstances. (In one instance, it is possible to see the influence of these changing fashions even on this genre of inscription: one later example, *IG* V.1 1320, includes not only the standard Spartan formula – in this case: Ὀναϊτελής | ἐν πολέμωι – but also the standard phraseology of later epitaphs: χαίρε.)[7]

Moreover, these inscriptions are not just chronologically persistent, but also geographically pervasive. Of the seventeen stones which have an attested provenance, just under half (eight) were found in, and immediately around, Sparta town. The other nine have turned up in widely scattered locations: at Pellana, Kefala, Sellasia, Geraki, Thalamai (on the edge of the Mani), Mari (in the foothills of Mt Parnon); and one even outside Laconia, at Alea in Tegea (see *Map* 1). How is this variation to be explained?

It has been argued that this geographical spread is a reflection of the basic function of these inscriptions: these stones, it is claimed, mark the graves of soldiers buried at the site of a battle. This explanation is particularly popular in the case of the two Sellasian examples, which could quite neatly be associated with the battle of Sellasia in 222 BC; it can then be extrapolated to all other cases.[8]

This is, however, an unsatisfactory solution, for various reasons. First, with the exception of Sellasia, it is far from easy to find a suitable battle for each attested findspot.[9] Second, there is one case where we seem to have extremely good evidence that the commemorated victim was not commemorated in the place where he died. *IG* V.1 1124 is the memorial of a certain Eualkes, who died ἐν πολέμοι, ἐν Μαντινέαι ('in war, at Mantineia'); it was found at the end of the nineteenth century in Geraki. The letter-forms of this inscription suggest a fifth-century date, and the obvious fifth-century date at which to place Eualkes' death would be 418: specifically, the battle of Mantineia.[10] This is one of the few Spartan battles where we have some explicit information about the fate of the Spartan dead: according to Thucydides (5.74.2) they were buried in neighbouring Tegea. If Thucydides is right, therefore, either Eualkes did not die in the Mantineia of 418, or this memorial does not mark the spot where he was buried.

Unless, that is – and this is the second possible explanation for this huge spread of material – Eualkes' memorial had moved between 418 and its discovery in 1882. In this particular case that explanation seems unlikely: the distances involved are just that bit too great (it is about 60 km in a straight line from Geraki to Tegea; another 20 km from Tegea to Mantineia). But it does not seem immediately out of the question that this stone, and the others, migrated from some central Spartan location to the *chōra* of Laconia. It is easy to see how the site of Sparta, once abandoned, could have become a convenient stone quarry for the surrounding area.[11]

An explanation based on chance distribution cannot, therefore, easily be discarded, and it would certainly be unsafe to claim that all these stones must originally have been located in (or even very near to) the places in which they were eventually found. Nevertheless, some of the distances involved here

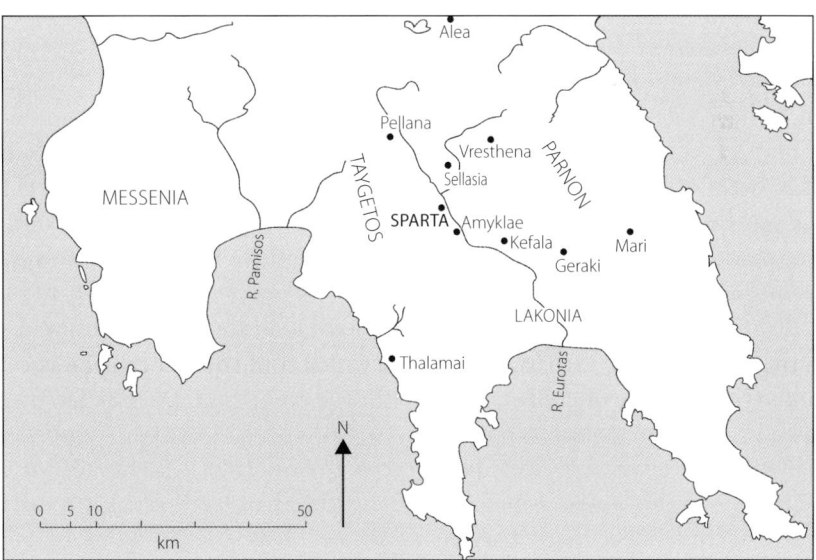

Map 1. Findspots of 'en polemoi' inscriptions.

do make it equally hard to believe that all these stones originated in a single location in Sparta town: moving a stone from Sparta to Geraki (*c.* 25 km) might perhaps be worth the effort; but it is easier to question the point of transporting something like this all the way out to Mari (*c.* 36 km), or over Taygetus to Thalamai (*c* .34 km). As a result, it is hard to picture a situation in which these stones originally formed part of 'some public burial ground that has its correspondence in the Athenian *Demosion Sema*.'[12] What seems more plausible is a situation in which the stones start off in a wide range of locations, and, it seems quite possible, in locations which are associated with perioikic as well as Spartiate habitation.[13]

So far, I have provided an extended and negative account of the roles of these monuments: they do not make a striking visual impression; they do not provide much information about the deceased; they do not mark the site of a battle; they do not combine to form a collective area of commemoration. And, to add another negative, they do not, in my opinion, mark the location of a burial. Almost all the literary evidence suggests that the Spartans regularly buried their war-dead at or near the site of the battle.[14] These monuments are not, therefore, directly connected with the immediate post-death treatment of the war-dead.

But if that is what these monuments do not do, is it possible to say anything positive about the function (or functions) they perform? Any assessment of the positive role of these stones should start from the characterization of their function which appears in the *Instituta Laconica*: they are μνημεία, 'memorials'; their primary function is to provide a focus for memory, and for commemoration. But if that viewpoint is accepted, then another question should immediately follow: what sort of commemoration is involved, and whose memories are being preserved? The best-known contemporary commemorative model – that of Athens – points clearly to one possible set of answers: the principal commemorating agent is the city; monuments to the war-dead are, above all, a state concern; and the commemoration of the war-dead is a collective activity, designed to reinforce the shared ideals and ideologies of the citizen body.[15]

In Sparta, on the other hand, it is quite hard to see how these monuments could perform that sort of function. It is not that there is no element of collectivity, or even of politicization, in these memorials. If the general thrust of the Plutarchan stories is to be believed, this style of inscribed monument was strictly regulated by the Spartan state.[16] And even if it should not be believed – if this *nomos* is much more custom than law – then it remains true that this is a peculiarly Laconian practice. I have already mentioned the strikingly large geographical spread of these ἐν πολέμῳ stones in Laconian territory, but something which is equally striking is that this spread stops abruptly at the border. With the exception of the single stone found just over the Laconian border in Tegea, this style of commemoration is found nowhere else in the Greek world.[17]

There is, then, a political aspect to these stones. But it is political in a broad sense: the sense of displaying a connection between the commemorated man and the political community of which he formed a part. Fighting, and dying, for one's *polis* is one of the most obvious ways to stake a claim to membership in that community,[18] but the assertion of a connection between community and individual could operate in more than one direction. The top-down model – the model which most easily explains Athenian practice – would, I think, give the initiative to the larger group: in Athens, and in some other Greek states, commemoration is primarily a collective act, marked (in Athens) by civic ceremony and (in other Greek states too) by the creation of public, collective, and centrally located monuments.[19] But the Spartan material, because of its scattered distribution and varied styles, seems to lend itself more easily to a bottom-up interpretation: these stones provide a medium through which individual Spartans – possibly even individual Laconians – can make a quite personal demonstration of, or even argument for, their relationship to the larger community.[20]

It is also easier, in the Spartan case, to add a third element to that model: another group which might have a stake in these monuments is the family of the dead soldier. It is true that this is something which has to be argued for not so much from any positive evidence as by a process of elimination: the dead man cannot put up his own gravestone; and, as has just been suggested, the diverse forms and locations of the stones suggest strongly that the state does not take a direct part in the creation of the monuments. The family is the most obvious remaining candidate,[21] and one which would have something to gain from the creation of such a memorial: the monument could act not only as a source of prestige, but also – if we are prepared to allow that even Spartans might have feelings – as a focus for mourning and for personal commemoration (something which might be thought to be particularly necessary in the absence of a body).[22]

Although, therefore, the existence of these stones can seem, and in some ways is, an indicator of extreme social control and conformity, they also point to a certain lack of centralization: there is an allowance for the small-scale, the local, the dispersed, and there is scope, too, for personal, affective meanings as well as larger political functions. All of this is quite strikingly different from the way in which such commemoration is managed in some other Greek states (most notably Athens).

But that group of inscriptions provides only half – or rather less than half – of the story of Spartan war memorials. If the focus of attention is shifted slightly, to the evidence for the collective burial and commemoration of the Spartan war-dead, then it becomes possible to find a set of Spartan practices which seem more obviously top-down, not just in their origins but also in their functions. These monuments represent a practical level of centralization and official control (the bodies of the dead have been collected, buried, and commemorated in a single place); they can also be argued to perform important political – power-political – functions after their creation. What is interesting, though, is precisely where we have to look in order to find monuments of that sort. This move from dispersal to centralization, from individual to group, perhaps from private to public, also involves a distinctive topographical shift, away from territory firmly within the boundaries of Laconia to the borderlands and beyond. It was striking that the ἐν πολέμῳ memorials are found (almost exclusively) only within Laconia, and it is no less noteworthy that this other form of Spartan war memorial appears (almost exclusively) only outside land which is incontestably Spartan (see *Map* 2).

This phenomenon might seem to be simply an inevitable consequence of two features of Spartan war-making: they buried their dead at the site of the battle; and those battles rarely took place inside Laconian territory. But even if this accounts for the origins of the peculiar geographical pattern of Spartan war memorials, it does not necessarily rule out the possibility that this pattern might have further consequences.

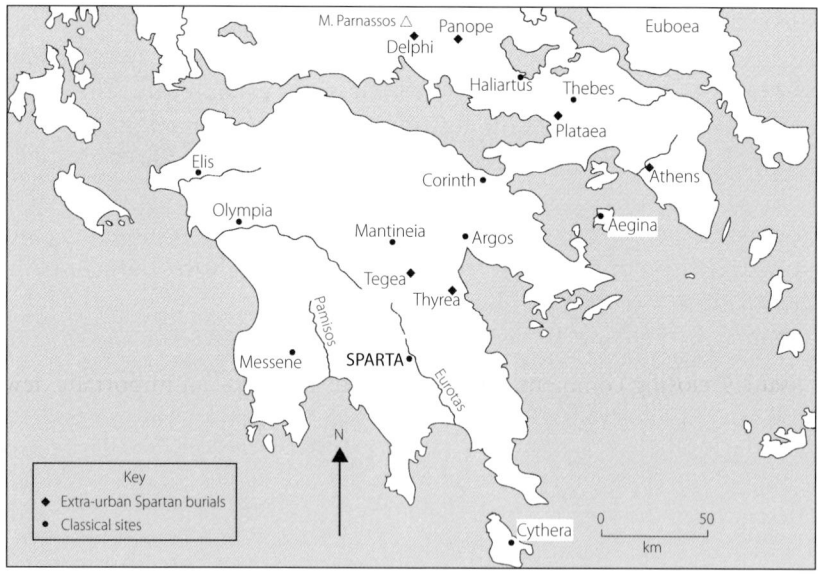

Map 2. Extra-urban Spartan burials.

Once more, the initial impetus for pursuing this line of thought comes from a Plutarchan story:

Ἀργείου ποτὲ εἰπόντος· 'πολλοὶ τάφοι παρ' ἡμῖν εἰσὶ Σπαρτιατῶν,' Λάκων εἶπεν, 'ἀλλὰ μὴν παρ' ἡμῖν Ἀργείων οὐδὲ εἷς,' ὡς αὐτῶν μὲν πολλάκις Ἄργους ἐπιβεβηκότων Ἀργείων δὲ τῆς Σπάρτης οὐδέποτε.

When an Argive once said, 'There are many tombs of Spartans in our country,' a Spartan said, 'But there is not a single tomb of an Argive in our country,' indicating by this that the Spartans had often entered Argos, but the Argives had come into Sparta. (*Lak. Apophth.* 20 = *Mor.* 233c)[23]

There is, therefore, – at least according to this imagined Spartan – a positive political spin which can be put not only on the absence of foreign dead in Sparta, but, more importantly, on the presence of Spartan dead in foreign territory. Far from being a sign of weakness, these burials are a marker of military prowess – something of which the Spartans can be, and are, proud.

The first example which might be used to support and expand on this suggestion is found on Sparta's borders, and forms a small part of a well-known story. That story is the so-called 'Battle of the Champions', the ritualized contest between 300 hand-picked Spartan warriors and 300 equally elite Argives for the control of the contested border territory of the Thyreatis.[24] There are various, not always consistent, accounts of the engagement, but the main point of interest here is not what really happened during the Battle of the Champions, but what happened afterwards. The key piece of information for this purpose comes in Pausanias (2.38.5):

ἰόντι δὲ ἄνω πρὸς τὴν ἤπειρον ἀπ' αὐτῆς χωρίον ἐστίν, ἔνθα δὴ ἐμαχέσαντο ὑπὲρ τῆς γῆς ταύτης λογάδες Ἀργείων τριακόσιοι πρὸς ἄνδρας Λακεδαιμονίων ἀριθμόν τε ἴσους καὶ ἐπιλέκτους ὁμοίως. ἀποθανόντων δὲ ἁπάντων πλὴν ἑνὸς Σπαρτιάτου καὶ δυοῖν Ἀργείων, τοῖς μὲν ἀποθανοῦσιν ἐχώσθησαν ἐνταῦθα οἱ τάφοι.

As you go up inland from here is the place where three hundred picked Argives fought for this territory with an equal number of specially chosen Lacedaemonian men. All were killed apart from one Spartan and two Argives, and the graves for the dead were raised here.

Pausanias' closing comment, as he leaves the site, adds an important new detail: ἀπὸ δὲ τῶν πολυανδρίων ἰόντι Ἀνθήνη τέ ἐστιν…, 'as you go from these common graves you come to [the village] Anthene…' (2.38.6). These burials are mass-burials, πολυάνδρια, the characteristic form of collective, public burial for those who die in war.

The evidence for the existence of this monument is, admittedly, exiguous (and only literary),[25] but it is nevertheless possible to develop a tentative argument about the possible significance of this burial – an argument which is particularly concerned with the question of territoriality. The Battle of the Champions was above all a contest over territory.[26] Even if it is not clear that the Spartans won the battle itself, there is no doubt that they gained and kept control of that piece of territory for most of the classical period,[27] and that they also regularly reasserted that control, by marching out from Sparta and celebrating the festival of the Parparonia at, or near, the site of the battle.[28]

It might, I think, be possible to fit Pausanias' *polyandrion* into that picture of a symbolically loaded struggle both to acquire territory, and to demonstrate continued ownership of it. To do so, two things have to be accepted. First: that there is frequently a connection between a city's war-dead and its heroes. The relationship is often quite hard to pin down, but it is certainly the case that many of the honours which are given to the collectively-buried war-dead show substantial overlap with the sorts of honours which are associated with heroization: regular offerings, associated festivals, burial and commemoration in particularly marked locations. This overlap in practice can be seen in a number of places in Greece (not just Athens, but also Thespiae and Megara, for example)[29] and it is not implausible that it might also apply in Sparta. If so, one of the distinctive features of dead heroes becomes relevant: that they act as defenders of a particular group (in this case, a particular city); and that this defensive capability is often closely connected with the presence of the physical remains of the hero, or heroes, in the land which they are meant to be protecting.

The *polyandrion* to the dead of the Battle of the Champions would, therefore, be a very nice example of the physical marking not only of a battle site, but also of a key piece of disputed territory – a tangible manifestation of the claim which Sparta is making to this border country. The monument to the dead continues, in perpetuity, to assert control of the land which those dead fought to secure, and which the dead still occupy. In this case, too, they can even be seen to perform a sort of limitary function: the *polyandrion* is, in some ways, a glorified *horos*, marking and patrolling the extent of Spartan control.

This argument is not, however, unproblematic. It requires a convenient forgetting of the fact that Pausanias talks not of a single *polyandrion* but of plural *polyandria*: if there are also Argive burials in this bit of land, what do we do with those (and what should we assume the Spartans did with them)? And, perhaps more importantly, it is based on an example which, in the context of Spartan mass burials, is not only atypical but arguably unique: the most common form of Spartan war burial is not the liminal but the entirely extra-territorial.[30] And so it seems to make sense to look at some of those more typical examples; examples which do not, I think, require the complete abandonment of the arguments developed so far, but which do provide them with rather more substance and point towards a slightly different line of interpretation.

It is worth starting by asking some further questions about the immediate implications of extra-territorial burial and commemoration. Burial at the site of the battle is sometimes represented as the logistically easy option. To an extent that is, obviously, true, but it does not follow that this practice was therefore entirely unproblematic, or straightforward. Burying bodies on the battlefield is not necessarily simply a matter of putting them in a convenient hole, wherever they happen to have fallen. The potential difficulties are, predictably, most visible when battles are lost. Losing a battle involves – indeed, is often marked by – losing control of the bodies of the dead. If the normal niceties of war are followed then the bodies should be recovered once the battle is over, but this need not mark an end to potential problems.

The aftermath of the battle of Haliartus provides a good example of the form those problems might take. After Sparta's defeat, and after some more than usually convoluted wrangling over the recovery of the Spartan dead, Pausanias is reported to have removed Lysander's body from the area:

τὸν δὲ Λύσανδρον ᾗ πρῶτον κομίζοντες ὑπὲρ τοὺς ὅρους ἐγένοντο τῆς Βοιωτίας ἐν φίλῃ καὶ συμμαχίδι χώρᾳ τῇ Πανοπέων κατέθεσαν, οὗ νῦν τὸ μνημεῖόν ἐστι παρὰ τὴν ὁδὸν εἰς Χαιρώνειαν ἐκ Δελφῶν πορευομένοις.

As soon as they had come beyond the boundaries of Boeotia with Lysander's body, they buried it in the friendly and allied territory of the Panopeans, where his monument now stands, by the road leading to Chaeroneia from Delphi.
(Plutarch *Lysander* 29.3)[31]

Spartan actions here might not seem to need much explanation: 'it is inconceivable', asserts one historian, 'that having received [Lysander's body, Pausanias] should bury it in hostile country.'[32] There are some practical reasons why such an action might be beyond conception: difficulty of further access to the tomb; the risk of desecration; the public relations problem of revealing the extent of your losses to the enemy.[33] It is also, however, important to recognize the potential symbolic significance of the location of such burials, and such monuments, and, most crucially, the potential for creating a positive message even from a monument which marked a defeat.

To identify that possible positive message, it is necessary to take a closer look at the story of the Panopean burial. Why create a burial, and erect a monument, in Panopean territory? The argument for convenience is, admittedly, a strong one: Panope, and Phocis more generally, are the closest areas of allied territory (around 40 km from the battlefield). But it is also worth remembering some of the background to this battle, and to the Corinthian War. Why are the Spartans fighting at Haliartus in the first place? There are various possible answers to that question, but the immediate reason for their intervention was a call for help from the Phocians, requesting Spartan assistance in repelling Locrian (and Theban) aggression.[34] The friendship and alliance to which Plutarch alludes in his account is not as settled as his casual reference might suggest; rather, it is something which is being established and strengthened at this precise moment. Leaving this burial in Phocian territory might not, then, be an entirely neutral action, but could have a more positive meaning: this is a marker of the connection between Sparta and Phocis; a symbol not just of the fact that Sparta believes that her dead are safe here, but also of the fact that Spartans have died on behalf of, and in defence of, this land.

This sort of behaviour is not restricted to the aftermath of lost battles: something similar seems to have happened after the battle of Mantineia in 418. The Spartans won this battle, put up a trophy, and gained control of their dead (including, presumably, the Eualkes whose ἐν πολέμῳ memorial was discussed above). What is of interest here, though, is what the Spartans are reported to have done with those bodies: not left them in Mantineia, but ἀπήγαγον ἐς Τεγέαν, οὗπερ ἐτάφησαν, 'brought them back to Tegea, and buried them there' (5.74.2).

Thucydides provides even less information than Plutarch, but some speculation is again possible. Even after a victorious battle, there might be a negative reason for Sparta's actions: a possible coyness over revealing to the world the extent of their losses is implied by Thucydides' statement on the difficulty of calculating Spartan casualties in the battle (5.74.3). But here too there is scope for a positive reading. Why Tegean territory?[35] When the causes of this battle are examined, it emerges that Tegea – and the Tegean relationship with Sparta – have played a prominent part in the story: the Tegeans are allies of Sparta but, according to Thucydides, have become increasingly agitated at Spartan failure to defend them against hostile Peloponnesian states. It is an explicit warning from the Tegeans that provides the immediate motivation for the Spartan invasion: the Spartans are at home, planning their next move when,

ἀφικνεῖται αὐτοῖς ἀγγελία παρὰ τῶν ἐπιτηδείων ἐκ Τεγέας ὅτι, εἰ μὴ παρέσονται ἐν τάχει, ἀποστήσεται αὐτῶν Τεγέα πρὸς Ἀργείους καὶ τοὺς ξυμμάχους καὶ ὅσον οὐκ ἀφέστηκεν. ἐνταῦθα δὴ βοήθεια τῶν Λακεδαιμονίων γίγνεται αὐτῶν τε καὶ τῶν Εἱλώτων πανδημεὶ ὀξεῖα καὶ οἵα οὔπω πρότερον.

word came from their friends in Tegea that, if the Spartans did not come quickly, Tegea would go over to the Argives and their allies, and already had all

but done so. Whereupon, help was sent, both of the Lacedaemonians themselves and of the helots, in full force, promptly and on such a scale as never before.
(5.64.1 f.)

There is a parallel between the roles of Tegea and Phocis in both these stories. In both cases, they are (in some sense) responsible for getting Sparta involved in a battle. In both cases, their territory becomes the location for the burial and commemoration of the dead of that battle. The existence of that parallel makes it tempting to wonder whether a similar motivation might lie behind Sparta's actions on both occasions. The decision to bury and commemorate in Panope, or in Tegea, is not simply a matter of convenience, but is intended to make a more positive political point. Greek alliances tended not to last, which makes the desire to create solid, tangible markers of those alliances perhaps slightly paradoxical, but also very understandable. These monuments have the potential to function as stabilizing forces – as a sort of groyne, protecting against the shifting and eroding tides of interstate politics.

There is an occasion when it is possible to see that potential being realized, although the people who attempt to realize it are not the Spartans, but those in whose land the monument has been left. The people are the Plataeans, and the monuments and burials are those of the Spartans who died at the battle of Plataea.[36] These dead seem to have been left in peace for around fifty years, before making another, dramatic, entrance into Greek history – or into Greek history as imagined by Thucydides. The Plataeans are reaching the climax of their defence speech, when they call upon their star witnesses:

ἀποβλέψατε γὰρ ἐς πατέρων τῶν ὑμετέρων θήκας, οὓς ἀποθανόντας ὑπὸ Μήδων καὶ ταφέντας ἐν τῇ ἡμετέρᾳ ἐτιμῶμεν κατὰ ἔτος ἕκαστον δημοσίᾳ ἐσθήμασί τε καὶ τοῖς ἄλλοις νομίμοις, ὅσα τε ἡ γῆ ἡμῶν ἀνεδίδου ὡραῖα, πάντων ἀπαρχὰς ἐπιφέροντες, εὖνοι μὲν ἐκ φιλίας χώρας, ξύμμαχοι δὲ ὁμαίχμοις ποτὲ γενομένοις... σκέψασθέ τε· Παυσανίας μὲν γὰρ ἔθαπτεν αὐτοὺς νομίζων ἐν γῇ τε φιλίᾳ τιθέναι καὶ παρ' ἀνδράσι τοιούτοις· ὑμεῖς δὲ εἰ κτενεῖτε ἡμᾶς καὶ χώραν τὴν Πλαταιίδα Θηβαΐδα ποιήσετε, τί ἄλλο ἢ ἐν πολεμίᾳ τε καὶ παρὰ τοῖς αὐθένταις πατέρας τοὺς ὑμετέρους καὶ ξυγγενεῖς...καταλείψετε;

Turn your eyes upon the tombs of your fathers, who were killed by the Persians and buried in our land, and whom we have honoured every year with a public offering of garments and other customary rituals; we bring the first fruits too of all that the earth has produced in season, a well-meaning gift from a friendly land and from allies to those who were once their companions in arms... Consider this: when Pausanias buried them he thought he was laying them in a friendly land and among friends; but, if you put us to death and make Plataea Theban territory, what would you be doing but leaving your fathers and kinsmen in a hostile land and among their murderers? (3.58.4–5)

This is a notoriously unsuccessful speech. But it need not follow (particularly not in the world of Thucydidean decision-making) that the arguments contained in it are therefore also necessarily bad or irrelevant.[37] It is, therefore, perhaps worth noting some of the themes used by the Plataeans here. Not only is there a repeated insistence on the importance of the dead being placed in friendly land, there is also the claim that the land must remain friendly: the presence of the Spartan dead in Plataean soil should almost, it seems, guarantee that this territory never becomes hostile.

The penultimate stop in this extended tour around mainland Greece is probably the second most famous Spartan burial (and also the only Spartan burial for which there is good archaeological evidence): the monument in the Athenian Kerameikos which contains the bodies of thirteen Spartans killed in the fighting of 404/3.[38] How does this burial compare to the pattern which is emerging from the other examples?

At the very broadest level, there is a parallel: all these burials and monuments are located well away from Spartan territory; and all of them function, or can be made to function, as some sort of permanent marker of the relationship between Sparta and the state which hosts the monument. But it is in the nature of that relationship that a key difference between the Athenian example and the others must be identified: at Panope, Tegea and Plataea the relationship from which the burial arises, and which is being preserved, is one of friendship and alliance. The monument at Athens was a result of outright hostility between the two sides: Athenians fighting Spartans, and, what is more, Athenians losing.

It might be possible to downplay the monument's hostile background, and to make it a more Atheno-friendly symbol. The best example of this process is Lysias' use of the burial in his *Epitaphios*, where – by some clever manipulation of language, and of history – the monument ceases to have anything to do with Spartan military success, and becomes instead a marker of an Athenian victory, and a testament to Athenian military and moral ἀρετή.[39] But this is, perhaps, not the most obvious reading of the monument – things would surely look quite different from a Spartan point of view. It is quite easy to see this monument as a fundamentally Spartan creation. Its most obvious identifier – the inscription associated with the burial (*IG* II² 11678) – is, in content and appearance, a Spartan text: the text, which is retrograde, is written in Laconian script, and is plausibly restored to have included the heading Λα[κεδαιμόνιοι], 'Lacedaemonians'; the preserved section names two Spartan polemarchs.[40] Moreover, it is a Spartan monument which occupies a prime position in a piece of foreign territory; territory belonging to a state on which Sparta has just inflicted a crushing defeat.

There are, therefore, some things about the Spartan monument in Athens which are much more reminiscent of the *polyandrion* in the Thyreatis, or of the response of Plutarch's Spartan, than they are of the monuments in Panope, Tegea or Plataea. Here is a physical marker which both commemorates a victory and acts as a perpetual reminder of that victory. And here, too, are the bodies of the Spartan dead, occupying in perpetuity this piece of land.

But, again, the parallel comes up against a hitch. The dead of the Thyreatis occupied a piece of conquered land; in fact, their very presence in that land – or so the argument went – functioned almost as a guarantee of its conquered status. The Thyreatis becomes a piece of Sparta because there are Spartans buried in it. Athens – demonstrably – does not actually become part of Sparta. Is there any way to resolve the contradiction?

The question is not easy to answer (and it might be that it does even need to be asked: the quest for a single explanatory model that can unproblematically be applied to every single example seems likely to be misguided). But if a solution is to be found then it would require a certain loosening, or redefining, of some theoretical structures or assumptions. There might, for example, be scope for playing with the concept of territoriality itself, so that it becomes less rigid, less 'container-like': might it be possible to imagine 'islands' of Spartan territory, spatially divorced from the central area, but ideologically part of the heartland?[41] Alternatively, a less dramatic explanation would make the point at issue not the absolute ownership of territory but the looser, but still potent, claim of 'friendship'. The idea of 'friendly territory' has recurred in these examples, and friendship, in Greek interstate relations, is a usefully fluid concept. It can be freely offered, but it can also be imposed.[42] In certain circumstances, it implies equality, in others, hierarchy. The precise implications of the general idea are highly context-dependent, and the contexts which appear here are almost infinitely variable: different monuments can do different things; the same monument can do different things, to different people, at different times.

That last point is illustrated most clearly by the most famous Spartan commemoration of all: the memorial to the 'Three Hundred' Spartiates who died at Thermopylae. This is a hard example to discuss with any certainty: the evidence for Spartan treatment of the dead of this engagement, while not as sparse as that for other memorials, is far from complete, and, more troublingly, not entirely consistent.[43] But the complexity of the evidence perhaps reflects, at least in part, the complexity of Spartan practice in this case: the dead of Thermopylae are commemorated, individually and as a group, in more than one place, in more than one way, and for more than one purpose.

At first sight, the commemoration of 'Three Hundred' is not inconsistent with the patterns of Spartan extra-territorial burial sketched so far, although the closest parallel comes not from Plataea but from the Thyrea. There is no extant evidence to suggest that the presence of the Spartan dead had much impact on the future shape of Spartan–Locrian diplomatic relations, but it is clear that the Spartans buried at Thermopylae were represented as occupying, even in death, the patch of ground which they were sent to defend. The pass at Thermopylae becomes a small island of Spartan εὐνομία (obedience to the laws) representing and patrolling the reach of Spartan authority (at least over her own citizens):

Ὦ ξεῖν', ἀγγέλλειν Λακεδαιμονίοις ὅτι τῇδε
κείμεθα, τοῖς κείνων ῥήμασι πειθόμενοι.

Stranger: go and tell the Spartans that we lie here obedient to their commands.
(Hdt. 7.228)[44]

But Thermopylae is not, of course, purely a Spartan story: the Spartans were not fighting only in self-defence, and, in contrast to their goals at Thyrea, were not hoping to establish a practical claim to ownership of this piece of territory. This absence of overall control is reflected in the nature of the monument established at the site of the battle. Although the epigram seems quintessentially Spartan in the sentiments it expresses, it was not straightforwardly, or perhaps at all, a Spartan creation: Herodotus (7.228) reports that the stelae were erected on the initiative of the Delphic Amphictiony, and it is not clear how much input the Spartans were allowed in either the form or the content of this memorial.[45] Moreover, if Strabo's description of the site is to be believed, then the Spartans did not have (or did not manage to maintain) sole occupation of this commemorative space: he reports seeing five stelae at the site, of which one (9.4.2) recorded the noble deeds of the Opuntian Locrians; another may have included the epitaph for the Thespian contingent.[46]

The danger of the dilution of the exclusively Spartan ownership of the sacrifice commemorated at Thermopylae, a danger whose severity would be magnified by the privileged status of the engagement, might help to explain the prominence of another strand to the Spartan commemoration of the battle: namely, the monuments and rituals established in Sparta itself. Not all of these are unparalleled in Spartan practice: the heroization of Leonidas corresponds both to honours awarded to other notable Spartan leaders, and to a consistent Spartan interest in using the burial of their kings to focus attention on the (physical) centre of the Spartan state.[47] But here too some specific points are worth noting. First, it is surely not without significance that Leonidas' body was not brought home immediately. The fact that it was thought worth going to the trouble of repatriating his physical remains reflects not only the basic importance attributed to placing the hero's body in the most appropriate location, but also, more interestingly if less clearly, the lack of consensus as to exactly where the most appropriate location was.[48] The second feature is much more unusual: in this one instance it is not just the leader but the whole military force who are allowed a collective presence in Sparta itself. The bodies of the 'Three Hundred' were not repatriated, but their names (and patronymics) were recorded on a monument in Sparta town (Paus. 3.14.1) and it seems possible, too, that they, along with Leonidas and Pausanias, were commemorated annually at a festival held in their honour.[49]

The treatment of the dead of Thermopylae demonstrates, therefore, not only the potential complexity of Spartan approaches to their war-dead, but also, at a more basic level, that the strict distinction between two categories of commemoration – domestic memorialization of individuals, and external burial of groups – implied by the structure of this chapter is, to at least some extent, misleading. Thermopylae is, of course, a special case, but I would argue that the variety of responses which it provokes can also be perceived in less historically significant contexts: the body of Eualkes of Geraki, for example, is perpetuating the Spartan presence at Tegea, at the same time as his memorial is perpetuating his own memory, and perhaps the status of his family, back in Laconia. Whether through accident or design the two aspects of Spartan commemorative practice are distinctively complementary: there is a predominantly private aspect, and a predominantly public; a method of commemorating the individual, and the group; a set of material with an internal focus, a different set with an external function. One might note in passing that, in comparison, Athenian practice can begin to seem strangely straightforward and inflexible. Spartan customs, certainly, start to look more multifaceted, and less exclusively dominated by the demands of the state. In this, as in other matters, I would suggest, Spartan practice is, in fact, less rigid, simplistic and unimaginative than it might at first appear.

Acknowledgements

I would like to thank the 5th Ephorate of Prehistoric and Classical Antiquities for giving me permission to examine epigraphic material related to this study. Mrs Stella Raftopoulou and the staff of the Sparta Museum, Helen Fields and the British School at Athens, and Dr John Lund of the National Museum of Denmark, have been extremely generous with their time and expertise and I am very grateful for their assistance.

Notes

[1] For detailed discussion of these conventions, see Pritchett 1985, part 2.

[2] The version given in the *Lycurgus* differs in two significant respects. First, it specifies two categories of Spartan to whom burial is allowed: the first is soldiers killed in war; the identity of the second is disputed (the manuscripts read γυναικὸς τῶν ἱερῶς or [in some versions] γυναικὸς τῶν ἱερῶν, but this is emended in most texts to γυναικὸς [τῶν] λεχοῦς, 'a woman who dies in childbirth'). Second, it makes a much closer connection between the memorial and a burial – implying, unlike the *Instituta*, that these monuments are gravestones. The textual uncertainty makes the reliability of the first variation hard to assess (there is epigraphic evidence, from the Hellenistic period and later, for commemoration of women who died in childbirth, but there is an obvious danger of circularity in using this material as supporting evidence for an emended text): for a summary of the issues, see Hodkinson 2000, 260–2, and for a more detailed discussion, Brulé and Piolot 2004. The reliability of the second variation is more relevant to the argument here, and also easier to assess: for a persuasive argument that this should be seen as a later elaboration of the, original and more accurate, version of the *Instituta*, see Hodkinson 2000, 249 f.; the case against seeing these monuments as grave markers is also set out later in this chapter.

[3] The details of publication, findspot and approximate date are:

IG V.1 701 (Magoula, C5); *IG* V.1 702 (no findspot, C5); *IG* V.1 703 (Acropolis, early C4); *IG* V.1 704 (Kefala, later C4); *IG* V.1 705 (Roman wall, C4); *IG* V.1 706 (North tower, C3/2?, retrograde; the reading of this stone is not totally secure); *IG* V.1 707 (Amyklai, C5?); *IG* V.1 708 (2 names; no findspot, C3?); *IG* V.1 709 (no findspot, C2?); *IG* V.1.710 (Artemis Orthia, C3/C2); *IG* V.1. 918 (Pellana, C3); *IG* V.1 921 (near Sellasia, C3?); *IG* V.1 1124 (Geraki, 418?); *IG* V.1 1125 (Geraki, C5/C4); *IG* V.1 1320 (Thalamai, Imperial?); *IG* V.1 1591 (Pellana, C4); Zavvou 1992–8, no. 1 (Mari, late C4); Zavvou 1992–8, no. 2 (Menalaos St, Sparta, C1); Papanikolaou 1976/7 (Vresthena, near Sellasia, C3?); *IG* V.2 251 (Alea, Tegea, C2). For these findspots, see *Map* 1.

Partially published or unpublished examples: Steinhauer 1992, 241, n. 8 (C1, no other details); Hodkinson 2000, 267, n. 40 (no details). There is at least one further (unpublished) fragment in the Sparta museum; another stone is reported to be in the museum at Mystra.

Note also *SEG* 47.352: a 5th-century gravestone found (near Sellasia) by the Laconia Survey; the (unbroken) stone has a name, but no ἐν πολέμῳ reference.

[4] *IG* V.1 708. There is no clue as to the relationship between the two men – something which would be very useful in assessing the function and origin of these stones.

[5] *IG* V.1 705 (though this is also among the most fragmentary).

[6] *IG* V.1 1320 (a shield and sword/spear), *IG* V.2 251 (hoplite), Steinhauer 1992, 214, n. 8 ('representation of a hoplite').

[7] On this fusion of funerary forms, see Tod and Wace 1906, 25. On changes in burial practice in Hellenistic and early Roman Sparta, see Cartledge and Spawforth 2002, 132 f.

[8] On the Sellasian material, see Papanikolaou 1976/7; for the extrapolation, see, for example, the decision of the editors of the *Lexicon of Greek Personal Names* to categorize Spartans known from these inscriptions as 'attested at' the findspot of their stone, rather than as originating from that place (vol. IIIa, *s.v.* Ἐχεμήδης, Τελέστωρ).

[9] Cartledge (1987, 234) does contemplate connecting *IG* V.1 703 with Epameinondas'

attack on Sparta in 370/69. It is also, of course, worth remembering that many military engagements do not leave a trace in our literary sources, and that it is possible that Spartan soldiers were involved in regular, low-intensity, conflict with the helots (for this suggestion, see Powell 2001, 235).

[10] The suggestion that the date is 418 is as old as the published history of the stone (it first appears in the first publication, Roehl 1882, no. 77b) and has never been seriously challenged.

[11] For a good example of the mobility of Spartan inscriptions, see the scattered findspots of the two fragments of the 'war fund' (found 11 km and 19 km away from Sparta town): Loomis 1992, 11–19.

[12] Clairmont 1983, 116 (similar assumption in Christou 1964, 129 f.).

[13] Cartledge (2002, 220 and 268) notes this, in relation to *IG* V.1 1124 (Eualkes, at Geraki).

[14] See below for further discussion.

[15] For this reading of Athenian practice, see above all Loraux 1986.

[16] Most scholars do seem to see this as being some form of 'funerary legislation', even if they doubt its Lycurgan credentials: e.g. MacDowell 1986, 120; Garland 1989, 13 f.; Toher 1991, 169 ff.

[17] Unless *ICret* II.xix.4 (3/2 cent. BC; from Phalasarna in W. Crete) is taken to be one such example; but the stone is very fragmentary, and the reconstruction extremely insecure.

[18] Another way of demonstrating value to the community – winning Panhellenic victories – also features on *IG* V 1.708 (compare the Olympic and Pythian victors in the 5th-century casualty list from Thespiae, *IG* VII 1888; stele b, lines 9 f.).

[19] The classic ancient account of Athenian practice is Th. 2.34; note also the 4th-century Thasian regulations for public commemoration of their war-dead (Sokolowski 1962, no. 64). For the archaeological and epigraphic evidence for Athenian commemoration, see most conveniently Clairmont 1983. Clairmont (*ibid*, ch. 7) also lists the evidence for non-Athenian collective commemoration; the cases of Megara, Thespiae and Tanagra are discussed in more detail in Low 2003.

[20] If the perioikic findspot of some of the stones is an accurate reflection of perioikic origin, then this argument could still work, and might become even stronger: the stones provide a medium by which those on the margins can make a claim for inclusion in the more narrowly defined political community.

[21] The *syssition* might be another, but this would leave the geographical spread unexplained.

[22] Suggested by Hodkinson (2000, 254 f.), although, as he makes clear, this does not have to entail family burial areas. Much depends on how much commemoration is envisaged for 'ordinary' Spartan dead: Parker (1989, 150) raises the possibility that these would have no grave-marker, and no subsequent commemorative rites at all; Hodkinson (2000, 254) proposes instead that the ban on commemoration applied only to *inscribed* memorials; other burials would have been simple but still 'distinguishable by a man's children and grandchildren'. (On the little that is known of Sparta's 'cemeteries', see Kourinou 2000, 215–19.)

[23] The same story is told in Plutarch's *Agesilaus* 31.6.

[24] The main ancient sources are Hdt. 1.82 and Paus. 2.38.5; Th. 5.41.2 adds some details on the subsequent history of the area. On the significance of the conflict, see

Brelich 1961, ch. 2; on its topography, Phaklarēs 1987; generally on symbolic conquest, de Polignac 1995.

[25] Enthusiastic attempts have been made to connect *SEG* 13.266 (found on Mt. Zavitsa) with the *polyandrion* (see Rômaiou 1950, 257 f.; Pritchett 1980, 110–16; Pritchett 1992, ch. 2; Cartledge 2002, 162), but discovery of a further fragment of that inscription makes the connection increasingly implausible (Kritzas 1985, 710–13; Phaklares 1990, 91 f.). According to Herodotus (1.82), the initial encounter between the chosen three-hundred was followed by a conventional battle, in which the Spartans were decisively victorious: if this is correct, then the burials which Pausanias sees need not (only) be those of the 'champions'.

[26] See esp. the version of the story in *Mor.* 231e: Polydorus has come to capture land, not a city.

[27] For a detailed discussion of the history of this territory, see Brelich 1961, ch. 2; on its status as borderland see Daverio Rocchi 1988, 201 ff.

[28] On the Parparonia, see, generally, Bölte 1929, 130–2. On the location of the festival site (near Karies) see Cavanagh et al. 1996, 279.

[29] Stupperich 1977, 62–70; Low 2003.

[30] Robertson (1983, 90 f.) argues, rather speculatively, on the basis of Paus. 8.37.9, 41.1 and 42.1, that another example can be seen in the Ariontia (and the Spartan-Arcadian conflicts over border territory at Phigaleia).

[31] Paus 9.32.5, 33.1 has a μνῆμα of Lysander at Haliartus: this could be explained either as a cenotaph (rather than burial: so Bommelaer 1981, 7 f.; Roesch 1982, 214, n. 37), or as a later, local, invention: 'the believing visitor may still be shewn a 'tomb of Lysander' at Haliartos to this day' (Austin 1931/2, 209).

[32] Austin 1931/2, 209. Plutarch is silent on the fate of the rest of the bodies: is the treatment of Lysander representative or exceptional? (Xen. *HG* 3.5.24 does at least imply that all the Spartan dead were carried outside Boeotia.) There is a tendency for accounts of burial to focus on the most important (compare, e.g., Hdt. 5.63 on the burial of the Spartan dead in Cynosarges: only Anchimolios' burial is described); this is presumably a historiographical feature (suggested by Pritchett 1985, 164), but might also reflect the fact that prominent Spartans do seem to have received more prestigious burials (Hodkinson 2000, 257).

[33] A fear visible especially in Pausanias' story (9.13.11) of Epameinondas' refusal to allow the Spartans to retrieve their dead immediately after Leuctra, on the grounds that the Spartans were 'always inclined to cover up their disasters'. Pritchett 1985, 189, detects a similar motivation in the Spartan treatment of their dead after Olpae (426/5). It might also be a factor at Tegea (see below).

[34] *Hell. Oxy.* 21 and Xen. *HG* 3.5 disagree on much, but not on this. Neither source mentions a pre-existing Spartan alliance with the Phocians.

[35] As Pritchett (1985, 195) points out, the Spartans were heading home anyway, to celebrate the Carneia (Th. 5.75.2–3).

[36] On the evidence for the burials, see Clairmont 1983, 103–6, 121 f.; Pritchett 1985, 174 f. The main testimony is in Herodotus (9.85), who reports three separate Spartan tombs: precisely which Spartans were in which tombs is disputed.

[37] The graves reappear in Isoc. *Plataicus* 61 (used to prove a relationship between Plataea and Athens: a good example of the potential for multiple meanings – something especially relevant to these Persian War examples, which can easily be endowed with

panhellenic as well as bilateral significance).

[38] On the tomb: Brueckner 1915; Karo 1930, esp. 90 ff.; Tod 1932/3; Van Hook 1932; Gebauer and Johannes 1937; Gebauer 1938; Ohly 1965; Willemsen 1977; Clairmont 1983, no. 60; Pritchett 1985, 208; Hodkinson 2000, 257–9 (emphasizing the social differentiation in the burial). The results of a comprehensive new study of the monument are forthcoming: see the initial report in *AR* 49, 8.

[39] Lysias 2.63: followed, perhaps, by modern scholars, who label the monument Athenian (Tod 1932/3; Cartledge 2002, 231); note also the (intermediate) position of Förtsch (2001, 62 f.), who sees the monument as an example of 'Spartas langer Arm', but would also like to include Athenian consent in the process by which it gets erected; Missoni (1986, 63) envisages a situation in which the Spartans commission the monument and the Athenians pay for it. Wolpert (2002, 89) argues that the monument would have been useful for those who wished to downplay the *stasis* element of the events of 404/3, since it would allow the presence of foreign enemies to be emphasized.

[40] In his account of the engagement and of this burial, Xenophon (*HG* 2.4.33) names the same two polemarchs (Chaeron and Thibracus) who appear on the extant part of the inscription. The retrograde form of the inscription is not necessarily distinctively Laconian by this point, but the alphabet certainly is: see Jeffery 1990, 198. The Laconian appearance of the text does not, however, necessarily imply that it was also created by the Spartans: Athenian monuments do use epichoric scripts and/or dialects, often apparently as a concession to those commemorated (e.g. Argive casualty list: *Agora* XVII.4; Pythagoras of Selymbria: *IG* I³ 1154).

[41] An argument central to the thesis of Schiller 1996; who follows (in part) Rousset 1994.

[42] On oppressive *philia*, see Mitchell 1997.

[43] Herodotus gives no details on the burial of the Spartan forces, but does mention the lion which commemorates Leonidas (7.225), and records (at 7.228) the epitaphs erected over their graves. The later appearance of the site is described by Strabo (9.4.2, 9.4.16). The main source for the memorials erected in Sparta is Pausanias 3.14. There is no good archaeological evidence for the commemorations at either site. For general discussions of the material, see Clairmont 1983, 114–16, 222–5; Pritchett 1985, 168–73.

[44] The accuracy of Herodotus' rendition of the epigram, and the reliability of its attribution to Simonides, is disputed: for a convenient summary of the possibilities, see Page 1981, no. 22b.

[45] Arguments from dialect are inconclusive: the MSS of the epigrams have a mixture of Doric and Ionic, and editors have tended to use preconceptions about authorship to establish the correct dialectal readings, rather than *vice versa* (see, for example, Legrand 1951, 227, n. 2).

[46] The Thespian epitaph is reported by Stephanos of Byzantium, s.v. Θέσπεια (= *GVI* no. 5); Page (1981, 78), questions its authenticity, but Clairmont (1983, 222–5) and Pritchett (1985, 171 f.) include it in their reconstructions of the epigraphic monuments at the site. On the problem of illicit incursions into commemorative sites, compare the pseudo-tumulus erected by the Aeginetans at Plataea, ten years after the battle (Hdt. 9.85.3).

[47] Pausanias reports, alongside the monument to Leonidas, a cenotaph of Brasidas, a tomb of Pausanias, commander of the Spartan army at Plataea (3.14.1), and a tomb of Eurybiades, commander of Sparta's fleet at Artemisium and Salamis (3.16.6). On the

post-mortem treatment of Spartan kings, see Hdt. 6.58, with Cartledge 1987, 337–42.

[48] Herodotus 7.225 describes the lion monument erected for Leonidas at Thermopylae in terms which imply that the monument stood over a burial (Pritchett 1985, 171). The transfer of the bones is recorded by Pausanias 3.14.1: τὰ ὀστᾶ τοῦ Λεωνίδου τεσσαράκοντα ἔτεσιν ὕστερον ἀνελομένου ἐκ Θερμοπυλῶν τοῦ Παυσανίου ('the bones of Leonidas were taken from Thermopylae by Pausanias, forty years after the battle'). The date and the name of the king are incompatible: Connor 1979 suggests that the 'forty years' is correct but the king's name is not, and that the transfer took place in 440 in the hope of reviving the battered reputation of the Agiad royal house; Corbett 1949 prefers to amend the date and accept the king, and argues for a connection with the revival of Sparta's anti-Persian ambitions at the turn of the fifth and fourth centuries.

[49] It is not clear if Pausanias' list is the same as that which Herodotus (7.224) claims to have seen: for discussion, see Ball 1976. Evidence for the festival is also problematic: Pausanias (*ib.*) implies that the speeches and festival honour only the individual leaders, but the 'Simonidean' epitaph reported at DS 11.11.6 suggests a more wide-ranging (and older) festival. Podlecki (1968, 257–62) doubts that it is possible to argue for a Spartan festival for all the dead of Thermopylae on the basis of this evidence; Ball (1976, 3 f.) argues persuasively that it might be.

Bibliography

Austin, R.P.
   1931/2 'Excavations at Haliartos 1931', *BSA* 32, 180–212.
Ball, R.
   1976 'Herodotus' list of the Spartans who died at Thermopylae', *Museum Africum* 5, 1–8.
Bölte, F.
   1929 'Zu lakonischen Festen', *RhM* 78, 124–43.
Bommelaer, J.F.
   1981 *Lysandre de Sparte. Histoire et traditions*, Paris.
Brelich, A.
   1961 *Guerre, Agoni e Culti nella Grecia Antica*, Bonn.
Brulé, P. and Piolot, L.
   2004 'Women's way of death: fatal childbirth or *hierai*? Commemorative stones at Sparta and Plutarch, *Lycurgus* 27.3', in T.J. Figueira (ed.) *Spartan Society*. Swansea, 151–78.
Cartledge, P.A.
   1987 *Agesilaos and the Crisis of Sparta*, London and Baltimore.
   2002 *Sparta and Lakonia. A regional history, 1300–362 BC*, 2nd edn, London.
Cartledge, P.A. and Spawforth, A.
   2002 *Hellenistic and Roman Sparta. A tale of two cities*, 2nd edn, London.
Cavanagh, W.G., Crouwel, J., Catling, R.W.V. and Shipley, G.
   1996 *The Laconia Survey*, Vol. 2, *Archaeological data*, London.
Christou, C.
   1964 'Σπαρτιατικοὶ ἀρχαϊκοὶ τάφοι καὶ ἐπιτάφιος μετ' ἀναγλύφων ἀμφορεὺς τοῦ Λακονικοῦ ἐργαστηρίου', *AD* 19.1, 123–63.

Clairmont, C.W.
1983   *Patrios Nomos: Public burial in Athens during the fifth and fourth centuries* BC, BAR International Series 161, Oxford.
Connor, W.R.
1979   'Pausanias 3.14.1: a sidelight on Spartan history, *c.* 440 BC?', *TAPA* 109, 21–7.
Corbett, P.E.
1949   'Λέων ἐπὶ Λεωνίδῃ', *Hesperia* 18, 104–7.
Daverio Rocchi, G.
1988   *Frontiera e Confini nella Grecia Antica*, Rome.
Förtsch, R.
2001   *Kunstverwendung und Kunstlegitimation im archaischen und frühklassischen Sparta*, Mainz.
Garland, R.
1989   'The well-ordered corpse: an investigation into the motives behind Greek funerary legislation', *BICS* 36, 1–15.
Gebauer, K.
1938   'Ausgrabungen im Kerameikos II', *AA*, 607–16.
Gebauer, K. and Johannes, H.
1937   'Ausgrabungen im Kerameikos', *AA*, 183–203.
Hodkinson, S.
2000   *Property and Wealth in Classical Sparta*, London.
Karo, G.
1930   'Archäologische Funde aus dem Jahre 1929 und der ersten Hälfte von 1930', *AA*, 88–167.
Kourinou, E.
2000   Σπάρτη. Συμβολή στη μνημειακή τοπογραφία της, Athens.
Kritzas, C.
1985   'Remarques sur trois inscriptions de Cynourie', *BCH* 109, 709–16.
Legrand, P.E.
1951   *Hérodote. Histoires*, vol. 8, Paris.
Loomis, W.T.
1992   *The Spartan War Fund. IG V.1, 1 and a new fragment*, Historia Einzelschriften 74, Stuttgart.
Loraux, N.
1986   *The Invention of Athens. The funeral oration in the classical city*, trans. A. Sheridan, Cambridge, Mass.
Low, P.A.
2003   'Remembering war in fifth-century Greece: ideologies, societies and commemoration beyond democratic Athens', *World Archaeology* 35, 98–111.
MacDowell, D.M.
1986   *Spartan Law*, Edinburgh.
Missoni, R.
1986   'Idealità e prassi degli spartani circa i caduti in guerra', in *Decima Miscellanea Greca e Romana*, Rome, 61–81.

Mitchell, L.G.
1997 'φιλία, εὔνοια and Greek interstate relations', *Antichthon* 31, 28–44.
Ohly, D.
1965 'Kerameikos-Grabung. Tätigskeitbericht 1956–1961', *AA*, 277–376.
Page, D.L.
1981 *Further Greek Epigrams*, Cambridge
Papanikolaou, A.D.
1976/7 ''Επιτύμβιον ἐξ ἀρχαίας Σελλασίας', *Athena* 76, 202–4.
Parker, R.C.T.
1989 'Spartan religion', in A. Powell (ed.) *Classical Sparta. Techniques behind her success*, London and Norman, Okla., 142–72.
Phaklares, P.V.
1987 ''Η μάχη τῆς Θυρέας (546 π.Χ.)', *Horos* 5, 101–19.
1990 Αρχαία Κυνουρία. Ανθρώπινη δραστηριότητα και περίβαλλον, 2nd edn, Athens.
Podlecki, A.J.
1968 'Simonides: 480', *Historia* 17, 257–75.
Polignac, F. de
1995 *Cults, Territory and the Origins of the Greek City-State*, trans. J. Lloyd, Chicago and London.
Powell, A.
2001 *Athens and Sparta. Constructing Greek political and social history from 478 BC*, 2nd edn, London.
Pritchett, W.K.
1980 *Studies in Ancient Greek Topography*, Part 3, *Roads*, Berkeley, Los Angeles, London.
1985 *The Greek State at War*, Part 4, Berkeley, Los Angeles, London.
1989 *Studies in Ancient Greek Topography*, Part 6, Berkeley, Los Angeles, London.
Robertson, N.
1983 'The collective burial of fallen soldiers at Athens, Sparta and elsewhere', *EMC/CV* 27, 78–92.
1992 *Festivals and Legends. The formation of Greek cities in the light of public ritual*, Toronto, Buffalo, London.
Roehl, H.
1882 *Inscriptiones Graecae Antiquissimae, praeter Atticas in Attica repertas*, Berlin.
Roesch, P.
1982 *Etudes béotiennes*, Paris.
Romaiou, K.
1950 ''Ερευνητική περιοδεία εἰς Κυνουρίαν', *Praktika*, 234–41.
Rousset, D.
1994 'Les frontières des cités grecques. Premières réflexions à partir du recueil des documents épigraphiques', *Cahiers du Centre G. Glotz* 5, 97–126.
Schiller, A.K.
1996 'Political territoriality of the classical Athenians, 508–338 BC', PhD diss., Wisconsin-Madison.

Sokolowski, F.
  1962   *Lois sacrées des cités grecques. Supplément*, Paris.
Steinhauer, G.
  1992   'An Illyrian mercenary in Sparta under Nabis', in J.M. Sanders (ed.)
         Philolakōn. Lakonian studies in honour of Hector Catling, London, 239–45.
Stupperich, R.
  1977   'Staatsbegräbnis und Privatgrabmal im klassichen Athen', Diss., Münster.
Tod, M.N.
  1932/3 'Greek inscriptions IV. A Spartan grave on Attic soil', *G&R* 2, 108–11.
Tod, M.N. and Wace, A.J.B.
  1906   *A Catalogue of the Sparta Museum*, Oxford.
Toher, M.
  1991   'Greek funerary legislation and the two Spartan funerals', in M.A. Flower
         and M. Toher (eds.) *Georgica. Greek studies in honour of George Cawkwell*,
         London, 159–75.
Van Hook, L.
  1932   'On the Lacedaemonians buried in the Kerameikos', *AJA* 36, 290–2.
Willemsen, F.
  1977   'Zu den Lakedämoniergräbern im Kerameikos', *MDAI(A)* 92, 117–57.
Wolpert, A.
  2002   *Remembering Defeat. Civil war and civic memory in ancient Athens*, Baltimore
         and London.
Zavvou, E.P.
  1992–8 ''Επιτύμβιες ἐπιγραφὲς ἀπὸ τὴ Λακωνία', *Horos* 10–12, 297–9.

4

WAS CLASSICAL SPARTA A MILITARY SOCIETY?

Stephen Hodkinson

Modern perspectives

The title of this chapter poses one of the fundamental questions that underlay the choice of 'Sparta and War' as the theme of this volume.[1] In modern scholarship the most common image of Sparta in the fifth and fourth centuries BC has been that of a society dominated by military elements: more like an army camp than the community of citizens to be found in other Greek poleis. Take, for example, the comments in several standard works on Sparta by British ancient historians. According to W.G. Forrest (1968, 54),

> it was Sparta's misfortune that [her institutions] were formalised at a time when military efficiency was the only concern of a state education; it was Sparta's fault...that they were then maintained, more or less unchanged, when other Greeks were discovering that there were other virtues besides the military.

For Geoffrey de Ste Croix (1972, 91), Sparta was 'a community of professional soldiers'. For Moses Finley (1986, 177), she was 'the model military state'. Paul Cartledge (1979, 156) argues that Sparta's 'new social system, in operation by the time of Herodotus, was characterized by an overriding emphasis on military preparedness and a reduction of non-military wants to the barest minimum'. Similarly, J.T. Hooker (1980, 135, 141) claimed that 'the discipline for which Spartan soldiers were famous...was inculcated in the camp-like conditions of their city'; and he subsequently referred to 'the relentless pursuit by the Spartans of the single aim of military efficiency'. Similar views have been common in works by a large number of scholars in other western European countries and the USA, especially during the second half of the twentieth century.[2]

These modern views are, of course, not without foundation in the ancient evidence. As we shall shortly discuss in more detail, they derive ultimately from statements by a number of classical writers, foremost amongst them Aristotle, whose criticism of the Spartan polity for its single-minded orientation towards war and military valour clearly underlies the views quoted above.[3] Nevertheless, current scholarly ideas of Sparta's military orientation appear to stem not just from a reading of the ancient sources, but also from certain features of the modern intellectual and political climate. It is indicative to contrast modern scholars' unquestioning acceptance of Aristotle's views on Sparta's military orientation with their more critical reactions to his views on other aspects of Spartan society, such as politics, land tenure and, above all, women.[4] The contrast between scholars' positive responses to Aristotle's criticism of the Spartans' supposed militarism and negative reactions to his censure of their alleged gynaecocracy is especially revealing, following as it does the fault-lines of modern sensibilities.[5]

Another sign of the influence of modern intellectual perspectives is the recurring tendency to ground the notion of Sparta's military orientation in associations with so-called 'primitive warrior societies'. In 1918 W.S. Ferguson's essay 'The Zulus and the Spartans: a comparison of their military systems' commenced with the assertion that 'both alike made war, and preparation for war, the primary aims of their association' (p. 197). Ferguson's comments were echoed in H. Michell's remark (1952, 232 n. 1) that 'The nearest approach to the military organization of Sparta is to be found in that of the Zulus under their warrior kings.' Subsequent studies have extended this specific comparison into wider general claims. According to A.H.M. Jones (1968, 34), 'the famous discipline of the Spartans...is undoubtedly very ancient fundamentally and has close analogies with the customs of many primitive warrior tribes throughout the world'. Reflecting on the Greeks' own comparison of Sparta and Crete, L.H. Jeffery (1976, 114) asserts that 'Modern scholarship...sets both places in the light of anthropology and finds the same practices, *mutatis mutandis*, reflected in...other warlike tribes'. Henri Marrou (1956, 14), too, claims that 'these countries still retained certain features of the old civilization which had everywhere else been lost'.

Space does not permit here a full survey of the development of the idea of Sparta's military orientation within modern historiography, a subject which itself needs setting within the broader framework of changing perceptions of Sparta in Western political and intellectual thought.[6] I have focused my own short introductory survey primarily on ancient historical works written since World War II in order to highlight the prevalence of the idea in recent scholarship. It is worth, however, briefly considering how far this recent scholarship has been influenced by Sparta's political association during the twentieth century with two major militaristic regimes: Nazi Germany and the Soviet Union.[7] Drawing upon earlier assimilations in Germanic thought between the Spartans and Germans as leaders of the Dorian and Nordic/ Aryan races, Nazi propagandists and German classicists in the 1930s and early 1940s grounded the ethos of the Third Reich in supposed precedents of Spartan militarism.[8] This association between Sparta and Germany was taken up eagerly in the United Kingdom, especially by liberal and socialist thinkers keen to portray Britain as the war-time equivalent of democratic Athens.[9] It has probably exercised a considerable influence upon the near-unanimous view of Sparta's military orientation among post-war British ancient historians, many of whom have been of left-wing political leanings. Subsequently, in discussions within the U.S. 'intelligence community', Sparta was repeatedly invoked as an ideal-type for modelling the militarized economy of the Soviet Union, especially during the Reagan administration of the 1980s.[10] This longstanding Sparta–Soviet association forms a suggestive backdrop to recent assertions regarding Sparta's militarism by a number of U.S. scholars, especially those in sympathy with Republican international politics.[11]

The potency of the military image of Sparta during the twentieth century, supported by powerful modern political analogies, helps to explain why this has been one of the few notions that has remained untransformed by the significant reassessments of the character of Spartan society produced by the last generation of scholarly research. It is time, therefore, to re-assess where the military image stands today. The last generation of research since the 1980s has produced, I would argue, a number of interrelated new insights which should call that image into question. Studies of a wide range of aspects of her society have provided a richer perception of the variety of Spartan life, with the result that Sparta's military features assume a less dominating position. Recent research has also frequently embodied a trend to 'normalize' Sparta, to rescue her from 'theme park' images,[12] based upon an increasing realization of the many respects in which her society – for all its peculiarities – was also characteristically Greek. From this perspective, images of Sparta such as that conveyed by Forrest – an atypical polis dominated by a uniquely military orientation – appear less plausible.

A further area of enhanced understanding has been an increase in anthropological sophistication which has undermined the simplistic analogies between Sparta and so-called 'primitive' societies. Research within African anthropology has shown that the supposedly primitive customs of warrior tribes used as comparisons with Sparta, were often recently-invented traditions of societies re-constructing their cultural identities in the face of Western colonialism and modernization.[13] Likewise, the latest research indicates that the alleged historical parallels between the military organization of early Sparta and Crete are the product of classical invention, dependent upon an artificial construct of the Cretan *politeia* developed in one of the fourth-century philosophical schools (Perlman 2005). It also has become clear that Sparta itself was not a static society, but was constantly undergoing change, adapting its institutions and practices to new circumstances, in every period from the seventh to the fourth century BC and beyond. This awareness does not necessarily preclude the idea that Spartan society had a special military orientation; but it undermines the notion that it resulted as a survival from a primitive warrior condition.

Finally, there has been a similar development of sophistication regarding representations of Spartan society in the ancient sources, with a keener perception of the distorting effects resulting from the phenomenon known as the 'Spartan mirage'. Owing to Sparta's long conflict with Athens during the later fifth century and creation of an empire in the early fourth, few of the Athenian or Athenian-influenced writers who provide the bulk of our evidence were in a position to write about the military aspects of Spartan society from a neutral perspective. Their statements, consequently, often require considerable contextualization and interpretation. My reassessment of Sparta's military image will therefore commence with the ancient sources' depiction of the character of Spartan society.

Before that, however, some remarks are necessary about a matter of terminology. Although the terms 'militarism' or 'militaristic' have often been applied to Spartan society in previous scholarly discussions,[14] I shall henceforth avoid their use in my discussion of Sparta's alleged military orientation, owing to the danger of historical anachronism. Although discussion of the military orientation of early modern absolutist monarchies was a significant feature of seventeenth- and eighteenth-century political debates, the term 'militarism' developed only in the mid-nineteenth century, following the decline of classical republican thought and the emergence of the state as a conceptual entity separate from its citizens.[15] A modern synthetic study of the history of the concept of 'militarism' divides it into two types, applicable to different kinds of societies.[16] The more recent type is the more straightforwardly anachronistic: that of the 'military-industrial complex' of certain recent and current industrialized, high-technology societies. The earlier, original, type of 'militarism' described some of the less industrialized societies of later nineteenth- and early twentieth-century Europe. Although some analysts included pre-modern societies in their discussions,[17] the term's primary frame of reference was those contemporary nation-states, especially the emerging Prusso-German state, which were judged to be characterized by a self-exclusive military sphere, an all-pervasive militaristic spirit, large-scale para-military organization, and a prioritization of military preparations entailing programmes of civilian austerity. Even this earlier type of 'militarism' presupposed a distinction between the civilian and the military spheres, and defined that state of affairs in which military men and matters were dominant over civilians and civil affairs.

Such conditions of 'militarism' were alien, not just to Sparta's community of citizen-soldiers, but to all Greek poleis, in which such a separation of civilian and military spheres did not exist:[18] hence the coining in some recent studies of phrases such as 'civic militarism' or 'le militantisme du citoyen' to reflect the distinctiveness of the ancient situation.[19] The earlier type of 'militarism' also included concerns which are distinct from the purely military concern of the winning of war. In the words of Alfred Vagts (1959, 15),

> an army so built that it serves military men, not war, is militaristic; so is everything in an army which is not preparation for fighting, but merely exists for diversion or to satisfy peacetime whims... In wartime...the pursuit of ends not identical with the winning of victory is militaristic.

Although the final sentence of this quotation might arguably apply to the behaviour of certain individual Spartan commanders, these characteristics of modern militarism do not apply to Spartan society or policy as a whole.[20] Even those ancient writers who characterized Spartan society as an army camp focused their criticisms, as we shall see, on what they claimed to be its excessive concentration on warfare and conquest, not on militaristic diversions like those outlined by Vagts.[21] My discussion in this essay will, consequently, focus on the significance of *military* aspects of Spartan social life: that is, on those aspects of her social institutions, practices and values which pertained to preparation for successful warfare. My aim is to assess their significance in comparison with aspects of polis life which were directed at other, non-military, goals: aspects that we may broadly characterize as 'civic'. Although Greek poleis did not possess the separation of civilian and military spheres characteristic of most modern Western societies, classical writers – as we shall shortly see – frequently expressed a distinction between the military and non-military aspects or activities of polis life, and between military and non-military virtues. Greek poleis were also thought to vary in the extent of their concentration on military virtues and preparation for war. In line with these contemporary distinctions, it is meaningful to ask how significant were the military elements in Sparta's citizen-soldier mix.

Ancient representations

I shall begin my discussion by examining the accounts of contemporary sources from the archaic and classical periods. As already indicated, the testimony of certain of these writers is often thought to demonstrate that Spartan society was excessively oriented towards military values and war. I shall suggest, however, that a somewhat different perspective emerges when this testimony is viewed in context and the full range of contemporary opinion taken into account.

Sparta's military orientation may appear to be demonstrated already in the archaic period in the poetry of Tyrtaios, above all in his comparison of military and other virtues in fragment 12.1–9:[22]

> I would not rate a man worth mention or account
> for skill in running or wrestling,
> not even if he had a Cyclops' size and strength
> or outstripped in the race the Thracian Boreas
> or if he surpassed Tithonos in good looks
> or Midas and Kinyras in their wealth
> or outshone Pelops son of Tantalos in kingliness
> or had Adrastos' gift of honeyed speech
> and every virtue, save a warrior's might...

Tyrtaios' evidence is especially important because it comes from a native Spartan, in contrast to the evidence of external commentators on which we are dependent for the classical period. There is no doubt about the emphasis of this passage on the priority of military prowess over non-military skills and personal attributes. Nevertheless, we should beware of over-interpretation. Tyrtaios was writing in the midst of Sparta's struggle to preserve her control over the rebellious Messenians, and his poems are in part a rallying-cry for Spartan citizens in that serious conflict.[23] Their military tone is explicable in context. Moreover, Tyrtaios does not dismiss non-military qualities outright: his argument is rather that he would not value them in men who did not also demonstrate military prowess. The very need for such sentiments implies a Spartan audience by no means convinced of their truth. That Tyrtaios' views were not a complete or uncontested statement of Spartiate values in the archaic period can be seen from other evidence attesting the Spartans' high regard for several of the non-military values that he mentions. Note, for example, the prominence in the sixth and early fifth centuries of private athletic dedications by runners and wrestlers and the public recognition which the polis gave to athletic success in the form of official victor lists (Hodkinson 1999, 152–7). Similarly, the significance of kingly qualities is also not in doubt, in view of the primary importance of the kings in archaic Sparta. Indeed, Tyrtaios himself emphasizes the merits of kingship in his other poems.[24]

What, however, about the use made of Tyrtaios' poetry in classical Sparta? Two fourth-century writers – Plato (*Laws* 629a–e) and the Athenian orator Lykourgos (*Against Leokrates* 106–7) – indicate that his poetry was recited to contemporary Spartans; and both portray his poems as praising and encouraging bravery in war. However, neither writer draws the inference that Spartan society was imbued with a dominant or distinctive set of military values. Plato explicitly contrasts Tyrtaios' focus on the single excellence of military valour with the laws laid down by the Spartan lawgiver Lykourgos, which he argues were enacted with a view to a more complete range of excellences, including justice, self-control, and wisdom (630d–e; cf. 630a).

The Athenian orator Lykourgos cites Tyrtaios' poems in his prosecution of Leokrates, a fellow-Athenian, for cowardice. The passage in question forms part of a longer invocation of normal standards of Athenian bravery which he accuses Leokrates of having sullied. Indeed, he links the military qualities described by Tyrtaios to these Athenian standards of bravery through the invented tradition that Tyrtaios was an Athenian by birth. Lykourgos, consequently, portrays the military values depicted by Tyrtaios, not as distinctively Spartan, but as common values shared also by Athenians. Finally, it is worth noting the context in which Tyrtaios' poems are said to be performed. Although Plato claims that the Spartans were surfeited with the poems, the only precise context of performance mentioned by either writer is Lykourgos' reference to the singing of the poems in the king's tent during campaigns. This reference receives support from a fragment of Philochoros (*FGrH* 328 F 216; ap. Athen. 630f), which also locates their performance in communal gatherings on campaign.[25] In other words, Tyrtaios' martial poems are described as being performed in the particular military context to which they were suited. There is no indication of their performance outside the context of military campaigns, still less that their influence was such as to instil military values throughout the entirety of citizen life.

Indeed, the depictions of Spartan society by our earliest sources from the classical period suggest that her military aspect was prominent but not dominant. In Pindar's brief characterization of Sparta (fr. 199 Maehler, ap. Plut. *Lyk.* 21.4) it appears as just one item among several salient features of Spartan life:

> There are councils of elders
> and the conquering spears of young men
> and choruses and the Muse and joyousness.

In his *Histories* Herodotus highlights the changes to their military organization as an important aspect of the Spartans' own account of the reforms of Lykourgos (1.65):

> He changed all the customs (τὰ νόμιμα πάντα) and took care that no one transgressed the new ones. Lykourgos afterwards established their affairs of war (τὰ ἐς πόλεμον ἔχοντα): the *enōmotiai* and *triēkades* and *syssitia*; and, besides these, the ephors and the *gerontes*.

These military changes, however, are presented as just part of, and subsequent to, a wider-ranging civic reform. Likewise, speaking to the Persian king Xerxes, the exiled Spartan king Damaratos emphasizes the Spartans' warlike prowess and extreme military commitment (7.104):

> So is it with the Lakedaimonians; fighting singly they are as brave as any man living, and together they are the best warriors on earth. They are free, yet not

wholly free: *Nomos* (Law) is their despot, whom they fear much more than your men fear you. They do whatever it bids; and its bidding is always the same, that they must never flee from the battle before any multitude of men, but must abide at their post and there conquer or die.

As the passage makes clear, Damaratos emphasizes that these military values are a product of the obedience of Spartan soldiers to the broader *Nomos* of the polis. A similar message emerges from the famous epitaph upon the Spartiate collective tomb at Thermopylai: "Stranger, go tell the Lakedaimonians that we lie here obedient to their commands" (Hdt. 7.228). In all these statements the Spartans' distinctive military elements and behaviour are presented as deriving from or subsidiary to their overall civic arrangements and discipline.

In other parts of the *Histories*, moreover, Sparta appears as a normal Greek *polis* whose citizens are involved in a wide range of private activities, influenced by personal and family ambitions and a desire for wealth: competing for advantageous marriage alliances or contracting marriages with close kin to preserve their property, participating in chariot-racing and in panhellenic games, engaging in foreign guest-friendships and in diverse kinds of economic and financial transactions, both legal and illicit.[26] Herodotus gives no indication that the military aspects of Spartan life exercised any impact upon these activities or upon the polis' non-military institutions. The sole respect in which military affairs are represented as impinging upon Spartan everyday life is in the ostracism of Aristodemos the 'trembler' after Thermopylai (7.229–31), a subject to which I shall return.

The idea that certain Spartan institutions were influenced by military concerns makes its first appearance in Thucydides (2.39):

We [sc. the Athenians] differ from our adversaries [sc. the Spartans] also in our military practices in this way. We throw open our city to the world, and never by expulsions of foreigners (*xenēlasiai*) exclude them from any opportunity of learning or observing, although the eyes of an enemy may occasionally profit by our liberality, trusting less in preparations and deceits than to the native spirit of our citizens; while in education, where our rivals from their very cradles by a laborious discipline seek after manliness, at Athens we live exactly as we please, and yet are just as ready to face the perils which they face.

The idea that the Spartans' practice of *xenēlasiai* and the nature of her public upbringing were essentially aspects of their military preparations and practice represents a clear development on previous ideas of the scope of military aspects of their society. It is significant, however, that this view first finds expression in the most politicized context conceivable: in Athens in 430 BC, at the end of the first year of war between the two poleis and at the state funeral for dead Athenian warriors. This significance is intensified by the fact that the comments are not Thucydides' own direct commentary, but part of the public oration he puts into the mouth of Perikles. Irrespective of the extent to which one judges the oration to be Thucydidean invention or a record of Perikles' actual words, his characterization of Spartan practice should not be taken to reflect Thucydides' own views.[27] Rather, it reads precisely like the kind of propaganda about an imperial adversary to be expected of such an occasion. Its tendentious nature is evident in the manner in which the customs of the two poleis are described in terms of such extreme contrast. Certainly, as Hornblower (1991–6, i.303–4) remarks, the impression given of the Athenians' easy-going military preparations is not only surprisingly naive but contradicted by other evidence suggesting that in reality Athenian late-fifth-century military training was much more professional.[28] The claim that Spartan training was so greatly different is correspondingly suspect. Similarly, as Thomas Figueira's recent study has shown, the assertion that the purpose of *xenēlasiai* was primarily military is stretching a point, and by no means the only interpretation of this practice, even in Thucydides' own text.[29] Once again, other evidence suggests that Spartan security measures at time of war were not unique.[30]

That the rhetoric of Sparta's opponents in the funeral oration cannot be taken as a straightforward depiction of the military orientation of Spartan institutions is further confirmed by the entirely different image Thucydides had already put into the mouth of the Spartan king Archidamos during his account of the debates in Sparta in 432 BC. Archidamos depicts Sparta's financial preparations for war as so haphazard that her public treasury was empty and her capacity to extract war funds from its citizens uncertain (1.80). Later in the same speech (1.84) the Spartans' warlike characteristics are said to be allied to more moderate qualities:

> We are both warlike and prudent (πολεμικοί τε καὶ εὔβουλοι) because of our sense of order (τὸ εὔκοσμον): warlike, because self-control is the greatest part of a sense of shame, and a sense of shame is the greatest part of courage (ὅτι αἰδὼς σωφροσύνης πλεῖστον μετέχει, αἰσχύνης δὲ εὐψυχία)...[31]

In this formulation, the warlike characteristics do not dominate, but are integrated with and based upon a number of civic qualities. The adjective 'warlike' (πολεμικοί) is balanced by an adjective describing a civic virtue ('prudent': εὔβουλοι); and both are said to depend upon 'our sense of order' (τὸ εὔκοσμον). The Spartans' warlike character and its associated quality 'courage' (εὐψυχία) are then said to derive from two further civic qualities: a sense of shame (αἰσχύνης), and ultimately from self-control (σωφροσύνης). Of course, Archidamos' speech, arguing against an immediate declaration of war, is itself as partisan as Perikles' funeral oration; but it confirms that

119

in his speeches Thucydides was capable of representing contrasting perspectives on the character of Spartan society without necessarily committing himself to either.

In other parts of his work, important aspects of the Spartan *politeia* are presented without reference to military concerns. When, in his very first reference to Sparta's internal society, Thucydides highlights the uniformity and simplicity of Spartan lifestyle and dress (1.6), he presents it as a measure of social rather than military cohesion: a cohesion all the more necessary given the personal rivalries and ambitions at which he – like Herodotus – hints throughout his work.[32] As for Sparta's military ideology, he records the surprise of other Greeks at the surrender of the Spartans trapped on the island of Sphakteria in 425 BC, the defensive reaction of one of the survivors when his bravery was impugned compared with that of the fallen, and the subsequent temporary *atimia* suffered by the survivors.[33] However, the ambiguities presented in this episode – the uncertainty shown by both the Sphakterians and the Spartans on the mainland about what they should do, the authorities' initial lack of action against the returnees, and the temporary nature of their *atimia* – are such as to leave the distinct impression that there are limits to the supposed Spartan ideology of conquest or death.[34] This is not the place for a full rehearsal of the arguments regarding Thucydides' presentation of Spartan attitudes to war-making, especially the interpretation of his controversial assertion that the Spartans were 'not quick to enter upon wars unless compelled to do so'.[35] However, the continual oscillation of the Spartan authorities and of individual commanders between initial spells of determination for military action and subsequent periods of inertia, vacillation, discouragement or fear is repeatedly highlighted in the historian's account.[36]

It is only in the fourth century that sweeping statements about the military character of Spartan society start to appear. The stimulus for these claims was also highly political: the sudden growth of Sparta's empire following the end of the Peloponnesian war. Some proponents of these claims were Spartan supporters seduced by their temporary imperial success. Aristotle *Politics* (1333b11–22) refers to a number of writers, among them a certain Thibron (probably the Spartan general), who praised the aim of the Spartan system on the grounds that their lawgiver had framed the whole of his legislation with a view to conquest and war.

Other proponents were critics of Spartan imperialism. Such generalizations about Sparta's military character appear a number of times in the works of Isokrates. In his *Busiris* (17–18), for example, Isokrates constructs a comparison with the careful regulation of Egyptian society to depict Sparta as a society with an overwhelmingly military focus:

> the Lakedaimonians govern their own city in admirable fashion because they

imitate certain of the Egyptian customs: for instance, the provision that no citizen fit for military service could leave the country without official authorization, the *syssitia*, and the training of their bodies; furthermore, the fact that, lacking none of the necessities of life, they do not neglect the edicts of the state, and that none engage in any other crafts, but that all devote themselves to arms and warfare, all these practices they have taken from there.

In his *Panathenaikos* Isokrates ascribes similar ideas to various laconizers. The Spartan sympathizer, responding to Isokrates' criticisms, argues (202, 216–17) that the Spartans deserved gratitude because they had discovered the best practices (τοῖς καλλίστοις τῶν ἐπιτηδευμάτων): namely, their physical exercises, training in courage, spirit of concord and, in general, their discipline for war (τὴν περὶ τὸν πόλεμον ἐπιμέλειαν). Finally, in his *Archidamos* (81) Isokrates lays the most striking emphasis upon this military focus through the speech of the young Spartan prince:

> This much, at any rate, is clear to all – that we have been superior to all the Hellenes, not because of the size of our *polis* or the number of its inhabitants, but because the *politeia* which we have established is like a military camp (τὴν πολιτείαν ὁμοίαν...στρατοπέδῳ), well administered and rendering willing obedience to its officers.

The rhetorical contexts of these portrayals of Sparta's military orientation should be noted.[37] The images in the *Busiris* and *Panathenaikos* accord with Isokrates' agenda against Spartan imperialism throughout his writings. The parallel between Sparta and Egypt in the *Busiris* is created in order to contrast the Egyptians' allegedly peaceful society with the Spartans' abuse of their single-minded military focus for imperial exploitation.[38] In the *Panathenaikos* the Spartan sympathizer's praise for their military qualities is constructed to enable Isokrates to criticize the Spartans' abuse of these qualities for unjust wars against other Greeks.[39] In the *Archidamos* the military camp comparison is wedded to a different but equally rhetorical context: one in which the Spartan prince is attempting to rouse his fellow citizens to take the scarcely credible step of abandoning their *polis* and forming themselves into an army on the move. The military camp comparison is the sole analogy that would provide full support for the case Archidamos wishes to make. Given the demands of the context, we should not treat it as a definitive or exhaustive perspective upon the nature of the Spartan *politeia*. Indeed, in the very same work Archidamos also presents a very different, non-military image of a society which places its highest priority upon the breeding of horses for chariot-racing while in the midst of suing for peace (55).

What about more analytical fourth-century commentators? While criticizing those writers who praised Sparta's military orientation (*Politics* 1333b14–35), Aristotle concurs that Sparta was a *polis* with a single-minded military intent. Near the start of his discussion of the Spartan *politeia* in Book 2 he classes the Spartans among 'the military and warlike races' (1269b25–6: τῶν στρατιωτικῶν καὶ πολεμικῶν γενῶν). At 1271b2–6 he elaborates by arguing that,

> Another criticism that may be made against the fundamental principle of the lawgiver is one that Plato has made in the *Laws*. The entire system of the laws is directed towards one part of excellence (πρὸς γὰρ μέρος ἀρετῆς), the warlike part (τὴν πολεμικήν), because this is serviceable for conquest. Owing to this they remained secure while at war, but began to decline when they had won an empire, because they did not know how to live a peaceful life, and had been trained in no other form of training more important than the art of war (μηδὲ ἠσκηκέναι μηδεμίαν ἄσκησιν ἑτέραν κυριωτέραν τῆς πολεμικῆς).

At 1324b7–9 he claims that 'both the system of education and the mass of the laws are framed in the main with a view to war'; and at 1334a40–b4 he asserts that the Lakedaimonians believe that the greatest goods are obtained by means of one particular excellence. Finally, at 1338b25–39 he comments that the Spartans had been superior to others because they alone used to implement training for their young men.

A number of observations should, however, be made which may serve to qualify the impact of these powerful assertions of Sparta's military orientation. First, Aristotle's account is couched in entirely generic terms without specific detail to substantiate his assertions. Secondly, the context in which some of these assertions are made does not always inspire confidence. For example, Aristotle's classification of the Spartans among 'the military and warlike races' at 1269b25–6 is connected with his disputable claim that Spartan males, like most such peoples, were under the sway of their women, who thereby managed a great deal of affairs during the Spartan empire. Thirdly, although Aristotle's characterization of Sparta as a militarily-orientated society appears to single her out from other Greek states, his comments exemplify a broader trend of late-fourth-century thought that was also applied to other poleis. Both 1269b25–6 – which is part of a long account of how female power undermined Sparta's citizen economy and manpower – and 1271b2–6 (quoted above) are linked to explanations of Sparta's imperial decline. Aristotle's contemporary, the historian Ephorus, had already asserted that the decline of another fourth-century power, Thebes, was due to her exclusive concentration on military excellence (μόνης δ'ἐπιμεληθῆναι τῆς κατὰ πόλεμον ἀρετῆς: *FGrH* 70 F 119, ap. Strabo 9.2.2). Aristotle's own work lends further credence to this indication that an excessive orientation towards military qualities had become a stock explanation for imperial decline. In *Politics* Book VII he argues that 'most of these poleis [sc. whose legislation is framed with a view to war] remain safe while at war, but perish when they have won their empire: in peace-time they lose their keen temper, like iron' (1334a6–9). Hence, far from viewing Sparta as unique in the extent of her military orientation, even Aristotle sees her as just one example among many.

Finally, Aristotle's emphasis upon Sparta's excessive military orientation is limited by other aspects of his characterization of Spartan society. In one passage he actually contradicts his own account of the Spartans' narrow concentration on a single part of excellence. In explaining the origins of the disciplined life of Spartan men, he states that when they gained their leisure at the end of these wars, 'they put themselves into the hands of their legislator in a state of preparedness brought about by the military life (for this embraces many parts of excellence)'.[40] Rather than Spartan citizen life being focused on a single narrow military excellence, their military life is here portrayed as inculcating a diversity of excellences required for their civic activities. Elsewhere Aristotle expresses another respect in which a military focus was only one part of Spartiate life, implying in particular that it exercised only a limited impact upon private behaviour. At 1270b32–35, for example, he comments that the official lifestyle is so harsh that the citizens secretly abandon it to enjoy pleasures of the body. Throughout his critique of the Spartan *politeia* in Book 2, he repeatedly remarks upon the Spartans' high level of uncontrolled private self-interest. The selection of *gerontes*, for example, is described as *dynasteutikē* (1306a18–91). In fact, elections to the Gerousia are said to exemplify the lawgiver's method regarding the entire *politeia*, that of making the citizens ambitious, a characteristic which Aristotle goes on to associate with acts of injustice and love of money (1271a13–18). Love of money (*philochrēmatia*) is a chronic feature repeatedly identified as a significant characteristic of Spartan citizens, the major weakness that he views as the source of Sparta's serious inequality of property and decline of citizen manpower (1270a11–b6; cf. 1269b23–4).[41] Indeed, developing the point already intimated by Thucydides, Aristotle concludes his critique by arguing that for individual Spartiates love of money even took precedence over the polis' demands for military finance.

> Public finance is also badly regulated by the Spartiates: they are obliged to undertake large-scale wars, but there is never any money in the public treasury; they pay *eisphorai* (εἰσφέρουσί) badly, for as most of the land is the property of the Spartiates themselves, they do not enquire too closely into one another's *eisphorai*. For the lawgiver, the outcome has been the reverse of useful: he has made the *polis* poor and private citizens lovers of money. (1271b10–15)

Although Aristotle himself acknowledges his dependence on Plato's *Laws* for his critique of Sparta's military focus, his overall depiction of the character of Spartan society in many ways resembles Plato's image of the Spartan-based timarchic regime described in the *Republic* (545a–550c). This regime, which in Plato's account emerges as a result of internal conflict among the Guardians of the ideal state, embodies a compromise involving, on the one hand, the distribution of land and houses to private ownership, on the other, the reduction of their subjects to the status of *perioikoi* and slaves, with the rulers devoting themselves to war and maintaining guard over their subjects. In keeping with its origins, the resulting regime involves a mixture of military and non-military features, which are expressed under three headings: features in which it resembles the ideal state, features peculiar to itself, and features which it shares with oligarchy. The first two headings include several militarily-orientated features: under the first heading, the abstention of the soldier class from farming, handicrafts and money-making, the maintenance of common messes, and the attention paid to gymnastics and to military contests (547d); under the second, a preference for simpler, hearty types who prefer war to peace and an admiration for and occupation with the tricks and stratagems of war (547e–548a). In contrast, however, its oligarchic features are entirely non-military. Its primary oligarchic feature is a love of property, leading to a secret lust for gold and silver, stored privately in domestic treasuries, thereby funding lavish expenditures within citizen households. The most salient features of the society are said to be contentiousness and ambition (548c: φιλονικίαι καὶ φιλοτιμίαι). A similar picture comes across in Plato's depiction of the timarchic individual. He is contentious and self-willed, desirous of power and honour (φίλαρχος δὲ καὶ φιλότιμος); also increasingly avaricious as he grows older (548d–549b). Ultimately, the accumulation of wealth, allied to the other non-military features, leads to the decline of timarchy to an oligarchic system character-ized by extravagance, disobedience to the law, envious rivalry and increasing differentiation between rich and poor (550d–551b). Hence, the *Republic* too, though – unlike Aristotle's *Politics* – not strictly a historical depiction of Sparta's contemporary development, suggests the primacy of private, non-military influences among Spartan citizens.

At first sight the *Laws* provides a more straightforward account of Sparta's military character. The most blunt statement appears in Book II during a dis-cussion between the Athenian and Kleinias, his Cretan interlocutor, about different types of song. The Cretan comments that neither his compatriots nor the Spartans would be able to sing any other song than those they had learnt in choruses; to which the Athenian replies:

> Naturally; for in truth you never attained to the noblest singing. For your *politeia* is that of an army camp (στρατοπέδου γὰρ πολιτείαν ἔχετε) rather than that of city-dwellers, and you keep your young people massed together like

a herd of colts at grass. None of you takes his own colt...and trains him...so that he may turn out not only a good soldier, but also able to manage a polis and cities – in short a man who (as we said at the start) is more of a warrior than the warriors of Tyrtaios (τῶν Τυρταίου πολεμικῶν εἶναι πολεμικώτερον), inasmuch as... he esteems bravery (τὴν ἀνδρίαν) as the fourth in order of excellences, not the first. (666e–667a)

This passage labels Crete and Sparta as military societies who train their citizens to place bravery above other values. The Athenian's apparently paradoxical criticism, that the man who places bravery below other excellences is actually more warlike and able to manage a polis and cities than the Spartan warriors (described by Tyrtaios) who place it first, reads like indirect comment on the Spartans' misgovernment of subject poleis which had contributed to the collapse of their empire. Plato's mention of Tyrtaios explicitly refers the reader back to his earlier, more extensive treatment of Sparta's military orientation at the start of Book I. In contrast to the uncompromising assertions of Book II, however, this earlier treatment exhibits a number of ambiguities, as well as certain apparent discrepancies with the passage just quoted. Kleinias and Megillos initially agree that the lawgivers of their two states had established both their public and private customs with a view to war (626a–c; cf. 628e). But the Athenian convinces them that they have mistaken their lawgivers' intentions: Lykourgos and Minos had framed their laws with an eye, not to the single excellence of bravery in war (*andria*) described by Tyrtaios, but to the full range of excellences (justice, self-control, wisdom, bravery), of which bravery was the least important (629a–632d, esp. 630d–631a). At this point, however, the argument takes a different direction. The Athenian decides to continue his discussion of the work of these lawgivers by examining institutions connected with bravery. Megillos and he outline a series of institutions – the common meals, the *gymnasia*, hunting, the *krypteia*, and tests of endurance – which they agree were devised with a view to war (633a–c). But later in the discussion, when the topic moves from bravery to self-control (*sōphrosynē*), Megillos briefly adds that the common meals and *gymnasia* were also devised to foster that excellence (635e–636a). This point, however, is not developed because at this juncture the Athenian is already engaged in a lengthy argument (extending to the end of Book I) that, while the two states effectively trained their citizens to master fear and pain, by entirely prohibiting pleasures such as drunkenness they failed to inculcate a similar bravery or capacity for self-control in the face of pleasures and disgraceful acts (633c–650b, esp. 633c–638e). The twists and turns of Plato's discussion briefly summarized above preclude a single message regarding the significance of Sparta's military aspects. Military considerations are presented as a significant influence over particular institutions, although some of these institutions are also argued to inculcate non-military values. But, despite initial thoughts – and in contrast to Book II – the *politeia* as a whole is presented as focused on the full range of citizen excellences;[42] and the concluding part of the chapter implies the existence of the kind of private sphere already viewed in the *Republic*, one dominated by personal pleasures and non-military values and behaviour.

Finally, we should consider the evidence of Xenophon's *Polity of the Lakedaimonians*, commencing with the work's opening comments (1.1–2):

> Once when I was pondering on the fact that Sparta, though among the most thinly populated poleis, became the most powerful and famous (δυνατωτάτη τε καὶ ὀνομαστοτάτη) in Greece, I wondered how this could have happened. However, once I had studied the institutions of the Spartiates (τὰ ἐπιτηδεύματα τῶν Σπαρτιατῶν), I wondered no more. Indeed, I admire Lykourgos, who gave the Spartans the laws in obedience to which they were outstandingly successful (ηὐδαιμόνησαν), and I think that he reached the utmost limit of wisdom. For, it was not by imitating the other *poleis*, but by adopting customs quite different from most, that he made his own native city pre-eminently prosperous (προέχουσαν εὐδαιμονίᾳ τὴν πατρίδα ἐπέδειξεν).

In his book on militarism and morality in the ancient world (1996, 103), Doyne Dawson cites Xenophon's *Polity* as the only surviving example of the pro-Spartan writers criticized by Aristotle 'who praised the Spartan system on the grounds that it was best suited for war and conquest', claiming that the work 'declares at the start' that 'Spartan military success proves the supe-riority of the peculiar Spartan institutions'. This, however, is to over-interpret Xenophon's words. His statement that the character of the Spartans' institu-tions *explains* why they had become most powerful and famous (δυνατωτάτη τε καὶ ὀνομαστοτάτη) is not the same as *praising* those institutions *on the grounds of* military success.[43] Moreover, it is by no means self-evident that Xenophon's conception of Sparta's success is focused exclusively, or even primarily, on her military or imperial hegemony. The fact that his reference to her power is paired with a reference to her fame suggests a broader concep-tion of the nature of Sparta's prominence; and, as the passage proceeds, war and conquest appear to recede further from Xenophon's mind. He goes on to say that Lykourgos' laws were responsible for her condition of *eudaimonia* (the word appears twice in different forms). As Michael Lipka's commentary (2002, 18–19) has recently argued, Xenophon's conception of *eudaimonia* both in the *Lak. Pol.* and in his other writings relates not to external power but to the internal character of society, above all embodying notions of restraint and self-control.

This opening sets the tone for the overall theme of the work. There are two references (at 2.7 and 4.7) to the aim of making the Spartans better fighting men and a number (1.10; 4.7; 5.9) to the aim of improving their physical condition. However, the primary focus is on how the Lykourgan system produced good internal social order and citizens with the right moral qualities (e.g. 2.2, 10, 14; 3.4). The most illustrative passage is 7.1–2:

> Nor does this exhaust the list of the customs established by Lykourgos at Sparta that are contrary to those of the other Greeks. In other poleis, I suppose, all men make as much money as they can (χρηματίζονται ὅσον δύνανται). One is a farmer, another a ship-owner, another a merchant, and others live by different handicrafts. But at Sparta Lykourgos forbade freeborn citizens to have anything to do with the acquisition of wealth (χρηματισμὸν). He insisted on their regarding as their own concern only those activities that promote freedom for poleis (ὅσα δὲ ἐλευθερίαν ταῖς πόλεσι).

Having listed various occupations of citizens in other poleis, Xenophon does not say 'but in Sparta all citizens are full-time soldiers'; instead, he refers more generally to those activities that promote freedom for poleis. Even chapter 9, dealing with the position of cowards, devotes more space to social than to military implications.

Xenophon does of course devote three chapters (11–13) to specifically military matters, in which he emphasizes the superiority of their military practices over those of other Greeks. However, it is relevant to note how he introduces this part of his work:

> These [i.e. the preceding] measures are general blessings both in peace and in war (καὶ ἐν εἰρήνῃ καὶ ἐν πολέμῳ). But if anyone wishes to discover in what respect their military practices (τὰς στρατείας) are better than those of others, it is also possible for him to hear these things. (11.1).

With these words Xenophon explicitly places his following account of Sparta's military practices in a separate compartment from his account in the earlier chapters of the work, which deals with Spartan society in times of both peace and war. In emphasizing that the measures discussed in earlier chapters were blessings common to both peace and war, Xenophon explicitly eschews any idea that they were specifically military in character.[44] Furthermore, in separating the military chapters from the preceding ones, he indicates that the practices described there operated without implications for the character of Spartan society at home. It is in keeping with this perspective that the last of these three chapters, chapter 13, which deals with the kings' power and honour on campaign (ἐπὶ στρατιᾶς…δύναμιν καὶ τιμὴν: 13.1) is also separated from the account in chapter 15 of their honours inside Sparta (αἱ τιμαὶ οἴκοι: 15.8).[45]

The above survey indicates that the representations of Spartan society and military affairs by contemporary classical writers lend, at best, only partial and qualified support to modern ideas of the dominance of military elements within Spartan society. The earliest classical commentators note Sparta's distinctive military characteristics, but depict them either as just one facet of her society or as stemming from Sparta's broader civic arrangements and ideology. There is no sense that they exercised a pervasive influence over her society as a whole. Only in the politically-charged atmosphere of Perikles' funeral oration does the notion of a broader influence begin to emerge; but the idea is not pursued in the rest of Thucydides' work. The notion of Sparta's singular military orientation developed fully only after the creation of Sparta's fourth-century empire. Her rapid acquisition of imperial domination after the Peloponnesian war led extremists on both sides (whether Spartan partisans or hostile critics like Isokrates) to attribute it to her exclusively military focus. But, even in the fourth century, among more detached observers opinions were divided. Earlier writers, whose careers spanned Sparta's imperial heyday as well as her subsequent decline, tended to take a more moderate line. Xenophon largely maintains the balanced view of Spartan society found before the Peloponnesian war. Some parts of Plato's writings reflect more recent views, acknowledging the strength of military elements and values; but elsewhere this is counter-balanced by a broader view of the Spartan *politeia* and an awareness of a powerful private sphere of non-military values and behaviour. Only in Aristotle's *Politics*, written a generation or more after Sparta's decline, does the attempt to identify weakness in the nature of the Spartan *politeia* lead to the unequivocal claim that one of its failings was a single-minded military orientation. But even Aristotle acknowledged the limited extent to which this orientation influenced the sphere of both private and public behaviour.

I have focused upon explicit references to Sparta's military characteristics as a means of assessing the extent to which contemporary writers perceived them as influencing the character of social relationships among the Spartiate citizens. It is relevant, however, to conclude my survey by briefly noting the significance of a non-military characteristic which several classical writers identify as underpinning Spartiate social relationships: a deep-rooted ethic of co-operative sociability. Since I have recently examined this ethic in detail elsewhere (Hodkinson 2005, 258–63), I shall confine myself to briefly outlining its prominence in contemporary sources. Thucydides' and Xenophon's accounts of the willing collaboration of the elite in establishing the uniformity and discipline of Spartan life depict the ethic as underpinning the very creation of Sparta's classical *politeia* (Thuc. 1.6; Xen. *Lak. Pol.* 8.1–2). Plato and Aristotle represent it as the basis of Spartan politics in their respective comments on the *philia* involved in Sparta's constitutional mixture (*Laws* 693b–e) and on the unanimity between classes in her political and social arrangements (*Pol.* 1270b21–6; 1294b19–29). Co-operative sociability is portrayed in operation in everyday life in Herodotus' reference to younger Spartiates' practice of giving way to their elders (2.80), in Kritias' account of sociability among fellow-drinkers in the common messes (fr. B6), and in Xenophon's and Aristotle's descriptions of the practice of communal property-sharing (*Lak. Pol.* 5.3, 6.3; Arist. *Pol.* 1263a26–40). In the fourth century these ideas crystallized in the widespread notion of Spartan *homonoia* (concord), which appears in several writers.[46] Both the contexts of the instances of co-operative sociability listed above and the contexts in which the idea of Spartan *homonoia* appears are almost invariably non-military.[47] The unanimity of classical writers regarding the prominence of this feature of civic life is further evidence that the overall picture of Spartan society in contemporary writings is not unduly dominated by the theme of military discipline. As Ducat (1999a, 47) has noted, the civic *homonoia* between Spartan citizens was viewed as an essential element in the Spartans' success, as in Lysias' statement (33.7) that,

> they alone live in homes that are unravaged and unprotected by walls, are free from internal unrest and unconquered and have always followed the same customs.[48]

Lysias' assertion juxtaposes Sparta's civic concord and stability alongside her military strength as the twin pillars of her pre-eminence.

The 'professionalism' of Spartan military practice

Having surveyed contemporary representations of the role of military elements in Spartan society, I shall now attempt a more synthetic discussion of the key issues. In organizing my discussion I shall make use of Xenophon's distinction between institutions and practices applying across the whole of Spartiate life – in his words, 'both in peace and in war' – and those pertaining solely to military campaigns. I shall deal only briefly with questions to do with the character and methods of the Lakedaimonian army on campaign – in particular, with the extent to which Spartan military practices were distinctive, what we nowadays call more 'professional', compared to those of other poleis – since these questions are only indirectly relevant to my central concern with the character of Spartan society.

The recent analysis by Hans van Wees (2004) suggests that in certain aspects the Lakedaimonian army was not altogether different from those of other poleis, especially in its composition and personnel. Like the armies of other poleis, though formed around a core of Spartiate troops, it also relied – indeed, became increasingly dependent – upon a large number of hoplites without full citizen rights, in the form of the *perioikoi* and helots.[49] The absence of mercenaries before the Peloponnesian war is striking, but is also true of Athens, which like Sparta possessed the capacity to raise large numbers of troops within its own alliance.[50] The elite unit of *hippeis* around the king is sometimes regarded as a distinctive feature;[51] but both Athens and the Boiotians had similar forces at Plataia in 479 BC and by the Peloponnesian war so did several other *poleis*. The only unusual aspect is the Spartan method of selecting its elite unit on merit, in contrast to the more usual method of recruitment from the rich.[52]

Where Spartan practice does appear distinctively professional is in the systematic organization of her campaigning – at least on land (Cartledge 1977, 17). Spartan military thoroughness commenced with the levy, which included specified age-classes not only of cavalry and infantry, but even of *cheirotechnai* (handicraftsmen: Xen. *Lak. Pol.* 11.2). Spartan armies were unique in having a centrally organized baggage train under its own commanders who attended the king's war council (*ibid.* 11.2; 13.4).[53] Another distinctive element was the systematic routine of sacrifices and divination, beginning at home and continuing throughout the campaign, which led Xenophon to pronounce that the Spartans were 'the only craftsmen of warfare' (μόνους τῷ ὄντι τεχνίτας τῶν πολεμικῶν: *ibid.* 13.5). Thucydides highlights the extraordinarily stratified system of military units, with their sub-divisions going right down to the platoon-size *enōmotiai* of 30-odd men, a corresponding uniquely hierarchical command structure (Thuc. 5.66), and standing arrangements for the nomination of substitute officers in case of the commander's death (*ibid.* 3.109; 4.38). A Spartan soldier was required to swear a special oath of obedience to his officers, right down to his *enōmotarchos*:[54] the contrast with the more egalitarian ethos of other Greek armies led to conflicts when Spartan generals were in command of troops from other *poleis*.[55] Spartan military professionalism was evident in other ways too: in their method of walking, not running, into battle in organized step without breaking formation (Thuc. 5.70); in the disciplined routine within Spartan camps;[56] and in the delegation of matters of justice, finance and booty to specially-appointed officials (Xen. *Lak. Pol.* 13.10–11). Xenophon claims that, 'it is almost impossible to find any detail in military matters that is overlooked by the Spartans' (*ibid.* 12.7).

A military society?

The key issues for our discussion, however, concern the implications of this distinctive military organization. These issues can be broken down into two aspects. One aspect is whether the 'professionalism' of the Spartans' approach to the conduct of war meant that military factors exercised an unusual level of influence over their policy-making in external affairs; whether the dynamics of Sparta's military preparations, to borrow a modern phrase, 'gained the upper hand over "the steady art of statecraft"'.[57] This aspect merits more detailed treatment than there is space for here; but it is worth noting the existence of a range of evidence against the proposition of any consistently pre-eminent military influence. For example, the conclusions of Van Wees' study of the justifications the Spartans gave for waging war and the motives underlying their decisions do not suggest any unusual military influence. The justifications for going to war advanced in the Spartans' three embassies to Athens preceding the Peloponnesian war conformed to standard Greek norms: justifications in terms of defending the gods against impiety, protecting their allies against injustice, and ensuring the freedom of fellow-Greeks.[58] Similarly, ancient accounts of their motivations for declaring war suggest that they were no different from those of other Greek poleis, being dominated above all by considerations of honour and prestige.[59] Further evidence is available in the history of Spartan foreign relations: for example, from the numerous occasions when they refused external requests for military assistance.[60] We should also note the Spartans' capacity to restrain their use of force against Athens between the Persian and Peloponnesian wars until exactly the right moments of opportunity (Powell 1980; 1988, 118–26): so much so as to provoke the Corinthians, in the speech Thucydides gives them before the Spartiate assembly (1.68–71), to accuse the Spartans of chronic inactivity and failure to defend their allies. Thucydides' own direct judgement (1.118), that the Spartans 'were not quick to go to war unless compelled to do so', has provoked a deal of scholarly controversy; but, even on a minimal interpretation, it does not betoken an approach to foreign affairs in which political judgements were overridden by military dynamic.

The other aspect – the one on which I shall concentrate – is the question of the effect of the Spartans' approach to military matters upon the character of Spartan society. Was Plato right, for instance, to claim that key institutions such as the common meals, the *gymnasia*, hunting and the *krypteia* were devised with a view to war? In a previous study (Hodkinson 1993) I have examined the impact of Sparta's prolonged engagement in warfare between 431 and 371 BC – during the Peloponnesian war and Spartan empire – upon the internal crisis of Spartiate society. In my discussion here I shall not attempt to differentiate this or any other period, but shall focus my attention on the classical period as a whole. It is arguable that military matters may have exercised a greater, or at least a different, impact upon Spartan society during the period of her imperial expansion. The evidence for many Spartan social institutions, however, is insufficiently detailed or specific to detect any changes in their character between different periods. Hence a separate examination of this period would require a different kind of approach, one whose scope lies beyond the limits of this present paper. One partial compensation is that an undifferentiated approach embracing the classical period as a whole enables us to address directly the assertions of the late classical sources, most of whom (like Plato and Aristotle) viewed the military characteristics of contemporary Spartan society, not as new phenomena deriving from her period of empire, but as the outcome of longstanding structural factors deriving from the basic nature of the Spartan *politeia*.

Before addressing the significance of military elements in particular spheres of Spartiate life, we need first to deal with one general issue which has contributed significantly to the military image of Spartan society: the question of their servile labour force, the helots. Scholars have often wanted to view the Spartans' need to keep the large helot populations of Lakonia and Messenia under permanent subjection as the major driving force behind their creation of a cohesive society of citizens sharing a common public lifestyle.[61] This hypothesis has naturally led scholars to assume that the society thus created must have been dominated by the requirements of military security. This view has received strength from the assertions of certain prominent classical writers (Thucydides, Plato and Aristotle) regarding the constant danger allegedly posed by the helots.[62]

However, as I have already argued elsewhere (Hodkinson 1997, 96–7), to ascribe the transformation and subsequent character of Spartan society to the helot problem is too extreme. Sparta was not unique in reducing a native population to a condition of servitude during the archaic period. Several similar subject populations existed under the domination of Greek poleis both in mainland Greece and in other parts of the Greek world;[63] and a number of them seem to have posed as much a threat of revolt as did the helots.[64] Aristotle himself (*Pol.* 1269a36–9) equates the revolts of the Thessalian *penestai* with those of the helots. Neither is it valid to claim (Raaflaub 1997, 56) that the Spartiates faced a permanent threat to their very existence not shared by poleis without a comparable native subject population. This is to underestimate the extent to which archaic and classical Greek warfare revolved around the capture of cities and the elimination, enslavement or dispersal of their populations.[65] The reality is that almost all Greek poleis faced the regular prospect of serious threats to their very survival, whether from internal or from external sources. Yet the fact that no other polis created a communal and publicly-orientated social system like that in Sparta suggests that considerations of military security arising from the helots are unlikely to have been the decisive factor. There was nothing inherent in the helot problem that demanded the radical transformation of Spartan society, had it not also been desirable in its own right as a response to other problems

– the prime candidate being chronic internal conflict among the Spartans themselves which is well-attested in the evidence for archaic Sparta.[66]

It is possible that shared solidarity against the helots was a factor in tilting the Spartans towards a communal solution to the problems within their citizen body; but that gives no grounds for assuming that this solution entailed the militarization of classical Spartan society. It is true that Thucydides (4.80) asserts that 'Lakedaimonian policy towards the helots was always largely determined by considerations of security'.[67] But this is a comment on Spartan policy, not on the nature of their social institutions; and, even as a generalization regarding policy, it is at odds with other parts of his narrative, which portray a much lower level of Spartan concern about the helots.[68] Likewise, other major classical writers, such as Herodotus and Xenophon, give a contrary impression of the Spartans' perception of the helots, treating them simply as part of the scenery (Whitby 1994). Indeed, so little were the Spartans normally in fear of a helot threat that they went about their daily lives unarmed.[69] As recent studies have suggested, there were many ways of keeping the helots under control other than through military means.[70] In sum, there are no grounds for assuming purely from the presence of the helots that Spartan society must have possessed an especially military character.

Clearly, there are some respects in which military affairs were more prominent in Spartiate life than within the life of citizens in other poleis. The most basic respect was that liability for military service, in its primary form of hoplite fighting, extended to all Spartiates between the ages of 20 and 60. No other Greek polis equated citizenship with military service to quite this extent; although it should be noted that, if one includes light-armed and other types of troops, all Greek poleis had very high rates of military participation (Van Wees 2004, 45–6). More importantly, being freed by the labour of the helots from the need to work for their subsistence, adult Spartiates were permanently available for military training, not just during campaigns as were the bulk of hoplites in other poleis. The evidence at first sight may suggest that military training was a frequent and regular part of Spartiate life. Thucydides' statement (5.70) regarding the Lakedaimonian custom of walking into battle in step to the tune of *auloi* without breaking ranks appears to exemplify a level of co-ordination based on long practice unknown to other armies. Xenophon's detailed description of the complex marching manoeuvres performed by Lakedaimonian troops and his insistence that they could carry out with ease things that hoplite instructors thought difficult (*Lak. Pol.* 11.8–10) might also seem to imply significant amounts of time spent on formation drill. Several post-classical military manuals describe a particular type of counter-marching manoeuvre known specifically as the *Lakōnikos exeligmos*.[71] Finally, the late Roman imperial writer Vegetius claims that the Spartans were the first to write on the art of war, to approach military affairs as a matter of discipline and study of skills rather than of courage or luck, and that they instructed drillmasters (*tactici*) to teach their youth the various fighting techniques (*Epitoma rei militaris* 3, preface).

Some important qualifications are, however, necessary. The statements by Thucydides and Xenophon relate to manoeuvres performed by the entire Lakedaimonian army.[72] However, the bulk of non-Spartiate troops within that army cannot have spent much time in Sparta itself, especially the *perioikoi*, most of whom were working farmers living in a number of different poleis scattered around her large territory.[73] Hence opportunities for them to congregate for peacetime military training must have been limited. Xenophon's description cited above may in fact confirm this probability. Although his comments on the ease with which the Lakedaimonians performed difficult manoeuvres (11.8) might appear to be evidence for regular drill practice, his emphasis on the uncomplicated nature of the Lakonian formation – 'so easy to learn that no one who knows man from man should go wrong' (*Lak. Pol.* 11.5–6) – could equally, as Noreen Humble (this volume) points out, be interpreted to signify that it could be mastered with comparatively little training. Given the absence of collective training by other Greek armies, with the exception of certain picked units, the Lakedaimonians' superiority in military drill could probably have been achieved with minimal practice. After all, the manoeuvres described by Thucydides and Xenophon were ones undertaken before battle was joined, not in 'the crunch of battle'. The evidence of the battle of Mantineia in 418 indicates that even during these preliminaries the Lakedaimonian army was insufficiently well-drilled to avoid the general tendency of Greek armies to veer to the right; and the fact that two Spartan officers who were ordered to march their *lochoi* from the right wing to fill up a gap near the left refused to do so suggests lack of confidence about their capacity to execute the manoeuvre successfully (Thuc. 5.71–2). As for manoeuvres during battle itself, the failed counter-march at the battle of Kerkyra in 374/3 (Xen. *Hell.* 6.2.20–3) provides an indication of the limits of the Lakedaimonians' supposed superiority of military drill.

The limited training opportunities available to perioikic troops had implications for the level of training undertaken by Spartiate soldiers, since from some point between the Persian and Peloponnesian wars – if not before – the *perioikoi* seem to have fought in the same military units as the Spartiate troops.[74] In these circumstances, the utility of regular formation training by the Spartiates themselves is unclear. Indeed, contemporary sources are silent about the provision of specialized military training for adult Spartiates. Not only, as we have seen, are the implications of the references to collective formation drill ambiguous; there is no mention at all of weapons practice or of any sort of mock combat training. It is true that during his discussion of army manoeuvres in the *Lak. Pol.* Xenophon comments that only 'those brought up under the laws of Lykourgos' (i.e. the Spartiates) find it easy to carry on fighting with any one next to them, even when the formation is in disorder (11.7). However, as Humble argues, it is unclear that Xenophon is ascribing this capacity to specialist collective training. The overall tone of his work suggests that he intends it as a social comment on the Spartiates' systematic training in obedience and their fear of the consequences of being deemed cowards.

Furthermore, the assertions of post-classical military manuals cannot be used to supply evidence of training lacking in contemporary sources. The information in the *Taktika* of Asklepiodotos, Aelian and Arrian is largely influenced by Xenophon's account and limited to the single tactic of the Lakonian counter-march: it says nothing about any broader or more systematic training. As for the claims of Vegetius, Everett Wheeler (1983) has shown that they are part of Sparta's post-classical military legend, propagated in particular by Roman attempts to associate their practices with Spartan antecedents. The origins of the legend of Spartan drillmasters (*tactici*) lay in post-classical conflation of various authentic but different classical phenomena. The first phenomenon was itinerant professional *hoplomachoi* (none of them Spartans), who themselves embraced two types of role: one akin to that of sophists, offering diverse military instruction, including weapons training, to paying pupils in their host poleis; the other that of mercenary drillmasters training the armies of other states. The second phenomenon was Sparta's longstanding practice from the late fifth century of sending individual Spartiates abroad as leaders of the armies of other poleis (or, from the mid-fourth century, allowing them to depart as mercenary leaders). During the Hellenistic period the twin roles of the *hoplomachoi* became more specialized. As many poleis came to replace the first type of *hoplomachoi* by hiring their own publicly-paid instructors, the functions of these institutionalized *hoplomachoi* (who included at least one Spartan) became more focused on training suitable to the *gymnasion* and *palaistra*.[75] In contrast, the mercenary military drillmasters focused exclusively on the practical tactical training of armies in times of war, becoming generally known as *tactici*. In Wheeler's words (1983, 15), 'Vegetius' view of Spartan *tactici*…mirrors in part the tradition of Spartan generals and mercenary commanders in foreign service, conflated with the Hellenistic innovation of the functional specialization of the two types of *hoplomachoi*.' The conflation of the war-time role of Spartan military leaders with the peace-time training provided by several classical *hoplomachoi* arose in this context. It offers no evidence for the existence of systematic military training in classical Sparta.

In fact, there is only one occasion on which Xenophon makes explicit reference to adult Spartiates' training for warfare:

> Lykourgos established the principle that for men of that age [sc. over 30], hunting was the noblest occupation, except when some public duty prevented, in order that they might be able to stand the fatigues of soldiering as well as the younger men (*Lak. Pol.* 4.7).

So concerned were the Spartan authorities to ensure the accessibility of hunting to all Spartiates that there were provisions for poorer citizens to borrow hunting dogs from their richer neighbours (*Lak. Pol.* 6.2). This evidence provides some support for Plato's claim of the connection in Sparta between hunting and war. However, in claiming that hunting was devised for military purposes, Plato is clearly over-playing his point. Although the authorities encouraged and facilitated citizens' participation, there is no suggestion that normal Greek hunting practices were modified to suit the requirements of military training. Sparta was not the only place where hunting was regarded as good military training due to its generic develop-ment of physical and mental toughness.[76] Instead, Plato's one-sided claim could equally be reversed to argue that in their focus on hunting Spartan preparations for war followed the Greek norm of unspecialized training. Taken together with the lack of evidence for specialized training, Xenophon's evidence suggests that Spartan preparation for war revolved primarily around not the inculcation of specific collective military skills but the ensuring of individual physical fitness.[77]

In this context we should also consider the role of dance. Several Roman imperial writers claim that dance in Sparta was specially connected to war. According to Lucian (*Peri Orchēseōs* 10), the Spartans conquered everyone with music and rhythm to lead them. Athenaios (*Deipnosophistai* 630e–631a) cites the classical writer, Aristoxenos of Taras, for the statement that the warlike dance known as the *pyrrhichē* received its name from the Spartan Pyrrhikos; and a number of late writers associate the dance with the Spartan heroes, the Dioskouroi.[78] Athenaios states that in his time the dance still persisted in its warlike form only in Sparta, where it was taught to all boys from age five onwards. Philostratos (*On Gymnastics* 19) claims that dance at Sparta was, like other contests, viewed as a preliminary training for war, involving avoiding and hurling missiles, leaping and handling a shield. Certainly, the Spartans were noted for their love of dance from an early date;[79] but we should be cautious of regarding it as providing specialized military training. Despite Lucian's grandiose (and perhaps intentionally comic) general assertion, the details he provides relate merely to the role of music in enabling the Spartans to march in step – the point already made by Thucydides (5.70) *à propos* of the battle of Mantineia. The evidence of Philostratos might appear at first sight more relevant to actual fighting. However, as Graham Anderson has observed, his work is not a technical treatise, but rather, 'the kind of composition that sophists prided themselves on being able to write with little reflection,' dignifying gymnastics and dance with the aura of something ancient, Spartan and military, under the influence of Sparta's post-classical military legend.[80]

The details of the dance described by Philostratos coincide with those of the *pyrrhichē*, as described by Plato (*Laws* 815a), and he may well have copied them from there, adding a Spartan attribution not in Plato's text. As the evidence of Athenaios indicates, the pyrrhic dance was one element of their supposedly ancient traditions assiduously fostered by the Spartans in Roman times, as part of their general re-invention of the *agōgē*.[81] In the classical period, in contrast, notwithstanding the comments of Aristoxenos, there was nothing peculiarly Spartan about the *pyrrhichē*. Ephorus ascribed its origins to Crete, as did the local Spartan historian Sosibios; and it was associated with a variety of other heroes or divinities beside the Dioskouroi.[82] Indeed, the *pyrrhichē*, like other armed dances, is attested throughout the Greek world, taking a variety of forms and serving a variety of purposes, military and non-military (Ceccarelli 1998): for example, the Pyrrhic dancers who appear frequently on fifth-century Attic vases are typically women rather than men.[83] As regards Sparta itself, there is no contemporary evidence mentioning the *pyrrhichē* by name in the archaic or classical period. This is not to deny the existence of Spartan dances performed with weapons or armour, perhaps including the choral dances at the festival of the Gymno-paidiai in which participants expressed their military prowess.[84] Neverthe-less, as Ceccarelli (1998, 99–108) has shown in her detailed examination of the subject, the inadequacies of the surviving evidence make it difficult to establish the exact context of these dances, still less their precise form or content. For the best descriptions of the classical *pyrrhichē* we are compelled to turn to non-Spartan sources: Plato, and before him Euripides (*Andromache* 1129–36). These read more like training in fitness, agility and dexterity, than specific training for hoplite warfare;[85] and no doubt they also provided psychological preparation and a sense of cohesion among the participants. If Plato's *pyrrhichē* draws inspiration from Spartan armed dances, this would be another case in which the Spartans shared the widespread Greek practice of generic physical and psychological preparation for warfare.

This impression of the character of Spartan training is reinforced by the fact that, in contrast to the absence of specialized military training in the daily routine of adult Spartiates, Xenophon provides explicit indications of official compulsion to undertake regular gymnastic exercise. In his *Memorabilia* the second item on the younger Perikles' list of the ways in which the Athenians fail to imitate the Spartans concerns their exercises for bodily fitness (3.5.15). In his *Polity* he outlines how these exercises were publicly regulated, with the most senior citizen in each *gymnasion* being given the responsibility of ensuring the right balance between the amount of physical exercise and quantity of permissible rations (*Lak. Pol.* 5.8–9). In Plato's *Laws* the *gymnasia* are described as one of the institutions devised with a view to war; but, as we have seen, they are also said to underpin the civic virtue of self-control (633a; 635e–636a). Indeed, Xenophon's description of the *gymnasia* portrays them as a civic institution in their own right: he gives no hint that they were designed for the specific purpose of military training.

This concentration on gymnastic activity was maintained even during wartime. During campaigns the only compulsory activity required of Spartan troops when not fighting was to practise gymnastics – twice each day (*Lak. Pol.* 12.5). Xenophon's comment on this regular exercise focuses not on its military effects but on its civic impact, making the troops 'more magnificent' (μεγαλοπρεπεστέρους) and 'more free-spirited' (ἐλευθεριωτέρους). In 396 BC, when King Agesilaos was training his troops in Ephesos during his Asian campaign, he allocated prizes to his hoplite units on the criterion of their physical condition, not their combat formation or co-ordination or their ability with weapons: hence the hoplites devoted themselves not to working as a military unit but to exercising in the *gymnasion* (Xen. *Hell.* 3.4.16).[86] It is in keeping with this approach that Spartiates who won athletic victories in the Crown Games were automatically promoted to one of the most prestigious roles in the entire army, a place in the kings' lifeguard.[87] These passages show a degree of interpenetration between gymnastic activities and military training, but not – as Plato claimed – in terms of the impact of the military on Spartiate life in times of peace. Rather, it was gymnastic activities that penetrated into their life in times of war. In general, it seems, Spartiate training for warfare was pursued through the standard pursuits of leisured elites throughout the Greek world.

These observations lead on to a further point. Although the daily routine of adult Spartiates was structured to some extent by official expectations of engagement in the *gymnasion*, hunting and the evening common meals, this regimentation had its limits. Evidence for their other daily activities suggests that adult Spartiates had sizeable amounts of time available for personal business, such as approaches to their patrons or pederastic partners, political negotiations, economic transactions in the *agora*, and supervision of their estates.[88] An adult Spartiate's daily life was not excessively dominated by his civic duties, still less by those aspects of his duties that pertained to his role as a warrior.

The period of a male Spartiate's life that was undoubtedly dominated by civic duties was, of course, his youth; and it is noteworthy that ancient writers' accounts of the Spartiates' focus upon training for war all locate it primarily in the upbringing.[89] Accordingly, the youngest soldiers could be given special responsibilities in battle: for example, service in the king's lifeguard and sorties from the phalanx in pursuit of mobile enemy troops.[90] The main accounts of the upbringing in Xenophon's *Polity of the Lakedaimonians* (chs. 2–4) and Plutarch's *Life of Lykourgos* (chs. 16–18) indicate that it included training in qualities such as physical endurance, tenacity, competitiveness, obedience and collective activity which formed a good grounding for participation in hoplite warfare. Once again, however, there is no strong evidence that the upbringing was dominated by training in specialist military skills. Advocates of this view sometimes cite the reported comments of a Spartan supporter, Prokles of Phleious, who in a speech in 369 BC to the Athenian assembly asserted that the Spartans 'carry on their training from their very boyhood with a view to war by land' (Xen. *Hell.* 7.1.8). The context of this statement, however, is a discussion, not of the focus of the upbringing, but of Sparta's focus on land rather than naval warfare. Although it confirms that military preparation was one element throughout the upbringing (which is not at issue), it does not say anything regarding its importance in comparison with the upbringing's other functions. Aristotle (*Politics* 1324b7–9), in contrast, does claim that the system of education was mainly framed with a view to war. However, the precise nature of this warlike focus is revealed in his subsequent discussion of this education (1338b24–29):

> And again we know that even the Lakonians, although so long as they persisted by themselves in their laborious exercises they surpassed all other peoples, now fall behind others both in gymnastic and in military contests (κἀν τοῖς γυμνικοῖς ἀγῶσι κἀν τοῖς πολεμικοῖς); for they used to excel not because they exercised their young men (τοὺς νέους γυμνάζειν) in this fashion, but only because they trained and their adversaries did not.

Aristotle indicates clearly that, as with Spartiate adults, the training of her young men (his use of the word *neoi* probably signifies men in their 20s) that produced Sparta's military success was essentially gymnastic and physical: hence the commencement of such training by other poleis had undermined Spartan pre-eminence in both spheres. Similarly, neither Xenophon's nor Plutarch's accounts, which cover the entire upbringing from age 7 to age 30, makes any mention of training in military drills or use of weapons.[91] Likewise, there is no attestation of simulated hoplite combat. The sole reference in Xenophon's account is to impromptu scuffles among the *hēbōntes*

(*Lak. Pol.* 4.4–6). Plato refers to collective battles, but these are explicitly stated to be with bare hands (*Laws* 633b). Plutarch mentions fighting among the young boys (*Lyk.* 16.5), but there is no indication that this was anything akin to mock warfare. The so-called 'mock battle' at the Platanistas, attested only in Roman sources, located on an artificial landscape and marked by an antiquarian evocation of divine and heroic beings, is almost certainly of post-classical origin.[92]

Although many aspects of the upbringing had a positive impact on adult Spartiates' subsequent performance in the army, to reduce the purpose and function of the upbringing to primarily a preparation for warriorhood is to underestimate its wide-ranging functions of socializing Spartan boys into all aspects of adult citizen life. Ducat (1999a, 44) hits, I think, the right note: 'ce n'est pas seulement le guerrier qu'elle veut former...c'est le citoyen, dont la guerre n'est qu'une des activités'. Indeed, as he rightly notes, certain aspects of the upbringing seem irrelevant or even ill-adapted to preparation for participation in warfare. Despite the rationalizing explanations of Xenophon, the systematic under-nourishment of the boys (*Lak. Pol.* 2.5–6) was counter-productive to the raising of powerfully-built soldiers;[93] and their consequent furtive thieving (2.6–7) no real training for obtaining supplies on campaign. It was features such as these which led Nigel Kennell in his book *The Gymnasium of Virtue* to remind us, rightly, of the ritual aspects of many of the socializing features of the Spartiate upbringing, 'a conglomeration of activities with fundamentally religious foundations, not merely a Lacedae-monian Sandhurst or West Point' (1985, 135; cf. 123).[94]

Perhaps the most notable case in point is the institution of the *krypteia*, in which selected young men lived a temporary period of privation in the remote countryside, targeting helots for murder as part of their task.[95] As we have seen, Plato (*Laws* 633b–c) claimed the *krypteia* as another of the institutions devised for war, on account of its function as a painful training in endurance (πολύπονος πρὸς τὰς καρτερήσεις). The claim is repeated, with a similar emphasis on its physical aspects, in a surviving scholion on the passage: 'it was also another form of exercise (γυμνασίας) for war'. This interpretation, it should be noted, is completely absent from those sources deriving from Aristotle and his school, who view it rather as an internal security measure against the helots.[96] Nevertheless, the notion of the *krypteia* as military apprenticeship has had a long hold within classical scholarship, going well beyond Plato's and the scholiast's emphasis on its role as physical preparation. Since the early nineteenth century several studies have likened the institution to the organized territorial patrols of the Athenian *peripoloi* and the *agronomoi* in Plato's imaginary Magnesia which served as a military apprenticeship for their future lives as hoplites.[97] Yet, as Jeanmaire almost a century ago (1913) and Ducat (1997a; 1997b), more recently, have pointed out, the activities of the *kryptoi* – sent out without specific instructions, operating on their own initiative distant from official supervision or control, barefoot, with only daggers for offensive weapons,[98] and hiding themselves from others' view with no facilities for reporting any information gained – were neither analogous to those of territorial patrols nor an apprenticeship for hoplite warfare. In the words of Vidal-Naquet, in this temporary period of ritual inversion common to many societies, 'the *kryptos* appears in every respect to be an anti-hoplite', the *krypteia* and the life of the hoplite 'symmetrical opposites' (1986, 147, 113). The essential irrelevance of the *krypteia* to the military training of Spartiate warriors is shown, above all, by the fact that it involved only a select minority of young men, for whom it appears most clearly as an intensive ritualized period of personal trials (one of which was the killing of helots) in an increasingly selective process of choosing Sparta's future leaders.[99]

Discussion of the ritual aspects of the upbringing raises the question whether the Spartiates' religious practices were especially marked by a military orientation, an issue explicitly addressed in Robert Parker's classic survey of Spartan religion (1989). It is clear that Spartan religion included a number of military elements, such as the festival called the Promacheia and several prominent armed statues (Athena Poliouchos on the acropolis, Apollo at Amyklai and Thornax, Aphrodite near Sparta itself).[100] The Spartan acropolis was a place of deities with multiple military connections. Besides Athena Poliouchos, it included a sanctuary of Aphrodite Areia and was used as a place of assembly for men of military age and a destination of an armed procession of young men. The archaeological record includes several dedications of military equipment.[101]

On the other hand, armed cult statues were by no means peculiar to Sparta;[102] and the associations of the acropolis were more than purely military. The deities of the acropolis included ones with eminently civic or non-military attributes, such as Zeus Kosmetas ('Orderer'), Zeus Hypatos ('Most High') and Athena Erganē ('Worker').[103] Military dedications at its sanctuaries in the archaic and classical periods are outnumbered by non-military votives, including items relating to athletic and equestrian success, as well as female dedications of mirrors and bronze bells.[104] At the sanctuaries of Artemis Orthia and the Menelaion, too, the lead figurines dedicated at the sanctuary in the sixth and fifth centuries include a notable series of hoplite warriors; but they are outnumbered by a range of other types. Their military role was just one of the aspects of citizen life for which Spartiates supplicated or thanked the gods.[105]

Likewise, military elements were only one aspect of Spartan festivals. The Gymnopaidiai commemorated the mid-sixth-century 'Battle of the

Champions' (Sosibios, *FGrH* 595 F 5); but, although its competitive dancing is characterized by Plato (*Laws* 663c) as a severe test of endurance, their military character is unclear, since the choirs danced 'unarmed' and included boys of pre-military and old men of post-military age.[106] Although the Karneia was described by the mid-third-century writer Demetrios of Skepsis as 'an imitation of military life' (ap. Athen. 141e), it also included musical and athletic contests. In general, as Parker (1989, 146) comments, 'the ethos of many Spartan festivals seems to have been closer to a *fête champêtre* than to the parade of tanks in Red Square'.[107] The same limited role of military features is evident in other religious contexts. The cult of Ares is not especially prominent; and, although the cult of the Dioskouroi had military connections, the twin gods were also associated with Spartan athletics.[108] Finally, there were central aspects of civic Spartan religious life without military connotations, such as the cult of Demeter (Parker 1988) and the priesthoods of Zeus Lakedaimon and Zeus Ouranios, the primary priesthoods of Sparta's kings (Hdt. 6.56).

One institution in which military organization was closely linked with civic life was the daily common meals, the *syssitia*. Herodotus includes them – alongside the *enōmotiai* and the otherwise unknown *triēkades* – among his list of military institutions created by Lykourgos (1.65).[109] Xenophon describes them by a name with military connotations, *syskēnia* (*Lak. Pol.* 5.2; 9.4; 13.1, 7; *Hell.* 5.3.20). Plato, as we have seen, included them among his list of institutions devised with a view to war (*Laws* 633a). It seems likely that the *syssitia* were closely connected to the organization of the smallest units of the army, the *enōmotiai*, with the members of two or more *syssitia* combining to form one *enōmotia*.[110] The idea of the penetration of an essentially military institution into everyday Spartiate life is most clearly expressed in Van Wees' judgement (2004, 108) that, 'the mess-groups which were elsewhere constituted informally for the duration of a campaign were a permanent feature of social life'.

However, it would be mistaken to view the *syssitia* in predominantly military terms. Aristotle twice indicates that the authentic Spartan name for the *syssitia* was not Xenophon's militarily-oriented term *syskēnia* but a non-military term, *phiditia* (*Pol.* 1271a26–7; 1272a1–4). In the second of these passages Aristotle states that the Spartans had originally called their messes by the more militarily-oriented Cretan name *andreia*. This statement is supported by Ephorus (*FGrH* 70 F 149, ap. Strabo, *Geography* 10.4.18) who cites the appearance of the older term in a passage of Alkman (fr. 98, Campbell) around 600 BC. Both writers indicate that this name had been abandoned by their day. As for *syskēnia*, not only was it not the authentic Spartan term, it is also not the sole term used by Xenophon, who in two separate passages employs the name *philitia* (*Lak. Pol.* 2.2; 5.6). These passages may well be the source of Plutarch's comments (*Lyk.* 12.1) that *philitia* and the Spartan term *pheiditia* were equivalents, signifying the civic virtues of friendship and friendliness, or alternatively of simplicity and thrift.[111] Whether Plutarch is right or not, these contemporary non-military names accurately reflect the essential civic roles of the *syssitia* in ensuring social cohesion and moderation in the consumption of food and drink (Xen. *Lak. Pol.* 5.4–7; Fisher 1989). Hence Plato also linked the *syssitia* to the virtue of self-control (*Laws* 635e–636a). A fragment of Kritias (fr. B6, Diels-Kranz, ap. Athen. 432d) nicely expresses the ideal of their atmosphere of friendly, well-ordered sociability. One element of this sociability was the voluntary additional donations of food known as the *epaikla*, which enabled citizens to share with their companions the products either of their surplus wealth or their success in the hunt, while in the process engaging in largesse and personal display.[112] This largesse was especially evident in the royal *syssition*, in which each king had an additional meal portion with which he could honour other citizens (Hdt. 6.57; Xen. *Lak. Pol.* 15.4; *Ages.* 5.1). In all these respects the *syssitia* served as *loci* for a range of civic and personal activities which owed little or nothing to a military function.

Indeed, a Spartiate's membership of a *syssition* was more closely linked to his civic position than to his role as a warrior. This is most evident with the royal *syssition*, whose membership in Sparta differed markedly from the membership of the royal tent on campaign;[113] and also with the *syssition* of the ephors, who dined together by virtue of their civic office.[114] The primacy of the link to civic rather than military position is also evident in the case of ordinary *syssitia*. Membership of a *syssition* was a criterion for the possession of citizen status: failure to make one's food contributions led to exclusion from citizenship (Arist. *Pol.* 1271a26–37; 1272a12–16). The *syssitia* included elderly men no longer in the army, and they were attended by youths not yet of age for military service (Xen. *Lak. Pol.* 3.5). Conversely, some Spartiates who had lost their citizen rights and were thereby excluded from a *syssition*, still fought in the army.[115]

In view of these considerations, it would be tempting to reverse Van Wees' judgement by saying that civic dining-groups, which were elsewhere constituted solely during peace-time, were in Sparta a permanent feature of military life. A more balanced judgement, however, is that the *syssitia*, like the upbringing, served a dual function, structuring both civic and military activity. The striking feature of Spartan society is the complementarity and integration of the two spheres in such a way that the Spartans' civic institutions and practices provided support for their military activities without being dictated by them. We have already seen examples of this in the selection of Olympic athletic victors for service in the king's bodyguard and in the use of hunting as the primary means of military training for citizens over age 30, supported by provisions extending access to hunting dogs to all citizens.

The nature of the relationship between the civic and military spheres can be seen most clearly by considering how the Spartans dealt with the two extreme forms of behaviour in war: cowardice and death in battle. Before doing so, however, we need to clear away one aspect of the Spartan mirage which has contributed significantly to misunderstanding of Spartan policy. The image of the ferocious Spartan mother, urging her sons into battle, burying them cheerfully on their glorious death or killing them on their inglorious return, has been for centuries a powerful image apparently symbolizing the dominance of military ideology over family maternal emotion. But we need to remember that the sources of these images (the *Lakainōn Apophthegmata* and various *exempla* in sources of Roman Imperial and Byzantine date) are all post-classical.[116] Their tone is redolent of Hellenistic and later moral and philosophical ideals, not the ethics of the classical Spartan polis (Hammond 1979/80). In particular, the famous saying of the Spartan mother to her departing warrior son 'Either this or on this [shield]' (*Lak. Apoph.* Anon. no. 16 = Plut. *Mor.* 241f) and stories of mothers burying their sons (Anon. nos. 2, 8 = *Mor.* 241a, c), cannot relate to authentic classical practice, since (as we shall see) fallen warriors were never brought back home for burial in Sparta in the classical period.

In contrast to this post-classical evidence, the classical sources make it clear that the issue of cowardice in battle (as Jean Ducat's article in this volume demonstrates) was not merely a matter for private judgement, but a public affair subject to official investigation and adjudication. Cowards suffered both social exclusion and juridical and political penalties, such as exclusion from office-holding, incapacity to conduct legal purchase and sale, lack of immunity against physical violence and, probably, prohibition against contracting a legitimate marriage.[117] However, when there were pressing countervailing circumstances, the Spartans usually put them above the strict application of military ethics. The case of those who surrendered at Sphakteria is instructive: they initially went unpunished (and some were even appointed to important posts), were subsequently made *atimoi* only due to fear of revolution, and their penalties were ultimately revoked (Thuc. 5.34). The numerous survivors of Leuktra who were adjudged to be *tresantes* were likewise let off without punishment, according to Plutarch (*Ages.* 30.2), due to fear of revolution. Similarly, it was decided not to inflict *atimia* upon the young men among the survivors of the defeat at Megalopolis, despite the opposition of Akrotatos, the heir to the Agiad throne (Diod. 19.70).

As for those who died 'la belle mort spartiate', to borrow the term of Nicole Loraux (1977), it is clear that death in battle brought prestige to the dead warrior's family. Xenophon's accounts of the Spartans' reception of the news of the defeats at Lechaion and Leuktra depict the dead soldiers' kin looking 'bright and happy', even going about 'like prize-winners' (*Hell.* 4.5.10; 6.4.16; cf. Plut. *Ages.* 29.5–7). The noble death of the young Kleonymos at Leuktra brought honour to his *erastēs*, Archidamos.[118] All those who died in battle received honorific official burial abroad in a collective tomb, or *polyandreion*.[119] However, the polis took steps to limit the impact on society at home. Some special fallen warriors – those from the 'Battle of the Champions' and from Thermopylai – were specially honoured in Sparta with annual ceremonies.[120] There was no cult of the war dead in general, no regular public ceremonial for ordinary military deaths to compare with the public funeral games and speeches for fallen warriors in classical Athens.[121] In addition, after *c.* 550 BC the collective burials of ordinary citizen warriors always took place abroad, on or close to the battlefield.[122] There was no role in the burial for the deceased's kin; no opportunity of a glorious family burial at home.[123] The sole distinctive privilege for a fallen warrior was that an inscription could be set up on a memorial stone.[124] A number of these memorials survive: the ΕΝ ΠΟΛΕΜΟΙ stelai studied by Polly Low (this volume), mostly very modest in size and decoration, bearing only the simplest of texts: 'X [died] in battle'. With this exception, there were no special military decorations to mark the deaths of fallen warriors. Indeed, all Spartiates, however they died, were entitled to burial in the crimson cloak, the *phoinikis*, which they wore in battle.[125] Once again, we have complementarity between the civic and military spheres, with efforts taken to prevent the domination of the former by the latter.

This combination of complementarity and control can also be seen in the case of Sparta's primary military leaders, the kings. As the studies of Carlier (1984, 240–324) and Cartledge (1987) have shown, the kings stood at the apex of Sparta's military hierarchy as they did in the political, religious and social spheres. Their command of Sparta's armies offered the kings the potential for the advancement of their political power. However, the polis took steps to limit the impact of military command upon internal politics and society. After *c.* 506 the declaration of war and the allocation of command to one or other of the kings were moved into the hands of other decision-making bodies (Carlier 1977). Two ephors supervised the king on campaign and prosecutions for misconduct were frequent.[126] Although those with business to transact dealt in the first instance with the king, there were state-appointed officials to whom he remitted matters to do with justice, finance or booty (Xen. *Lak. Pol.* 13.10–11). Doubtless on some occasions a king could influence the way these officials handled their business. However, the evidence regarding the official booty-sellers (*laphyropōlai*) suggests that in general their presence severely restricted a king's capacity to dispose of booty to his own advantage.[127] As in life, so in death. It is notable that the greatest occasions of kingly ceremonial, royal burials, appear to have been free of military aspects and were attended not just by Spartan warriors but by all sections of the population of Lakedaimon, including a man and woman from each free household, and even helots too (Hdt. 6.58).

Conversely, ordinary Spartiates seem to have maintained a distinction between their role as soldiers and their political role as citizens. As already noted, the Lakedaimonian army was organized in an extraordinarily stratified fashion. Individual soldiers, moreover, swore a special oath of obedience to their officers.[128] It has often been hypothesized that these habits of obedience dictated the tenor of Spartan politics. 'Can we imagine', Moses Finley asked, 'that the obedient, disciplined Spartan soldier dropped his normal habits when he was assembled not as a soldier but as a citizen…?'[129] To a large extent, the answer to Finley's rhetorical question seems to be the opposite of what he intended. The classic case in point is that of 418 BC, when King Agis II made an unpopular truce with the Argives (Thuc. 5.60, 63). The army accepted his decision in obedience to the law, but already began to complain bitterly amongst themselves. Their indignation, still active on their return to Sparta, subsequently boiled over when the truce proved to have failed. Agis only marginally escaped personal punishment and had his authority limited by the imposition of ten advisers without whose agreement he was not empowered to act. In this incident 'the Spartans were well able to distinguish the roles of soldier and citizen' (Andrewes 1966, 3), to differentiate between their duty of military obedience to Agis and their right to political dissent.[130] Similarly, in 431 the majority of Spartiates rejected the arguments of the experienced general King Archidamos in favour of those of the ephor Sthenelaidas (Thuc. 1.79–87). This political distancing from military leaders was not limited to occasions when they were advocating less bellicose policies. During the siege of Phleious in 381 many of the Lakedaimonian troops expressed their political disagreement with King Agesilaos' aggressive policy (Xen. *Hell.* 5.3.16). In winter 379/8, despite his many years of military success, the king felt compelled to decline the command against the Thebans due to the expected adverse reactions of other citizens (5.4.13). Such independence of mind is evident even with regard to more purely military decisions. The annals of Spartan warfare show several examples of subordinate officers, and even ordinary soldiers, dissenting by word or deed from the actions of their commanders.[131] This is not, of course, to argue that Spartan decision-making was conducted along democratic lines. As recent analyses have shown, leading Spartiates, especially the kings and *gerontes*, wielded immense social and economic influence over political affairs.[132] The oligarchic character of Spartan politics owed more to such factors than to unthinking obedience on the part of the Spartiate soldier.

Overall, then, the military elements in Spartan society were clearly significant, but not dominant over other aspects of polis life in the way that has often been claimed. It is true that Sparta society was capable of producing warlike leaders. The classic example is Klearchos, whom Xenophon's *Anabasis* (2.5.1) characterizes as 'a man who was both fitted for war and fond of war to the last degree'. But Xenophon himself did not think that all Spartiates were like Klearchos (Tuplin 2004, 27); and the fact that to indulge his pursuit of warfare he had to spend his final years in exile illustrates the dissonance between his attitudes and those of other citizens.[133] For most citizens, their role as warriors was only part, albeit an important part, of a wider range of citizen activities. To characterize the Spartans as 'a community of professional soldiers' is consequently too narrow. Notwithstanding the professionalism of the Spartan army, a Spartiate was, in the words of Jean Ducat (1999a, 36), not so much 'un guerrier professionnel' as 'un *citoyen* professionnel'. Classical Sparta was far more than simply a 'military society'.

Notes

[1] To my knowledge the issues I shall address have been raised only in one recent account: an excellent chapter by Jean Ducat published, not as a scholarly article, but in a manual aimed at French students preparing for the *Agrégation* (Ducat 1999a). I am grateful to Paul Cartledge and to my co-editor, Anton Powell, for their stringent critiques of my argument; to Paul Christesen for assistance regarding the use of Spartan militarism in U.S. intelligence analysis; and to audiences at Austin, Copenhagen, Manchester, Sparti, Torun and Warsaw for many helpful comments and suggestions.

[2] Cavaignac 1948, 25; Kahrstedt 1948, 6–7; Passerini 1952, 71; Marrou 1956, 14–25; Kiechle 1963, 246–7; Snodgrass 1980, 109; Ducrey 1985, 68–9; Bengtson 1988, 68; Powell 1988, 215; Garlan 1989, 14, 144; Hanson 1989, 38; Kagan 1990, 72; Damsgaard-Madsen 1993, 55; Rahe 1994, 125–6; Briant and Lévêque 1995, 197; Kagan 1996, 19; Martin 1996, 71, 75, 77; French 1997, 244; Orrieux and Schmitt Pantel 1999, 73–4; Fornis 2003, 74.

[3] *Pol.* 1269b25–6; 1271b2–6; 1324b7–9; 1334a40–b4; 1338b25–39.

[4] Contrast, for example, scholarly assumptions that Aristotle's analysis of her military orientation reflects a fundamental characteristic of Spartan society with the view that his assessment of the minimal influence of Sparta's kings reflects only contemporary circumstances (e.g. contrast Ste Croix 1972, 91 with 138–9) or that his account of private landownership describes only recent corruptions (David 1982/3). Similarly, contrast the authority implicitly accorded by Hooker to Aristotle's comments on Spartan militarism with his marginalization of the same writer's account of the divisibility of Spartiate estates (contrast Hooker 1980, 141 with 116 and 142–3). For other examples

of the marginalization of Aristotle's evidence on Spartiate land tenure, Hodkinson 2000, 105 n. 6.

⁵ For qualification of Aristotle's account of Spartan women on the grounds that his 'quintessentially sexist' approach led him to over-estimate the extent of female influence, Cartledge 1981, esp. 104–5; cf. also Millender 1999, 371. His 'misogynistic perspective' is criticized even by sympathetic modern interpreters (e.g. Pomeroy 2002, 151 and 160).

⁶ I shall provide such a survey in a forthcoming book examining issues of Spartan militarism in comparative historical perspective.

⁷ The following is a brief summary of Hodkinson 2006a.

⁸ On German self-identification with Sparta under the Third Reich, and its antecedents, Rawson 1969, 306–43; Christ 1986; Rebenich 2002, 330–2, with extensive references; and generally Losemann 1977. Academic portrayals of Spartan militarism in Berve 1937; von Vacano et al. 1940.

⁹ Cf. Crossman 1937, 239; Murray 1946, 202, 204: a lecture to the Royal Society of Arts in 1941, especially interesting for its association of Sparta both with German militarism and with primitive savages. The linkage of Spartan militarism with Nazism is also evident in French thought: Marrou 1956, 23.

¹⁰ Greenslade 1970, 9–10; Hildebrandt 1985, 18 and 139–40, citing statements in October 1984 by former Chairman of the National Intelligence Council, Henry S. Rowen; Congressional Information Service 1984, 27 (testimony of Robert M. Gates, Deputy Director of Intelligence, CIA, on 21 November 1984, to the Congress Joint Economic Committee, Subcommittee on International Trade, Finance, and Security Economics; cf. Gates 1996, 318–19); Bernstein 1989 (a study prepared for the Director of Net Assessment, Office of the Secretary of Defense); 1997, 275–6. The reservations about the analogy expressed by the Rand Corporation analyst, Abraham S. Becker, in a report prepared for the United States Air Force (Becker 1981, 4 and 35) exercised no apparent brake upon its subsequent recurrence.

¹¹ Cf. Hanson 1989, 38: 'Sparta's closed militaristic society'; Kagan 1990, 72: 'Sparta was a military state'; 1996, 19: 'The entire system was designed to produce soldiers'; Rahe 1994, 125: 'turning the city into a camp, the *pólis* [*sic*] into an army; and the citizen into a soldier'. Suggestive backdrop: Bernstein was taught by Kagan and his 1997 article was published in the latter's *Festschrift* (Hamilton and Krentz 1997); Rowen and Kagan are both members of the *Project for the New American Century*, as was Bernstein until his death in 2001; Rahe too was a pupil of Kagan, dedicated his book to him (and to W.G. Forrest!) and also contributed to his *Festschrift*. On Hanson, cf. the title of his National Public Radio interview on March 13, 2004: 'Ancient Sparta and the U.S. War Against Terrorism'.

¹² I owe the phrase to P.J. Rhodes 1997, 3.

¹³ Kennell 1995, 143–5.

¹⁴ The terms are used in an especially indiscriminate fashion in modern discussions aimed at a non-academic audience: e.g. Murray 1946, 202; Bernstein 1989, v.

¹⁵ Cf. Vagts 1959, 13–17; Dawson 1996, 4, 189–91.

¹⁶ Berghahn 1981, 105–18, esp. 116.

¹⁷ e.g. Herbert Spencer's *The Principles of Sociology* (1882, 568–602): although Spencer himself did not use the term 'militarism', but the phrase 'militant type of society'.

¹⁸ Ducat 1999a, 45–7.

[19] Dawson 1996, 4; Ducat 1999a, 47, citing P. Veyne.

[20] Cf. Finley 1986, 171–3 (though he mistakenly characterizes Sparta's fourth-century critics as condemning her for being excessively militaristic). Even the Spartans' ethic of preferring a noble death in battle to a life in disgrace was allied to the proposition that such behaviour actually led to less loss of life (Xen. *Lak. Pol.* 9.1–2), a sentiment already present in Tyrtaios fr. 11.11–13 (Gerber).

[21] Supporters of Spartan imperialism also applauded her for the same hard-headed focus on military conquest condemned by their critics (Aristotle *Politics* 1333b11–22).

[22] Cf. also frs. 10 and 11 (Gerber).

[23] Cf. esp. frs. 5, 8–12, with Testimonia 1–12 (Gerber).

[24] Cf. frs. 2, 4, 5 (Gerber).

[25] Athenaios' own commentary adds that they were also sung on the march; but the context again is on campaign.

[26] Marriage alliances: Hdt. 5.39; 6.61–2, 65, 71; 7.205 (although several of these incidents concern the royal houses, other leading families are also thoroughly implicated). Chariot-racing and panhellenic games: 6.70, 103. Guest-friendships: 5.63, 70, 90; 9.9, 76. Economic and financial transactions: 1.153; 6.62, 86; 9.81; cf. also bribery: Hdt. 3.56, 148; 5.51; 6.50, 66, 72, 82; 8.5.

[27] For a balanced discussion arguing that Thucydides' speeches should be viewed neither wholly in terms of 'what was really said' nor 'what was appropriate', see Hornblower 1987, 45–72, concluding with the judgement that 'whether Thucydides reported or invented the speeches, or did something in between, the sentiments contained in those speeches can never be used as evidence for his own opinions'.

[28] Cf. Cawkwell 1972, 262 n. 4; Siewert 1977; Vidal-Naquet 1986, 97–8.

[29] Figueira 2003, esp. 58–9. Cf. 1.144, where the practice is juxtaposed by Perikles to Athenian measures in the Megarian decree.

[30] Refs. in Figueira 2003, 59 n. 59.

[31] I follow Hornblower's translation and interpretation of 'this difficult passage' (1991–6, i.128–9).

[32] Thuc. 4.108; 5.16; 8.12, 32, 38.

[33] Thuc. 4.37–40; 5.34.

[34] Ducat (this volume) provides an extensive analysis; see also Hodkinson 1983, 272 n. 98 for fuller remarks on the uncertainties in the decision to surrender.

[35] 1.118; cf. the 'hawkish' interpretation of this statement in Ste Croix 1972, 94–5.

[36] I have discussed these oscillations in detail in Hodkinson 1983, 265–76, with details of Thucydides' presentation at 265–7 and 269–72; cf. also Westlake 1968, 122–65, 277–307.

[37] The following comments are an abbreviated version of my discussion in Hodkinson 2005, 257–8.

[38] *Busiris* 19–20. For criticism of Spartan imperialism in Isokrates' other works, *Panegyrikos* 103–5, 122–32; *Plataikos* 12–15, 40–1, 62; *Areopagitikos* 7; *On the Peace* 95–103; *To Philip* 47–50. Cf. Cloché 1933; Ollier 1933, 326–71.

[39] *Panathenaikos* 218–29; cf. Gray 1994, 230–1, 267.

[40] 1270a4–6: παρεῖχον τῷ νομοθέτῃ προφδοπεποιημένους διὰ τὸν στρατιωτικὸν βίον (πολλὰ γὰρ ἔχει μέρη τῆς ἀρετῆς).

[41] Cf. also 1307a34–6: Sparta, 'where properties keep coming into the hands of a few',

is cited as a prime example of acquisitiveness by the *gnōrimoi*.

⁴² Later in the work, at 688a and 705d, the Athenian reminds his interlocutors of their earlier statements, but he does not engage in further discussion of the character of Spartan society.

⁴³ In this context it is worth noting that the underlying premise of Dawson's view, that Xenophon's *Polity* is a pro-Spartan work, has been subject to renewed challenge in recent years. For recent arguments for the work's critical approach to Sparta, Proietti 1987; Humble 1997; 1999; 2004; for older arguments, Strauss 1939; Higgins 1977.

⁴⁴ As noted by Lipka (2002, 188), although he deems Xenophon's comment to be tendentious in the face of the insistence of his contemporaries upon the preponderance of the warlike element.

⁴⁵ I adhere to the manuscripts' placing of the chapter of criticism as ch. 14: also defended recently by Humble 2004.

⁴⁶ Xen. *Memorabilia* 3.5.15–16; Ephorus, ap. Diod. 7.12.2–4; Dem. *Against Leptines* 107–8; Isok. *Panathenaikos* 178, 217, 258.

⁴⁷ Of the sources cited in the previous note, Xenophon contrasts Spartan *homonoia* with Athenian quarrelsomeness in politics and the law; Isokrates with the *stasis*, property redistribution and revolution in other poleis. Demosthenes praises *homonoia* among elite citizens. Ephoros links *homonoia* with bravery (*androsynē*); the subject in question, however, is not military discipline but the laws of Lykourgos and the right form of government.

⁴⁸ On the last point, cf. also Isokrates, *Archidamos* (61): 'we still remain faithful to the laws and ways of life which we established here in the very beginning'.

⁴⁹ Van Wees 2004, 83–5; cf. Hunt 1998. One might qualify this generalization due to the status of the *perioikoi* as full Lakedaimonians, though not Spartiates. Cf. Millender (this volume).

⁵⁰ Van Wees 2004, 73–4.

⁵¹ On the *hippeis*, see Figueira, this volume.

⁵² Van Wees 2004, 59.

⁵³ Cf. the careful guarding of the baggage train during battle: Van Wees 2004, 105, with refs. at 280 n. 12.

⁵⁴ Van Wees 2004, 98, 243–4. Strictly speaking, the evidence for this oath relates only to the battle of Plataia in 479, but it is likely that it was a more longstanding feature of Spartan practice. The oath was backed up with a special punishment for indiscipline, of standing holding one's shield (Xen. *Hell.* 3.1.9).

⁵⁵ Pritchett 1974–91, ii.243; Hornblower 2000, 57–60; Van Wees 2004, 108–13, esp. 111 (with ancient source refs. at 282 n. 35).

⁵⁶ Xen. *Lak. Pol.* 12.5–7; Van Wees 2004, 108–10.

⁵⁷ Berghahn 1981, 105.

⁵⁸ Van Wees 2004, 20–2. The texts are Thuc. 1.127, 139.

⁵⁹ Van Wees 2004, 22–5; cf. Hdt. 7.148–9, 157–62; Xen. *Hell.* 3.2.21–2, 26; 3.3.5.

⁶⁰ e.g. Hdt. 3.148; 5.49; 6.84, 108; Thuc. 1.109; 5.82.

⁶¹ e.g. Grundy 1948, i.219; Ste Croix 1972, 89–94; Hornblower 1983, 99; Cartledge 1987, 160–79.

⁶² Thuc. 4.80; Plato, *Laws* 777b–c; Arist. *Pol.* 1269a36–9.

⁶³ Finley 1986, 174–5; Garlan 1988, 101–6; Van Wees 2003; 2004, 30.

⁶⁴ Cf. the revolts of the Kyllyrioi at Syracuse and the Penestai in Thessaly (Hdt. 7.155;

Xen. *Hell.* 2.3.36). For full details of other revolts, Van Wees 2003, with a convenient summary on pp. 72–3.

[65] See the convenient summary of instances in Van Wees 2004, 124–6, with refs. to ancient sources and modern studies, to which add Kulesza 1999.

[66] Cf., recently, Van Wees 1999, 2–6; Hodkinson 2000, 2.

[67] αἰεὶ γὰρ τὰ πολλὰ Λακεδαιμονίοις πρὸς τοὺς Εἵλωτας τῆς φυλακῆς πέρι μάλιστα καθειστήκει. I follow the commentaries of Gomme (1956, 547–8) and Hornblower (1991–6, ii.264–5) in adopting the minimalist reading of the phrase, rather than that most Lakedaimonian institutions were designed to guard against the helots.

[68] Thucydides indicates that, when the Athenians had first occupied Pylos, the Spartans had treated the news with complacency, completing their festival without any sense of urgency or threat (4.6). Neither had the Athenian forces, apart from Demosthenes, initially foreseen any great potential for helot revolt (4.3–4). Only when the Messenians began to achieve some success in fomenting helot desertions did the Spartans become fearful that these troubles might spread (4.41, 55). This is not the only occasion when Thucydides' 'editorial comment' is at odds with his reporting of events: cf. the contradictions between his editorial judgements and reporting regarding the popularity of Athenian imperialism: Ste Croix 1954/5.

[69] This is implied both in Xenophon's account of the conspiracy of Kinadon (one of Kinadon's arguments for the feasibility of his plot is that agricultural and craft implements would be adequate weapons for the rebels against men who were unarmed: *Hell.* 3.3.7) and in Kritias' remarks (fr. B37, ap. Libanius, *Orations* 25.63) on the precautions taken by individual Spartiates against their helots (his comment that Spartans on campaign always carried a spear implies that they did not do so in their everyday lives at home).

[70] Hodkinson 2000, 113–35; 2003.

[71] Asklepiodotos, *Taktika Kephalaia* 10.13–15; Aelian, *Taktika* 27–8, 34.3–5; Arrian, *Technē Taktikē* 23–4; 31–2.

[72] Cf. Xenophon's use of inclusive terminology in his references to the '*Lakōnikē taxis*' (11.5) and '*Lakedaimonioi*' (11.8), in contrast to 'those brought up under the laws of Lykourgos' (11.7)

[73] The '*kaloi kagathoi* among the *perioikoi*', who were free to volunteer for Agesipolis' campaign against Olynthos in 381 (Xen. *Hell.* 5.3.9), were, as the text implies, a leisured minority untypical of the bulk of perioikic soldiers. Note that, when levied, the perioikic troops normally had to journey from their own poleis scattered throughout Spartan territory: e.g. Thuc. 4.8.

[74] The exact level of unit at which the *perioikoi* were integrated is unclear: refs. to the extensive bibliography on this subject in Hodkinson 1983 255 n. 41, to which add Cartledge 1987, 37–43. Lazenby's argument (1986) that the *perioikoi* were not incorporated in the army until after Leuktra has not met with wide agreement. In fact, Spartiate-perioikic integration may have begun earlier than usually thought. The 'thousand picked Lakedaimonians' at Thermopylai already included 700 *perioikoi* alongside the 300 Spartiates; and even at Plataia their separation is not as clear as usually thought (sources and discussion in Van Wees 2004, 83–4 and 275 nn. 25–6).

[75] On Laidas the Spartan, honoured for his instruction of the citizens of Gytheion, *IG* V.i.1523.

[76] See the comments of Xenophon, *On Hunting* 1.18; 12.1–9; cf. J.K. Anderson 1985, 17–29; Barringer 2001, 10–69.

77 Cartledge 1977, 17 n. 51 [= 1986, 402 n. 51] argues that 'the Spartans even had a word for the condition of being under military discipline (*taga*)', citing Chadwick 1969, 234. Although this is true, in the relevant passage (Aristop. *Lys.* 105) the context – the women's complaints about their husbands' absence on military service – indicates that the word refers to periods of active service on campaign (as Chadwick notes), not to a state of military discipline at home.

78 Refs. in Ceccarelli 1998, 99–100 with nn. 45–6.

79 Pratinos fr. 709 (Campbell), ap. Athen. 14.632f–633a.

80 G. Anderson 1986, 269–72 (quotation from p. 269).

81 On Roman Sparta's re-invention of the *agōgē*, Kennell 1995.

82 Ephorus, *FGrH* 70 F 149, ap. Strabo 10.4.16; Sosibios, *FGrH* 595 F 23, ap. scholion on Pindar, *Second Pythian* 2.127. Range of heroes and divinities associated with the dance: Ceccarelli 1998, 25.

83 On the *pyrrhikē* in Athens and female participation, Borthwick 1970; Goulaki-Voutira 1996. For criticism of the idea that Athenian practice represents an evolution from an earlier (Spartan) military version of the dance, Ceccarelli 1998, 25–6.

84 *Instituta Laconica* 15, ap. Plut. *Mor.* 238a–b; cf. *Mor.* 544e; Plut. *Lyk.* 21.1–2.

85 Wheeler 1982, 229–33. As he notes (ibid. 230), the same is true of other descriptions of warlike dances: e.g. Xen. *Anab.* 6.1.9–10.

86 Agesilaos was leading a largely non-Spartiate force, but his approach to military training evidently followed standard Spartiate practice.

87 Plut. *Mor.* 639e; *Lyk.* 22.4. Cf. the comments of Figueira (this volume).

88 The key texts are Xen. *Hell.* 3.3.5 (the conspiracy of Kinadon), 5.4.28–33 (the episode of Sphodrias); Plut. *Lyk.* 25.1.

89 Thuc. 2.39; Xen. *Hell.* 7.1.8; Arist. *Pol.* 1324b8–9; 1338b9–14, 24–39.

90 Service in the *hippeis*: sources in Figueira (this volume). Sorties: Xen. *Hell.* 4.5.14–16, 6.10; cf. Billheimer 1946: in both episodes the troops aged 30–34 were also involved, on the latter occasion after the initial sortie by the 20–29 year-olds had failed.

91 Modern scholarship has perpetrated some gross misunderstandings regarding their evidence. Marrou (1956, 21) claims that 'very soon the boy began to do real military training…learning how to move with others in formation, how to handle arms, how to fence and throw the javelin and so on'. He cites 'Xen., *Lac.* 2'; but there is none of this in the text.

92 Kennell 1995, 55–9. The sources are Cicero *Tusculan Disputations* 5.27.77; Pausanias 3.14.8–10, 20.2, 8; Lucian *Anacharsis* 38.

93 As Xenophon himself perhaps implies by placing this feature soon after his account of the contrary practice of feeding young girls better than usual so that they would become healthier future mothers (1.3). Contemporary medical literature pointed out the harm done by insufficient food: refs. in Lipka 2002, 124.

94 On the non-functional elements of the upbringing, see also Ducat 1999b, esp. 59–62.

95 The most recent discussions are those of Ducat 1997a and b. He argues convincingly that there are only four authentic ancient references: Plato, *Laws* 633b–c; the scholion on that passage; Herakleides fr. 10 Dilts = Arist fr. 611.10 (Rose) = 143.1,2, 10 (Gigon); Plut. *Lyk.* 28.1–3 = Arist. fr. 538 (Rose) = 543 (Gigon).

96 Refs. in previous note.

97 Koechly 1881 [1835], 587–8; Wachsmuth 1844, i.462; ii.304; cf., more recently,

Piérart 1974, 259–91; Lévy 1988.

[98] Set against the precise reference to *encheiridia* in Plutarch's quotation from Aristotle, the reference to *hopla* in Herakleides' précis of the Aristotelian *Lak. Pol.* is probably a simple error (Ducat 1997a, 50, 65).

[99] In contrast to most previous scholarship, which views the *kryptoi* as drawn from among the whole group of 18–19 year-olds, Ducat (1997a, 63–4) argues from their description as *neoi* in Plutarch's quotation from Aristotle that they were drawn from among the *hēbōntes*, probably from the *hippeis*, who already formed an elite among the 20–29 year-olds.

[100] Promacheia: Sosibios *FGrH* 595 F 4, ap. Athen. 674a–b. Armed statues: Aristop. *Lys.* 1320; *BSA* 28, 1926/7, 78 fig. 19.8 (Athena Poliouchos on the acropolis); Paus. 3.10.8 (Apollo at Thornax); 15.10 (Aphrodite); 19.2–3 (Apollo at Amyklai).

[101] Aphrodite Areia: Paus. 3.17.5. Place of military assembly and armed procession to Athena Chalkioikos: Plb. 4.22.8; 35.2. Military dedications: Hodkinson 2000, 292, with refs.

[102] Parker 1989, 146 with refs. at 165 nn. 18–19.

[103] Paus. 3.17.4–5. Athena Erganē could be interpreted as a patroness of makers of bronze armour, but equally of other crafts, female as much as male.

[104] Hodkinson 2000, 291–3, with refs.

[105] Lead figurines, Wace 1929. On bronze dedications in general: Hodkinson 1998; 2000, 271–302, with discussion of the lead figurines on p. 290.

[106] Details in the studies listed in Parker 1989, 167 n. 37.

[107] Parker 1989, 146, with refs., to which add Pettersson 1992.

[108] Cf. the refs. in Parker 1989, 166 n. 22 (Ares) and 26 (the Dioskouroi).

[109] Note also Polyainos' list of army units in 371: *morai, lochoi, enōmotiai, syssitia* (2.3.11).

[110] The best collection of the evidence remains Bielschowsky 1869, 32–4. For different views about the number of *syssitia* to an *enōmotia*, Toynbee 1913, 267–8; 1969, 369; Cartledge 1987, 41–2; Singor 1999, 71–2. For some doubts about the link between them, especially in the fourth century when the number of Spartiates in each army regiment (*mora*) was significantly reduced: Lazenby 1986, 13.

[111] Plutarch also reports a variant version, according to which the name was *editia*, referring simply to meals and eating.

[112] On the donation of *epaikla*, Xen. *Lak. Pol.* 5.3 and the sources cited in Athen. 140e–141e.

[113] The royal *syssition* in Sparta included, besides the invited honorand, the two Pythioi selected by each king (Hdt. 6.57; Xen. *Lak. Pol.* 15.5), who are not mentioned as attending the king's tent on campaign. Conversely, the latter included the *polemarchoi* and three other citizens (Xen. *Lak. Pol.* 13.1), who are not attested in the *syssition* in Sparta. The other key difference, after *c.* 506, is that the kings dined together in Sparta, but only one king was present on campaign.

[114] Plut. *Kleom.* 8.1; 9.4; Aelian *NA* 11.19.

[115] Cf. the comment of the conspirator Kinadon, who was almost certainly a Spartan 'Inferior', that he and other non-Spartates fought in the army (Xen. *Hell.* 3.3.7). Ducat (this volume) suggests that Spartiates disfranchised through cowardice did not normally retain their place in the army, but it seems likely that those who had dropped out of the *homoioi* due to inability to meet the required food contributions still did so.

116 For refs. to these sources, Hodkinson 2000, 253.

117 Thuc. 5.34; Xen. *Lak. Pol.* 9.5; cf. also MacDowell 1986, 44–6.

118 Xen. *Hell.* 5.4.33. Discussion in Hodkinson, 2006b.

119 The evidence is discussed by Pritchett 1974–91, iv.243–6; Hodkinson 2000, 252–3; Low (this volume).

120 For the evidence, Hodkinson 1983, 259 n.61.

121 Pritchett 1974–91, iv.106–24; Loraux 1986.

122 Cf. Hodkinson 2000, 251–2, with refs.; Low (this volume). The situation regarding fallen kings is uncertain. Herodotus' statement (6.58) that an image (*eidōlon*) was used in the funerary ceremony, presumably in place of the absent corpse, may be an extrapolation from the singular case of the ceremony for Leonidas, whose dead body was not recoverable immediately after Thermopylai (7.225, 238). We have no information about the burial of other kings who died in battle. However, the bodies of two other kings, Agesipolis I and Agesilaos II, who died abroad – though not in war – were brought home to Sparta (Cartledge 1987, 334, with refs.).

123 Contrast the evidence from early Sparta, which suggests burial at home to the glory of the dead warrior and his lineage: Tyrtaios 12.27–34 (Gerber).

124 *Instituta Laconica* 18 = Plut. *Mor.* 238d. Note (i) that although this text is post-classical in date, it evidently elaborates (and perhaps draws upon) the late-fourth-century account in the Aristotelian *Lak. Pol.*, as preserved in summary form in a passage of Herakleides Lembos (373.13 Dilts); (ii) that the account of Plut. *Lyk.* 27.2 is derivative on the *Inst. Lac.*, but makes a critical alteration in associating the inscription with the burial of the fallen soldier: cf. Hodkinson 2000, 249–55.

125 *Inst. Lac.* 18; Plut. *Lyk.* 27.1. Against the later claims of Aelian *VH* 6.6 that only supremely brave soldiers were permitted burial in the *phoinikis*, Hodkinson 2000, 247–8.

126 On the supervision of the ephors, Xen. *Lak. Pol.* 13.5; *Hell.* 2.4.36. List of known royal trials (most of them following military campaigns) in Ste Croix 1972, 350–3.

127 Pritchett 1974–91, V.375–416; Hodkinson 2000, 358–9. Hence the subterfuge that Agesilaos had to perform, in order to make profits for his friends during his Asian campaign in the mid-390s (*Ages.* 1.18–19.)

128 Thuc. 5.66; Van Wees 2004, 243–4.

129 Finley 1986, 170.

130 There has been considerable debate about whether these debates took place in the assembly or *Gerousia* (Andrewes 1966, 3; Ste Croix 1972, 133, 151; Lewis 1977, 39; Kelly 1981, 49 n.5). The essential point, for my argument, is that wherever the actions against Agis were played out politically, they derived from widespread dissatisfaction by no means confined to a few leading men.

131 List in Kelly 1981, 56. He rightly notes the standard practice of Spartan commanders consulting their subordinate officers right down to the relatively low level of the *pentēkontēres*.

132 Ste Croix 1972, 124–50; Cartledge 1987, 116–59; Hodkinson 2000, 335–68.

133 The sources for Klearchos' exile from Sparta provide conflicting accounts: Xen. *Anab.* 2.5.2–4; Diod. 14.12.2–9. This view is not incompatible with the likelihood that the Spartans made veiled use of the exiled Klearchos in their assistance to Cyrus, as Ellen Millender argues (this volume). For an argument that Klearchos was affected by post-traumatic stress disorder, Tritle 2004.

Bibliography

Anderson, G.
1986   *Philostratus: Biography and belles lettres in the third century AD*, Beckenham.

Anderson, J.K.
1970   *Military Theory and Practice in the Age of Xenophon*, Berkeley and Los Angeles.
1985   *Hunting in the Ancient World*, Berkeley and Los Angeles.

Andrewes, A.
1966   'The government of classical Sparta', in E. Badian (ed.) *Ancient Society and Institutions: Studies presented to Victor Ehrenberg on his 75th birthday*, Oxford, 1–20.

Barringer, J.
2001   *The Hunt in Ancient Greece*, Baltimore.

Becker, A.S.
1981   *The Burden of Soviet Defense: A political-economic essay*, Santa Monica.

Bengtson, H.
1988   *History of Greece: From the beginnings to the Byzantine era*, Ottawa. Trans. of the German 4th edn, Munich, 1969.

Berghahn, V.R.
1981   *Militarism: The history of an international debate, 1861–1979*, Cambridge.

Bernstein, A.H.
1989   *Soviet Defense Spending: The Spartan analogy*, Santa Monica.
1997   'Imperialism, ethnicity and strategy: the collapse of Spartan (and Soviet) hegemony', in C.D. Hamilton and P. Krentz (eds.) *Polis and Polemos*, 275–301.

Berve, H.
1937   *Sparta*, Leipzig.

Bielschowsky, A.
1869   *De Spartanorum Syssitiis*, Berlin.

Billheimer, A.
1946   'Τὰ δέκα ἀφ' ἥβης', *TAPhA* 77, 214–20.

Borthwick, E.K.
1970   'P. Oxy. 2738: Athena and the Pyrrhic dance', *Hermes* 98, 318–31.

Briant, P. and Lévêque, P. (eds.)
1995   *Le monde grec aux temps classiques:* Tome 1, *Le V siècle*, Paris.

Carlier, P.
1977   'La vie politique à Sparte sous le règne de Cléomène 1er. Essai d'interprétation', *Ktema* 2, 65–84.
1984   *La Royauté en Grèce avant Alexandre*, Strasbourg.

Cartledge, P.A.
1977   'Hoplites and heroes: Sparta's contribution to the technique of ancient warfare', *JHS* 97, 11–27. Reprinted in German translation, with addendum, in K. Christ (ed.) *Sparta*, Darmstadt, 1986, 387–425, 470.
1979   *Sparta and Lakonia: A regional history 1300–362 BC*, London; reprinted, London and New York 2001.
1981   'Spartan wives: liberation or licence?', *CQ* n.s. 31, 84–105. Reprinted in his *Spartan Reflections*, London 2001, 106–26.

1987 *Agesilaos and the Crisis of Sparta*, London.

Cavaignac, E.
1948 *Sparte*, Paris.

Cawkwell, G.L.
1972 'Epaminondas and Thebes', *CQ* n.s. 22, 254–78.

Ceccarelli, P.
1998 *La pirrica nell'antichità Greco romana: Studi sulla danza armata*, Pisa and Rome.

Chadwick, J.
1969 'ταγά and ἀταγία', in *Studi Linguistici in Onore di Vittore Pisani* I, Brescia, 231–4.

Christ, K.
1986 'Spartaforschung und Spartabild. Eine Einleitung', in id. (ed.) *Sparta*, Darmstadt, 1–72. Reprinted in id. *Griechische Geschichte und Wissenschafts-geschichte*, Stuttgart, 1996, 9–57, 219–21.

Cloché, P.
1933 'Isocrate et la politique lacédémonienne', *REA* 35, 129–45.

Congressional Information Service
1984 *Allocation of Resources in the Soviet Union and China, 1984, Part 10* (U.S. Congress, Joint Economic Committee, Continuation of annual hearings before the Subcommittee on International Trade, Finance and Security Economics), 86-J841–4 Testimony no. 1, November 21, 1984, 2–119.

Crossman, R.H.S.
1937 *Plato Today*, London.

Damsgaard-Madsen, A.
1993 *Graekenlands Historie*, Aarhus.

David, E.
1982/3 'Aristotle and Sparta', *AncSoc* 13/14, 67–103.

Dawson, D.
1996 *The Origins of Western Warfare: Militarism and morality in the ancient world*, Boulder and Oxford.

Ducat, J.
1997a 'La cryptie en question', in P. Brulé and J. Oulhen (eds.) *Esclavage, guerre, économie en Grèce ancienne: hommages à Yvon Garlan*, Rennes, 43–74.
1997b 'Crypties', *Cahiers Glotz* 8, 9–38.
1999a 'La société spartiate et la guerre', in F. Prost (ed.) *Armées et sociétés de la Grèce classique: aspects sociaux et politiques de la guerre aux Ve et IVe s. av. J.-C.*, Paris, 35–50.
1999b 'Perspectives on Spartan education in the classical period', in Hodkinson and Powell (eds.) *Sparta: New perspectives*, 43–66.

Ducrey, P.
1985 *Guerre et guerriers dans la Grèce antique*, Paris.

Ferguson, W.S.
1918 'The Zulus and the Spartans: a comparison of their military systems', *Harvard African Studies* 2, 197–234.

Figueira, T.J.
2003 '*Xenelasia* and social control in classical Sparta', *CQ* n.s. 53, 44–74.

Finley, M.I.

1986   'Sparta', in *The Use and Abuse of History*, 2nd edn, London, 161–78 = B.D. Shaw and R.P. Saller (eds.) *Economy and Society in Ancient Greece*, London 1981, 24–40 = J.-P. Vernant (ed.) *Problèmes de la guerre en Grèce ancienne*, Paris 1968, 143–60.

Fisher, N.R.E.

1989   'Drink, *hybris* and the promotion of harmony in Sparta', in A. Powell (ed.) *Classical Sparta: Techniques behind her success*, London, 26–50.

Fornis, C.

2003   *Esparta*, Barcelona.

Forrest, W.G.

1968   *A History of Sparta 950–192 BC*, London.

French, V.

1997   'The Spartan family and the Spartan decline: changes in child-rearing practices and failure to reform', in Hamilton and Krentz (eds.) *Polis and Polemos*, 1997, 241–74.

Garlan, Y.

1988   *Slavery in Ancient Greece*, Ithaca and London. English trans. of *Les esclaves en Grèce ancienne*, Paris, 1982.

1989   *Guerre et économie en Grèce ancienne*, Paris.

Gates, R.M.

1996   *From the Shadows: The ultimate insider's story of five Presidents and how they won the Cold War*, New York.

Gomme, A.W.

1956   *A Historical Commentary on Thucydides. Volume III: Books IV–V 24*, Oxford.

Goulaki-Voutira, A.

1996   'Pyrrhic dance and female pyrrhic dancers', *Repertoire International d'Iconographie Musicale (Research Center for Musical Iconography, Newsletter)* 21, 3–12.

Gray, V.J.

1994   'Images of Sparta: writer and audience in Isocrates' *Panathenaicus*', in A. Powell and S. Hodkinson (eds.) *The Shadow of Sparta*, London, 223–71.

Greenslade, R.V.

1970   'The many burdens of defense in the Soviet Union', *Studies in Intelligence* 14.2, 1–12.

Grundy, G.B.

1948   *Thucydides and the History of his Age*, 2nd edn, Oxford. Original edn, London, 1911.

Hamilton, C.D. and Krentz, P. (eds.)

1997   *Polis and Polemos: Essays on politics, war, and history in ancient Greece in honor of Donald Kagan*, Claremont, Calif.

Hammond, M.

1979/80   'A famous *exemplum* of Spartan toughness', *CJ* 75, 97–109.

Hanson, V.D.

1989   *The Western Way of War*, New York.

Higgins, W.E.

1977   *Xenophon the Athenian*, Albany, N.Y.

Hildebrandt, G.C. (ed.)

1985   *Rand Conference on Models of the Soviet Economy, October 11–12, 1984*, Santa Monica.

Hodkinson, S.

1983   'Social order and the conflict of values in classical Sparta', *Chiron* 13, 239–81.

1993   'Warfare, wealth and the crisis of Spartiate society', in J. Rich and G. Shipley (eds.) *War and Society in the Greek World*, London and New York, 146–76.

1997   'The development of Spartan society and institutions in the archaic period', in L.G. Mitchell and P.J. Rhodes (eds.) *The Development of the Polis in Archaic Greece*, London and New York, 83–102.

1998   'Patterns of bronze dedications at Spartan sanctuaries, *c.* 650–350 BC: towards a quantified database of material and religious investment', in W.G. Cavanagh and S.E.C. Walker (eds.) *Sparta in Laconia: The archaeology of a city and its countryside*, Proceedings of the 19th British Museum Classical Colloquium, British School at Athens Studies 4, London, 55–63.

1999   'An agonistic culture? Athletic competition in archaic and classical Spartan society', in Hodkinson and Powell (eds.) *Sparta: New perspectives*, 147–87.

2000   *Property and Wealth in Classical Sparta*, London.

2003   'Spartiates, helots and the direction of the agrarian economy', in N. Luraghi and S.E. Alcock (eds.) *Helots and their Masters in Laconia and Messenia: Histories, ideologies, structures*, Cambridge, Mass. and London, 248–85.

2005   'The imaginary Spartan *politeia*', in M.H. Hansen (ed.) *The Imaginary Polis* (Acts of the Copenhagen Polis Centre, vol. 7), Copenhagen, 222–81.

2006a   'The modern mirage of Spartan militarism', *Omnibus* 52 [September].

2006b   'The episode of Sphodrias as a source for Spartan social history', in N. Sekunda (ed.) *Corolla Cosmo Rodewald*, Gdansk.

Hodkinson, S. and Powell, A. (eds)

1999   *Sparta: New perspectives*, London.

Hooker, J.T.

1980   *The Ancient Spartans*, London.

Hornblower, S.

1983   *The Greek World, 479–323 BC*, London. 3rd edn, 2002.

1987   *Thucydides*, London.

1991–6 *A Commentary on Thucydides*, 2 vols., Oxford.

2000   'Sticks, stones, and Spartans', in H. van Wees (ed.) *War and Violence in Ancient Greece*, London, 57–82.

Humble, N.M.

1997   'Xenophon's view of Sparta: a study of the *Anabasis*, *Hellenica* and *Respublica Lacedaemoniorum*', Diss., McMaster.

1999   '*Sōphrosynē* and the Spartans in Xenophon', in Hodkinson and Powell (eds.) *Sparta: New perspectives*, London, 339–53.

2004   'The author, date and purpose of chapter 14 of the *Lakedaimonion Politeia*', in C.J. Tuplin (ed.) *Xenophon and his World*, Stuttgart, 215–28.

Hunt, P.

1998   *Slaves, Warfare, and Ideology in the Greek Historians*, Cambridge.

Jeanmaire, H.
 1913 'La cryptie lacédémonienne', *REG* 26, 121–50.
Jeffery, L.H.
 1976 *Archaic Greece*, London.
Jones, A.H.M.
 1968 *Sparta*, Oxford.
Kagan, D.
 1990 *Pericles of Athens and the Birth of Democracy*, London.
 1996 *On the Origins of War and the Preservation of Peace*, New York.
Kahrstedt, U.
 1948 *Geschichte des griechisch-römischen Altertums*, Munich.
Kelly, D.H.
 1981 'Policy-making in the Spartan assembly', *Antichthon* 15, 47–61.
Kennell, N.M.
 1995 *The Gymnasium of Virtue: Education and culture in ancient Sparta*, Chapel Hill and London.
Kiechle, F.
 1963 *Lakonien und Sparta. Untersuchungen zur ethnischen Struktur und zur politischen Entwicklung Lakoniens und Spartas bis zum Ende der archaischen Zeit*, Munich.
Koechly, H.
 1881 *Cryptia: De Lacedaemoniorum Cryptia Commentatio*, in his *Opuscula Philologica* I, Leipzig, 580–91. Repr. of the original 1835 publication.
Kulesza, R.
 1999 'Population flight: a forgotten aspect of Greek warfare in the sixth and fifth centuries BC', *European Review of History* 6, 151–64.
Lazenby, J.F.
 1986 *The Spartan Army*, Warminster.
Lévy, E.
 1988 'La cryptie et ses contradictions', *Ktema* 13, 245–52.
Lewis, D.M.
 1977 *Sparta and Persia*, Leiden.
Lipka, M.
 2002 *Xenophon's* Spartan Constitution. *Introduction, text, commentary*, Berlin and New York.
Loraux, N.
 1977 'La belle mort spartiate', *Ktema* 2, 105–20. Reprinted as 'The Spartans' "Beautiful Death"' in her *The Experiences of Tiresias: The feminine and the Greek man*, Princeton, 1995, 77–91 (translation of French original, Paris 1989).
 1986 *The Invention of Athens: The funeral oration in the classical city*, Cambridge, Mass. Trans. of French original, Paris 1981.
Losemann, V.
 1977 *Nationalsozialismus und Antike. Studien zur Entwicklung des Faches Alte Geschichte 1933–1945*, Hamburg.
MacDowell, D.M.
 1986 *Spartan Law*, Edinburgh.

Marrou, H.
1956   *A History of Education in Antiquity*. Trans. of French original, Paris 1948.
Martin, T.R.
1996   *Ancient Greece from Prehistory to Hellenistic Times*, New Haven and London.
Michell, H.
1952   *Sparta*, Cambridge. Repr. 1964.
Millender, E.G.
1999   'Athenian ideology and the empowered Spartan woman', in Hodkinson and Powell (eds.) *Sparta: New perspectives*, 355–91.
Murray, G.
1946   *Greek Studies*, Oxford.
Ollier, F.
1933   *Le Mirage spartiate: Étude sur l'idéalisation de Sparte dans l'antiquité grecque de l'origine jusqu'aux Cyniques*, I, Paris.
Orrieux, C. and Schmitt Pantel, P.
1999   *A History of Ancient Greece*, Malden, Mass. and Oxford. Trans. of French original, Paris, 1995.
Parker, R.
1988   'Demeter, Dionysus and the Spartan pantheon', in R. Hägg, N. Marinatos and G.C. Nordquist (eds.) *Early Greek Cult Practice*, Stockholm, 99–103.
1989   'Spartan religion', in A. Powell (ed.) *Classical Sparta: Techniques behind her success*, London, 142–72.
Passerini, A.
1952   *Questioni di Storia Antica*, Milan.
Perlman, P.
2005   'Imagining Crete', in M.H. Hansen (ed.) *The Imaginary Polis* (Acts of the Copenhagen Polis Centre, vol. 7), Copenhagen, 282–334.
Pettersson, M.
1992   *Cults of Apollo at Sparta: the Hyakinthia, the Gymnopaidiai and the Karneia*, Stockholm.
Piérart, M.
1974   *Platon et la cité grecque*, Brussels.
Pomeroy, S.B.
2000   *Spartan Women*, New York.
Powell, C.A.
1980   'Athens' difficulty, Sparta's opportunity: causation and the Peloponnesian war', *AC* 49, 87–114.
1988   *Athens and Sparta: Constructing Greek political and social history from 478 BC*, London and New York. 2nd revised edn 2001.
Pritchett, W.K.
1974–91   *The Greek State at War*, 5 vols., Berkeley, Los Angeles and London.
Proietti, G.
1987   *Xenophon's Sparta*, Leiden.
Raaflaub, K.
1997   'Soldiers, citizens and the evolution of the early Greek *polis*', in L.G. Mitchell

and P.J. Rhodes (eds.) *The Development of the Polis in Archaic Greece*, London and New York, 49–59.

Rahe, P.A.
1994   *Republics Ancient and Modern*, I: *The Ancien Regime in Ancient Greece*, Chapel Hill and London. Reprint of the original 1992 single-volume edition.

Rawson, E.
1969   *The Spartan Tradition in European Thought*, Oxford. Paperback repr. 1991.

Rebenich, S.
2002   'From Thermopylae to Stalingrad: the myth of Leonidas in German histori-ography', in A. Powell and S. Hodkinson (eds.) *Sparta: Beyond the mirage*, London and Swansea, 323–49.

Rhodes, P.J.
1997   'Introduction', in L.G. Mitchell and P.J. Rhodes (eds.) *The Development of the Polis in Archaic Greece*, 1–8.

Ste Croix, G.E.M. de
1954/5 'The character of the Athenian empire', *Historia* 3, 1–41.
1972   *The Origins of the Peloponnesian War*, London.

Siewert, P.
1977   'The ephebic oath in fifth-century Athens', *JHS* 97, 102–11.

Singor, H.
1999   'Admission to the *syssitia* in fifth-century Sparta', in Hodkinson and Powell (eds.) *Sparta: New perspectives*, 67–89.

Snodgrass, A.M.
1980   *Archaic Greece*, London.

Spencer, H.
1882   *The Principles of Sociology*, vol. II, London.

Strauss, L.
1939   'The spirit of Sparta and the taste of Xenophon', *Social Research* 6, 502–36.

Toynbee, A.J.
1913   'The growth of Sparta', *JHS* 33, 246–75.
1969   *Some Problems in Greek History*, Oxford.

Tritle, L.
2004   'Xenophon's portrait of Clearchus: a study in post-traumatic stress disorder', in C. Tuplin (ed.) *Xenophon and his World*, Stuttgart, 325–39.

Tuplin, C.
2004   'Xenophon and his world: an introductory review', in C. Tuplin (ed.) *Xenophon and his World*, Stuttgart.

Vagts, A.
1959   *A History of Militarism: Civilian and military*, London.

Van Wees, H.
1999   'Tyrtaeus' *Eunomia*: nothing to do with the Great Rhetra', in Hodkinson and Powell (eds.) *Sparta: New perspectives*, 1–41.
2003   'Conquerors and serfs; wars of conquest and forced labour in archaic Greece', in N. Luraghi and S.E. Alcock (eds.) *Helots and their Masters in Laconia and Messenia: Histories, ideologies, structures*, Cambridge, Mass. and London, 33–80.

2004   *Greek Warfare: Myths and realities*, London.

Vidal-Naquet, P.

1986   *The Black Hunter: Forms of thought and forms of society in the Greek world*, Baltimore and London. English trans. of French original, Paris 1981.

von Vacano, O.W., John, E.W., Berve, H., Harder, R. and Rumpf, A.

1940   *Sparta. Der Lebenskampf einer nordischen Herrensicht*, Kempten.

Wace, A.J.B.

1929   'The lead figurines', in R.M. Dawkins (ed.) *The Sanctuary of Artemis Orthia at Sparta*, London, 249–84.

Wachsmuth, W.

1844   *Alterthumskunde: Hellenische Alterthumskunde aus dem Gesichtspunkte des Staats*, 2nd edn, 2 vols., Halle.

Westlake, H.D.

1968   *Individuals in Thucydides*, Manchester.

Wheeler, E.L.

1982   '*Hoplomachia* and Greek dances in arms', *GRBS* 22, 223–33.

1983   'The *hoplomachoi* and Vegetius' Spartan drillmasters', *Chiron* 13, 1–20.

Whitby, M.

1994   'Two shadows: images of Spartans and helots', in A. Powell and S. Hodkinson (eds.) *The Shadow of Sparta*, London, 87–126.

5

THE LACEDAEMONIAN STATE: FORTIFICATIONS, FRONTIERS AND HISTORICAL PROBLEMS

Jacqueline Christien

The present paper gives me a welcome opportunity to collect and develop ideas and information on the ancient Peloponnese which have so far been scattered and sometimes difficult of access.[1] Much is owed to the publications of other archaeologists.[2]

The archaeological data is plentiful, at times embarrassingly so. Much of it is well known. However, in addition to offering certain new material, we can hope to provide for the first time an overall vision of the fortified places which framed Lacedaemonian territory. And by 'Lacedaemonian territory' we here mean the area of the Spartan state at its most extensive, as it was in the period between the acquisition of Kynouria and the loss of Messenia; that is, between 550 and 370. Our focus will be on the frontier as it existed in the early fourth century, and on how the nature of that frontier affected Spartan society.

FUNDAMENTALS OF METHODS AND DATA

My own collection of data was begun long ago.[3] From the start I was aware that Sparta was the most important of all Greek states, and that much about it was – unsurprisingly – beyond our comprehension. The inspirational work of Ollier (1933, 1940) on the Spartan mirage supplied part of the explanation as to why this should be so, but also created in me an ambition to view a Sparta free of mirage. To attain such a view, I believed it necessary to work not on the period of Sparta's expansion but on a later time, the time of Sparta's difficulties, for which we have solidly historical, albeit fragmentary, information. This was the information which, in my view, could be found in ancient texts which claimed to present a world without chronology, the world of model Spartan education which always kept a mythical dimension. Like Kennell (1995),[4] I came to believe that we could detect a distinctively Spartan reality playing out in the late classical and early hellenistic periods.

To be able to proceed, research had to be founded on what survived of ancient reality. It had to proceed from the terrain rather than from texts, and elements of the terrain had to be understood together, even when texts gave no immediate help. Texts revealed not any full reality, but merely what seemed important at particular periods, to their authors.

From the time of the Peloponnesian War, and more so still after the battle of Leuktra, Sparta was on the defensive. Accordingly, I looked for her defences. The city of Sparta itself was not an immediate object of defence. Sparta, as Thucydides indicates (1.10.2), was not a typical city; for one thing, the existence of Amyklai, away to the south on the plain, made it impossible to include all the main inhabited districts within a single wall, on classic lines. When eventually Sparta was provided with a defensive wall (at a date as yet undetermined), any hope of defending Amyklai thereby had to be abandoned. All this had a certain logic. The Spartan state was a regional affair, and what mattered most was to defend the whole region. But for a historian this raised a huge practical problem; we have to deal with this region in its full, impressive, extent – of some 8400 square kilometres.[5]

The district least understood in recent times is the east coast of Lakonia, an area which in antiquity lay on important sailing-routes towards Africa and the West. Accordingly I began my research on that east coast, working systematically from north to south. Certain literary texts encouraged the search; best-known is Thucydides' evidence that the Spartans began to fortify their east coast during the Archidamian War (4.57). And we were duly rewarded by the discovery, on Parnon, of not one but two lines of defence, running from north to south[6] (*Map* 1).

Next, I proceeded to the coast of Messenia. There, on the west coast, I found a single line of defence. We know, from Thucydides again (4.3.3), that at the date when the Athenians occupied Pylos-Koryphasion (425), the place was uninhabited.[7] But a further surprise met us to the west of Taygetos, in the form of a double-entry system of fortifications[8] (*Map* 2). All of this raised various questions.

(1) These defensive systems must have controlled roads: but which roads? From early on I had been struck by the presence, in two places, of rail-like features at the edge of a town.[9] Such had been described as scattered about the countryside, by the travellers[10] and archaeologists[11] whose works had become my bedside reading.

As I collected information about these surviving features, from earlier writers but above all from my own systematic autopsy, gradually there appeared a road network. These were without doubt the remains of ancient Greek wagon-roads, *hamaxitoi*, a term which we find for example applied by

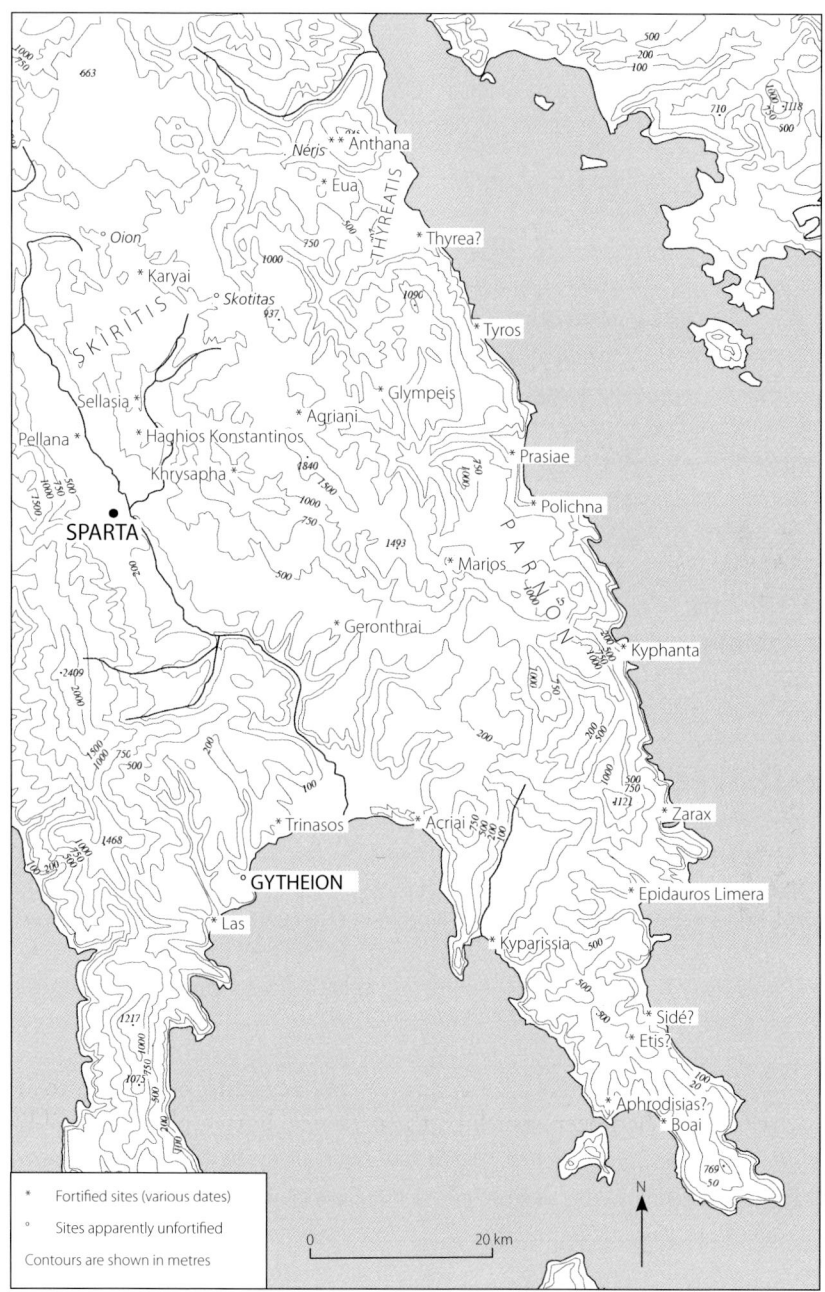

Map 1. Eastern Lakonia.

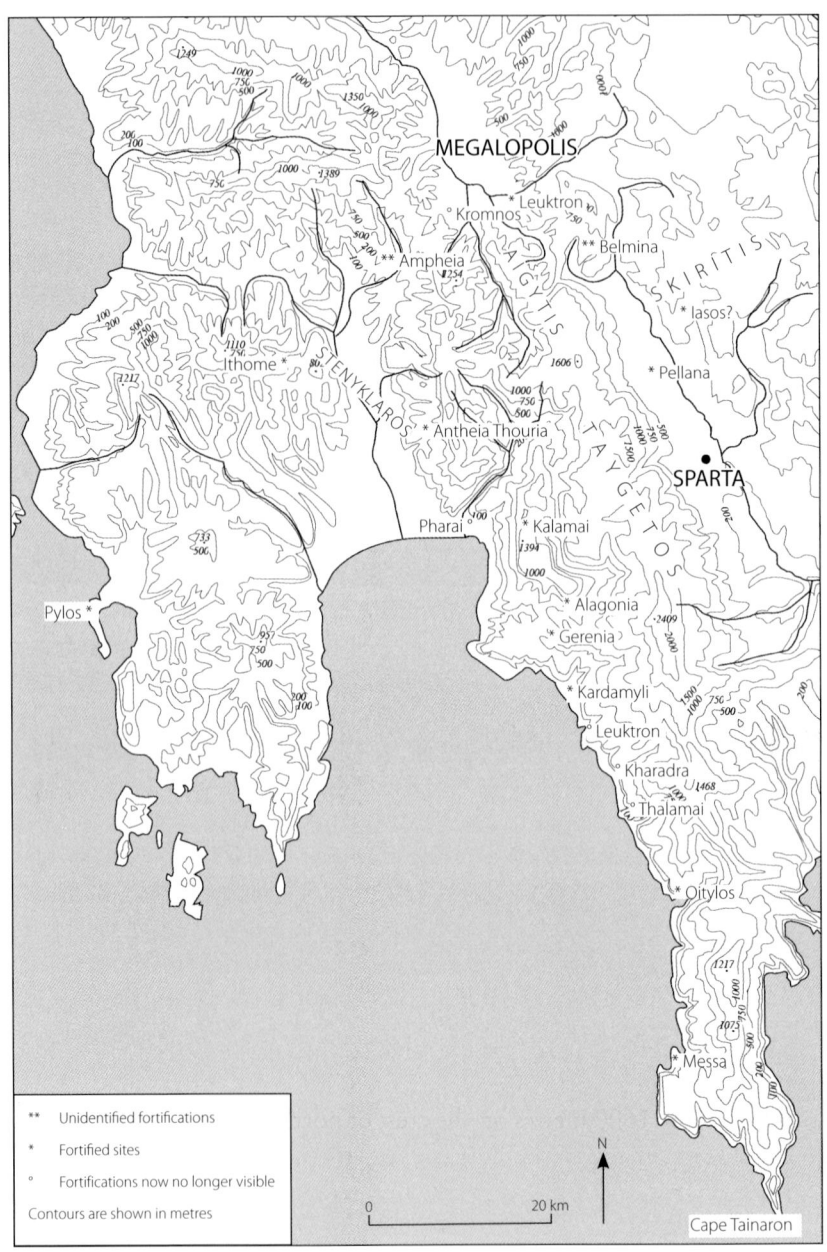

Map 2. Western Lakonia and Messenia.

Xenophon to the border areas of Lakonia.[12] The road leading to Epidauros Limera can be followed, albeit fragmentarily, from the crossing over the Eurotas as far as the coast, via Leukai (the furthest point of the plain of Molai) and the shrine of Apollo Hyperteleatas.

On Parnon we determined that these roads went boldly across hillsides. We found traces at an altitude of around 1200 metres, on the road leading from the Thyreatis to Lakonia, after following the faint remains of the road from Eua (Helléniko, above Astros) towards Karyai.

Fig. 1. 'The Dragon's Footprint' – grooves showing an ancient road from the Thyreatis. The site is between the sources of the Tanos and the Skotitas. Photo by the author.

There are similar traces (now gradually being destroyed) going up from the shrine of Maleatas behind Geraki, and likewise from Sparta in the direction of Glympeis.[13] These, I concluded, formed part of the mountain roads.

On Taygetos there are remains of what seems to have been the road from Aigytis and from the upper Messenian plain. These traces can be found at an altitude of some 1600 metres on the crest of north Taygetos, and again near the Kastro of Kamara overlooking the Aigytis valley, and also near Kokkala (ancient Ampheia?), a fortress on the western flank of north Taygetos controlling the route down to the plain. This road, which allowed swift access to the plain of Stenyklaros, may have allowed Spartans of the fourth century to swoop on to the plain and to intimidate the state of Messenia which Epameinondas had recently created – albeit that they never succeeded in gaining control of the fortress which guarded the pass between Aigytis and

Fig. 2. Grooves on ancient road, north Taygetos. Photo by the author.

the plain of Stenyklaros. This wild spot, which was to become the Kastro of medieval times, was an eyrie which made it possible to plunder the plain of Messenia. Again, we should like to know whether these roads existed during the classical period.

The only literary texts to give much guidance were those of Xenophon (*Hellenica*) and Diodorus (= Ephorus), in their accounts of the Theban invasion of Lakonia in 370/69. Xenophon had a reasonable knowledge of Lakonia, given that he had met many Spartans and had certainly visited Sparta itself. He also had the advantage of being a contemporary of the invasion, even though, as a refugee at Corinth, he apparently had less than full information. He was constrained by a desire to write nothing which might damage the reputation of his admired Sparta. In spite of his silences, what he does say is of inestimable value. Diodorus has a similar importance, in spite of his rhetorical excesses, since his account reacted to and amplified that of Xenophon, which Ephorus considered incomplete and partisan. For once, then, we had fairly helpful texts to guide us.

In the event I was able to discover on the ground traces of what appeared to be the invasion routes indicated by our two texts – particularly near Karyai, a place subsequently deserted and occupied today only by a small church beside the Saranda Potamos, at the corner of an attractive plain. In the nineteenth century traces of this ancient road were visible for several kilometres, since the later road took a more westerly line and thus had not obliterated the signs of its ancient predecessor. Now, we know that there were wagon-roads leading out of Lakonia. Xenophon says explicitly (*LP* 11.2) that in the rear of the army there followed its baggage on wagons or on pack animals. Herodotus (8.124) tells of how Themistokles left Lakonia on 'the finest chariot in Sparta', and was escorted by the 300 *hippeis* as far as the border with Tegea. In all probability this was the road that he took; this is the direct route from Lakonia to Tegea (*Map 3*).

It is likely, too, that these wagon-roads were in use earlier than the fifth century, and that several such roads not only led in and out of Lakonia but also gave access to remote areas of the Spartan state: Epidauros Limera, the Thyreatis, Boiai, Messenia. And along these roads lay fortifications, in two lines of different periods. But to understand the general system was not easy.

Map 3. Karyai and district, showing three ancient roads (ancient place names in capitals).

(2) It became clear that we were dealing with fortifications of several different kinds. Dating posed a problem here too.

(a) Along the east coast

Many of the sites seem to date from the fortification of the area at the time of the Peloponnesian War. But why the double line? The answer, it seemed to me, was that the frontiers themselves were moved over time.

In the case of the Thyreatis, which was returned permanently to Argive control in 338, the system should be constructed as follows.

To belong to Sparta: Anthana on the side of Mt. Zavitsa, i.e. right on the border with the Argolid, and Thyrea. (The site of Thyrea is now unknown, though traces may remain of the associated port built by Aiginetans or Spartans at Paralia Astros in 424. Sparta had strengthened the Thyreatis by settling there Aiginetans who had been ejected from their island in 431. The creation of this port was a cause of anger to Athens.)

To belong to Argos: Eua, in the mountains on the Parnon road, and the Paralia Haghios Andreas, the ancient name of which is unknown but which was perhaps a new Thyrea, marking the frontier with the Spartan site at Tyros.

All sites along the southern coast are fortified, as far as Haghios Phokas (ancient Side?) to the south of Epidauros Limera. But Zarax and Kyphanta have their own distinctive 'Macedonian' layout, no doubt connected with the Argive control of the area (as far as Zarax) from 265 to 219.[14] This period of Argive rule saw the fortification of Glympeis (or Glyppia), on the site of which the ancient walls have almost disappeared, and of Marios, the border with Spartan territory lying at the time in the interior of Parnon.

(b) In Messenia

There seems to have been systematic fortification of every place that the Spartans might have been able to reach after 369, and a blocking of all entry-points. Many of these fortifications have disappeared, and are known only from literary evidence or, in the case of the three 'Boiotian' sites Thalamai, Kharadra and Leuktron, through the existence of vast quarries.[15] Of Oitylos, Kardamyli and Pharai there are barely-detectable traces. More significant remains exist for Messa, on the Tigani peninsula of south-western Mani, and above all for the points which controlled the routes towards Lakonia: Gerenia and Alagonia on the route from Kardamyli to Sparta, Kalamai on the route to Pharai and Sparta, Thouria on the route between Sparta and Messene. The case of Ampheia (Kokkala) is not quite certain, but there exist the remains of a large ancient wall and of an ancient road.[16] This would have been an appropriate route for the road from Sparta to northern Messenia.

All this looks like a defence-system created by Messenians in the fourth century, though conceivably there had been defences created earlier at places such as Oitylos, Kardamyli and Pharai which were exposed to Athenian attacks from the sea. It is also conceivable that small forts had been created along the roads (as, for example, between Geraki/Geronthrai and Marios, and between Krysapha and Agriani. Alagonia may be a similar case.) However, the fact that there are forts blocking every route, taken with Strabo's reference to Boiotians settling around the Lesser Pamisos, implies that the main purpose was defence against Sparta.

(c) The North

There are more questions than answers. Karyai was fortified, after the Theban invasion of Lakonia. The fortification wall is built over houses from the early fourth century.[17]

Oion seems also to have been fortified, but clarity is lacking. We can make out the shape of a gateway facing Lakonia, but it cannot be dated. Pritchett (1965, 64) pointed out that Sellasia is fortified.[18] The town was captured in the course of Epameinondas' invasion of Lakonia and held for four years before the Spartans retook it, which shows that it was fortified, at least during the period 369–5. But there is at present no explanation available for the two great fortresses of Mt. Khelmos north of Pellana and of Haghios Konstantinos over-looking Sellasia on the Spartan side.[19] For Pellana, there is recently-discovered evidence, as yet unpublished, of a fortification apparently from the late fourth century. For Aigys, Strabo (8.5.4) reports a fortification, which now, however, has disappeared.[20] Leuktron, at the furthest point of Taygetos (Leondari), was the site of a medieval fortification; no ancient remains are known.

It is predictable that this region should present a confusing overall picture. It was an area of perennial dispute between Arcadians and Spartans after the foundation of Megalopolis; the border was subject to much alteration. Interpretation of what remains on the ground is made extremely difficult by the fact of successive acts of destruction. Our research gives rise to the following historical reconstruction.

FRONTIERS IN THE FOURTH CENTURY

1. Post 369

Taken together, our information indicates the following frontiers.

(a) The frontier with Argos (according to the latest evidence)

The Argives used to be thought not to have had a share of the spoils of Lakonia at the time of Epameinondas' invasion. Pausanias (2.38.6) makes clear that they did not gain control of the Thyreatis until the time of Philip II, a point seemingly confirmed by the excavations of the cemeteries at Eua, from which most of the Greek material was dated to the end of the fourth and the beginning of the third centuries. However, several graves where a double burial had taken place posed a problem, since the initial burial belonged to an earlier part of the fourth century.[21] C. Kritzas has now presented (in Paris, March 2006) his first findings concerning bronze tablets found recently at Argos, which make clear that the Argives did indeed gain control of the Thyreatis in 369.[22]

Argos had pressing business elsewhere, helping the Thebans establish the new state which thenceforward would naturally be their ally and would outflank the Spartans. While Epameinondas was recognized as *oikist*, our sources make clear that the Argive general Epiteles played an important part in the decision to found Ithome, the Messenian strong point, later known as 'Messene', and that the Argives took part in the foundation ritual, sacrificing to Hera of Argos and to Nemean Zeus before Thebans, Argives and Messenians all joined in swearing an oath in the name of the Heroes of Messenia.[23] Concern with establishing their influence in Messenia[24] perhaps caused the Argives to do too little in Thyreatis. In any case, Sparta was apparently able to wrest that territory back from them fairly rapidly. (Perhaps this occurred in 357. Some such dramatic coup on the part of Arkhidamos would help to explain why Isokrates composed a 'Letter to Arkhidamos', and also why the Thebans unleashed such aggression against Sparta at Delphi in 357/6.) There was similar turbulence on Sparta's other frontiers.

(b) The frontier with Tegea

This ran, for a short time, to the south of Sellasia. Justification for this was no doubt derived from the way in which the Lacedaemonian state had traditionally been arranged – a subject now largely obscure, with the exception of two helpful passages of Xenophon. He refers to Sellasia as πλησίον τῆς Λακωνικῆς, 'near Lakonia' (*Hell.* 2.2.13). Likewise when referring elsewhere to Pellana (*Hell.* 7.5.9), he states that Agesilaos 'had left Lakonia…and was already at Pellana'. These north Lacedaemonian districts were no doubt the area in which the Skiritai were recruited. In any case, they were Lacedaemonian rather than Lakonian. Sellasia was to stay in the control of the Arkadians (or the Boiotians?) until 365, but Karyai was retaken much sooner. Oion (like Belmina, Malea, Leuktron and Iasos) and Kromnos (like Aigys and Karystos) took part in the foundation of Megalopolis.[25]

The creation of Megalopolis, by a process of *synoikismos*, seems to have been more problematic than that of Ithome, which was a new foundation, designed as the political centre of a Messenia which extended from Oikhalia to Ithome itself, even though recent excavations have shown that the site

Figs. 3 and 4. Fortification walls of Ithome (Messene). Photos by the author.

had previously been inhabited. (On the akropolis was a sanctuary of Zeus Ithomatas; there was also apparently a shrine to Messenian Asklepios.) While the origins of Megalopolis are not well defined, it was presumably fear of the Spartans that compelled the populations of small border towns to abandon their dangerously-exposed homes. On the other hand, in Kromnos we apparently have a town which remained inhabited and whose citizens did not flee the Spartans.[26] In any case the frontier, which must have been to the north of Pellana, apparently soon reverted to its traditional line to the north of the Skiritis. On this front the Spartans seem from 365 to have regained virtually all of their lost territory, if not all of its inhabitants. But Megalopolis held out and survived. So that, even without any loss of their territory, the Spartans were left with a major embarrassment: from now on, the simplest route out of Lakonia was controlled by an enemy city all the more intractable because its very existence was under threat from Sparta.

(c) The frontier with Messenia

In addition to the founding of heavily-fortified Ithome (above, *Figs.* 3 and 4), fortifications were created at every point where a route from Lakonia descended into Messenian territory, and existing populations were reinforced with garrisons. One such fortress was even given the name 'Leuktron', to commemorate the battle of Leuktra and thereby insult Sparta. The occupants of three fortresses were called 'the Boiotians' (see n. 15), which makes clear their region of origin.[27] This area of upper Mani is fertile (at least around Leuktron and Kardamyli), but very small. Why, then, were so many military resources bestowed on it? The answer has to do with the fact that the Messenians clung to the idea that they lived under the protection of the Dioscuri who, according to one form of the myth, were born at Thalamai (Paus. 3.26.3) and therefore haunted the region.

Especially important was the road from Sparta to Stenyklaros, traces of which survive (at an altitude of 1660 metres) on north Taygetos, then – further on – near Kamara and in the Kokkala pass. In this last place remains of a fortification wall, which have survived in spite of the medieval *kastro*, strongly suggest that this was ancient Ampheia. The Spartans, in their reconquest of the most northerly parts of their state, managed to get control of the Aigytis. They were then in a position to make devastating raids against the plain of Stenyklaros and to prevent the Messenians of Ithome from exploiting it properly. We can see why the propagandists of Messenia regarded this place as so special. The 'Pseudo-History' of Messenia[28] compiled in the third century very likely reflects the still-painful memory of these fourth-century conflicts while retrojecting them to a more distant era.[29]

This permanent threat from Sparta probably meant that in reality rather few Messenians returned from the western Mediterranean or from Cyrenaica to repopulate the new state. Isokrates puts the following into the mouth of Arkhidamos:

> ...if the true Messenians were to be brought back, that would be an injustice, but at least there would be some excuse for doing us this harm. But in fact the people being settled on our borders are our own helots. The most painful thing for us is, not the thought of being robbed of our territory, but the sight of our own slaves as its new masters.[30]

This passage implies that very few Messenians answered the call of Epameinondas to return to their own homeland. Why, indeed, would they have left Tyndaris or the towns of Cyrenaica where they had settled? Rather, Isokrates' text suggests, most of the population of the new state were people who had previously lived there as helots, and who now lived alongside Boiotians, Argives and also Arcadians who had come as reinforcements to settle in the most threatened areas. It may also be that helots defected from Lakonia, attracted by the idea of freedom, and came to reinforce the new towns, especially all those situated where roads descended from Taygetos. Such exposed places had their Boiotian or Argive garrisons but must have been short of volunteers from Messenia itself.

2. Sparta adapts: the Krypteia

The above history may explain changes to Sparta's militaristic education system and also the creation of the Krypteia which, as I have suggested elsewhere, may belong in this context.[31]

The Krypteia has a special place in French scholarship.[32] Recent contributions to this tradition have been made by Lévy (1988) and preeminently by Ducat (1997a, 1997b and 2006). We are, therefore, in a good position to see everything that *ancient writers* have to say on the subject. However, the questions posed by Lévy and Ducat essentially repeat the attempts of Jeanmaire and others to explain the Krypteia as an element of the Spartan constitution. I venture now to propose a new theory.

First, certain fundamental facts. Xenophon knows the *hippeis* of Sparta, but shows no knowledge of the *krypteia*. Likewise earlier writers – Herodotos, Thucydides, and the mischievous Aristophanes – all show no awareness of this institution. The term *krypteia* appears first – albeit out of context and reinterpreted for the author's own purposes – in Plato's *Laws* (633b), a work perhaps of the 350s. Subsequently it was used by Aristotle,[33] or so we are told. It does not appear, however, in his *Politics*. The occasion where we can see the *kryptoi* at work in a historical context is in the third century, where they act as specialist troops in the army of Kleomenes III (Plut. *Kleom.* 28.4). We owe to Plutarch much information – and some misinformation – on Sparta.

Elsewhere he locates the *krypteia* in the ahistorical context of the reformer Lycurgus, but indicates that he himself had no confidence that the institution was of such great antiquity.[34] Moreover, in his work the *kryptoi* duplicate the role of the *hippeis*. Like the latter, the former are young people in the bloom of youth, between the ages of 20 and 30; they are not ephebes. They are, however, picked men – like the *hippeis*. The difference is that, whereas the *hippeis* displayed themselves in the broad light of day as an arm of the regime, to intimidate the subject population, the *kryptoi* achieve their own form of terror by hiding. Now, to kill the workers on whom your own or your neighbour's family depended would have been absurd. But if the designated victims were former helots, now of independent Messenia, or were Laconian helots who had taken refuge there, the killing would have made far more sense. To protect their *kryptoi* from being polluted by murder (as they would have been polluted, without the ritual declarations needed to explain the fact of war to gods and men), and to make them effective at all stages of the year, the ephors made the due declaration and gave them authority to conduct their war of the shadows. The purpose was to make life impossible for the inhabitants of the newly-independent state. Obviously they had to hide, and to operate at night whenever possible. Similar operations exist today; those who carry them out are called 'special forces'. I suggest that the reason why the term *krypteia* is not found before Plato's *Laws*, before 369, is that before that time the institution itself did not exist.

After 369, Lacedaemonian territory was hemmed in, reduced in scale – intolerably – by a half, threatened on all frontiers, struggling to preserve its social structure and even its very existence. In a study of Isokrates' *Arkhidamos*, a work which for long baffled interpreters, Azoulay[35] has produced a theory which I find utterly convincing. The implicit backdrop to the work, Azoulay argues, is the *krypteia*. The guerrilla war which Isocrates describes is in fact that of the *kryptoi*. Now, the work was written in 366. And it has long been known that Isokrates, the head of a school of political orators, was a close observer of current affairs.[36] There was no name yet available to him, to apply to this novel form of warfare, but he had quickly realized that the Spartans had invented a form of war very different from that of hoplites. Faced with disaster, it is readily understood that the Spartan regime should have adapted. During the Theban invasion, Sparta had freed a number of helots and had reformed the citizen body;[37] it would not be surprising if she had also adapted so as to produce the *krypteia*. Such evolution was characteristic of Sparta, at all periods.

Freed from its modern image as an initiation rite, and properly set in a historical context, the *krypteia* fits very well into the period following the loss of Messenia. For thirty years or more Sparta stubbornly refused to accept the fact of that loss, until the rise of Philip II profoundly changed inter-state relations, even in the Peloponnese.

3. The crisis of 338 and the evolution of the frontier[38]

Philip had no obvious reason for hostility towards Sparta which, after Leuktra, had kept far away from the coasts of Macedonia. Philip even seems to have acted to restrain those who, after the Sacred War, sought to exact reprisals from Sparta. It may be that between Philip and the Spartans there had been secret negotiations, since Arkhidamos is found after 346/5 to lose interest in the affairs of mainland Greece and to seek alliances elsewhere.

From 344 Philip was linked by alliances to Argos, Messenia and Megalopolis. However, none of these states was present at the battle of Khaironeia; was it understood that the king's ambitions extended only to central Greece, or was the whole Peloponnese perhaps concentrating at the time exclusively on events in the West? Both explanations may be relevant: in taking up a position at Corinth and summoning there all the cities of Greece, Philip showed the speed of political judgement and of action that Demosthenes had inveighed against.[39] No one at the time was in a position to stop him, whereas to have waited would have allowed the Greeks to reorganize and perhaps to evade his control. And astutely he made only a single demand: to be declared *hēgemōn* of the Greeks, to resurrect the panhellenic alliance and to reverse the flow of history by having the West invade the East. Such thinking had been in the air for some time.

What was not predictable was that the Spartans, even after they lost Arkhidamos, should have refused. Philip had overlooked the fact that to be *hēgemōn* of an alliance had been Sparta's own political Big Idea and that Sparta could not countenance its passing to others, still less themselves to submit to the hegemony of another power.

Angry at seeing his own grand project thus jeopardized, Philip made a display of force in the direction of Lakonia (which clearly was quite incapable of withstanding him), but his political instinct ruled otherwise: it would not be wise to crush personally the state which of old had defeated the Persians at Plataia. He chose instead the sly device of requiring the *synedrion*, which included many of Sparta's enemies, to see to the punishment of the Spartans. Thus Sparta lost almost everything that Arkhidamos had won back.

(a) To the north-east

Argos – fatherland of the Macedonian Argead kings, according to legend – this time managed to recover the Thyreatis. This is the period, no doubt, to which belong the fortifications of Eua (Helleniko), along with the outpost of Spathokoumeno. Together these two strong points, far from the frontier, blocked any descent to the plain by an enemy.[40]

(b) To the north of Lakonia

Tegea and Megalopolis no doubt shared the spoils. Tegea on this occasion may have laid claim to the Karyatis and the Oiontis. (Oion is much closer to the plain of Tegea than to that of Megalopolis, the synoikismos of which had led to Oion's annexation. Pausanias may contain traces of a Tegean claim on this area.[41] However, Tegea apparently did not succeed in obtaining these places, since in 331 we find the Tegeans supporting the Lacedaemonian revolt.

On the other hand, Sellasia probably remained under Spartan control; it lies far closer to Sparta than to Tegea or even to Karyai. Likewise, while the Belminatis and the Aigytis no doubt passed into the control of Megalopolis, Pellana was successfully retained by Sparta;[42] the paian of Isyllos (*IG* 4².1.57) says that Philip was stopped by Asklepios at Pellana.

(c) The west

In earlier publications I have tried to show that the Messenia of Epameinondas' day included all the western slopes of Taygetos. However, it seems that in the west generally, in spite of Messenian claims to territory, Sparta suffered less than in other areas. The frontier ran along the Little Pamisos river, south of Kardamyli. Thus southern Mani, including the disputed shrine at Thalamai, remained in Spartan hands. On the other hand, the Messenians must have recovered the Dentheliatis (Tac. *Ann.* 4.43): that is, the valley of the river Nedon and its tributary and also the temple of Artemis Limnatis on the road from Antheia-Thouria to Sparta. Thus one side got Artemis, while the other got the Dioscuri. The Messenians seem not to have been satisfied with this arrangement, even though they could indulge in fanciful tales about this shrine of Artemis, to which young Spartan girls had come (Strabo 8.4.9, Paus. 4.4.2–3).

The fact that Messenia fared relatively badly was perhaps due to the rather negative policy that she adopted towards Macedonia after allying with Athens in 342. Messenia apparently exiled local pro-Macedonian politicians, who were to be recalled in the reign of Alexander (Dem. 17.4). This negativity towards Macedonia may be related to a shift in the policy of the Spartans themselves, who seem at this time to have formally accepted the loss of their former Messenian territory. But Messenia's policy towards Macedonia may also be explained by events in the West. The Corinthians in Sicily and the Spartans in southern Italy were effectively working in the interests of Messenia, which itself had links with cities of the West. Unfortunately our historical sources, with their frequently-Athenian perspective, say too little about all this. In any case, free now from the outright hostility of Sparta, Messenia was far from positive towards Macedonia. Hegemony and symmachy: these no doubt brought back bad memories for the Messenians.

As for the Spartans, they had lost half of the space which separated their city from their frontiers. And their neighbours had gained a similar amount as buffer teritory.

CONCLUSION

We are at last in a position to give a general view of the fourth-century changes to Sparta's frontiers and to her society. In the face of such upheavals, there was bound to be a certain adaptation. We have argued that one such was the creation, in this period, of the *krypteia*. I believe that Sparta had undergone similar adaptations in the fifth century, but our source material does not allow us easily to identify the relevant historical contexts. With Sparta, we are dealing with a society which preferred to fuse its various changes into a seamless constitution which officially had no history.

From the fifth century, we have signs of Spartan society adapting to the economic conditions which followed the negotiations whereby the Messenian revolt was brought to an end. Such were the coming into existence of the category of *nothoi*, bastard Spartiates, the sons of Spartan citizen women,[43] and the first appearance in our sources of the *neodamōdeis*.[44] The disappearance of the *neodamōdeis*, and the appearance of the *krypteia*, are likewise signs of a society restructuring itself in order to survive in an intensely hostile environment. From now on, Sparta had to create a new form of army and to protect a territory hemmed in by enemies. Her response to this new situation was, to ease the fear which now hung permanently over her own weakened and exposed territory by exporting terror to her new Messenian neighbours. Against the new state the Spartans practised not hoplite war but a form of state terrorism. That, I hold, is one conclusion which emerges from our study of Sparta's frontiers.

Notes

[1] My own work has appeared regularly in the journals of learned societies specializing in Peloponnesian studies: *Peloponnesiaka* and *Lakonikai Spoudai*. I thank Greek colleagues for their supportive interest in this regard. Two such articles are reprinted in Gengler and Marchetti 2000.

[2] Cf. Catling, ibid.; Cavanagh et al. 2002, 211–56; Shipley 2000, 369–90.

[3] My first examination of the landscape was in 1978.

[4] I do not, however, share all of Kennell's conclusions.

[5] Cf. Ehrenberg 1976, 61, who compares the territory of Athens (2650 square kilometres) of Corinth (880 square kilometres) and of modern Luxembourg (2600 square kilometres).

[6] For a description see Christien 1992b 7.

[7] Though note that, while Koryphasion was uninhabited, Thucydides (4.118.4) also allows us to infer that inhabited places lay nearby. A clause of the truce between Sparta

and Athens stipulated that the troops stationed at Koryphasion should not go as far as Bouphras and Tomeus. The likelihood that these were Messenian villages has now been confirmed by the work of Alcock et al. (2005, 147–209), which shows that the fertile areas to the north and east of Koryphasion were inhabited. However the period which our archaeologists have identified, 480–323, does not correspond with any historical development. The historical break occurred in 369. Thus while the 'Archaic' map at op. cit. 160 is helpful, the map of the 'Classical Period' may reflect patterns of Messenian population after 369.

[8]   Cf. Christien 2000, 163–5.

[9]   At Paralia Haghios Andreas in the southern Thyreatis and at the site of Oion in the south-eastern plain of Tegea. The latter site has since been concreted over for the building of a church.

[10]   Leake 1830 identified several such features, in the north of the plain of Helos and at the foot of Kourkoula east of Akriai. General Joachmus (1857) noted on his map 'Lakonia and Kynouria', a long surviving section near Karyai.

[11]   Especially Hope Simpson 1966, whose maps show traces of road around Pharai. One such road corresponds with the paved road which runs from the heart of Taygetos and which was guarded by the small fort at Kalamai. The other, slightly further south, disappears curiously into the mountain – either because erosion has obliterated further remains or because the road was never intended to cross Taygetos. Local guides have not been available in this area, which earthquake has caused to be uninhabited in modern times.

[12]   Xen. *Hell.* 7.4.22; near Kromnos.

[13]   I became aware of these remains only after publishing Christien 1989. One road crossed Parnon directly from Sparta to Glympeis (and no doubt then went further, heading for the coast by a northerly route which took it to the southern Thyreatis); another road headed for the south, towards Prasiai.

[14]   Christien 1987b, 111–24.

[15]   Strabo 8.4.4: 'Leuktron, a colony of Boiotian Leuktra', and (a few lines later) 'Leuktron, Kharadra and Thalamai, which, nowadays, are called "the Boiotian places"'. What is meant by 'nowadays'? Is Strabo repeating a phrase used in the testimony of Ephorus?

[16]   Christien 1998, 442.

[17]   Rhomaios (1957), in his disappointment at not finding the sanctuary of Artemis Karyatis on the akropolis of this site, concluded that it was not Karyai. My own view, however, is that we should return to the topographical conclusion of Loring (1895); see Christien 1987, with which now Shipley 2000, esp. 369–76.

[18]   He refers to a thick wall on the summit of Palaiogoulas hill.

[19]   Loring 1895. Additional information supplied by The Laconia Survey (vol.1, 169) only deepens the problem, as I see it.

[20]   However, medieval – and some ancient – remains above Kamara are perhaps to be identified with Strabo's *phrourion*; cf. Shipley 2000, 371–2.

[21]   Abadie and Spyropoulos 1985, 393 grave 6; p. 418, grave θ; p. 420, grave I; p. 424, grave IE. In each case there are two burials, the earlier datable to the 360s, the later post-338.

[22]   Kritzas' lectures concerned the discoveries at Argos and the interpretation of texts already reconstructed and deciphered. Further information can be expected.

[23] Grandjean 2003 gives full documentation on the founding of Ithome; v. esp. pp. 49–59.

[24] We may be able to detect, in the traditions and the names of certain towns of the Messenian *perioikis* (Oitylos, Antheia), traces of the Argive presence.

[25] For bibliography (albeit lacking reference to articles in French), see Shipley 2000.

[26] Xenophon makes clear (*Hell.* 7.4.21–2; 22–8) that the anti-Spartan alliance fought fiercely over Kromnos; its site, so far as we know, lay on the direct route between Megalopolis and Messenia. Kromnos, more than any other Lacedaemonian town, was affected by what happened on the plain of Megalopolis.

[27] I cannot accept the theory of Grandjean (2003, 69) which limits the Messenia of Epameinondas' day to Ithome and the neighbouring plain. Admittedly Cape Akritas and the west coast lay beyond the control of the Messenians. However, the whole Lacedaemonian *perioikis* on the western slopes of Mt. Taygetos was, in my view, provided with fortifications and garrisons, so as to make possible the working of the Messenian plain. Even so, the Messenians for long afterwards must have lived in a state of fear. It is, in any case, inconceivable that the western slopes of Taygetos were allowed to remain under Spartan control. It was to limit Spartan raids that these slopes were thoroughly protected by fortifications and by garrisons of Boiotians and Argives.

[28] Pearson 1962, 29.

[29] This is the case even if these stories contain some elements which go back beyond the fourth century; cf. Ogden 2004.

[30] Isok. 27–8. Cf. Ogden 2004, 135, 177–80.

[31] Christien 1997, 70–2.

[32] This point is well analysed by Birgalias (1999, esp. pp. 97–117). I have not seen the extensive treatment of the Krypteia in Ducat (2006).

[33] Heraclides Lembus fr. 373, 10 Dilts = Arist. Frag. 538 Rose.

[34] *Lyc.* 28.13. The author, as moralist, gives a moralizing reason for doubting that Lycurgus could have created the *krypteia*; but as an eminently learned man he may well have been influenced by a sense that the term was not to be found in the oldest texts.

[35] Azoulay, (forthcoming).

[36] See Matthieu 1925.

[37] Amouretti et al. 2000, 170.

[38] Cf. Roebuck 1948 (=1984).

[39] So *Second Philippic* 4: 'he is all action, you are all talk'; *Third Philippic* 47–50.

[40] Piérart (2001) treats the whole question and sets it in a broad context.

[41] Paus. 8.45.1. The eight populations which make up Tegea include the Karyatai and the Oiatai.

[42] My researches in the area of Karyai now lead me to revise the opinion expressed in Christien 1985, 463 n, 62, to reject the theory of Rhomaios who towards the end of his life conducted a minor excavation on this site, and to adopt once more the topographic identification proposed by Loring (1895). I must likewise revise the view expressed in Christien 1989, n. 57. Pellana is, after all, on the site of Kalyvia Georgitsi, even though the remains of a temple which used to be visible there were not *in situ*. The site of Kalyvia Georgitsi, currently Pellana, has recently been excavated, but the conclusions of the excavator have led to controversy in the Greek archaeological service and have not yet been published.

[43] Christien 1993.

[44] Amouretti et al. 2000, 147–9.

Bibliography

Abadie, C. and Spyropoulos, T.
1985   'Fouilles à Helleniko', *BCH* 109, 385–454.

Alcock, S., Berlin, A., Harrison, A., Heath, S., Spencer, N., Stone, D.
2005   'Pylos Regional Archeological Project, VII', *Hesperia* 147–209.

Azoulay, V.
Forthcoming   'L'*Archidamos* d'Isocrate: une politique de l'espace et du temps'.

Birgalias, N.
1999   *L'Odyssée de l'éducation spartiate*, Athens.

Catling, R.W.V.
2002   'The survey area from the Early Iron Age to the Classical Period', in Cavanagh et al., *The Laconia Survey*, Vol. I, 175–256.

Cavanagh, W., Crouwel, J., Catling R.W.V. and Shipley G. (eds.)
2002   *Continuity and Change in a Greek Rural Landscape: The Laconia survey, I: Methodology and interpretation*, London.

Christien, J.
1987a   'L'invasion de la Laconie et les routes du nord de l'état spartiate', *Praktika du IIIe Congrès international des Péloponnesiakon Spoudon*, Vol. II (Kalamata, September 1985), 325–36.

1987b   'Les forteresses de la côte orientale de la Laconie et la guerre de Chrémonidès', *Ktema* 2, 111–24.

1989   'Les liaisons entre Sparte et son territoire malgré l'encadrement montagneux', in J.-F. Bergier (ed.) *Montagnes, fleuves, forêts, dans l'histoire*', St. Katharinen, 18–44.

1992a   'Le mythe spartiate. Essai en historiographie', *Lakonikai Spoudai* 10 (Mélanges V. Vayakakos), 93–104.

1992b   'De Sparte à la côte orientale du Péloponnèse' *Polydypsion Argos*. BCH Suppl. 22, 157–72.

1993   'Les bâtards spartiates', *Mélanges P. Lévêque*, Vol. 7, Paris, 33–40.

1997   'Les temps d'une vie', *Métis* 12, 45–79.

1998   'Sparte et le Péloponnèse après 369', *Praktika du Ve congrès des Peloponnesiakon Spoudon*, (Argos-Nauplia, September 1995), 433–67.

2000   'Sparte', in M.C. Amouretti, J. Christien, F. Ruzé, P. Sineux: *Le regard des Grecs sur la guerre*, Paris, 127–78.

Christien, J. and Della Santa, M.
2001/2 'Pausanias et Strabon : La route du Taygète et les carrières de marbre laconien', *Praktika du VIe congrès international des Peloponnesiakon Spoudon*, Vol. 2, Tripolis, September 2000, 203–16.

Christien, J. et Spyropoulos, T.
1985   'Eua et la Thyréatide', *BCH* 109, 455–66.

Ducat, J.
1997a   'La cryptie en question', in P. Brulé and J. Oulhen (eds.) *Esclavage, guerre, économie: Hommages à Yvon Garlan*, 43–74.

1997b   'Crypties', Cahiers du Centre Gustave Glotz, VIII, 9–38.

2006   *Spartan Education. Youth and society in the classical period*, Swansea.

Ehrenberg V.
1976   *L'état grec*, Paris.

Gengler, O. and Marchetti, P.
2000   'Sparte hellénistique et romaine. Dix années de recherche 1989–1999', *Topoi* 10, 57–86.
Goester Y
1993   'The Plain of Astros', *Pharos* I, 39–112.
Grandjean C .
2003   *Les Messéniens de 370/369 au Ier siècle de notre ère; monnayage et histoire*, BCH Supp., Paris.
Hope Simpson, R.
1966   'The seven cities offered by Agamemnon to Achilles', *BSA* 52, 113–32.
Joachmus,A.
1857   'Commentaries', *Journal of the Royal Geographical Society* 27, 1–53.
Kennell, N.M.
1995   *The Gymnasium of Virtue: Education and culture in ancient Sparta*, London.
Leake, W.M.
1830   *Travels in Morea*, London.
Lévy, E.
1988   'La Kryptie et ses contradictions', *Ktema* 13, 245–53.
Loring, W.
1895   'Some ancient roads in the Peloponnese', *JHS* 15, 25–89.
Matthieu, G.
1925   *Les idées politiques d'Isocrate*, Paris.
Ogden, D.
2004   *Aristomenes of Messene; Legends of Sparta's nemesis*, Swansea .
Ollier. F.
1933, 1940   *Le mirage spartiate. Etude sur l'idéalisation de Sparte dans l'Antiquité grecque*, 2 vols., Paris.
Pearson, L.
1962   'The pseudo-history of Messenia and its authors', *Historia* 11, 397–426.
Piérart, M.
2001   'Argos, Philippe II et la Cynourie (Thyreatide) Les frontières du partage des Héraclides', in R. Frei-Stolba and K. Gex (eds.) *Recherches récentes sur le monde hellénistique*, Berne, 27–43.
Pritchett,W.K.
1965   'The battle of Sellasia, 222 BC', *Studies in Ancient Greek Topography* I, Berkeley.
Rhomaios, K.
1957   'Iasos –Iasaia', Ἑλληνικά 15, 65–75.
Roebuck, C.
1948   'The settlement of Philip II and the Greek states in 338 BC', *CPh*. Reprinted in *Economy and Society in the Early Greek World*, Chicago, 1984, 132–50.
Shipley, G.
2000   'The extent of Spartan territory in the late classical and Hellenistic period', *BSA* 95, 367–90.

6

AMOMPHARETOS, THE *LOCHOS* OF PITANE AND THE SPARTAN SYSTEM OF VILLAGES

Marcello Lupi

There is an ancient historiographical dispute regarding the alleged existence of a detachment of the Spartan army named the Pitanate *lochos*. In his Book I, while stating his research method, Thucydides denies that the *lochos* of Pitane ever existed. It is generally acknowledged that the target of his argument was Herodotus, who, in the ninth Book of his *Histories*, dwells on the role that this detachment played in the course of the battle of Plataia and in particular on the behaviour of its commander, the *lochagos* Amompharetos, son of Poliades.

The uncertainties of the ancients are inevitably reflected in modern studies; yet, despite the greater confidence that is usually placed in Thucydides, there generally prevails – or rather there has long prevailed – the opinion that such a battalion did in fact exist. According to this thesis, at the time of the battle of Plataia the Spartan army was organized in the 'obal' way: each of the five villages (*ōbai*) alleged to make up the *polis* of Sparta provided a *lochos*; thus Pitane, considered one of these five villages, provided the military contingent Herodotus refers to as the Pitanate *lochos*. An attempt has been made to justify the presumed error of Thucydides – who is too sure of what he says to be easily set aside – by claiming that the *lochos* of Pitane was officially named differently, and that therefore Herodotus was right from a factual point of view, Thucydides from a formal one.[1]

The present work sets out to question both this interpretation of the *lochos* of Pitane and the prevailing thesis on the distribution of the Spartan citizens by villages on which the interpretation depends;[2] in particular, it aims to frame differently the role of Pitane within the *polis* of Sparta. It is important to keep in mind that the reliability of Herodotus' account rests on another passage from his work (3.55.2), in which he claims to have been at Pitane – incidentally defined as *dēmos*, i.e. village, township – where he had met the Spartan Archias, whose grandfather bravely met his death at Samos during the Spartan expedition against Polykrates. The facts that Herodotus had been to Pitane and had also been acquainted with a Pitanate *lochos* have seemed not to be coincidental, and this has in turn strengthened the hypothesis of a 'Pitanatenquelle', according to which Archias is to be identified as Herodotus' source on the *lochos* of Pitane;[3] it has also been claimed that, given the presence of this Pitanate source, 'the onus of proof is firmly on those who wish to support Thucydides in denying that such a unit had ever existed'.[4] The solidity of this hypothesis, however, depends on the strength of the assumption on which it rests: if one accepts the idea that the citizens of Sparta were distributed into five villages and served in their respective battalions, it is natural to believe that, since Herodotus had been to Pitane, he would have certainly received information about the *lochos* that came from there. Yet, there is a risk of circularity, since it is precisely Herodotus' passage on the Pitanate *lochos* that constitutes one of the most significant pieces of evidence in support of the thesis of a city formed from five villages and five *lochoi*. If this thesis is rejected, the coincidence of Herodotus' being at the same time a visitor to Pitane and a witness to the Pitanate *lochos* may be explained differently.

I. Amompharetos and the traditions on the battle of Plataia

In order to judge Herodotus' evidence correctly it is necessary to set the role that the *lochos* of Pitane would have played during the battle of Plataia within the context of the description of the battle that Herodotus provides. This means tackling at least some of the problems in Herodotus' description of the tactical course of the battle. Many attempts have been made to put forward a reconstruction which on the one hand makes use of the information provided by Herodotus – especially the topographical data, which is often far from clear – and on the other hand rationalizes Herodotus' account by purging it of those elements judged to be less convincing, and by eventually integrating it with information from other sources.[5] More recently, however, greater attention has been paid to interpreting Herodotus as a literary text. This approach has engendered scepticism regarding the possibility of coming to a trustworthy reconstruction of what really happened;[6] all the more so because, having to gather information a few decades after the battle, Herodotus' text inevitably reflects different traditions, each concerned to provide a biased description of the event.[7] In examining closely events concerning the *lochos* of Pitane and its commander, as narrated by Herodotus, it will be necessary to consider how far the account is characterized by literary devices and biased traditions, and whether it is possible to save some of the 'factual' data that may prove useful for an assessment of the *lochos* itself.

Herodotus tells how, after originally encamping in the territory of Erythrai at the foot of Kithairon (9.19.3), the Greeks took courage and descended towards Plataia, deploying along the bank of the Asopos, in a position judged to be more suitable for pitching camp and with a more abundant water supply thanks to the presence of the Gargaphia spring (9.25). Here the two armies faced each other for several days until – exposed to continual harassment by the Persian cavalry and with the Persians having cut off their supplies as well as having made turbid the waters of the Gargaphia spring – Pausanias and the other Greek commanders met together and decided on a plan of retreat: if the Persians let that day pass without joining battle, the Greeks would withdraw under cover of darkness to the place called 'Island', considered more readily defensible (9.50–2). With night falling, and after the centre of the Greek formation had already completed its retreat, Pausanias ordered the Spartans to take their arms and to continue with the retreat (9.53.1). The figure of Amompharetos – the 'Unblameable', as his name says – comes on to the scene at this point: while the other officers obey Pausanias without hesitation, only 'Amompharetos, son of Poliades, who commanded the *lochos* of Pitane' refuses to flee from the foreigners and declares he would never willingly bring shame upon Sparta (9.53.2). Herodotus, moreover, maintains that Amompharetos had not been present at the previous meeting of the Greek commanders, and consequently did not know that a retreat had been planned. Pausanias judged Amompharetos' attitude intolerable, but nevertheless decided not to abandon him, fearing that left alone the *lochos* of Pitane would have been completely wiped out. Rather, he tried to persuade him to change his mind (9.53.3–4), but their discussion turned into an open quarrel to the point that Amompharetos took up a rock with both his hands and 'setting it before the feet of Pausanias said that with this vote (*psēphos*) he voted not to flee before the foreigners', while for his part Pausanias rebuked Amompharetos as 'mad and out of his mind' (9.55). Herodotus also adds that by dawn the discussion had not yet finished, and that at this point Pausanias decided to carry out the retreat, convinced, as later events proved correct, that Amompharetos, if left alone, would decide to follow him (9.56). And in fact when he realized he had been abandoned, Amompharetos did lead his *lochos* towards the rest of the Spartan army, which in the meantime had stopped so as to be able to help should the need arise. At the very moment of their rejoining forces the Persian cavalry attacked the Spartans, and the battle began (9.57).

At this point in Herodotus' account Amompharetos disappears and we hear nothing further of him until Herodotus, upon completing the description of the battle, focuses on those who had most distinguished themselves and had fallen in combat. In chapters 71–2 he writes that the Spartans were outstanding among all the Greeks for their bravery and mentions in particular Poseidonios, Philokyon and Amompharetos; while of a fourth Spartiate, Kallikrates, whose beauty is also mentioned incidentally, Herodotus takes

187

care to state that he died before the battle, being struck by an arrow while Pausanias performed the ritual sacrifices. Further on, at chapter 85.1–2, when dealing with the burial of the Greeks at Plataia, Herodotus begins by mentioning the Spartans, who distributed their dead among three tombs. The first, where Poseidonios, Amompharetos, Philokyon and Kallikrates were buried, was reserved for those whom the transmitted text indicates as 'priests' (ἱρέες; but a long-accepted emendation prefers the reading ἱρένες);[8] in the second were buried the other Spartiates, and in the third the helots.

There seems an obvious inconsistency, though one seldom explored by scholars, between the Amompharetos who blatantly disobeys Pausanias – who, besides being commander-in-chief of the Greek army, was in particular Amompharetos' direct commander as regent of Sparta – and the Amompharetos who was honoured for his death by the Spartans, and most likely with the approval of Pausanias himself. Unless we imagine two persons of the same name,[9] the explanation for the inconsistency must be sought in the context of the traditions that refer to Amompharetos. In other words, what are Herodotus' sources in chapters 53–7 on the one hand, and 71–2 and 85 on the other?

The account of chapters 53–7 has raised many doubts, which years ago Peter Green summed up with the following question: 'Could anything be more jejune or implausible?'[10] In particular, the quarrel between the Spartan commanders that goes on through the whole night before the battle is implausible and, as has been observed, it is partly constructed on the Homeric model of the quarrel between Agamemnon (Pausanias) and Achilles (Amompharetos).[11] Nor does it seem reasonable that, after finally deciding to abandon Amompharetos, Pausanias stopped in order to wait for him, nor that Amompharetos, after so much stubbornness, had so quickly consented to withdraw after having being abandoned. Recently, however, it has been argued that 'real life is messy, chaotic, and unpredictable', so that Herodotus' account should not be rejected merely on the grounds that Amompharetos' behaviour hardly appears rational.[12] But such an argument seems rather weak: it may even be admitted, leaving aside the less likely details of Herodotus' account, that Amompharetos disobeyed and a quarrel with Pausanias ensued; but is it then believable that, after so blatantly disobeying the orders he had received, Amompharetos could have been judged by the Spartans as one of their most courageous warriors and buried with honour?[13] Moreover, and this is what counts most, the simple recognition that an Athenian source is behind these chapters is enough to make the entire account suspect. The pro-Athenian inclination of the source cannot be doubted: Herodotus observes that while Pausanias tried to persuade Amompharetos to retreat the Athenians did not move from their position 'knowing the mind of the

Spartans who think one thing and say another' (9.54.1). The Athenians then dispatch a herald to the Spartans, and it is before him that the most dramatic scene of the quarrel between Amompharetos and Pausanias takes place (9.55). Therefore, not only does Herodotus' source have an unfavourable attitude towards the Spartans, but the historian himself in fact admits, by having the figure of the herald intervene, that his information on the quarrel comes from an Athenian source.[14]

In the case of the 'other' Amompharetos, who is praised for his courageous behaviour and then buried in the first of the three Spartan tombs, we are certainly dealing with Spartan traditions which exalted the Spartan dead and mentioned their burial. Herodotus claims that, although the Tegeates and the Athenians had also behaved courageously, it was the Spartans who had distinguished themselves far more than the others; moreover, the historian makes explicit reference to a discussion in which the Spartiates who had been present at the events expressed the opinion that the most courageous of all had been Poseidonios. Consequently, the source for chapter 85 must also be Spartan, both because we meet there with the same four Spartiates that Herodotus had mentioned in chapters 71–2, and because the order in which the burials are mentioned corresponds to their respective degrees of courage: first the Spartans, then the Tegeates and the Athenians.

It has been rightly observed that the passages quoted here belong to the restricted number of occasions in which it is possible to infer Herodotus' source for the campaign of Plataia from the historian's account itself: 'Details within the theatrical anecdote of Amompharetos' refusal to retreat suggest an Athenian source for this story, while the report that the Spartans present at Plataiai decided who was worthy of the prize for valour implies a Spartan source.'[15] It follows from this that the figure of Amompharetos has the privilege of appearing both in a passage where an Athenian source is clearly recognizable, as well as where the tradition is certainly Spartan. The two images are in open contradiction: in the Spartan tradition Amompharetos is a brave warrior, honoured for the courage shown in battle and buried in a way suited to such courage; in the Athenian tradition he is the commander of the *lochos* of Pitane, who has disobeyed Pausanias and, in refusing to retreat, has unintentionally created the conditions for the Greek victory at Plataia. The unresolved contrast between these two images should not be cause for any surprise, since it shows Herodotus' adherence to the principle of *legein ta legomena*: namely, to report the traditions which he has learned about, without his necessarily believing them (7.152).

If this interpretation is correct, the thesis of a 'Pitanatenquelle' does not hold. Since the notion of a Pitanate *lochos* appears only in the chapters that depend on an Athenian source, we can infer that in all likelihood it has been elaborated in an Athenian setting.[16] It is not my intention to deny that Herodotus may have used some data from a Spartan source – including possibly the idea that Amompharetos was the commander of the *lochos* of Pitane – and imported it into a context dependent on an Athenian tradition,[17] but the burden of proof is on those who wish to pursue this hypothesis. In any case, the fact that Thucydides denies the existence of such a battalion so resolutely is an excellent argument against the thesis that the notion of a *lochos* of Pitane depends on Spartan tradition, and this in turn reduces considerably the possibility of using this notion in order to reconstruct the organization of the Spartan army. But even if Herodotus' evidence has to be used with caution, there is no reason to doubt that Amompharetos was in fact the commander of a unit of the army, and there certainly must be some reason why the Athenian tradition has indicated this unit by the name of Pitanate *lochos*. Nor is there any reason to doubt that such a *lochos* performed the movements that Herodotus ascribes to it. If we consider these movements for what they are in themselves – leaving aside how the tradition followed by Herodotus attempts to justify them, and consequently ignoring the episode of the quarrel between Amompharetos and Pausanias – it is possible to surmise that the *lochos* of Pitane acted as a rearguard. As such it delays its withdrawal in order to protect the retreat of the rest of the army and, in accordance with a tactical scheme used at other times by the Spartans,[18] finally retreated by making the enemy's attack converge on itself. The interpretation of the *lochos* of Pitane as rearguard has been advanced several times in the last century,[19] and, although we may never achieve certainty about the tactics of the battle, it deserves consideration.

II. How old was Amompharetos? The *eirenes* puzzle

In the identification of the detachment of the army that Herodotus calls the *lochos* of Pitane, a decisive part is played by the subject of Amompharetos' age; if we read ἰρένες into Herodotus 9.85, we are obliged to admit that this *lochos* was commanded by a young man, with the inevitable consequences for the identification of the battalion: at Sparta, in fact, the young men who had reached the age of twenty were called εἰρένες (or ἰρένες),[20] and remained in this age-grade probably until reaching their thirtieth year.[21] Indeed, among the arguments most frequently put forward to reject the presence of ἰρένες in the Herodotean text there is the claim that, as commander of the *lochos* of Pitane, Amompharetos would necessarily have had to be more than thirty years old.[22] But this argument, too, works only if one accepts the thesis of the 'obal' army: if in fact the *lochos* of Pitane was one of the five batallions into which the entire Spartan army was subdivided, it would be natural to expect it to be led by a man of mature age, since the Spartan institutions entrusted the most important *archai* to men over the age of thirty years.[23] But the term *lochos* was also used to indicate a military detachment of a smaller size,[24] and it is possible that Amompharetos led a battalion made up only of young men. Moreover, the likelihood that the tradition concerning the *lochos* of Pitane recorded in Herodotus is Athenian, makes it hard to imagine that the term *lochos* is being used in the technical Spartan sense, which in turn precludes a too mechanical association of the Pitanate *lochos* with the Spartan *lochoi* attested in Thucydides, Xenophon and Aristotle.[25]

It is not worth dwelling very long on the philological difficulties, both because they have already been treated in some recent studies,[26] and especially because no definitive solution is possible at a purely philological level. Suffice it here to note that the manuscripts of Herodotus 9.85.1–2 are unanimous in presenting the following text:

> Λακεδαιμόνιοι μὲν τριξὰς ἐποιήσαντο θήκας· ἔνθα μὲν τοὺς ἰρέας ἔθαψαν, τῶν καὶ Ποσειδώνιος καὶ Ἀμομφάρετος ἦσαν καὶ Φιλοκύων τε καὶ Καλλικράτης· ἐν μὲν δὴ ἑνὶ τῶν τάφων ἦσαν οἱ ἰρέες, ἐν δὲ τῷ ἑτέρῳ οἱ ἄλλοι Σπαρτιῆται, ἐν δὲ τῷ τρίτῳ οἱ εἵλωτες.

> The Lacedaemonians made three graves: in one they buried the *irees*, among whom were Poseidonios and Amompharetos and Philokyon and Kallikrates; in one of the tombs then were the *irees*, in the second the other Spartiates, in the third the helots.

Since ἰρέες is the Ionian form used by Herodotus in place of ἱερεῖς, it follows that the transmitted text presents the 'priests' as being buried in the first tomb. Yet, leaving aside a recent edition of the ninth Book of Herodotus,[27] all editors accept an emendation proposed by L.C. Valckenaer in the mid-eighteenth century that involves the correction of ἰρέας/ες to ἰρένας/ες. Underlying the emendation is the presence of the entry εἰρήν in a lexicon of Herodotean terms that have come down to us through certain manuscripts. Since the only place in which such an entry – in the variant ἰρήν – could be present, is Herodotus 9.85, the acceptance of the emendation can readily be understood. In Valckenaer's view, the emended text appeared more plausible than the transmitted one, since the reference to priests buried separately from other Spartiates clashed with the general silence of the sources on particular Spartan priesthoods as well as on particular burials for priests killed in battle.[28] The correctness of the emendation was seriously questioned in the 1950s by Willem den Boer, but only in recent years has the opinion that the manuscript reading must be preferred begun to prevail.[29] So it seems appropriate to consider all the arguments on which support for the manuscript reading is based, and to evaluate their strength.

There is no doubt that the presence of the term in an Herodotean lexicon does not have decisive weight. In fact two λέξεις Ἡροδότου have come down to us: the first, ordered by books and containing almost exclusively Herodotean material, does not present the entry εἰρήν. The word is instead attested only in the second lexicon, which unfortunately includes a substantial number of entries absent from Herodotus' text. Quite rightly it has been stated that 'it is therefore not correct to say that ἰρήν occurs in Herodotus because it is found in the Λέξεις'.[30] Nonetheless, it would be equally incorrect to argue that the term did not occur in Herodotus simply on the grounds that these lists of entries also contain non-Herodotean material: the first lexicon is mutilated in the final part and does not present entries belonging to the ninth Book of Herodotus; thus, the absence of the item εἰρήν in such a list is hardly relevant. Next, a point of method has been raised, namely that 'it is methodologically wrong to ignore the consensus of the MSS and to prefer a glossa on a word that does not exist in the text of Herodotus'.[31] However, such a methodological principle is not convincing: the consensus of all the manuscripts ensures, beyond any doubt, that the lesson ἰρέας/ες was already present in the archetype of the manuscript tradition, but this archetype does not go back beyond the Middle Ages when, as is virtually certain, a considerable number of corruptions must have already altered Herodotus' text. It seems to me that the question is to be posed differently: it is clear that if the lexicons in question contained only entries coming from Herodotus, it would be necessary to consider the forms ἰρένας/ες as a variant present in the indirect tradition; and since such a variant would naturally be preferable as *lectio difficilior*, in the Spartiates buried in the first grave we should unhesitatingly recognise the *eirenes*. The fact that these lexicons contain some non-Herodotean material weakens the case for the emendation and leads us to register a *non liquet* from a *textual* viewpoint. In order to offer a satisfactory solution to the problem, it is thus necessary to consider the *contextual* arguments and to judge whether these really require the emendation.

The main contextual argument is the almost total absence of evidence on Spartan priesthoods.[32] It has been rightly objected that the scarcity of knowledge about such priesthoods is not a sufficient reason for emending a text,[33] but the arguments put forward in defence of the transmitted text do not appear particularly strong: hardly convincing, for example, is the reference to the tripartite Indo-European ideology to justify the fact that one of the three tombs was destined for priests.[34] Methodologically doubtful, too, is the thesis that we should accept the manuscript text, attributing nevertheless to the ἰρέες a different meaning from that commonly found in Herodotus, and in particular the sense of 'heroes'.[35] Yet a simple check on the use of the term ἰρεύς in Herodotus would have shown that the text of the manuscripts is inherently implausible with respect to its *usus scribendi*. In the 56 certain occurrences of the term, Herodotus always relates individual priests with the specific sanctuaries to which they are assigned: this feature is absent only in Herodotus 9.85.[36] Had Herodotus simply wished to say that the soldiers buried in the first tomb were not really priests, but more generically, 'holy' men – whatever this might mean in Spartan culture – he would have used the term ἱροί, as he does elsewhere in his *Histories*.[37] But, since he did not do so, it is necessary to acknowledge that the transmitted text implies a reference to some priests as holders of a specific cult, without Herodotus ever making any reference to these cults or ever qualifying these alleged 'priests' except for their courage and beauty.

Thus, despite the growing consensus towards the restoration of the text transmitted by the manuscripts, in my view this text continues to be unsatisfactory, and I intend here to offer a series of arguments to show either that the Spartiates buried in the first tomb were young men or that young men were at any rate the components of the *lochos* of Pitane. None of these arguments claims to be particularly original, and probably none taken individually may be considered decisive; taken together, however, they have a decisive weight.

(1) An account of why Spartan citizens fallen in battle were buried separately requires us to identify the categories the Spartan culture used to make distinctions within their own citizen body. While we cannot justify a separation between priests and other citizens, the generational distinction between young adults under thirty years of age and mature men, is well attested in Spartan society.[38] Also we should recall how the first ten conscription classes, that is the young men in their twenties, constituted a discrete unit to which the more risky military duties were assigned, such as hurling itself against the enemy at double speed while the rest of the army advanced at a regular pace.[39] Thus, an age-based burial, with the young adults in one tomb and the other Spartiates in another one, seems quite possible.

(2) Since a considerable number of scholars believe, in my view rightly, that the battalion led by Amompharetos acted as a rearguard of the Spartan army and took on the particularly risky task of making the Persian army's attack converge on itself, it is very probable that such a rearguard was made up of young men, since, as has just been noticed, the youngest conscription classes had to perform the manoeuvres reputed to be the most dangerous.

(3) One of the Spartiates buried in the first tomb, Kallikrates, is said to be the most handsome man (ἀνὴρ κάλλιστος) amongst all the Greeks present at Plataia (Hdt. 9.72.1). It has been argued that Kallikrates, being an *anēr*, could not be an *eirēn*, because Xenophon would not include the *eirenes* age class among the *andres*.[40] This is not quite right, both because the presence of the term *eirēn*, which is absent from all the manuscripts of Xenophon, is very

dubious,[41] and also because Xenophon himself qualifies as *andres* all the young men in their twenties, whom he calls *hēbōntes* (Xen. *Lak. Pol.* 4.3). There is no reason, therefore, why Herodotus could not have regarded Kallikrates as an *anēr* if the latter were a young man who, as *eirēn*, had passed the age of twenty, and it is certain that Herodotus did not intend to say that Kallikrates was the most handsome only within a specific age group. Rather, here the word that counts is not *anēr*, but *kallistos*. The Greek conception of beauty in fact makes it very unlikely that Kallikrates could be considered the most handsome of the Greeks present at Plataia, had he not been a young man.[42]

(4) Also significant, moreover, is the mintage during the third quarter of the fourth century of some coins that present the legend Πιτανατᾶν περιπόλων in the Dorian alphabet. It has long been shown that such coins, found in the Samnite area, take on meaning if interpreted in the context of the traditions which ascribe a Spartan (and in particular Pitanate) origin to the Samnites and to other Italic populations: these traditions were undoubt-edly elaborated in the Spartan colony of Taras, interested in ingratiating itself with the Samnites by attributing to them a Spartan origin to the point of claiming that some Samnites were called Pitanates (Strabo 5.4.12).[43] For our purposes the reference to the 'frontier guards' (*peripoloi*) is especially notable, as the task of patrolling the frontiers was chiefly performed in the Greek world by young men.[44] Thus, since calling the Samnite youth *Pitanatai peripoloi* seems clearly to imply a reference to the stories regarding the *lochos* of Pitane and to its role in the battle of Plataia, it follows that the tradition on the Pitanate origin of the Samnites entailed the awareness that the Pitanate *lochos* was made up of young men.

(5) In the same way, the Emperor Caracalla must also have known about this: it is said by Herodianus that when in his pro-Hellenic fervor Caracalla wanted to institute a *lochos* of Pitane, he had some young men (νεανίαι) summoned from Sparta.[45]

(6) Finally, a decisive argument that supports the thesis that the members of the Pitanate *lochos* were young has been provided by Douglas H. Kelly, who has offered a new, albeit in some ways obvious, interpretation of the passage where Thucydides denies its existence (1.20.3). It is thus worth considering the text in its entirety:

πολλὰ δὲ καὶ ἄλλα ἔτι καὶ νῦν ὄντα καὶ οὐ χρόνῳ ἀμνηστούμενα καὶ οἱ ἄλλοι Ἕλληνες οὐκ ὀρθῶς οἴονται, ὥσπερ τούς τε Λακεδαιμονίων βασιλέας μὴ μιᾷ ψήφῳ προστίθεσθαι ἑκάτερον, ἀλλὰ δυοῖν, καὶ τὸν Πιτανάτην λόχον αὐτοῖς εἶναι, ὃς οὐδ' ἐγένετο πώποτε.

On many other matters, belonging to the present and not obscured by time, the other Greeks too have wrong opinions, as the fact that the kings of the

Lakedaemonians cast not one vote each, but two, and that they have the *lochos* of Pitane, which has never existed.

Kelly has observed that the usual interpretation of the expression καὶ τὸν Πιτανάτην λόχον αὐτοῖς εἶναι, according to which αὐτοῖς should be referred to the Lacedaemonians, does not respect the syntax of the text, since 'the subject of the infinitive προστίθεσθαι just before is Λακεδαιμονίων βασιλέας and, as these phrases are linked with τε...καὶ, αὐτοῖς too should be taken as referring to the Spartan kings'.[46]

Kelly's argument, which is unavoidable from a syntactical point of view and implies that the *lochos* of Pitane belonged to the kings, has two further consequences: first, that the Thucydidean controversy clearly revolves around the prerogatives of the Spartan kings, which in turn allows the controversy to be viewed in a new perspective, as I will try to show in the next section; a second consequence derives from an acknowledgement that the only detachment of the army which had a specific relationship with the two kings is the corps of three hundred *hippeis*, which acted as a sort of royal guard – and it follows, therefore, that some form of overlap had to exist between the *lochos* of Pitane and the corps of the *hippeis*. The fact, explicitly attested in several sources, that the *hippeis* were selected from among the young men not yet thirty years old[47] also shows that Thucydides' passage, if read in its correct syntax, implies a *lochos* of Pitane composed totally of young men. Therefore, the *lochagos* Amompharetos also had to be young.

In light of all these arguments, I believe it is legitimate to consider the presence of the εἰρένες in Herodotus' text as highly probable; but even those who wish to continue to support the reading offered by the manuscripts will have to agree that the mysterious ἱρέες of Herodotus – whether they were 'priests', 'heroes' or something else – were, by sheer accident, also young men.

III. Herodotus and Thucydides on the Pitanate *lochos*

Despite the merits of his interpretation, Kelly built on it a highly improbable hypothesis: by assuming again that Herodotus must have obtained information on the Pitanate *lochos* during his stay at Pitane, Kelly inferred that the historian had misinterpreted the information he had received from the Spartan Archias, who would have praised the valour of 'the young men of Pitane who, at least in Archias' opinion, always dominated the competitive selection of *hippeis*. So Herodotus came away with the impression that the *hippeis* were called the Pitanate *lochos*'.[48]

We have already indicated the weakness of the basic assumption: the probability that the Herodotean tradition on the *lochos* of Pitane is Athenian undermines speculation on the boasts of the Pitanates, with which Kelly tries to justify the erroneous identification made by Herodotus between the *lochos* of Pitane and the body of the *hippeis*. As a matter of fact, a different reconstruction may be formulated by carefully analysing the context in which Thucydides denies the existence of the *lochos* of Pitane. At the end of the so-called *archaiologia* Thucydides notes how difficult it is to trust information about the past, since men are accustomed to accept oral traditions regarding past events without submitting them to verification, even when these traditions regard events of their own country. He supports this assumption by claiming that most Athenians wrongly believe Hipparchos was killed by Harmodios and Aristogeiton when he was tyrant, not knowing that the actual tyrant was Hippias, since he was the eldest among the sons of Peisistratos (1.20.1–2). To this Athenian example Thucydides adds the two examples taken from Spartan institutional history mentioned above, relating to the votes of the Spartan kings and to the *lochos* of Pitane.

To put side by side examples taken from Athenian and Spartan history seems natural for one who attempted to write the 'contemporary' history of the great war between Athens and Sparta; but it is worth observing that the parallelism operating in the passage is not perfect. With regard to Athens, Thucydides makes it clear that it is the Athenians themselves who have the wrong opinions about their past, whereas in the case of Sparta his formulation is less clear and he introduces his observations with the sentence 'the other Greeks too have wrong opinions'. Strictly speaking, these 'other Greeks' should be 'others' with respect to the Athenians, but they certainly were not the Spartans, since it seems highly unlikely that the Athenian Thucydides would have been in a position to correct the Spartans on their own past, let alone their institutions. Generally the problem has been avoided by imagining that with the expression the 'other Greeks' Thucydides in fact had in mind only one other Greek, namely Herodotus of Halikarnassos.[49] Thucydides would restrict himself, therefore, to criticizing what Herodotus had written regarding the *lochos* of Pitane (9.53) and the votes the Spartan kings had at their disposal in the *gerousia* (6.56.5). To my mind, however, the question is more complex: even admitting that Thucydides' criticism was aimed at two far-removed passages of Herodotus' text, a quick comparison of all the passages in question suffices to show that there could hardly be a direct connection between that of Thucydides and those of Herodotus, inevitably raising the problem of the forms of intertextuality between the two historians.[50]

As has been noted, their texts presuppose among the public to which they are addressed 'a large contextual competence we fatally lack'.[51] On the *lochos* of Pitane, in particular, Herodotus and Thucydides are to be considered as users of traditions which their public at least in part would know; and it is in the context of these traditions – only partially reconstructable through their accounts – that the substance of the controversy has to be examined. Thus, if it is true that the very notion of the *lochos* of Pitane belongs to the Athenian tradition, it is not completely correct to claim that Thucydides is criticizing Herodotus: as a matter of fact he is criticizing an Athenian tradition that Herodotus had accepted and which he believes instead should be rejected; and if Herodotus had learned it at Athens during his stay in the 440s, it is unlikely that Thucydides would have known about it solely through the mediation of Herodotus.[52] Even on the votes of the Spartan kings it seems difficult to believe that Thucydides is simply replying to the text of Herodotus which we read today. Thucydides' controversy is addressed against those who claim that the Spartan kings had two votes in the *gerousia* at their disposal, but Herodotus says something different, namely that if the kings are not able to take part in the meetings of the *gerousia*, those among the *gerontes* who are closer to them through family ties have two votes at their disposal as well as their own as a third. The sense of Herodotus' text is far from clear,[53] but, unless we accept that Thucydides meant to provide an extremely simplified interpretation of it, we must conclude that he did not have Herodotus' text in front of him.[54] On the contrary, Thucydides is criticizing the untrustworthiness of the oral tradition, and it would indeed be strange if he supported his criticism by reporting an example taken from a written text. Thucydides' criticism, rather, was to be addressed towards the oral traditions in circulation at Athens, including among these the traditions that had spread through the public lectures that Herodotus held at Athens, and at which Thucydides quite likely had been present.

I noted above that Thucydides' controversy revolves around the topic of the privileges of the Spartan kings even when it deals with the *lochos* of Pitane; consequently, the fact that Herodotus dwelt on such privileges in the sixth Book (chs. 56–9) can hardly be considered a coincidence and represents the starting point for reconstructing the intertextual relationship between the two historians as regards the Pitanate *lochos*. It is in these chapters that Herodotus tackles the theme of the votes of the Spartan kings in the *gerousia* in the ways indicated above, and even if apparently no explicit reference to the *lochos* of Pitane is present, there is clearly a reference to a military corps having a specific relationship with the kings. As a matter of fact, Herodotus writes that during the military campaigns the kings had at their disposal a selected corps of a hundred men (6.56: ἑκατὸν δὲ ἄνδρας λογάδας ἐπὶ στρατιῆς φυλάσσειν αὐτούς [i.e. τοὺς βασιλέας]). Within a few lines, therefore, Herodotus alludes both to the kings' votes in the *gerousia* and to a military corps closely linked to the kings of the Lacedaemonians, precisely the two traditions criticized by Thucydides.[55] So, rather than identify the *lochos* of Pitane with the total number of the *hippeis*, it is more feasible that it was only a part, just as Pitane was only a part of Sparta. It is unequivocally evidenced by Xenophon that the corps of the three hundred *hippeis* was institutionally divided into three sections: its selection, in fact, came about through the nomination by the ephors of three *hippagretai*, each with the task of choosing a hundred men (*Lac. Pol.* 4.3). Since it appears certain that the hundred men who accompanied the king during the military campaigns are to be identified with one of the three groups making up the *hippeis*, Herodotus' testimony must mean that only one third of the *hippeis* constituted the kings' bodyguard in the strict sense.[56] These hundred men must then be recognized as underlying the Athenian notion of the Pitanate *lochos*. Consequently Amompharetos, as commander of the *lochos* of Pitane, is to be identified with one of the three *hippagretai*.[57]

It is true that Herodotus does not refer to these hundred men with the name of *lochos* of Pitane and that, therefore, the criticism of Thucydides would not make sense if directed towards Herodotus' text as we have it today. But this objection fails if we keep in mind that Thucydides did not intend to tackle this version of the text, but the one read publicly by Herodotus very likely in the presence of Thucydides himself.[58] Since we do not have this other text, the observations which follow are inevitably speculative, but it is worth observing that Herodotus' chapters on the privileges of the Spartiate kings contain some notable features: on the one hand, Herodotus takes care to inform us that this subject has been overlooked by 'others' and that he is the first to gather material on it (6.55); on the other, it has been noticed that behind these chapters must be a Spartan document that Herodotus would have reproduced by transcribing it in Ionian dialect. In particular, it has been observed that chapters 56 and 57, with the singular sequence of 22 infinitives, present the syntactical structure typical of some Spartan legislative texts, the same that characterizes the so-called 'Great Rhetra'.[59] Both such a claim of originality and this documentary care rarely perceptible in Herodotus' text make it likely in my view that Herodotus is responding to accusations levelled against him at the level of documentary reliability. In other words, when – relatively late in his life – Herodotus decided to write down his work, he found himself competing with Thucydides and aware of some of the criticisms that had been levelled against him by his Athenian rival, levelled, that is to say, against the content of his public lecture.[60] The choice of publishing a Spartan document, limiting himself to giving it an Ionian veneer in order to make it accessible to a non-Dorian audience, protected him from all criticism on the documentary level. In this way, however, his text on the privileges of the Spartan kings no longer contains any reference to the *lochos* of Pitane, and cannot contain any for the simple reason that at Sparta there did not exist a battalion officially called the Pitanate *lochos* and no official document could consequently make reference to it.

If this hypothesis is correct, we may reasonably infer that on the occasion of his public readings Herodotus did not read the document at his disposal on the privileges of the Spartan kings but interpreted it: on the basis of the current Athenian tradition he assigned the name *lochos* of Pitane to the hundred *hippeis* set to guard the kings and offered a very personal reading of the law on the votes cast by the kings during the councils of the *gerousia*. This is the 'text' against which Thucydides polemicizes. However, when Herodotus set down his definitive text, he adhered to a greater documentary sobriety and, while continuing to make reference to the *lochos* of Pitane in his account of the battle of Plataia, he struck out this reference from the sixth Book of his *Histories*. He had finished by admitting that Thucydides was at least in part right.

IV. Dorian tribes and Spartan villages: toward a new approach

The reconstruction here proposed has two results: first, the notion of the *lochos* of Pitane had been elaborated in an Athenian setting, and so Thucydides must be right when he states that a *lochos* of Pitane, understood literally, had never existed at Sparta; second, it must be acknowledged that by this notion the Athenian tradition had intended to refer to a detachment of the Spartan army that really had existed and had played an important role in the battle of Plataia, and it is possible to identify this detachment with the hundred men who made up the king's bodyguard.

It remains to be understood why these hundred men, who represented a third of the entire corps of the *hippeis*, were known, at least according to a tradition circulating at Athens, as the *lochos* of Pitane. The selection of the three hundred *hippeis* into three groups, in fact, does not seem to have any relationship with the distribution of the Spartiates by villages; rather, it appears reasonable to assume that a Spartan military battalion made up of three hundred men, divided into three groups and led by three commanders relates to the three Dorian tribes.[61] The custom of organizing the army by distributing the citizens according to the tribes to which they belong is attested by Tyrtaeus (fr. 19.8 West), and whatever is the origin of the three hundred *hippeis* in chronological terms, it seems likely that at the time of the battle of Plataia the *hippeis* still reflected this criterion of distribution, even if the rest of the army was at that time organized differently.[62]

The identification of the tribe whose hundred *hippeis* made up the king's bodyguard does not present particular difficulties: it must have been the same tribe to which the two kings belonged, and it is generally admitted that the kings were included in the tribe of the Hylleis.[63] In fact, the ideology at the root of Dorian identity claimed that during their migration into the Peloponnese the Dorians had been accompanied by the descendants of Herakles, the Herakleidai. For our purposes the question of the historicity of the Dorian migration and of the origin of the three tribes is irrelevant; it suffices to observe, in the light of this ideology, that the tribe of the Hylleis, which took its name from Hyllos son of Herakles, was imagined to represent the Herakleides branch, whereas the other two represented the Dorians in a strict sense.[64] Thus, since the main function of the tribes in historical times was clearly that of segmenting the civic body,[65] such a segmentation must have been consistent with the ideology underlying the Dorian identity, and both the ruling families at Sparta, insofar as they claimed to descend from Herakles,[66] had to be included in the tribe of the Hylleis.

It is evident, then, that the only way to reconcile the two theses that the *lochos* of Pitane was equivalent to the hundred men making up the king's guard and that these men were the contingent of the *hippeis* coming from the tribe of the Hylleis, is to admit that a relationship existed between the tribe of the Hylleis and the village of Pitane. I do not mean to say that it is necessary to posit a mechanical correspondence between the tribe and the village, but rather that those who elaborated the tradition on the Pitanate *lochos* were aware of the fact that the soldiers who made up this battalion came mostly from the area of Pitane. If, as I believe, this is correct, a radical revision of the prevailing opinion regarding the segmentation of the Spartan citizen body is necessary. In what follows I will attempt to show that – independently of the *lochos* of Pitane – there are excellent reasons for believing that the prevailing opinion is inadequate, and I will indicate the general outline of an alternative hypothesis.

According to the opinion still prevailing today – based on an antiquarian interpretation of the most celebrated archaic Spartan document: the 'Great Rhetra'[67] – Spartan citizens were distributed within two intersecting structures: the inherited order of the tribes and a local structure of the villages. In fact, the *rhētra* refers to a division of the civic body into *phylai* and *ōbai*, respectively identified with the three traditional Dorian tribes (Hylleis, Dymanes and Pamphiloi), and with the four villages (Pitane, Mesoa, Limnai, Kynosoura) that supposedly formed the city of Sparta, while only later, as the result of the expansion of Sparta in the early-archaic age, would Amyklai have been added, some kilometres south of the town itself. However, while the presence of the three *phylai* is explicitly attested in archaic times in the poems of Tyrtaeus, the identification of the *ōbai* with these five villages is the result of a reconstruction that has exploited all the available evidence but has also quite problematically treated each source without taking into account its date.

The cornerstones of this theory can be summarized as follows. Thucydides' authoritative testimony explicitly asserts that the *polis* of Sparta had not achieved urban unification and its citizens followed a residential model that he considers old-fashioned and summarizes in the expression *polis kata kōmas*: the Spartiates, that is to say, were distributed in a plurality of villages (1.10.2). Thucydides never uses the Spartan technical term *ōbai*, but the lexicographic sources bear out an equivalence between *ōbai* and *kōmai*.[68] Moreover, Pausanias the Periegete, referring to the origins of the cult of Artemis Orthia, bears witness to a division of the Spartan citizens into inhabitants of the villages of Pitane, Mesoa, Limnai and Kynosoura (3.16.9), and this same subdivision is substantially confirmed by Roman-period inscriptions primarily belonging to competitive contests, in which such communities are called *ōbai*.[69] Finally, a further inscription of the Roman period calls *ōba* the community of Amyklai, while attributing to it a status of semi-autonomy with respect to Sparta (*IG* V.1.26). The five *ōbai*, as thus specified, would account for the presence of the number five in certain Spartan magistracies, especially in the ephorate, as well as the already-mentioned subdivision of the Spartan army into five *lochoi* attested in certain sources.[70] This reconstruction, which by and large interprets the *ōbai* of the 'Great Rhetra' through documents of the Roman imperial age, was clearly formulated by L. Pareti in 1910 and in fact emerged as an orthodoxy in Spartan studies subsequently, especially through the works of V. Ehrenberg and H.T. Wade-Gery.[71]

A minority opinion has sometimes opposed this orthodoxy, suggesting that the *ōbai* of the *rhētra* indicated a descent-defined internal subdivision of the *phylai*.[72] This alternative thesis, moreover, took advantage of the interpretation offered by A.J. Beattie in the early fifties of an inscription from the area of ancient Amyklai. The inscription is now lost, but its text was transcribed by the French antiquarian Fourmont in the mid-eighteenth century.[73] Fourmont has never enjoyed a good reputation for the quality of his transcriptions, and the interpretation of this particular inscription, datable between the late sixth and early fifth century, is problematic to say the least: following Beattie's study, however, no doubts exist that it makes reference to an '*ōba* [ōϝά] of Arkaloi', thus raising the problem of how it was possible that on the territory of the *polis* of Sparta – and indeed in the neighbourhood of one of the five alleged *ōbai* – a further and unknown *ōba* was located. Despite the attempts to save the orthodoxy by admitting that in the classical age the *ōbai* were more than five or that Arkaloi was in fact a perioikic community,[74] it can be reasonably hypothesized that in late-archaic and classical Sparta the *ōbai* were not villages, but rather an internal subdivision of the *phylai*. Nevertheless, this hypothesis has never been formulated in detail, and it remains an open question whether the prevailing opinion has stood more because of the absence of a valid alternative paradigm rather than for its intrinsic explanatory capacity.

Finally, it should also be noted that some recent studies have shown a growing scepticism towards the theory of the 'obal' army, and the relationship between the number of the ephors and the *ōbai* has seemed somewhat opaque.[75] No one, however, as far as I know, has ever doubted the idea that the *polis* of Sparta was made up, as early as the archaic and classical age, of five villages; at most it has been claimed that Amyklai was in fact a perioikic city, and that therefore the classical city was made up of four villages.[76] To my mind, a solution of the problem of the *lochos* of Pitane can only be reached if one begins to question this assumption; to question, in other words, the idea that Sparta kept unaltered a system of four or five villages for a period of time ranging from about the age of the 'Great Rhetra' until the beginning of the third century AD. It is likely that such trust in an almost millennial continuity has benefited from reputed Spartan conservatism,[77] but more recent studies on Sparta have revealed the continuous changes to which the society and the institutional organization of Sparta were subject,[78] and there is no reason to believe that only the distribution of the civic body remained unaltered. Moreover, although it has been claimed that the subdivisions of the civic body in the Greek *poleis* were generally conservative and that most of the innovations concerning them took place in the archaic period during the age of the tyrants, M.H. Hansen has recently warned against such a continuistic approach, stating that in fact they were subject to constant transformations.[79]

So, if late evidence is left aside, it is easy to realize that the thesis of a Sparta divided into four villages, as bequeathed to us by Pausanias and the inscriptions of Roman times, has no foundation in classical sources.[80] Two of these villages (Mesoa and Kynosoura) are completely unknown to the most ancient sources, apart from being localized in Spartan topography only conjecturally. A third village (Limnai) may with certainty be identified in the marshy area situated to the east and south-east of the acropolis where the temple of Artemia Orthia (Paus. 3.16.7) was erected, but it too is absent from the sources. Only Pitane may be localized with certainty in the area immediately west of the akropolis,[81] and it alone is attested in classical sources. In consideration of this there is no reason for regarding it as certain that the *kōmai* of Thucydides must correspond to the districts which made up Roman Sparta. Rather, it is the famous passage of Thucydides that deserves reconsideration: it has been observed that, since at the beginning of the fifth century Sparta had a population of 8,000 Spartiates of military age, the alleged five villages of Sparta must have been inhabited in this period by a total population – including women, children, men not of military age and urban slaves – on the order of some tens of thousands. Consequently, also excluding the inhabitants of Amyklai, we may deduce that the four villages comprising Sparta should have been inhabited, at least in the period of the city's maximum demographic expansion, by a population such that they could not constitute separate villages, but rather had to form a conurbation.[82] Personally, I wonder whether Thucydides, faced with a city made up of a conurbation where the great mass of the citizens dwelt and only a single village was situated apart, could in fact have written of a *polis* organized *kata kōmas*, structurally different from Athens. In my opinion Thucydides' expression should at least generate the suspicion that the organization of the space of the archaic and classical *polis* was different from that of Roman Sparta, and that consequently the area within which the *kōmai* of Thucydides are to be situated was in fact larger than the claimed conurbation of four villages.

In this regard it is worth reflecting on the long-observed presence of a *vacuum* around Sparta, as the nearest among the cities that the ancient sources present as inhabited by *perioikoi* were located at a considerable distance from Sparta.[83] Must we therefore conclude that in the archaic and classical period the fertile and extensive plain of Sparta was occupied, not to mention the farms inhabited by the helots, only by the two settlements of Sparta and Amyklai? Unfortunately, the *Laconia Survey*, whose data are now available, is of no great help, since the area subject to investigation is situated entirely on the eastern side of the Eurotas, while the plain spreads out especially on the western side, where Sparta and Amyklai are in fact situated.[84] Despite these limitations the survey provides important data: particularly interesting is the identification of the site of Thornax, mentioned in some sources as situated a little to the north of Sparta and known above all for a sanctuary of Apollo Pythaeus where the statue of the god had the same form as that of the Apollo of Amyklai (Paus. 3.10.8). The survey tentatively identifies Thornax with the site of Gedalari, located some four kilometres to the north of Sparta.[85] Unless we are ready to believe that Thornax too was a perioikic community, this location creates some difficulties for the thesis of the four villages.[86] Moreover, can we actually be certain that on the eastern bank of the Eurotas, where the so-called Menelaion is situated, there was not, besides the sanctuary, also a built-up area? In fact, given the particular geological history of the Eurotas valley, many classical sites could not be identified through surface investigations.[87] Finally, it is useful to remember that when, in 370, Epameinondas marched down through Lakonia along the eastern bank of the Eurotas, he encountered many houses filled with goods, and when, after crossing the Eurotas opposite Amyklai, he went north again in the direction of Sparta, his Arcadian allies turned to plunder other houses (Xen. *Hell.* 6.5.27–30). Were these houses little pieces of *polis* organized *kata kōmas*?

To sum up briefly, the picture I propose here is that of a *polis* created in the archaic age through the political *synoikismos* – without this implying the cohabitation of the whole free population in a single urban centre – of a series of villages spread out over the middle of the Eurotas valley: a *polis kata kōmas*, just as Thucydides describes it. Among these villages was Amyklai to the south, where the most important city festivity (the Hyakinthia) took place; Thornax to the north, and certainly a number of small villages situated along that tract of the Eurotas enclosed by the two sanctuaries of Apollo at Amyklai and Thornax. And, obviously, there was the real and proper centre of the *polis*: Pitane. The Roman city, on the other hand, is the result of the well-known phenomenon of urbanization in Hellenistic and Roman times,[88] which must have brought about the formation of other quarters around the nucleus of Pitane so as to form the four *ōbai* which we find in sources of the Roman period.

V. The centrality of Pitane in the Spartan system of villages

I have already noted that, while there is no reference to the *ōbai* of Limnai, Mesoa and Kynosoura in classical sources, in contrast Pitane is well attested. Besides the reference to the Pitanate *lochos* in Herodotus and Thucydides, this toponym is present also in Pindar, Herodotus and Euripides; moreover, Pitane is further attested in some fragments of a commentary to Alkman, and this makes it almost certain that Alkman himself mentioned such a village. This clear disparity between Pitane and the other three *ōbai* of Sparta has generally been overlooked by scholars, who have been at most inclined to believe that Pitane was the most renowned Spartan village.[89] But to the latter, reductive, view it is possible to oppose an alternative picture: in my opinion the centrality of Pitane in the most ancient sources depends on the fact that it represents the real and proper urban centre of Sparta. In a *polis* constituted by villages, Pitane was therefore the main village and the political and cultic centre of the city.

This interpretation is bolstered by ancient indications of a certain equivalence between Sparta and Pitane. First, there is a passage of Euripides' *Troades* (1110–13) where Pitane, called *polis*, is related to the temple of Athena Chalkioikos and refers by metonymy to the whole of Sparta. For his part, Herodotus utilizes the term Sparta in a topographical sense many times, but in the only case in which he makes reference not to traditions about Sparta but to his personal presence in the city, he writes that he had been in the village (*dēmos*) of Pitane. It is worth observing that the historian never mentions Sparta in this passage: he simply says that he had been to Pitane and had met there, as we already know, the Lacedaemonian Archias (3.55.2). It is also interesting to note that while Pausanias the Periegete, in presenting mythical traditions about Lakonia, makes Sparta the daughter of the river Eurotas (3.1.2), a local tradition, attested by the learned Spartan Sosibios and probably already known to Pindar, maintained that Pitane was Eurotas' daughter.[90] Therefore, rather than interpreting this evidence by agglutination and imagining both Sparta *and* Pitane as daughters of Eurotas, it is much better to think of Pitane as playing in older local tradition the role that Sparta did in the later tradition related by Pausanias.

On this view, the correspondence we have postulated between the *lochos* of Pitane and the hundred selected men of the kings' guard takes on a special significance: the centrality of Pitane derived evidently from the fact that it was the political and cultic centre of the *polis* of Sparta, and as such it was the village where the akropolis of Sparta with the temple of Athena Chalkioikos was located and to which both royal families would have belonged. This hypothesis requires, however, that both the Agiadai and the Eurypontidai resided at Pitane.

Pausanias' evidence (3.14.2) that the tombs of the Agiadai lay in proximity to the so-called *leschē* of the Krotanoi, who were a part (*moira*) of the Pitanates, strongly suggests that the Agiadai were Pitanates. It is not so easy to establish where the Eurypontidai resided: Pausanias records that their tombs were situated near the city walls at the end of Aphetais street (3.12.8). In spite of the well-known difficulty of reconstructing Spartan topography on the basis of Pausanias' information, this means that they probably lay in the southern zone of the Roman city.[91] On the other hand, both the tomb of king Theopompos and the house of king Ariston, both of the family of the Eurypontidai, were located near the *hērōon* of Astrabakos in the marshy area of Limnai.[92] These two pieces of information do not appear readily compatible, which has caused a certain oscillation in scholars' opinion with regard to the residence of the Eurypontidai, although the thesis of a tie with Limnai prevails.[93] It is certain, however, that in the context of the Roman city the tombs of the Eurypontidai did not lie in the *ōba* of Pitane. But this fact is only apparently in contradiction with the thesis of a relationship between the family of the Eurypontidai and Pitane, as shown by a passage from Strabo (8.5.1), which records that the Spartans called Limnai the area of the city which once (τὸ παλαιόν) was marshy and which constituted the suburb (προάστειον) of Sparta. A definition of Limnai as 'suburb' appears completely unreasonable if used to refer to one of the four villages which claimed to form together the city of Sparta, but it accords perfectly with the image of a *polis* made up of a series of villages spread over the territory, one of which, as *asty*, acted as political and cultic centre. On this view, it is reasonable to presume that Limnai, being located very close to Pitane and to the akropolis of Sparta, was regarded as a part of Pitane.

I believe that the picture outlined here has the twofold advantage of better explaining our classical sources and of providing an interpretative key regarding the function of the Dorian tribal system in the *polis* of Sparta. Oswyn Murray has reminded us that the division of the Greek *polis* into segments of citizens corresponds above all to a need to rationalize the city organization.[94] In this way, the introduction of the three Dorian tribes on the one hand reflected the elaboration of a Dorian ideology that tied the birth of the city to the return of the Herakleidai and to the arrival of the Dorians. On the other hand, the three Dorian tribes provided an instrument to organize rationally within a unitary structure, for military purposes also, a heterogeneous citizen body made up of the inhabitants of villages of different sizes and histories. It appears likely that when it was necessary to carry out this division of the citizen body it was not possible, or convenient, to ignore the territorial reality;[95] and this entailed that the village of Pitane, as political and cultic centre of the city, was set within a single tribe. It is equally likely that the tribe of the Hylleis, namely those who claimed to descend from Hyllos son of Herakles, came to include the two families which had assumed a leading role within the city and which, obviously, had to be interested in emphasizing their own descent from Herakles: two families which resided within or near the area of Pitane.

Finally, there is evidence which in my view confirms decisively the hypothesis of a relative overlapping between tribal structure (Hylleis) and territorial unity (Pitane). In 1957 the publication of the 24th volume of the Oxyrhynchus papyri extended our knowledge of Alkman's poetry and, as a consequence, of the city as it was in his day, thanks to the discovery of several fragments from a commentary to the poet. In one fragment, unfortunately preserved in a very lacunose state, there is a reference to Pitane and to two distinct choruses of girls, the one made up of *Dymainai*, that is girls belonging to the Dorian tribe of the Dymanes, and the other of Pitanatides, namely girls coming from the village of Pitane.[96] According to the textual reconstruction offered by W.S. Barrett, the commentator was explaining that the girls of the tribe of the Dymanes arrived at Pitane to dance together with the girls of Pitane;[97] despite the uncertainty of this reconstruction, the fact remains that the fragment quotes in the same context two choruses of girls apparently belonging to two different orders of organization.[98] Different explanations to justify this singular juxtaposition between the Dymanes and the village of Pitane have been put forward,[99] but it is evident that the most economical explanation is that the two choruses belonged to a single order of organization of the citizen body, the tribal one, and that consequently the chorus of the girls of Pitane was perfectly homologous to that of the *Dymainai*. This entails an equivalence between the inhabitants of Pitane and the members of one of the three Dorian tribes, and, since obviously this tribe cannot be that of the Dymanes, it follows that it was probably that of the Hylleis.[100] What Alkman's commentator says, then, fits well with the interpretation here provided of the Pitanate *lochos*: on the one hand, this denomination indicates that the members of this military unit came from the village of Pitane; on the other, that they belonged formally to the tribe of the Hylleis. The centrality of Pitane within the *polis* of Sparta clearly explains, in my view, why the territorial denomination took preference over the tribal one, and why in the Athenian tradition followed by Herodotus the corps of one hundred men selected from the tribe of the Hylleis had the name 'Pitanate *lochos*'.

VI. Amompharetos son of Poliades: an epilogue

It is appropriate, in ending, to reserve one final reflection for Amompharetos, or better, for the name of his father: Poliades. This name, not otherwise attested at Sparta,[101] is built upon the term *polis* and is probably the Spartan equivalent of *politēs*, in the same way that the Laconic *damōdēs* is equivalent to *dēmotēs*;[102] its meaning, therefore, is that of 'member of the *polis*' (alternatively, the relationship between Poliades and *polis* could be mediated by the adjective *polias*, an epithet notoriously reserved for some divinities as protecters of the *polis*).[103] But the *polis* to which the father of Amompharetos claims through his own name to belong is not yet the political community. It has been observed that 'the protection afforded by the *Polias, Poliatis* or *Poliouchos* deity...could be understood as protection extended to the town, not to the city as a whole, for the *polis* element in those epithets could be taken to refer only to the urban center.'[104] We can infer that those who, in the mid-sixth century, gave to the future father of Amompharetos the name of Poliades, intended to emphasize the relationship with the *polis* in the pre-political meaning of the term, and it is interesting to observe that the only known Spartiate who received a name explicitly referring to the notion of urban centre and to the sanctuary of the deity that was the protector of such a centre, was of Pitane. In the light of what has been here claimed, this was no accident.

Notes

[1] The theory of the 'obal' organization of the Spartan army goes far back in time. It found its most complete formulation in Wade-Gery 1944, 116–21, and, although sometimes criticized (e.g. Chrimes 1949, 314–19; Lazenby 1985, 50–3), it still has many supporters: Jones 1987, 119; Cartledge 1987, 427–31; Singor 2002, 259–65. Wade-Gery believed that Thucydides had wrongly inferred from the absence of the *lochos* of Pitane at his time that it had never existed; according to the same scholar, moreover, the

single *lochoi* were named by nicknames: thus, the *lochos* made up of the inhabitants of Pitane 'may not have been called Πιτανάτης λόχος' (1944, 121). Among the commentators on Thucydides , Gomme 1945, 138, prefers not to take up a definitive position, while more recently Hornblower 1991, 58, defends Thucydides' viewpoint: 'when, as here, he offers a firm statement he is I believe to be preferred to Hdt., who may have been speaking loosely'.

[2] For a more detailed description of this thesis, see below.

[3] The thesis of a 'Pitanatenquelle' has long been and still is now a recurring motif among scholars; it has also been accepted by some of these who, preferring to believe Thucydides, doubt the existence of a Pitanate *lochos* (Cozzoli 1979, 108; Kelly 1981, 37). But see Jacoby 1913, 463, who advised caution and Macan 1908, 709 (see below n. 16), who excluded it completely.

[4] Cartledge 1987, 429.

[5] This approach dates back at least to Grundy 1901, 408–52,1 and Munro 1904; cf. also Mele 1955 and Wallace 1982. Among the more recent studies of the battle of Plataia see Lazenby 1985, 97–111, and 1993, 217–47; Green 1996, 239–77.

[6] Cf. particularly Flower and Marincola 2002, 20–2.

[7] Cf. Osborne 1996, 337.

[8] A detailed analysis of this textual problem is developed below.

[9] Lazenby 1985, 49: 'the easiest way out of the problem...but that would surely be too much a coincidence'.

[10] Green 1996, 263.

[11] Flower and Marincola 2002, 201.

[12] Flower and Marincola 2002, 20–1; cf. also Tritle 2006, 219.

[13] Cf. Lazenby 1993, 237. It is worth recalling that on the occasion of the battle of Mantineia in 418 BC. the two polemarchs who refused to obey king Agis were exiled (5.71.3–72.1). The case of Amompharetos is certainly different since he died in combat, but we should remember that just after the battle of Plataia the Spartans refused to honour Aristodemos as, although he had performed great achievements and had fallen bravely, he abandoned his post in the phalanx and willingly sought death (Hdt. 9.71.2–4). In the same way we can infer that, if indeed Amompharetos had refused to obey Pausanias' orders, he certainly would not have been honoured.

[14] It is an unquestionable and long-recognized fact that some episodes of Herodotus' account of the battle of Plataia reflect an Athenian view (see also the exchange of positions in the battle array between Athenians and Spartans in Hdt. 9.46–7): cf. Mele 1955, 25–7; Lazenby 1985, 107; Prandi 1988, 75; Nyland 1996, 87–89. With that in mind it is useless to speculate on minor details: Amompharetos alleges, for example, that the rock set before the feet of Pausanias was the *psēphos* with which he voted not to flee before the foreigners and, since the Spartiates voted by acclamation and not, as at Athens, by using the *psēphoi*, it has been claimed that Herodotus must have drawn on an Athenian tradition. But Flower and Marincola 2002, 205, are right when they claim that this interpretation 'is too literal'; observe that Herodotus uses the term *psēphos* in reference to the vote of the *gerontes* (6.57.5).

[15] Nyland 1992, 88.

[16] Cf. Macan 1908, 709: 'It is a superficial inference that Hdt. got this story of Amompharetos in Pitane, during his visit to Sparta: the story is plainly not a Spartan story, it is almost plainly an Athenian.'

[17] The knowledge of Amompharetos' patronymic could imply a Spartan source, but the Athenian tradition itself may have had access to this knowledge. One may also suspect that his family had a tie with Athens, since a certain Amompharetos is among the five Spartan arbitrators in the Atheno-Megarian dispute for the possession of Salamis (Plut. *Sol.* 10.6): cf. Macan 1908, 708.

[18] Cf. Hdt. 7.211; Pl. *Laches* 191c.

[19] Cf. Woodhouse 1898, 54; How and Wells 1912, II 312; Mele 1955, 26; Burn 1962, 532; Lazenby 1993, 237; Green 1996, 265. *Contra* Flower and Marincola 2002, 201.

[20] Plut. *Lyc.* 17.2. That the form ἰρένες is a variant of εἰρένες is not a hypothesis (*pace* Gilula 2003, 82 n. 16), but a fact easily deducible from some inscriptions from Lakonia and Messenia (*IG* V.1 1120 e 1386). These inscriptions attest the existence of an age grade of τριτίρενες and, whatever is the relationship between such *tritirenes* and the Spartan age grades (cf. Ducat 2006), it follows that the form ἰρένες must have been a variant widespread throughout Lakonia.

[21] Whether the *eirenes* were only the young men in their twenty-first year of age or all those in their twenties (as is claimed especially by Tazelaar 1967; cf. MacDowell 1986, 164–6, Lupi 2000, 39–40), is disputed. Note that Kennell 1995, 120, who believes that in the Hellenistic and Roman period the *eirenes* were only the men in their twenty-first year, recognizes that in classical Sparta the term was used to indicate all the Spartiates who still did not enjoy all the rights of citizenship, that is up to the age of thirty.

[22] Busolt and Swoboda 1926, 696 n. 3; den Boer 1954, 292; Flower and Marincola 2002, 256.

[23] Xen. *Lak. Pol.* 4.7; cf. Hodkinson 1983, 251; Lupi 2000, 34–5; Lipka 2002a, 146–7.

[24] e.g. Xen. *Cyr.* 6.3.21; cf. Cartledge 1987, 429, Van Wees 2004, 278 n. 29.

[25] Cf. Van Wees 2004, 98 e 248, who regards *lochos* as 'the generic Greek term' and not as a Spartan technical word. It is to be observed that in classical Athens the term *lochos* had a technical value and corresponded to a detachment of approximately 100 men (Van Wees 2004, 100). On the *lochoi* in the Spartan army see particularly Lazenby 1985; Van Wees 2004, 243–9.

[26] Den Boer 1954, 288–98; Gilula 2003, 81–5; cf. also Nafissi 1991, 302–3 n. 108.

[27] Flower and Marincola 2002, 255.

[28] Valckenaer's position is reported in detail by den Boer 1954, 289–90.

[29] Kennell 1995, 14–15; Toher 1999, 118–21; Hodkinson 2000, 258; Flower and Marincola 2002, 255; Gilula 2003, 81–5. In a forthcoming publication, however, Andronike Makres again defends Valckenaer's emendation.

[30] Den Boer 1954, 291.

[31] Gilula 2003, 83.

[32] There is no doubt, obviously, that there were priests at Sparta, but no source makes reference to their having played a formal role in the army such as to justify a separate burial. Den Boer 1954, 294–8, and more recently Toher 1999, 122–6, believed they could identify these priest-soldiers in a textually problematic passage of Plutarch (*Lyc.* 27.2), but see the inescapable objections of Brulé and Piolot 2004, 156–7.

[33] Gilula 2003, 85.

[34] Kennell 1995, 15.

[35] Richer 1994, 64–70, who regards the ἰρέες as 'men whose *aristeia* was particularly marked'. In my view it is highly problematic to accept the transmitted text without

conceding that the term ἰρέες had the only meaning which we find in Herodotus. Indeed, to hypothesize a different meaning never attested in ancient texts is a far more speculative procedure than emending a text on the basis of an entry from a Herodotean lexicon. On the many proposals of emendation see Lupi 2000, 48 n. 2; suffice it here to observe that the very number of these proposals shows the difficulty of accepting the manuscript text.

[36] Unsurprisingly, in 52 of these 56 occurrences the reference is to the Egyptian priests frequently cited by Herodotus in the second and at the beginning of the third Book. The other occurrences refer to the Chaldean priests (1.181) and to the priest of the Heraion of Argos (6.81).

[37] Cf. e.g. 6.97.2, where the inhabitants of Delos are defined as 'holy'.

[38] I have dwelt at length on this generational distinction in Spartan society in Lupi 2000; cf. Ducat 2006.

[39] On the first ten conscription classes – the so-called τὰ δέκα ἀφ' ἥβης – cf. Billheimer 1946.

[40] *Lak. Pol.* 2.11; cf. den Boer 1954, 292; Toher 1999, 120–1; Gilula 2003, 84.

[41] Cf. Lupi 2003. It is surprising that Gilula 2003, who gives so much importance to the principle of the consensus of all the manuscripts, seems to ignore this fact.

[42] Cf. Lazenby 1985, 49. On the beauty of the young warrior cf. Vernant 1985.

[43] On these coins and their interpretation cf. Mele 1981, 81; Tagliamonte 1996, 23–8; Cerchiai 2002/3.

[44] It is well known that at Athens the role of *peripoloi* was performed by ephebes: cf. Vidal-Naquet 1968.

[45] Hdn. 4.8.3. Cf. Chrimes 1949, 318 n. 2; Cerchiai 2002/3, 160.

[46] Kelly 1981, 32.

[47] According to Xen. *Lak. Pol.* 4.3 they were selected from among the *hēbōntes*; cf. Dion. Hal. *Ant. Rom.* 2.13.4.

[48] Kelly 1981, 37.

[49] Kennelly 1994, 128–32, has recently opposed this consensus.

[50] The question of intertextuality between Herodotus and Thucydides has recently been the object of several studies: cf. in particular Hornblower 1992 (as well as 1996, 19–38, where he rejected the hypothesis of Kennelly 1994, who claimed that Thucydides did not know Herodotus' text and consequently did not polemicize against him). Hornblower, who has also listed all the passages where one might suppose Thucydides' knowledge of the text of Herodotus (1996, 137–45), imagines a model of close intertextuality to the point of believing that Thucydides had Herodotus' book open before him (1992, 141); cf. Luraghi 2000, 231–2.

[51] Luraghi 2000, 227.

[52] Gomme 1945, 137: 'Thucydides therefore almost certainly has other writers, and common opinion, in mind as well as Herodotus'.

[53] For possible solutions to this intricate question cf. Carlier 1984, 271–2.

[54] Cf. Kennelly 1994, 131.

[55] Hornblower 1991, 42, has reasonably supposed that knowledge of Herodotus' chapters on the privileges of the Spartan kings lay behind Thucydides' reference to the privileges of the hereditary *basileiai* (1.13.1).

[56] Cf. Cozzoli 1979, 86; Carlier 1984, 261; Lipka 2002a, 145; Scott 2005, 235.

[57] Kelly 1981, 35–6, who nevertheless, following Tazelaar 1967, 150, believed that, as

hippagretēs, Amompharetos must have been more than thirty years old. But Xenophon (*Lak. Pol.* 4.3) attests explicitly that the ephors chose the *hippagretai* from within the group of the *hēbōntes*; the fact that the *hippagretai* were selected in particular among the *akmazontes* merely indicates that they were the oldest of the *hēbōntes*, namely young men in their late twenties: cf. MacDowell 1986, 67; Lupi 2000, 36; Lipka 2002a, 143–4.

⁵⁸ On Thucydides as listener to Herodotus cf. Canfora 1982.

⁵⁹ Cf. Carlier 1984, 251; Lipka 2002b; Link 2004.

⁶⁰ On the idea that Herodotus wrote down his *Histories* only at an advanced age and thus at the same period as Thucydides, see now Rösler 2002. Hornblower 1992, 141, acknowledged the possibility that 'the two men were in a real sense contemporaries and rivals'.

⁶¹ Cf. Chrimes 1949, 314; see also Figueira in this volume.

⁶² It is not important here whether the *hippeis* were always selected in accordance with the tribe to which they belonged: after all, the ten Athenian *strategoi*, originally chosen one for each tribe, from the fourth century onwards were elected *ex hapantōn*. However, on the occasion of the battle of Plataia the three groups of a hundred *hippeis* were still selected in accordance with the three Dorian tribes.

⁶³ Chrimes 1949, 404; Carlier 1984, 307; Lazenby 1985, 69.

⁶⁴ On the emergence of a Dorian identity at Sparta and on ways in which this identity was constructed, see Hall 2002, 73–89.

⁶⁵ Cf. Davies 1996 and 1997, 30–1.

⁶⁶ Hdt. 7.204; 8.131.

⁶⁷ As is well known, the text of the 'Great *Rhetra*' is quoted by Plutarch (*Lyc.* 6). Although its authenticity seems by now beyond doubt, the dating continues to be uncertain: according to prevailing opinion it is to be fixed in the mid-7th century, but recently Van Wees 1999 has claimed that Tyrtaeus fragment 4 West does not presuppose the existence of the *rhētra*, which consequently can be set in the first half of the 6th century.

⁶⁸ Hsch. s.vv. ὠάς, ὠβάι and ὠγή.

⁶⁹ *IG* V.1.674–88.

⁷⁰ Cf. Cartledge 1987, 431. The names of five Spartan *lochoi* are attested in Schol. Arist. *Lysistr.* 453 and Schol. Thuc. 4.8, which depend on the lost *Lakedaimonion Politeia* of Aristotle (cf. Hsch. s.v. λόχοι = Aristot. fr. 541 Rose); yet, only one of these names seems to recall the name of a Spartan village, so that it has been supposed that four out of the five *lochoi* of the 'obal' army were known by their nicknames. See above n. 1.

⁷¹ Pareti 1910 and 1917, 173–87; Ehrenberg 1937; Wade-Gery 1944. Cf. also Oliva 1971, 78–87, and Jones 1987, 118–23.

⁷² Kiechle 1963, 119–27; Roussel 1976, 237–8; Levy 1977, 91–4.

⁷³ *IG* V.1.722; cf. Beattie 1951.

⁷⁴ Huxley 1962, 47–9, and Forrest 1968, 42–6, both hypothesize a system of nine *ōbai*, each made up of three phratries; this allows them to reconcile the *phylai* and *ōbai* of the 'Great Rhetra' with the 27 phratries attested at Sparta on the occasion of the festival of the Karneia (Demetrios of Skepsis, fr. 1 Gäde = Athen. 141e–f). On the Spartan phratries see now Lupi 2005. For Kennell 1995, 166, the *ōba* of Arkaloi has to be identified with a Lakonian community not integrated in the *polis* of Sparta.

⁷⁵ Lazenby 1985, 51–2; Kennell 1995, 166–7.

[76] Kennell 1995, 162–9. I do not have space here to tackle the question of the status of Amyklai; generally speaking, however, it must be said that to assume the presence of a perioikic community at only 5 km from Sparta – and right in the middle of a plain occupied to a great extent by the *klēroi* of the Spartiates – creates more problems than it solves.

[77] Spawforth 1996, 1433, describes the division of Sparta into four villages as 'an old-fashioned pattern persisting into Augustan times'.

[78] See, for example, Kennell 1995 and Hodkinson 2000 on the changes taking place, respectively, in Spartan educative and property systems.

[79] Hansen 2003, 271; the thesis according to which most transformations took place during the age of the tyrants dates back to Jones 1987, 12–13.

[80] Pausanias (3.16.9) put the four *ōbai* of Pitane, Mesoa, Limnai and Kynosoura in relation with an epoch previous to Lykourgos, but this is clearly 'an etiological phantasy' which meant 'to furnish a Lycurgan pedigree for a contest that dated only from the Hellenistic period' (Kennell 1995, 40).

[81] Cf. Paus. 3.14.2; *IG* V.1.917 (brick stamps with the inscription Πιτανατᾶν).

[82] Hansen 1995, 54–5; cf. also Forrest 1968, 43.

[83] Hampl 1937, 22–3; Shipley 1997, 193.

[84] Catling 2002, 235, assumes *a priori* that there were only these two settlements, on the basis of the fact that 'the revision of previous orthodoxy about archaic and classical Sparta has not gone so far as to suggest that Spartiates resided anywhere but in the villages of Sparta and the town of Amyklai'.

[85] Shipley 1996, 355–7.

[86] Cf. Shipley 2004, 576: 'So close to Sparta, it cannot have had a corporate existence unless it was part of the *obe* of Pitana'; in my view the suggestion that Thornax could be part of Pitane reveals the difficulty of setting within the orthodoxy a more complex territorial reality.

[87] Wilkinson 1999.

[88] Cf. Alcock 1993.

[89] Cf. Stibbe 1989, 80.

[90] Schol. Pind. 6.46 ff. (= Sosibios *FGrHist* 595 F 21); cf. Pind. *Ol.* 6.28–31. See also Calame 1987, 55–6.

[91] Cf. Musti and Torelli 1991, 203.

[92] Hdt. 6.69.3, to be compared with Paus. 3.16.6.

[93] For Limnai see Cartledge 1979, 106; Lazenby 1985, 66; Pettersson 1992, 109; Mesoa is supported by Stibbe 1989, 69.

[94] Murray 1990.

[95] On the territorialization of the tribes see Nagy 1987, 254–6.

[96] *P.Oxy* XXIV.2389, fr. 35; cf. Calame 1983, 69–70.

[97] Barrett 1961, 687.

[98] Cf. Calame 1997, 219–21, who emphasizes that what really counts in this fragment, apart from the interpretation adopted, is the close connection between the girl choruses and the political structures of the city.

[99] Harvey 1967, 70–1, argued, on the basis of Hsch. s.v. Δύμη, that the Dymanes quoted in the fragment were the inhabitants of the *ōba* of Dyme, to be added to those already known; for Forrest 1968, 44, the commentator was referring to a chorus of girls of Dymainai belonging to the *ōba* of Pitane.

[100] The alternative is that Pitane corresponds to the tribe of the Pamphyloi; yet, if the hypothesis of Jones 1980 is correct, the Pamphyloi occupy the last position in the original order of the three Dorian *phylai*, and it is consequently unlikely that Pitane, given its connection with the akropolis and the two royal families, can be identified with the *phylē* of the Pamphyloi.

[101] Cf. Poralla 1913, 107 (no. 618), and Fraser and Matthews 1997, 366.

[102] Hsch., s.v. δαμώδεις, makes certain that δαμώδης is Spartan form for δημότης; cf. also the term νεοδαμώδεις, first attested by Thucydides (5.67.1). As personal name Πολιάδης has its equivalent in Πολίτης, which in Homer is the name of a son of Priam (*Il.* 2.791 *et alibi*).

[103] But observe that Athena Chalchioikos, worshipped on the Spartan akropolis, was known by the epithet of Πολιᾶχος, as Damonon's stele attests (*IG* V.1.213; cf. Paus. 3.17.2: Πολιοῦχος).

[104] Polignac 1995, 86–7. The original significance of *polis*, as is evinced from Homeric poetry, seems to have been that of 'stronghold'; cf. Lévy 1983, 73: '*Polis*, peut-être liée au départ à l'enceinte fortifiée, est la ville vue de l'extérieur...donc surtout comme contenant et comme lieu.'

Bibliography

Alcock, S.E.
  1993   *Graecia Capta. The landscapes of Roman Greece*, Cambridge.

Barrett, W.S.
  1961   Review of *The Oxyrhynchus Papyri. Part 24* (London 1957), *Gnomon* 33, 682–92.

Beattie, A.J.
  1951   'An early Laconian *lex sacra*', *CQ* n.s. 1, 46–58.

Billheimer, A.
  1946   'Τὰ δέκα ἀφ'ἥβης', *TAPhA* 77, 214–20.

Brulé, P. and Piolot, L.
  2004   'Women's way of death: fatal childbirth or *hierai*? Commemorative stones at Sparta and Plutarch, *Lycurgus*, 27.3', in T. Figueira (ed.) *Spartan Society*, Swansea, 151–78. Translation of French original published in *REG* 115, 2002, 485–517.

Burn, A.R.
  1962   *Persia and the Greeks: The defence of the West, c. 546–478 BC*, London.

Busolt, G. and Swoboda, H.
  1926   *Griechische Staatskunde, II*, Munich.

Calame, C.
  1983   *Alcman. Introduction, texte critique, témoignages, traduction et commentaire*, Rome.
  1987   'Le récit généalogique spartiate: la représentation mythologique d'une organisation spatiale', *QS* 26, 43–91.

Canfora, L.
  1982   'Tucidide erodoteo', *QS* 16, 77–84.

Carlier, P.
  1984   *La royauté en Grèce avant Alexandre*, Strasbourg.

Cartledge, P.
 1979   *Sparta and Lakonia: A regional history, 1300–362 BC*, London.
 1987   *Agesilaos and the Crisis of Sparta*, London and Baltimore.
Catling, R.W.V.
 2002   'The survey area from the early iron age to the classical period', in W. Cavanagh, J. Crouwel, R.W.V. Catling and G. Shipley (eds.) *Continuity and Change in a Greek Rural Landscape: The Laconia survey, I: Methodology and interpretation*, London, 115–256.
Cerchiai, L.
 2002/3 'Pitanatai peripoloi', *AION(archeol)* n.s. 9–10, 159–61.
Chrimes, K.M.T.
 1949   *Ancient Sparta: A re-examination of the evidence*, Manchester.
Cozzoli, U.
 1979   *Proprietà fondiaria ed esercito nello stato spartano dell'età classica*, Rome.
Davies, J.K.
 1996   'Strutture e suddivisioni delle *poleis* arcaiche. Le ripartizioni minori', in S. Settis (ed.) *I Greci. Storia Cultura Arte Società, 2/I. Una storia greca. Formazione*, Turin, 599–652.
 1997   'The "Origins of the Greek *polis*". Where should we be looking', in L.G. Mitchell and P.J. Rhodes (eds.) *The Development of the* Polis *in Archaic Greece*, London and New York, 24–38.
den Boer, W.
 1954   *Laconian Studies*, Amsterdam.
Ducat, J.
 2006   *Spartan Education: Youth and society in the classical period*, Swansea.
Ehrenberg, V.
 1937   'Obai', *RE* XVII, 1693–1704.
Flower, M.A. and Marincola, J.
 2002   *Herodotus. Histories: Book IX*, Cambridge.
Forrest, W.G.
 1968   *History of Sparta*, London.
Fraser, P.M. and Matthews, E.
 1997   *Lexicon of Greek Personal Names, Vol. III A: The Peloponnese, Western Greece, Sicily and Magna Graecia*, Oxford.
Gilula, D.
 2003   'Who was actually buried in the first of the three Spartan graves (Hdt. 9.85.1)? Textual and historical problems', in P. Derow and R. Parker (eds.) *Herodotus and his World. Essays from a conference in memory of George Forrest*, Oxford, 73–87.
Gomme, A.W.
 1945   *A Historical Commentary on Thucydides*, vol. 1, Oxford.
Green, P.
 1996   *The Greco-Persian Wars*, Berkeley and Los Angeles. Revised edition of *The Year of Salamis*, London, 1970.
Grundy, G.B.
 1901   *The Great Persian War and its Preliminaries: A study of the evidence, literary and topographical*, London.

Hall, J.
2002   *Hellenicity: Between ethnicity and culture*, Chicago.
Hampl, F.
1937   'Die Lakedämonischen Periöken', *Hermes* 72, 1–49.
Hansen, M.H.
1995   '*Kome*. A study in how the Greeks designated and classified settlements which were not *poleis*', in M.H. Hansen and K. Raaflaub (eds.) *Studies in the Ancient Greek Polis* (Papers from the Copenhagen Polis Centre 2), Stuttgart, 45–81.
2003   '95 theses about the Greek *polis* in the archaic and classical periods. A report on the results obtained by the Copenhagen Polis Centre in the period 1993–2003', *Historia* 52, 257–82.
Harvey, D.
1967   'Oxyrhynchus papyrus 2390 and early Spartan history', *JHS* 87, 62–73.
Hodkinson, S.
1983   'Social order and the conflict of values in classical Sparta', *Chiron* 13, 239–81.
2000   *Property and Wealth in Classical Sparta*, London and Swansea.
Hornblower, S.
1991   *A Commentary on Thucydides, I: Books I–III*, Oxford.
1992   'Thucydides' use of Herodotus', in J.M. Sanders (ed.) ΦΙΛΟΛΑΚΩΝ. *Lakonian studies in honour of Hector Catling*, London, 141–54. Reprinted in Hornblower 1996, 122–37.
1996   *A Commentary on Thucydides, II: Books IV–V.24*, Oxford.
How, W.W. and Wells, J.
1912   *A Commentary on Herodotus*, 2 vols., Oxford.
Huxley, G.L.
1962   *Early Sparta*, Cambridge, Mass.
Jacoby, F.
1913   'Herodotos', *RE* suppl. II, 205–520.
Jones, N.F.
1980   'The order of the Dorian *phylai*', *CPh* 75, 197–215.
1987   *Public Organization in Ancient Greece: A documentary study*, Philadelphia.
Kelly, D.H.
1981   'Thucydides and Herodotus on the Pitanate Lochos', *GRBS* 22, 31–8.
Kennell, N.M.
1995   *The Gymnasium of Virtue: Education and culture in ancient Sparta*, Chapel Hill and London.
Kennelly, J.J.
1994   'Thucydides' knowledge of Herodotus', Diss., Brown University.
Kiechle, F.
1963   *Lakonien und Sparta*, Munich.
Lazenby, J.F.
1985   *The Spartan Army*, Warminster.
1993   *The Defence of Greece, 490–479 BC*, Warminster.
Lévy, E.
1977   'La Grande Rhètra', *Ktema* 2, 85–103.

1983   '*Astu* et *Polis* dans l'*Iliade*', *Ktema* 8, 55–73.

Link, S.

2004   'Die Ehrenrechte der spartanischen Könige', *Philologus* 148, 222–44.

Lipka, M.

2002a   *Xenophon's Spartan Constitution. Introduction. Text. Commentary*, Berlin and New York.

2002b   'Notes on the influence of the Spartan Great Rhetra on Tyrtaeus, Herodotus and Xenophon', in A. Powell and S. Hodkinson (eds.) *Sparta: Beyond the mirage*, London 2002, 219–25.

Lupi, M.

2000   *L'ordine delle generazioni. Classi di età e costumi matrimoniali nell'antica Sparta*, Bari.

2003   'I presunti *eirenes* di Senofonte (*Lakedaimonion Politeia* 2.5 e 2.11)', *AION(filol)* 25, 157–69.

2005   'Il sacrificio della fratria a Sparta (Hsch., *s.v.* ἐπιπαίζειν)', *Incidenza dell'Antico. Dialoghi di storia greca* 3, 199–214.

Luraghi, N.

2000   'Author and audience in Thucydides' *Archaeology*. Some reflections', *HSCPh* 100, 227–39.

Macan, R.W.

1908   *Herodotus. The Seventh, Eighth, and Ninth Books*, 2 vols., London.

MacDowell, D.M.

1986   *Spartan Law*, Edinburgh.

Mele, A.

1955   'La battaglia di Platea', *Annali della Facoltà di Lettere di Napoli* 5, 5–41.

1981   'Il pitagorismo e le popolazioni anelleniche d'Italia', *AION(archeol)* 3, 61–96.

Munro, J.A.R.

1904   'Some observations on the Persian wars, 3. The campaign of Plataea', *JHS* 24, 144–65.

Murray, O.

1990   'Cities of reason', in O. Murray and S. Price (eds.) *The Greek City from Homer to Alexander*, Oxford, 1–25.

Musti, D. and Torelli, M.

1991   *Pausania: Guida della Grecia, Libro III: La Laconia*, Milan.

Nafissi, M.

1991   *La nascita del kosmos. Studi sulla storia e la società di Sparta*, Naples.

Nagy, G.

1987   'The Indo-European heritage of tribal organization: evidence from the Greek *polis*', in S.N. Skomal and E.C. Polomé (eds.) *Proto-Indo-European: The archaeology of a linguistic problem. Studies in honor of Marija Gimbutas*, Washington, 245–66.

Nyland, R.

1992   'Herodotos' sources for the Plataiai campaign', *AC* 61, 80–97.

Oliva, P.

1971   *Sparta and her Social Problems*, Amsterdam and Prague.

Osborne, R.
1996   *Greece in the Making, 1200–479 BC*, London and New York.
Pareti, L.
1910   'Le tribù personali e le tribù locali a Sparta', *RAL* 19, 455–73.
1917   *Storia di Sparta arcaica, Parte I. Dalle origini alla conquista spartana della Messenia*, Florence.
Pettersson, M.
1992   *Cults of Apollo at Sparta. The Hyakinthia, the Gymnopaidiai and the Karneia*, Stockholm.
Polignac, F. de
1995   *Cults, Territory, and the Origins of the Greek City-State*, Chicago. Translation of French original, Paris, 1984.
Poralla, P.
1913   *Prosopographie der Lakedaimonier bis auf die Zeit Alexanders des Grossen*, Breslau. Rev. edn edited by A.S. Bradford, Chicago, 1985.
Prandi, L.
1988   *Platea: momenti e problemi della storia di una polis*, Padua.
Richer, N.
1994   'Aspects des funérailles à Sparte', *CCG* 5, 51–96.
Rösler, W.
2002   'The *Histories* and writing', in E.J Bakker, I.J.F. de Jong and H. van Wees, *Brill's Companion to Herodotus*, Leiden, Boston, and Cologne, 79–94.
Roussel, D.
1976   *Tribu et Cité. Études sur les groupes sociaux dans les cités grecques aux époques archaïque et classique*, Paris.
Scott, L.
2005   *Historical Commentary on Herodotus Book 6*, Leiden and Boston.
Shipley, G.
1996   'Site catalogue of the survey', in W. Cavanagh, J. Crouwel, R.W.V. Catling and G. Shipley (eds.) *Continuity and Change in a Greek Rural Landscape: The Laconia survey, II: Archaeological data*, London, 315–438.
1997   '"The other Lakedaimonians": the dependent perioikic *poleis* of Laconia and Messenia', in M.H. Hansen (ed.) *The Polis as an Urban Centre and as a Political Community* (CPC Acts 4), Copenhagen, 189–281.
2004   'Lakedaimon', in M.H. Hansen and T.H. Nielsen (eds.) *An Inventory of Archaic and Classical Poleis*, Oxford, 569–98.
Singor, H.
2002   'The Spartan army at Mantinea and its organisation in the fifth century BC', in W. Jongman and M. Kleigwegt (eds.) *After the Past: Essays in ancient history in honor of H.W. Pleket*, Leiden, 235–84.
Spawforth, A.
1996   'Sparta (site)', in S. Hornblower and A. Spawforth (eds.) *The Oxford Classical Dictionary*, 3rd edn, Oxford, 1433.
Stibbe, C.M.
1989   'Beobachtungen zur Topographie des antiken Sparta', *BABesch* 64, 61–99.
Tagliamonte, G.
1996   *I Sanniti. Caudini, Irpini, Pentri, Carricini, Frentani*, Milan.

Tazelaar, C.M.
   1967   'Παῖδες καὶ ἔφηβοι. Some notes on the Spartan stages of youth', *Mnemosyne* 20, 127–53.
Toher, M.
   1999   'On the εἴδωλον of a Spartan king', *RhM* 142, 113–27.
Tritle, A.A.
   2006   'Warfare in Herodotus', in C. Dewald and J. Marincola (eds.) *The Cambridge Companion to Herodotus*, Cambridge, 209–23.
Van Wees, H.
   1999   'Tyrtaeus' *eunomia*. Nothing to do with the Great Rhetra', in S. Hodkinson and A. Powell (eds.) *Sparta: New perspectives*, London, 1–41.
   2004   *Greek Warfare: Myths and realities*, London.
Vernant, J.-P.
   1985   *La mort dans les yeux. Figures de l'Autre en Grèce ancienne*, Paris.
Vidal-Naquet, P.
   1968   'Le chasseur noir et l'origine de l'éphébie athénienne', *Annales ESC* 23, 947–64.
Wade-Gery, H.T.
   1944   'The Spartan Rhetra in Plutarch, *Lycurgus* VI. C. What is the Rhetra?', *CQ* 38, 115–26.
Wallace, P.W.
   1982   'The final battle at Plataia', in *Studies in Attic Epigraphy, History and Topography presented to Eugene Vanderpool* (*Hesperia*: Supplement XIX), Princeton, 183–92.
Wilkinson, K.
   1999   'Geoarchaeological studies of the Spartan acropolis and Eurotas valley', in W.G. Cavanagh and S.E.C. Walker (eds.) *Sparta in Laconia: The archaeology of a city and its countryside* (Proceedings of the 19th British Museum Classical Colloquium), London, 149–56.
Woodhouse, W.C.
   1898   'The Greeks at Plataiai', *JHS* 18, 33–59.

7

WHY THE SPARTANS FIGHT SO WELL, EVEN IF THEY ARE IN DISORDER – XENOPHON'S VIEW

Noreen Humble

Among the topics Xenophon discusses in his *Lakedaimoniōn Politeia* are the military practices of the Spartans. In the chapters devoted to describing these the following comment stands out: 'nevertheless the fact that even if they are in disorder, they fight equally with whoever is next to them, this order is no longer easy to learn except for those educated by the laws of Lykourgos' (11.7).[1] The latest two commentators on the work (Rebenich 1998 and Lipka 2002) have shown no interest in the statement.[2] In fact Lipka goes so far as to argue that everything after chapter 10 of the work was not part of the original plan of the work and was added piecemeal (14, 11–13, 15) afterwards.[3] His main argument is that Xenophon has given us no real indication that he was going to devote a few chapters to military affairs. But given that Xenophon was looking at how such a small state as Sparta became so renowned and powerful it would have been fairly surprising, given the Spartans' long-standing reputation as soldiers,[4] if he had not included some discussion of military matters.

Perhaps these commentators are silent because they feel the statement is self-explanatory, or perhaps too difficult. It seems to me, however, that the comment raises two questions: what exactly is special about Lykourgos' laws that brings such steadfast fighting about, and is Xenophon forgetting that the Spartans do not always fight well in disorder, for example, at Sphakteria in 425 (Th. 4.31–36) and Lechaion in 390 (Xen. *HG* 4.5.17)?[5] It might also be added that they do not seem to learn from disaster and adapt: at both Sphakteria and Lechaion they were essentially defeated by peltasts. Because Xenophon seems a careful, not a careless, writer, I presume in the first instance that the answer is to be found inside the treatise and in the second instance that he is not forgetting these Spartan disasters, since he narrated one of them himself, and so he must have some reason for phrasing the comment as he did and bringing them to his reader's mind.[6]

The silence of the recent commentators is all the more surprising since earlier commentators (particularly Luppino Manes 1988, Proietti 1987, Ollier 1934) have attempted to explain at least partially what is going on in this passage and in some cases have noted problems with it. In the end, however, as will be shown, they either did not take their explanations far enough or did not address the questions their analyses threw up. Yet, when their different views are taken into consideration with a closer examination of the passage within the context of the whole work, this small remark[7] proves key to understanding Xenophon's presentation of Spartan military practices and their efficacy.

To understand the comment both the wider and the immediate context need to be kept in mind. My own view is that the chapter containing the comment under discussion is perfectly integrated with the earlier part of the work and complete understanding of the comment to hand and answers to the questions it raises are simply not attainable without reference to the whole work.[8] To this end I will lay out a brief overview of the topics discussed in the whole work, then take a closer look at the immediate context of the comment, noting any peculiarities and previous attempts, if any, to explain these. Finally, an alternative explanation will be presented which will take into consideration the issues raised by the context of the passage, by other commentators, and by the very comment under question.

Xenophon states his purpose at the beginning of the work, wondering how such an oliganthropic state could have become so very powerful and renowned. His examination finds that the Spartans prospered by obeying the laws set down by Lykourgos which differed completely from those of other states (1.1–2). Key areas of difference are then discussed: the begetting of children (including regulations for women) (1.3–10), the education of boys aged 7–14 (2), regulations for those aged 14–20 (3), for those aged 20–30 (4.1–6), and finally for those over 30 (4.7), the syssitia (5), certain communal practices (all men had authority over all boys; borrowing of possessions) (6), regulations to prevent accumulation of wealth (7), obedience to magistrates, especially ephors (8), willingness to fight to the death (9), the gerousia (10.1–3), the practice of public virtue (10.4–7), preparation of the army and basic manoeuvres (11), how they set up camp (12), role of kings in war (13). Chapter 14 explains why the Spartans no longer prosper and the final chapter (15) deals with the kings' role in peacetime. Xenophon also signals a shift at 11.1 from talking about affairs that pertain both to peacetime and war to those relating more specifically to military matters.

The more immediate context of the statement within chapter 11 itself is as follows. After comments on how the levy is conducted and the uniform of the army (11.2–3), comes a brief description of the division into *morai* and how the officers are divided up in citizen *morai* (11.4). Then come the following remarks:

[5] As to what the majority think, namely that the Lakonian order (τάξιν) under arms is most complex, they have supposed the very opposite of the truth; the foremost men in the Lakonian battle rank are officers, and each row has everything it needs to provide for itself. [6] It is so easy to learn this battle order (τάξιν) that no one who is able to tell men apart could make a mistake; to some it is granted to lead, to others it is ordered to follow. Deployments are announced by the *enōmotarch* acting as a herald <and> the phalanxes become thin and deeper; none of these things is in any way whatever difficult to learn.[9] [7] Nevertheless the fact that even if they are in disorder, they fight equally with whoever is next to them, this order (τάξιν) is no longer[10] easy to learn except for those educated by the laws of Lykourgos. [8] The Lakedaimonians do those things too most easily, which things seem very difficult to *hoplomachoi*;

There then follows a long and detailed account of standard manoeuvres of the marching army if the enemy approach from the front, back or either side (11.8–10).

A number of observations need to be made about this passage. The first thing to note is that there is an extraordinary emphasis here on the ease of many of these movements. This has been variously interpreted depending upon the overall view taken of the work. Thus Ollier understood Xenophon to be defending Spartan manoeuvres against those who criticized them as too difficult because he sees the work as one of praise and defence.[11] This explanation seems inadequate if on no other grounds than that it is not clear why such a point would need to be defended. Why not say they are superior soldiers because they carry out with ease difficult manoeuvres no one else can manage? Luppino Manes is on stronger ground because of her overall theory that the work is a project for reform. She implies, therefore, that Xenophon emphasizes the ease of formations to show that they could be adopted by anyone contrary to what might be thought, but that others must follow the Lykourgan way as set out in the treatise in order to be able to hold their ground in battle like the Spartans.[12] This explanation of the passage is more coherent than Ollier's but there are significant problems with regarding the whole work as a project of reform: it still requires a fundamental belief in the superiority of the Spartan system which Xenophon cannot be shown to have.[13]

It is also worth noting that this is the only place in the chapter (and indeed in chapters 11–13) where disorder is mentioned. It stands out because of the emphasis on orderliness in the preceding and succeeding passages, i.e. not just in marching formation or basic manoeuvres, but also in army preparation and command levels. Further the setting up of camp and the procedures followed by the king on campaign (12–13) are also very orderly. Though this notion of disorder is not expanded on, it plants a questioning seed and the instances of Spartans not fighting well in disorder come to mind.

Striking too is the contrast between those educated under the laws of Lykourgos in 11.7 and Lakedaimonians in 11.8. This shift in terminology is important (though not entirely unproblematic). The term *Lakedaimonioi* is favoured by Xenophon from chapter 11 on (11.2, 11.8, 12.5, 12.7, 13.5, 13.8, 14.2, 15.9), whereas he seems to have preferred the term *Spartiates* prior to that (1.1, 5.2, 5.9). The obvious explanation, as Proietti noted, is that Xenophon switches to the more general term because the army also contains non-Spartiates.[14] Proietti further argues, then, that 'the highly standardized tactical manoeuvres are necessary because the non-Spartan Lakedaimonians are not so reliable as soldiers'; only the Spartiates are able to cope with fighting when confusion reigns.[15] This is an important point since it was not a rare occurrence to find only one or a few full Spartan citizens leading an army composed of some combination of *perioikoi*, ex-helots, allies, and mercenaries.[16] The first striking example of this is Brasidas in 424, commanding helots and Peloponnesian mercenaries (Th. 4.80.5). Just before the battle in which he falls, Thucydides attributes to him the knowledge that his troops are inferior to the Athenian force, not in numbers but in quality (Th. 5.8.2). It appears, in fact, that there are only two full Spartiates, he and Klearidas (governor of Amphipolis, Th. 4.132.3), fighting in this particular battle (Th. 5.10.1–12) – a number hardly likely to have had much of an effect if they had had to stand their ground in the midst of disorder.

The final observation to note about the passage concerns what follows immediately upon the last sentence quoted above. In 11.8–10 we are presented, in seemingly excessive detail, with a description about how the marching army manoeuvres when the enemy attacks either in front, from behind, from the right or the left. The length of the description makes one wonder why such fairly standard manoeuvres need to be presented so thoroughly,[17] particularly in such a short work when wheeling movements have already been mentioned (11.6), and when other topics have been treated so briefly (see below). One common answer is that Xenophon wishes to prove that they are easy, as a dig against opposite claims by *hoplomachoi*.[18] Given Xenophon's generally disparaging comments about *hoplomachoi* elsewhere,[19] this certainly seems to be part of what is going on here. Moore's suggestion, however, that Xenophon 'underestimates the difficulty of executing them in the face of the enemy',[20] is surely not correct, if for no other reason than that Xenophon provides examples of success and of failure in executing these movements in the *Hellenika*.[21] Proietti, again, is a bit closer to the mark. He argues that the details show that 'the Lacedaemonians are fully prepared for any encounter with the enemy' and that this is meant to try to prevent the disorder which only Spartiates can cope with.[22] The order of presentation in the text does indeed suggest that the manoeuvres in 11.8–10 are meant to try to prevent the disorder mentioned in 11.7. Further, since it is generally thought that at least by Xenophon's time *perioikoi* and Spartiates were integrated in the same military units,[23] this precaution seems eminently sensible. However, it seems to me that Xenophon must expect his reader to notice that these detailed manoeuvres do not cover *every* encounter with the enemy, let alone deal with changing topographies or varied enemy formations.[24] Thus, the passage leads to the observation that there is still likely to be a significant number of instances when disorder is going to reign on the battlefield despite the precautions taken for the integration of non-citizen troops.

To try to explain all these issues coherently and to understand why it is that Xenophon presents his material in such a way that he almost appears to be undermining himself, it is first necessary to look at what exactly Xenophon thought was special about being brought up under Lykourgos' laws, i.e. what enabled the Spartans to fight equally with whoever was at their side in disorder (ignoring for a moment the doubts this comment raises). Of all the commentators the only one to examine what it means to be educated under the laws of Lykourgos in this particular context is Luppino Manes. She argues that Spartiates were accustomed to being blindly obedient, and, therefore, were able to fight when disorder reigned. She is right to emphasize this, though she does not refer for support to the rest of Xenophon's text, but instead reaches out widely to other authors instead (e.g. Herodotus, Thucydides, Isocrates and Plutarch).[25]

But if we do look back earlier in the text, we can see without a shadow of a doubt that, in Xenophon's view, obedience is the most important aim of the upbringing under Lykourgos' laws. Virtually every aspect of the system is concerned with instilling obedience. But although the rewards of being obedient are not absent, they are always overshadowed by comments about punishment for disobedience. Further, it is evident that constant supervision plays a strong role in enforcing obedience. So, for example, boys (aged 7–14) are constantly watched over by all manner of people: a παιδονόμος (educational supervisor) and his group of youths who deal out whipping as punishment (2.2); any citizen in fact could punish boys in the absence of the παιδονόμος (2.10), not just grown men but also other youths who were chosen as leaders (2.11); later Xenophon notes that all fathers have authority over all children (6.1–2) and complaining about punishment by someone else's father leads to further punishment by one's own. What exactly leads to punishment is for the most part left unclear. All Xenophon gives us are the following phrases: 'if anyone should slack off' (εἴ τις ῥᾳδιουργοίη, 2.2) and 'if they should do any wrong' (εἴ τι ἁμαρτάνοιεν, 2.10). Youths (aged 14–20) are punished for shirking from the unspecified but unceasing toil they are to carry out (public authorities and relatives are said to be the supervisors here, 3.1–3). Young men (aged 20–30) fight among themselves to keep fit but are bound to obey anyone who separates them, or receive punishment (4.3–6). *Syssitia* keep men in the public eye to prevent slacking (5.2). Obedience to the law of not accumulating money was achieved through making the system of coinage bulky and through punishment if hoarding of wealth was discovered (7). General obedience was further encouraged through threat of punishment from the ephors, those officers having been given the power to punish anyone on the spot (8.3–4); and by making obedience an act of impiety (8.5). Obedience regarding keeping one's post in battle was gained through fear of punishment (9).

Two other related concepts are also encouraged, though they are not mentioned as frequently as obedience. First, αἰδώς is also an aim.[26] Boys acquire it from the punishment meted out to them (2.2) and from the fact that they are under such constant supervision and in such fear of punishment (2.10). Youths are made to walk about in silence with eyes cast down and hands tucked away to promote αἰδώς as well (2.4). Secondly, ἐγκράτεια (self-control) is encouraged. Boys, for example, are to become accustomed to sparse clothing and little food (2.3–6, 2.14). In fact the provision allowing them to steal to supplement their diet is the only one said to pertain specifically to training for war (τοὺς παῖδας ποιεῖν καὶ πολεμικωτέρους, 'to make the boys more warlike', 2.7). Self-control is also encouraged by the *syssitia* system (though the term is not used in chapter 5).

For Xenophon, another notable aspect of the Spartan upbringing and way of life is a concern for general fitness, particularly for adult males. Men aged 20–30 keep fit because they are constantly at war with one another (4.6). Men over 30 must also keep fit by hunting so that on campaign they can keep up with the younger men (4.7). General exercising is encouraged and there are elders in the gymnasium to make sure everyone exercises their legs, arms and necks as much as is necessary (5.8–9). Lykourgos, it is said, made it more honourable to toil with one's body to help comrades rather than to spend money on them (7.4). Women are made to exercise too because of the belief that if both parents are strong, so too will the offspring be (1.4). And the Spartans are ordered by the law to exercise (γυμνάζεσθαι) in the army camps while on campaign (12.5–6).

What is striking, however, is that while Xenophon does note an obsession with physical fitness, he is not particularly forthcoming about what precisely this entailed. For example, there is no hint as to what specific exercise boys and youths carry out,[27] and he certainly does not suggest that the Spartans practised military exercises or manoeuvres, which might have been expected since he does say how easy their manoeuvres are. As Van Wees points out, that Agesilaos, while training troops in Asia Minor in 395 BC, judges hoplites by the state of their bodies, not by their skill as swordsmen (*HG* 3.4.16), suggests that 'all-round athletic exercise in the gymnasium... was far more prominent than either formation- or weapons-drill'.[28] The reason why there are such few details on this front is very likely simply because Spartan practice differed from other states in this regard only in degree, not in substance.[29] Xenophon does make it clear at the beginning of the work that it was precisely the laws which were different from those in other states that led to Spartan renown. Two main differences, therefore, between Sparta and other states are the creation of an atmosphere in which fear of punishment through constant supervision ensures obedience, and a greater emphasis on keeping fit.[30]

These features alone would tend to make the Spartans more prone to stand their ground and fight equally well with whoever is at their side in disorder but there is one additional piece of social conditioning which ensures that they do. The only specific reference to action in battle before chapter 11 is in chapter 9 where there is a discussion about how Lykourgos caused Spartans to prefer an honourable death to a disgraceful life. Xenophon first points out that it is observable that the Spartans lose fewer men by staying and fighting than those who flee when in danger (9.1); valour more than cowardice brings escape from premature death; and, of course, such valour brings with it glory and glory attracts allies (9.2). Then he remarks: 'by what means, however, he contrived that this would happen, this is not good to pass over. Accordingly Lykourgos clearly procured for brave men happiness, and for cowards, misfortune' (9.3). There follows then a long list of dishonours accorded a coward (9.4–5). The section concludes with Xenophon saying: 'I am in no way surprised, when such dishonour is laid upon cowards, that they prefer death before so dishonourable and disgraceful a life' (9.6).

This section is not only central to understanding the comment at hand but also provides a good example of the technique Xenophon uses when setting forth the list of Lykourgan institutions which caused the Spartans to win such renown. The general pattern of presentation is as follows: Xenophon remarks on a Lykourgan law which is worthy or admirable, presents a short treatment of its positive benefits, but then expatiates on the punitive measures set up to impose adherence to it, apparently because the positive benefits are not themselves strong enough to induce the Spartans to behave in the desired way. Each time he reveals a weakness in the system which could – and did eventually – lead to its collapse.[31] In this instance then we have the practice of fighting to the death which clearly brought long-lived fame to the Spartans. The battle of Thermopylai alone is ample evidence that glory does attend such action and it is likely that the events there played no small part in securing more goodwill to and allies for the Spartans in the Peloponnesian war than perhaps would have accrued otherwise. But in chapter 9 far more space is devoted to showing how this fame-bringing practice is brought about in a negative way. There is, for example, no list of honours accorded brave men, only punishments for cowards. The punishment is public shaming in front of peers, involves exclusion from customary honours, and even relatives are compelled to bear the disgrace. In other words, Lykourgos could find no philosophical reason which would make men stand their ground in battle. Apparently that fewer men were lost and that glory attended such valour were not enough themselves to ensure that men stayed their ground. They were made to do so by the imposition of harsh and shameful punishments. The text further compels us to note that if circumstances changed (e.g. if constant supervision were taken away, or opportunities were presented to live outside Sparta) such punitive measures would lose their force because they do not necessarily result in internalization of the behaviour they are trying to reinforce. It is significant too that the punishments for cowardice are given in much more detail than the punishments for any other misdemeanour. This suggests that cowardice is considered the greatest of all crimes. A further comment at 10.6 to the effect that cowardice is a crime against the whole city-state and therefore attended by the greatest penalties reinforces this point.

This pattern of presentation is repeated throughout the work. For example, in chapter 7 is a discussion of how desire for wealth is suppressed. First it is said that Lykourgos forbade citizens to engage in banausic activity; instead he had them direct their energies towards activities which promoted freedom for cities (7.1–2). How could wealth be an object of desire, Xenophon asks (7.3–4), when there was the same standard of living for all and toiling with one's body to help one's fellow citizens was more worthy of praise than spending money on each other? There then follow two measures designed to discourage saving money (7.5–6). First, coinage was made impossibly bulky and secondly, searches for gold and silver hoards were instituted and punishments meted out if any were found. So, while it was admirable that he did away with desire to compete in terms of wealth, the equal way of living by itself did not altogether remove the desire for wealth. Therefore, Lykourgos was compelled to instigate more punitive measures to make the Spartiates obey through fear of being found with wealth. The pattern is the same and a weakness in the system is revealed.[32]

Is the pattern discernible in chapter 11, and if so what is the weakness revealed? It is clearly admirable that the Spartans are highly organized when it comes to preparations for battle: equipment is gathered and levies are made according to a well laid out pattern (11.2–4). Their clear ease at marching and carrying out basic manoeuvres in an orderly fashion and the fact that a strict hierarchy of command facilitates this organization is also praise-worthy (11.5–6). It also makes perfect sense given the type of upbringing the Spartiates have had: one in which at every turn they have had to practise obedience to someone or other. The manoeuvres are not difficult, they are simply the result of superior organization and a better capacity for obedience, however negatively such obedience is obtained.

But the specific reference to the Spartiates and behaviour which only they can carry out with ease, stands out and invites contemplation. To fight equally with anyone beside them in disorder is only easy for Spartiates. Why? Well, because they are the only people for whom cowardice is so dishonourable that death is preferable. They will fight steadfastly no matter what the situation rather than suffer crippling public disgrace. Xenophon himself provides plenty of examples of Spartiates fighting to the death when the battle has essentially been lost: e.g. Mindaros in 410 BC at Kyzikos dies fighting (*HG* 1.1.17–22). Peisandros at the battle of Knidos in 394 BC holds his ground and dies fighting in a losing battle (4.3.12). Anaxibios, on campaign in Asia Minor in 389 BC, having had his army surprised in ambush, stands his ground with the words 'men, it is good/noble (καλὸν) for me to die here' (4.8.32–9). The sentiment is also well expressed by Kallikratidas who engages, against advice, in the sea battle at Arginousai in 406 BC. He is reported to have said that Sparta would be no worse off if he died, but that to flee was shameful (1.6.32). Mnasippos dies fighting in 373 at Kerkyra (6.2.22–3), and Kleombrotos is persuaded to fight at Leuktra in 371 when his friends remind him that he is in danger of suffering the worst penalty at the hands of the city if he lets the Thebans escape (6.4.5).

Aside from the question of whether or not such steadfastness was always sensible, what about occasions when they are in disorder and do not fight well or to the death? Sphakteria is certainly one example but an even better instance is the disaster of the *mora* at Lechaion in 390 as described by Xenophon himself (*HG* 4.5.10–17). Spartan hoplites were returning to their garrison after escorting Amyklaean soldiers home when they were attacked by Iphikrates' peltasts. The detailed manoeuvres described at 11.8–10 deal only with standard hoplite warfare. Here the enemy peltasts attacked and withdrew and picked off many of the hoplites without losing many men themselves. The hoplites, even when joined by cavalry, were unable to alter their standard way of attacking and so continued to lose men. Many were killed and at the last stand some flung themselves into the sea and a few were saved by the horsemen. Contemplation of the statement in 11.7, therefore, engenders unease in anyone familiar with Spartan military history.

The immediately following details of the standard hoplite manoeuvres (11.8–10) do nothing to dispel this unease. At first glance the description of the manoeuvres seems to suggest continuing attention to detail, an admirable awareness of the fact that many in a Lakedaimonian army are not full-citizens, and a worthy attempt to counter this. Yet it is obvious that the detailed manoeuvres here presented cover only a very few, very standard situations and beg the question what happens if the circumstances of a battle do not fit these carefully defined parameters. If only Spartan citizens fight well in disorder then presumably others do not. In fact, in most cases, they flee. Consider again the example of Anaxibios, he and 12 harmosts died together, the rest of his army (mercenaries, Lakedaimonians, and Abydian hoplites) who had not been killed, fled (4.8.39). While Mindaros was fighting to the death, the rest fled (1.1.18); Kallikratidas' Peloponnesian allies turned tail when he fell overboard (1.6.33); Peisandros' troops fled while he fought to the death (4.3.12); and Mnasippos is similarly abandoned and falls fighting (6.2.22, though in this instance his appalling generalship also contributes to the lack of steadfastness of those under his command).[33] Further, the very rigidity of the detailed manoeuvres shows that the Spartans limited themselves to coping with only one type of battle situation. No lessons appear to have been learned from Sphakteria. In a state where obedience and, hence, conformity are paramount, this conservatism is perhaps not surprising.

So while there are enormous benefits to such an ordered system, benefits which brought power and renown to Sparta, there are also problems which arise from the integration of a small number of elite citizen troops who will behave one way, steadfastly fighting to the death in any situation through fear of public disgrace, with a larger number of non-citizen troops. These latter may be able to carry out basic manoeuvres when integrated with the Spartiates but only a limited number of standard battle situations are catered for, and without the same social conditioning these troops are generally bound to flee at the first sign of disorder. The growing reliance on such troops reduces the strengths of the Spartan system. Further, if an enemy force were to become more orderly, as the Thebans eventually did, the advantages of the Spartan system would be negated. Xenophon, thus, at the same time as he is telling us what led to Sparta's renown, is subtly drawing attention to the flaw in the system by the very way in which he presents his narrative.

Later in chapter 13 he remarks that 'upon watching you would consider all others improvisers (αὐτοσχεδιαστὰς) in the art of campaigning, but the Lakedaimonians alone craftsmen (τεχνίτας) in warfare' (13.5). Again this comment, as with much of the material in the *Lakedaimoniōn Politeia*, is not as straightforward as it first appears. The term αὐτοσχεδιαστής can certainly be used to mean without any real skill,[34] and so in one way the statement would seem to support the view of the Spartans as skilled craftsmen in the arts of war. It can, however, also be taken more positively to mean taking the initiative and improvising, activities not encouraged by the Spartan system as laid out by Xenophon. Agesilaos, for example, uses it in this sense when he defends Phoibidas on the grounds that he showed initiative in capturing the Kadmeia (*HG* 5.2.32).[35] The point is precisely that the Spartan system was well-ordered but not particularly adaptable.

Xenophon's view of Spartan military practices is, thus, more nuanced than most commentators have noticed. As he states in 11.7, the Spartiates fight well with whoever is beside them in disorder because they have been conditioned to do so by their upbringing. Their upbringing, as presented by Xenophon earlier in the text, shows a remarkable emphasis on instilling obedience and keeping fit. Generally the ways in which obedience is gained are negative, i.e. there are harsh punishments for non-conformity and indeed some of the harshest punishments are meted out for showing cowardice. They stand their ground because if they did not, life back home would be intolerable. The comment at 11.7 also compels us to reflect upon the instances where the Spartans did not fight well in disorder. That it does so is not an accident. Xenophon, throughout the *Lakedaimoniōn Politeia*, presents the renown-bringing laws of Lykourgos in an ambiguous way. In each instance he shows us both the aspects of the laws which led to Sparta's renown as well as pointing us towards their shortcomings. The shortcomings here include the observations that Spartiates cannot really cope with disorder other than by fighting to the death; and the limited body of easy manoeuvres which help the other Lakedaimonians merge with the Spartiates only works in very orderly battle situations. The other Lakedaimonians, the *perioikoi*, not having been brought up to believe death is better than flight, are liable to flee in disorderly situations and Lykourgos' laws can do nothing about this. Nor does there seem to be a willingness to try to adapt to changing methods of warfare. These shortcomings along with others throughout the work lead to the situation described in chapter 14, the supposed chapter of disillusion.[36] A basic understanding of 11.7 is impossible, therefore, without reference to the rest of the work and thus the whole text is much more closely integrated than commentators, like Lipka, would allow.

In short, Xenophon is not trying to defend the Spartan practice (as Ollier says) or to encourage others to practise Spartan ways (as Luppino Manes says). He is showing the features of the Spartan system which won them great renown and success while at the same time pointing out the weaknesses in the system and how these eventually contributed to the Spartans' downfall – as any diligent political philosopher would do.

Acknowledgements

Thanks, as ever, are due to the editors of the volume both for the invitation to speak at the Celtic Conference in Rennes in 2004 and for their insightful comments on the ensuing paper. Thanks are also due to Hans van Wees and Keith Sidwell, discussion with whom helped clarify my arguments.

Notes

[1] 11.7: τὸ μέντοι κἂν ταραχθῶσι μετὰ τοῦ παρατυχόντος ὁμοίως μάχεσθαι, ταύτην τὴν τάξιν οὐκέτι ῥᾴδιόν ἐστι μαθεῖν πλὴν τοῖς ὑπὸ τῶν τοῦ Λυκούργου νόμων πεπαιδευμένοις.

[2] Rebenich 1998, 128 passes by the statement completely, while Lipka 2002, 197 only cites in comparison a passage from Plutarch (*Pelopidas* 23.3) in which Plutarch describes the Spartans as having trained to move from disorder to an orderly array, fighting beside whoever they find themselves next to. In the following passage Plutarch notes that this procedure was of no use against Pelopidas and Epaminondas (23.4).

[3] Lipka 2002, 27–31.

[4] Whether or not the reputation was justified, it was to Sparta that other states came for military aid and alliance. For example in Herodotus alone see 1.56–69 (by Croesus), 1.152 (by Aeolians and Ionians), 6.84 (by Scythia), 5.49 (by Miletus), 7.161 and 8.2 (Sparta is the popular choice to lead against Xerxes); see How and Wells 1912, 92 for further examples.

[5] Hodkinson 1983, 266–7.

[6] It might be argued that Xenophon wrote the *Lakedaimoniōn Politeia* before the disaster at Lechaion (Lipka 2002, 13, for example, dates the work to *c.* 394 BC) and that by the time he wrote Book 4 of the *Hellenica*, which from 2.3.11 at least is generally assumed to be a late work (see, e.g., Tuplin 1993, 29–31 and Dillery 1995, 14), he had become disillusioned with the Spartans. But he cannot be ignorant of Sphakteria. For a discussion of the various attempts at dating the *Lakedaimoniōn Politeia*, and the suggestion that it is difficult to be more precise than sometime between 394 and 371 BC, see Humble 2004, 219–20.

[7] An 'epigramme' as Ollier (1934, 58) calls it.

[8] Unlike most commentators I read the work as political philosophy, not panegyric; see Humble 2004, 220–6.

[9] There is a small lacuna in this last sentence but no agreement on what is missing; on which see Lipka 2002, 197.

[10] The sense of οὐκέτι ('no longer') is variously dealt with by translators. The best explanation seems to be that it sharpens the contrast between what is easy to learn (11.5) and what is not. It might also suggest that in Xenophon's view non-Spartans used to be able to fight well with one another even in disorder in the past. If this is the case, what precisely he is referring to is difficult to say, possibly the ideology of the pure citizen militia? On the ideal of the pure citizen militia see Van Wees 2004, 77–85.

[11] Ollier 1934, xxvi.

[12] Luppino Manes 1988, 97 (on 11.7) and more generally 19–31.

[13] See Tuplin 1993; Humble 2004.

[14] Proietti 1987, 64. This explanation works well in most cases though there are

instances where we might have expected Xenophon to have referred only to Spartiates (e.g. 13.5: the Lakedaimonians are master craftsmen of war; 14.2: formerly the Lakedaimonians preferred to live at home; 14.9: kings of the Lakedaimonians).

[15] Proietti 1987, 66.

[16] See on this Van Wees 2004, 45, 82–3, and especially 265 n. 2 for examples of Spartan expeditions where only one or a few Spartiates commanded armies composed of non-Spartiates.

[17] There has been disagreement about the precise nature of the movements Xenophon is describing here. For the most recent discussion see Lipka 2002, 198–201 (with diagrams, 265–8). Lipka also, 201, rightly points out that 'X. simply enumerates a number of tactical movements, whereby the difficulty of the Spartan manoeuvre (not the ground or enemy formation) is the main issue'.

[18] As Ollier 1934, 52 and Moore 1983, 115 suggest.

[19] For example, compare *Mem.* 3.1 and *Cyr.* 1.6.12–14.

[20] Moore 1983, 115. Lipka 2002, 198 seems to lean in the same direction when he comments on the example of Mnasippos at Kerkyra in 374 as an example that 'the Spartans did not always execute these tactical movements as successfully as X. wants us to believe'.

[21] Success: Agesilaos at Koroneia (*HG* 4.3.18); failure: Mnasippos at Kerkyra (*HG* 6.2.20–3).

[22] Proietti 1987, 65–6.

[23] Van Wees 2004, 84.

[24] See n. 17 above.

[25] Luppino Manes 1988, 97.

[26] As Cairns 1993, 1–4, notes, translating *aidōs* is difficult. He gives as a guide the English concepts of shame, modesty, respect and a sense of honour (455). See Humble 1999 on Xenophon's understanding of it. More generally on *aidōs* in Sparta, see Richer 1999.

[27] By way of contrast, in Xenophon's description of the Persian system in the *Cyropaedia* boys are said to learn to shoot and throw a spear (*Cyr.* 1.2.8), and young men either go out hunting or stay at home practising shooting bows and hurling spears, constantly engaging in contests (1.2.9, 12).

[28] Van Wees 2004, 92. This goes against the grain of the normal assumption that it was continual practice of military manoeuvres which made the Spartan performance of them look easy (see, for example, Anderson 1970, 107; Pritchett 1974–91, 4.63, n. 164; Powell 2001, 232).

[29] Aristotle (*Pol.* 1338b24–9) says that the Spartans differed in that they simply made their young engage in gymnastic and military contests while other states did not; as soon as others states started doing the same the Spartans lost their advantage. See also Kraut 1997, 186 on this passage.

[30] See also the comments Xenophon puts in Pericles' mouth at *Mem.* 3.5.15–16, 21, which echo the key features of the Spartan system which he draws out here: 'when will the Athenians take physical exercise, like the Spartans? Not only do they neglect their own fitness, but they make fun of people who look after themselves. When will they thus obey their leaders, those who exult in looking down upon their leaders? … In military affairs, where self-discipline, orderliness, and obedience are most vital, they devote themselves to none of these things' (translation adapted and expanded from Van Wees

2004, 88).

   [31] See further Humble 1997, 187–240, and 2004.

   [32] See Humble 2004, 224–5 on this passage in relation to chapter 14 of the work.

   [33] See n. 20 above.

   [34] LSJ *s.v.* αὐτοσχεδιαστής.

   [35] See also Th. 1.138.3 where Thucydides uses it in a positive sense about Themistocles.

   [36] See Humble 2004 for arguments as to why this chapter is also fully integrated with the rest of the work and is not an addendum added by a disappointed Xenophon after Leuktra.

Bibliography

Anderson, J.K.
   1970   *Military Theory and Practice in the Age of Xenophon*, Berkeley.
Cairns, D.L.
   1993   *Aidos*, Oxford.
Dillery, J.
   1995   *Xenophon and the History of his Times*, London.
Hodkinson, S.
   1983   'Social order and the conflict of values in Classical Sparta', *Chiron* 13, 239–81.
How, W.W. and Wells, J.
   1912   *A Commentary on Herodotus, Vol. 1 (Books I to IV)*, Oxford.
Humble, N.
   1997   'Xenophon's view of Sparta', Diss., McMaster University, Hamilton.
   1999   '*Sōphrosynē* and the Spartans in Xenophon', in S. Hodkinson and A. Powell (eds) *Sparta: New perspectives*, London, 339–53.
   2004   'The author, date and purpose of chapter 14 of the *Lakedaimonion Politeia*', in C. Tuplin (ed.) *Xenophon and his World*, Stuttgart, 215–28.
Kraut, R. (trans. and ed.)
   1997   *Aristotle. Politics. Books VII and VIII*, Oxford.
Lipka, M.
   2002   *Xenophon's Spartan Constitution*, Berlin.
Luppino Manes, E.
   1988   *Un progetto di riforma per Sparta*, Milan.
Moore, J.M.
   1983   *Aristotle and Xenophon on Democracy and Oligarchy*, 2nd edn, London.
Ollier, F.
   1934   *Xénophon*. La République des Lacédémoniens, Paris.
Powell, A.
   2001   *Athens and Sparta. Constructing Greek political and social history from 478 BC*, 2nd edn, London.
Pritchett, W.K.
   1974–91   *The Greek State at War*, parts 1–5, Berkeley.
Proietti, G.
   1987   *Xenophon's Sparta*, Leiden.

Rebenich, S.
    1998   *Xenophon. Die Verfassung der Spartaner*, Darmstadt.
Richer, N.
    1999   '*Aidōs* at Sparta', in S. Hodkinson and A. Powell (eds.) *Sparta: New perspectives*, London, 91–115.
Tuplin, C.
    1993   *The Failings of Empire: A reading of Xenophon Hellenica 2.3.11–7.5.27*, Stuttgart.
Van Wees, H.
    2004   *Greek Warfare. Myths and realities*, London.

8

THE POLITICS OF SPARTAN MERCENARY SERVICE

Ellen Millender

Mercenary service was long a feature of the Greek world. Ionian Greeks served together with Carians for the Egyptian Pharaoh Psammetichus I *c.* 650,[1] and the seventh-century lyric poet Archilochus seems to express concern that he might be called a Carian ἐπίκουρος 'mercenary' (fr. 216 West; cf. fr. 15).[2] It was not until the late fifth and fourth centuries, however, that mercenaries began to figure prominently in Greek warfare, as a consequence of several interrelated historical developments. Athens' fifth-century thalassocracy depended upon a navy that increasingly employed mercenaries, especially during the Peloponnesian War (431–404), when the Athenians competed with their Peloponnesian rivals for both hegemony in the Aegean basin and the mercenaries needed to achieve it. In the destabilized and war-torn Greek mainland left in the wake of Athens' defeat, ambitious leaders such as the Sicilian tyrant, Dionysius I, and the Persian prince, Cyrus the Younger, found a ready supply of would-be professional soldiers and *poleis* willing to trade alliance and aid for money and friendship. These and other factors, such as the repeated revolts of Persia's satraps against King Artaxerxes II and the Carthaginian intervention in Sicily during the first few decades of the fourth century, collectively gave rise to the 'Greek mercenary explosion' of the late classical period.[3] Although we must allow for the ancient sources' exaggeration of the numbers, references to the 11,000 Greek hoplites and additional special troops gathered by Cyrus in 401 (cf. Xen. *Anab.* 1.2.9) and the thousands of mercenaries hired by Dionysius I two years later (Diod. 14.43.2–3) demonstrate both the availability of and demand for such soldiers.

Like their Athenian rivals and many other Greeks, the Spartans took advantage of the rise in mercenary numbers at home and abroad, but neither their contributions to the development of mercenary warfare in ancient Greece nor the effects of such warfare on Sparta have received much scholarly attention.[4] This chapter examines the evidence for Spartan involvement in mercenary warfare during the late fifth century and the first half of the fourth century and considers the political, social, and economic ramifications of

Spartan mercenary service. At first glance, the sources' largely isolated reports of Lacedaemonians leading and employing mercenary forces appear to provide a limited picture of Spartan mercenary activity. I will argue, however, that such reports, when studied together and in the context of Sparta's development, maintenance, and loss of its hegemony in both the Peloponnesus and the Aegean, provide an important window on to the Spartans' foreign policy and domestic troubles during this period. They suggest that mercenaries played a more important role in Spartan statecraft and had a far more significant impact on Sparta's dramatic rise and decline in the fourth century than scholars have so far suggested.

The first section of the chapter, which focuses on the gradual increase of Spartan participation in the mercenary 'industry' from the 420s to the 370s, reveals that the Spartans effectively exploited both the growing supply of professional soldiers and other states' increasing dependence on mercenaries. There is little to no evidence of rank-and-file Spartiate hoplites serving as mercenaries. Instead, individual Spartiates functioned as military advisers, commanders, and overseers of Peloponnesian mercenary forces sent abroad, almost always with the approval of the authorities at home. Even more surprising, perhaps, is the Lacedaemonians' veritable conversion of the Peloponnesus into a large mercenary market to support their hegemonic aspirations and to aid their most valued allies, such as Dionysius I and Cyrus the Younger. The Spartans' employment of mercenaries, service as mercenary commanders, and trafficking in Peloponnesian hoplites enabled them to develop their short-lived Aegean empire (404–394) and to bolster their domination over mainland Greece during the 380s and 370s.

While such mercenary activity allowed the Spartans to pursue their imperialistic agenda without having to commit their own shrinking supply of manpower, it ultimately undermined the power that it had helped to create. As the second section of this chapter shows, the Spartans' involvement in mercenary warfare had negative repercussions on both Spartan foreign policy and the Peloponnesian League during the 380s and 370s. It contributed to the nexus of institutional problems that led to Sparta's decline into a second-rate power after the defeat by Thebes at Leuctra in 371.

I. The Development of Spartan Mercenary Service
1. The Peloponnesian War

The earliest evidence for Spartan employment of mercenaries during the fifth century comes from Thucydides' account of the Peloponnesian War. Mercenaries participated in Spartan expeditions during the Archidamian phase of the war, perhaps as early as 426, when the general Eurylochus led a force for a long period to distant Acarnania (Thuc. 3.100.2–102, 105–9). Thucydides labels part of this force as 'mercenary followers' (τὸν μισθοφόρον ὄχλον: 3.109.2), but his description of the force at 3.109.3 neither clearly delineates the identity of these paid soldiers nor specifies whether they were employed by the Spartans or their Ambraciot allies.[5] Thucydides' account of this expedition is nonetheless significant, because it suggests that the participation of such mercenaries was standard practice.

The next – and far better – attested instance of Spartan employment of mercenaries occurred a few years later, during Brasidas' Thracian expedition of 424–422.[6] According to Thucydides, the Spartan authorities, for both military and political reasons, sent out seven hundred helots to serve with Brasidas. The rest of his hoplite force was comprised of Peloponnesians 'persuaded by pay' (μισθῷ πείσας), whom Brasidas himself recruited in the Peloponnesus (4.80.5).[7] Given the usual geographical and temporal scope of intra-Greek warfare and the Spartans' general hesitation to commit troops to extended campaigns abroad, it is no wonder that they turned to mercenaries and other 'outsiders' like the helots, who would have to be compensated for participating in such a long and risky venture.[8] While the former received monetary payment for their services, the latter group received remuneration in the form of freedom. In his account of Brasidas' series of successes in northern Greece, Thucydides also reveals that Brasidas' forces were eventually reinforced by light-armed soldiers (4.110.2–111.2, 123.4), but he does not make it clear whether these men were mercenaries or allied soldiers. The five hundred Peloponnesian hoplites and three hundred Chalcidian peltasts that Brasidas put under the command of Polydamidas at Mende (Thuc. 4.123.4; cf. 4.129.3, 130.3–4, 131) may also have been mercenaries, but Thucydides is again unclear on this point.[9] Later, in his account of the Battle of Amphipolis in 422, however, we find Brasidas commanding a force that included 1,500 Thracian mercenaries, the Edonian army of cavalry and peltasts, and 1,000 Myrcinian and Chalcidian peltasts (5.6.4).[10]

Brasidas' responsibility for maintaining his force with allied help (cf. Thuc. 4.80.1, 83.6) occasionally created problems. His dependence on foreign aid forced him to serve as a veritable mercenary himself for the Macedonian Perdiccas in a campaign against Arrhabaeus, king of the Lyncestian Macedonians (4.124–8; cf. 4.83.4–6). Nevertheless, it has been widely recognized that Brasidas' soldiers, who formed such an attachment to their leader that they came to be unofficially known as the 'Brasideioi' (Thuc. 5.67.1, 71.3, 72.3), gave him an unusual degree of independence and the power to craft Spartan foreign policy. Brasidas' relatively free hand in the Thraceward region ultimately irritated the leading men back home, who were either jealous of his success or interested in ending the war (4.108.7). However, his achievements set a precedent for ambitious Spartiates looking for routes to power denied to them at home.[11]

Later, during the Sicilian Expedition (415–413), the Spartan commander Gylippus assumed overall command of the Syracusans' force, which included a significant number of mercenaries (Thuc. 7.13.2, 48.5, 58.3). Otherwise, the Spartans appear to have made little use of such 'hired help' during their struggle with Athens until the final phase of the Peloponnesian War, when mercenaries served as rowers in the Peloponnesian fleet and also began to shoulder militarily some of the Spartans' hegemonic ambitions around the Aegean.[12] Already in 412 we hear of the Lacedaemonians putting under the command of Pedaritus, the Spartan harmost of Chios, Peloponnesian mercenaries that they had taken over from the Persian rebel Amorges (Thuc. 8.28.4–5, 38.3, 55.3). According to Diodorus, Clearchus, the harmost of Byzantium, also made use of both Peloponnesian forces and mercenaries in his defense of that city against the Athenians in 408 (13.66.5). One may counter that Xenophon does not include mercenaries in his description of the forces serving alongside Clearchus, which included *perioikoi*, emancipated helots, Megarians, and Boeotians (*Hell.* 1.3.15). Xenophon's account of Clearchus' ill-considered decision to leave Byzantium in search of pay for his soldiers, however, suggests that the Spartans needed to hire at least some of the contingent that garrisoned this post so far from home (*Hell.* 1.3.17).[13]

The last decade of the Peloponnesian War also witnessed the Spartans' export of military expertise, rather than Spartan soldiers, to aid valued allies and thus bolster interests abroad, especially in Sicily. This practice may have begun with Sparta's dispatch of Gylippus to Sicily in 414 (cf. Thuc. 6.93.2).[14] Diodorus, or rather his source, the fourth/third-century Sicilian historian Timaeus, provides interesting evidence concerning a certain Dexippus, a *perioikos* (cf. Xen. *Anab.* 5.1.15). Dexippus supposedly enjoyed great repute at Gela because of his Lacedaemonian origins (13.85.3) and at Acragas because of his military expertise (13.87.5). According to Diodorus, Dexippus raised a thousand mercenaries and took them to Acragas in southern Italy in 406 to stem the Carthaginians' advance into Sicily from the west (13.85.3–4, 87.4–5, 88.7). We next find Dexippus back in charge of Gela, at the request of the Syracusans, where he posed an obstacle to the ambitious Dionysius' bid for tyranny (Diod. 13.93.1). Diodorus claims that Dionysius first undercut Dexippus' power at Gela by paying his mercenaries their arrears and thus winning their loyalty (13.93.2). After Dionysius failed to win over Dexippus to his cause, he sent him back to Greece later in 406, lest the Lacedaemonian frustrate his political plans by restoring the Syracusans' freedom (13.96.1).

Both Dionysius' surprisingly lenient treatment of Dexippus and the oddly formal 'return' of the Lacedaemonian commander to Greece suggest, as Paul Cartledge has argued, that Dexippus had likely been sent to Gela and later Acragas as 'part of an official Spartan policy of sending (limited) aid to the

Sicilian Greeks with a view to receiving reciprocal aid in the war against Athens'.[15] This interpretation of Dexippus' – and the Spartans' – activity in the West receives support from an inscription belonging to the first half of 406, which records the Athenians' friendly overtures to the Sicilian Greeks' Carthaginian enemies.[16] Diodorus also claims that the Spartans later sent Aristus (or Aretes) to Syracuse (in 404) to aid Dionysius' establishment of his tyranny in the hope of receiving like benefactions from him (14.10.2–3; cf. 14.70.3).[17] As we shall see below, the Spartans continued to send such military experts to aid Dionysius at least down to 396, and this policy helped to forge the close alliance that later benefited the Spartans in the dark days following Leuctra.

2. Spartan adventures abroad: Lysander, the Cyreians, and the Persian expedition

It was not until their defeat of Athens and the development of their own naval *archē*, however, that the Spartans truly began to exploit the opportunities offered by the growing phenomenon of Greek mercenary service. Mercenaries first figure prominently in the Spartans' interference in Athenian politics after the conclusion of the Peloponnesian War. When the Thirty at Eleusis asked the Lacedaemonians for support against their democratic rivals in 403, Lysander arranged a loan of 100 talents, very likely to facilitate the purchase of mercenaries (Xen. *Hell.* 2.4.28; cf. 2.4.43). After being appointed governor, Lysander also directly proceeded to Eleusis, where he raised a large force of Peloponnesian hoplites (Xen. *Hell.* 2.4.28–9; cf. Lys. 12.59–60; Diod. 14.33.5), whom Xenophon later seems to identify as mercenaries (μισθοφόροις: *Hell.* 2.4.30).

Under the continuing influence of Lysander, the ambitious architect of Sparta's imperialist program and established *xenos* of Cyrus the Younger, the Spartans once again exported their military expertise and employed Peloponnesian mercenaries in support of the Persian prince's attempted coup against his brother, Artaxerxes II, in 401.[18] At first glance, the Spartans appear to have played only a supporting role in the adventures of the force that Cyrus collected and that had to make its way out of Asia following his death at Cunaxa in the summer of 401. However, a careful reading of the sources, especially Xenophon's *Anabasis*, reveals that the Spartans actually maintained close contact with – and perhaps a great deal of control over – the Ten Thousand until they formally assumed command over the remnants of Cyrus' force in the spring of 399.[19] As we shall see, a series of Lacedaemonian generals commanded the Cyreians, and the Spartan admirals (*nauarchs*) and governors that operated in the Hellespontine region from 401 to 399 continually monitored this force.

According to Xenophon, Cyrus called on his various Greek *xenoi* to aid his war, sent money to several friends to raise troops, and successfully appealed to the Spartans to 'show themselves as good friends to him as he had been to them in their war against the Athenians' (*Hell.* 3.1.1; cf. Diod. 14.19.4; Plut. *Artax.* 6.3). The Spartan *polis* fulfilled its bonds of *xenia* with Cyrus (cf. Xen. *Hell.* 2.1.14) by offering aid in a variety of forms that may help to explain both Ephorus' belief that the Lacedaemonians and Cyrus were making secret plans for a joint campaign against Artaxerxes (Diod. 14.11.2 = *FGrH* 70 F 70) and Isocrates' repeated claims that the Spartans were intimately involved in Cyrus' attempted coup (8.98; 12.104–5; cf. 5.95–7).[20] Xenophon states that the ephors, seeing the justice of the Persian prince's request, ordered the *nauarch* Samius to put himself and his fleet at Cyrus' disposal (*Hell.* 3.1.1).[21] The Spartan authorities also sent a force of seven hundred Peloponnesian mercenaries under the command of the Spartan Cheirisophus (Xen. *Anab.* 1.4.3; cf. Diod. 14.19.5, 21.1).[22] These Peloponnesian mercenaries, though officially sent by Sparta, became full participants in Cyrus' expedition. Their leader, Cheirisophus, who had been personally summoned (μετάπεμπτος) by Cyrus (Xen. *Anab.* 1.4.3) and was thus likely another *xenos* of the Persian prince,[23] also eventually became commander of the 10,000 after the death of his compatriot, the Spartan exile, Clearchus (Xen. *Anab.* 6.1.32–3; cf. Diod. 14.27.1).

Clearchus, the former harmost of Byzantium, entered Cyrus' service after he had been exiled and condemned to death in 402 for insubordination.[24] As Xenophon makes clear, Clearchus, unlike the other Greek *stratēgoi* serving under Cyrus, was not one of Cyrus' established *xenoi* but received his 'commission' to hire mercenaries (ξενολογεῖν) for Cyrus, because the Persian prince admired the Lacedaemonian.[25] It is entirely possible that Cyrus respected Clearchus' military experience, and the two men did establish a *xenia* (Xen. *Anab.* 1.3.2–6).[26] Nevertheless, Cyrus likely valued more highly the support of the Spartans, the new hegemons in the Aegean. Both Cyrus and the Spartans, moreover, would have recognized Clearchus' suitability as a military adviser to Cyrus. Clearchus had gained an unusual degree of familiarity with the Hellespont through his position as *proxenos* of Byzantium, his numerous commands in that region from 412 to 410, and his governance of Byzantium in 408. To these appointments we must add Clearchus' later – and less clear – activity in that region in 403, which, according to Diodorus, included his successful recruitment of a large body of mercenaries and establishment of his own tyranny at Byzantium.[27]

There is also good reason to believe that the Spartans supported and even connived at Cyrus' appointment of Clearchus as his second-in-command, even if we do not accept Isocrates' repeated assertion that the Spartans sent

Clearchus to Cyrus (8.98; 12.104–5) or Plutarch's claim that they sent Clearchus instructions (*Artax.* 6.5).[28] As an exile, Clearchus was an outsider whom the Spartans could employ discreetly and disavow if necessary, as they hedged their bets regarding Cyrus' attempted coup. The Spartan authorities did not interfere with Clearchus' recruitment of an army and military activity in the Thracian Chersonese (*Anab.* 1.1.9, 1.2.9), despite the area's strategic importance and Clearchus' earlier despotic behavior.[29] The sources, moreover, do not report any difficulties between Clearchus and the Spartan commanders officially sent to support Cyrus. As Sherylee Bassett has suggested, Xenophon's claim that Clearchus was the only one of Cyrus' generals who knew the real aim of the campaign (*Anab.* 3.1.10) may further support the theory that the Spartan authorities at the very least co-operated with Clearchus. It is unlikely that the Spartan authorities – and especially Lysander, Cyrus' *xenos* – would have sent a force to Cyrus without knowledge of his true intentions, which they might have shared with the exiled Spartiate.[30]

Xenophon shows that Clearchus became Cyrus' favorite among the Greek commanders who joined his expedition, at least by the trial of Orontas, the prominent kinsman of the king who arranged a plot against Cyrus (*Anab.* 1.6).[31] Clearchus was the only Greek allowed to attend the trial of Orontas (Xen. *Anab.* 1.6.5) and was asked first among Cyrus' counselors for his opinion concerning Orontas' punishment (Xen. *Anab.* 1.6.9). Clearchus' position as Cyrus' chief commander became clear at Cunaxa, when Cyrus put him in charge of his force's right wing and gave him alone the instructions for battle.[32] The Spartan exile retained this position after Cyrus' death at Cunaxa (Xen. *Anab.* 2.2.5) until he was put to death by Tissaphernes, the satrap of Sardis.[33]

The Spartan general Cheirisophus, as mentioned above, then took charge of the Cyreians and was later elected by them as sole commander-in-chief (Xen. *Anab.* 6.1.32–3; cf. Diod. 14.27.1).[34] Cheirisophus' supreme command of the Ten Thousand, in turn, was short-lived, since only six or seven days later the Arcadians and Achaeans formed a separate force, a split that led to the subsequent creation of another force under Xenophon (Xen. *Anab.* 6.2.12–16). Cheirisophus, however, continued to lead the Cyreians, at least nominally, even after the various contingents reunited (Xen. *Anab.* 6.4.9). After his death the command of the mercenary army passed to another Lacedaemonian, the *perioikos* Neon (Xen. *Anab.* 6.4.11, 23), Cheirisophus' erstwhile lieutenant (Xen. *Anab.* 5.6.36).[35] Neon remained in charge until the bulk of the army joined the Thracian king Seuthes, and Neon thereafter remained with the Spartan forces at Perinthus (Xen. *Anab.* 7.2.1, 17, 29; 7.3.2, 7). The Cyreians, consequently, remained under Lacedaemonian leadership throughout most of their expedition.

The other Lacedaemonian who figures prominently in the *Anabasis* is the *perioikos* Dexippus, the aforementioned military adviser operating in Sicily in 406 (5.1.15). Xenophon paints Dexippus as a thoroughly duplicitous and self-serving adventurer (cf. Diod. 13.87.4–5, 88.7), who was put in command of a penteconter borrowed from the people of Trapezus to capture ships that would transport the Cyreians home by sea. Dexippus, however, used the ship to escape the Black Sea and thereby forced his stranded comrades to march by land along the coast (*Anab.* 5.1.15; 6.6.5, 22–3). Having developed an animosity toward Xenophon (Xen. *Anab.* 6.1.32; 6.6.11, 15), he later used his connections with Anaxibius, the Spartan *nauarch* operating in the Hellespontine region (Xen. *Anab.* 6.1.32), and Cleander, the Spartan harmost of Byzantium, to frustrate the Cyreians' attempt to get home safely (Xen. *Anab.* 6.6.6–34). While Xenophon does not clarify Dexippus' position, both his command over the Trapezan penteconter and his connections with the leading Spartans in the region suggest that he was part of the force Sparta sent out under the command of Cheirisophus in 401 (Xen. *Anab.* 5.1.15).[36]

Although the Spartans aided Cyrus in numerous ways and several Spartans served as commanders of his force, scholars have tended to downplay direct Lacedaemonian involvement in the expedition of the Ten Thousand. Cheirisophus and Neon were officers sent by the Spartan state, but Dexippus' role in the expedition is far less clear, and Clearchus could be viewed as a 'rogue' Spartiate.[37] Moreover, the *Anabasis* mentions only two other Lacedaemonian members of this force. Xenophon records the death of an otherwise unknown Cleonymus, whom he describes in general terms, as ἀνὴρ ἀγαθὸς Λακωνικός (*Anab.* 4.1.18). Draconтius, a presumably rank-and-file Spartiate, receives mention twice in the *Anabasis* (4.8.25–6; 6.6.30). His status as an exile – because of an accidental homicide committed when he was a boy (*Anab.* 4.8.25) – may suggest that he was simply another mercenary who sought employment with Cyrus.[38] It is striking, however, to find yet another Spartan exile participating in the expedition. Perhaps the Spartans once again encouraged an estranged and thus 'deniable' Spartan to help them pursue their indirect support of Cyrus.[39]

Spartan support for the Cyreians, moreover, was inconsistent and often lukewarm, at best. The Spartan authorities would have had good reason to support Cyrus' attempted coup, particularly given their debt to Cyrus (cf. Xen. *Hell.* 3.1.1; Diod. 14.19.4) and the obligations that individual Spartiates – especially Lysander and Cheirisophus – owed to their *xenos*, Cyrus.[40] However, as Diodorus suggests later in his account (14.21.2; cf. Just. *Epit.* 5.11.6–7), they also would have been wary of alienating Artaxerxes in the event of Cyrus' failure.[41] As Cartledge has pointed out, the Spartans' response to Cyrus' summons allowed them at once to balance these considerations and to bolster their hegemony.[42] All of these factors help to explain the rather ambivalent nature of the Spartans' support for Cyrus: their dispatch of a few Spartan (and perioikic) commanders, the limited involvement of the Spartan *nauarch* and his fleet,[43] and their at least tacit blessing on Cyrus' appointment of the exiled Clearchus.

Cyrus' death and the increasing likelihood of Artaxerxes' anti-Spartan backlash would have further dampened Spartan support for the 10,000. Xenophon's account of the Cyreians' ensuing adventures includes descriptions of Spartan generals and authorities in the eastern Aegean who showed little interest in aiding the Cyreians and often demonstrated outright hostility to that mercenary force, even though it was under the command of fellow Lacedaemonians. The Cyreian commander Cheirisophus, for example, failed to persuade the Spartan *nauarch* Anaxibius, his supposed friend (Xen. *Anab.* 5.1.4; Diod. 14.30.4), to supply the mercenaries with ships to take them back to Greece (Xen. *Anab.* 6.1.16; Diod. 14.31.3). Cleander, the Spartan governor at Byzantium, was also rumored to be bringing triremes and merchant ships to help transport the Cyreians (Xen. *Anab.* 6.2.13, 4.18, 6.1), but he took a long time to reach the mercenaries and arrived with only two triremes (Xen. *Anab.* 6.6.5). Cleander later added insult to injury by threatening to punish those Cyreians who had gotten into a conflict with Dexippus by outlawing the 10,000 from the Spartan empire (Xen. *Anab.* 6.6.9). Soon thereafter, Anaxibius and Cleander together forced the mercenaries out of Byzantium and almost precipitated a battle between the mercenaries and the Lacedaemonian forces at Byzantium (Xen. *Anab.* 7.1.2–4, 7–31, 36, 38–40). Aristarchus, Cleander's successor at Byzantium, in turn, sold into slavery (on Anaxibius' orders) four hundred Cyreians who were left behind at Byzantium and blocked Xenophon's efforts to transport the remnants of the Ten Thousand to Asia.[44] Xenophon, finally, records the threats to his life posed by Aristarchus (*Anab.* 7.2.12–14) and Thibron, the Spartan commander sent to Ionia in 400 to protect the Greeks of Asia Minor from Tissaphernes (*Anab.* 7.6.43).

The evidence provided by the ancient sources, nevertheless, reveals that both the Spartan authorities and individual Lacedaemonians had a continued stake in the mercenary army that Cyrus had collected, from its inception to its return to Greece. Both the fact that Spartiates deemed fit for military service required official authorization before leaving the Peloponnesus (Isoc. 11.18) and the evidence that Diodorus provides for the Spartan authorities' continued oversight of mercenary commanders abroad (14.78.1) suggest that the Lacedaemonian generals who led the Ten Thousand did so only with their home authorities' approval.

Lacedaemonian interest in the oversight of this force is particularly clear in Xenophon's account of the Cyreians' appointment of the Spartan Cheirisophus as commander-in-chief (*Anab.* 6.1.16–32). According to the *Anabasis*, the mercenaries expressed their desire to nominate Xenophon. The Athenian *stratēgos*, however, turned down the command in favor of Cheirisophus, ostensibly because he believed that the appointment of Cheirisophus (or any Lacedaemonian for that matter) would alone please the Spartans now dominating the Aegean (Xen. *Anab.* 6.1.26–31).[45] After accepting the command, Cheirisophus delivered a speech that further revealed the Spartans' interest in maintaining at least a modicum of control over the Cyreians. Cheirisophus claimed that Dexippus had falsely accused Xenophon of attempting to deprive the Lacedaemonians of the command over 'Clearchus' army' (τοῦ Κλεάρχου στρατεύματος: Xen. *Anab.* 6.1.32).

While it made sense for the Spartans to keep their eye on a large force operating in such a militarily and politically sensitive region and to maintain its allegiance to Sparta (cf. Xen. *Anab.* 6.6.34), both the authorities at home and their commanders abroad also remained aware of the possible advantages of exploiting this rich military resource. Individual Spartiates such as Anaxibius, Cleander, and Aristarchus may have occasionally looked upon the Ten Thousand with suspicion and impeded their *katabasis* to placate Pharnabazus, the Persian satrap of Hellespontine Phrygia, and perhaps to avoid instability in the sensitive Hellespontine region.[46] Cleander, however, eventually declared – but never realized – his interest in both joining and leading the Cyreians back to Greece (Xen. *Anab.* 6.6.34–7). According to Xenophon, Cleander became especially eager to command the Ten Thousand after witnessing the troops' excellent discipline (Xen. *Anab.* 6.6.35). Even more noteworthy are Anaxibius' repeated promises of regular pay for the Cyreians (Xen. *Anab.* 6.1.16; 7.1.2–3). These promises, together with Anaxibius' unrealized (or fictitious) arrangement for the Cyreians' transfer into the employment of Cyniscus, a Lacedaemonian general operating in the Chersonese against the Thracians (Xen. *Anab.* 7.1.13), suggest Spartan interest in utilizing the Cyreians to effect Spartan policies in the East. Xenophon also claims that Neon, the perioikic commander who replaced Cheirisophus, wanted to put the Cyreians under the control of the Lacedaemonians in the Chersonese in order that he might gain leadership over the whole army (Xen. *Anab.* 7.2.2). Aristarchus, the governor of Byzantium, later attempted to force the Ten Thousand to march to the Chersonese and thus unwittingly pushed them into the arms of the Thracian Seuthes.[47]

Soon thereafter, when the Spartans were ready to commit themselves to an aggressive policy in Asia Minor, they took the big step of openly hiring the survivors of Cyrus' Greek mercenary force to help fight against Artaxerxes. The remaining Cyreians passed into Spartan employment in spring 399, when Thibron employed them to fight Tissaphernes in a force reminiscent of Brasidas' fifth-century Thracian expedition in its mixture of *neodamōdeis*, allies, and mercenaries (*c.* 5000: Diod. 14.37.1–4).[48] They later fought under Thibron's successor, Dercylidas (Xen. *Hell.* 3.1.8; 3.2.6–7), and developed such a close relationship with this leader that they received the unofficial tag 'Dercylideioi,' which they kept even after they came under the leadership of Agesilaus II in 396 (*Hell. Oxy.* 21.2).[49] After serving with Agesilaus (and his subordinate commander, Herippidas) during his abortive campaign against Artaxerxes in 395 (Xen. *Hell.* 3.4.20; Isoc. 4.144), many of the remaining Cyreians accompanied the Eurypontid king back to Greece in 394 (Xen. *Hell.* 4.2.5), fought at Coroneia later that year (Xen. *Hell.* 4.3.15–17; *Ages.* 2.10–11), and appear to have remained in Spartan service at least until the battle of the Long Walls that linked Corinth and Lechaeum in 392 (Polyaen. 3.9.45). While the Spartans' – and particularly Lysander's and Agesilaus' – renewed interest in campaigning against Artaxerxes likely accounts for their open employment of the Cyreians in 399, the Spartans had never fully relinquished their interest in and claim on this unique mercenary force.

3. The further development of Sparta's mercenary 'industry' in the 390s

To meet their growing hegemonic needs and ambitions, the Spartans further exploited the demand for military expertise and the ready supply of mercenary soldiers that had contributed to the creation of the 10,000. The benefits of trading on their military reputation and leadership of Peloponnesian armies had become very clear, and the Spartans continued to provide commanding officers for mercenaries overseas, most notably in Sicily for Dionysius I, as mentioned above.[50] Dionysius I repeatedly looked to Sparta for military expertise, receiving Aristomenes at some point after 397 (Polyaen. 2.31.1). In 396 the Spartans sent Pharacidas (or Pharax) as admiral of an allied contingent of ships from the Peloponnesus and Italy to aid Dionysius against the Carthaginians.[51] Like his predecessor, Aristus/Aretes (404 – Diod. 14.10.2–3; cf. 14.70.3), Pharacidas supported Dionysius' tyranny against the wishes of the latter's Syracusan subjects (Diod. 14.70.2–3). During that same year, the Lacedaemonian general, Aristoteles, commanded mercenary troops for Dionysius during his campaign against the Carthaginians. Dionysius, however, came to fear these mercenaries and sent Aristoteles back to Sparta to face trial among his fellow citizens (Diod. 14.78.1–2). By exporting their military expertise, the Lacedaemonians furthered their interests indirectly and at little cost to Sparta.

Another indirect and cost-effective way to achieve Spartan policies both at home and abroad appeared in the increasingly large and attractive pool of mercenaries from Sparta's Peloponnesian League allies. The sources demonstrate that both the Greeks and rulers all over the Mediterranean looked to the Peloponnesus for their mercenaries.[52] Thucydides, for example, mentions Arcadian mercenaries serving under Pissuthnes, the Persian satrap of Sardis, in 427 (3.34.2), whose bastard, Amorges, later employed Peloponnesian mercenaries in his rebellion against Darius II (8.28.4).[53] When Cyrus later began to collect the force for his march against his brother, he specifically ordered the commanders of all the garrisons (φρούραρχοι) under his control to recruit Peloponnesians – as many as possible and of the best quality (*Anab.* 1.1.6).[54] A high percentage of the Cyreians, moreover, came from the Peloponnesus – especially from Arcadia and Achaea (cf. Xen. *Anab.* 6.2.9–12, 16).[55] In fact, twelve of Cyrus' fifteen generals, fifteen of his twenty-eight captains (λοχαγοί), and seven of thirteen known enlisted men were Peloponnesian.[56] Both the Peloponnesian domination of Cyrus' force and its continued leadership by Lacedaemonian commanders likely explain its adoption of many elements of Spartan military organization, such as the λοχαγοί and the ἐνωμοτία.[57] Dionysius I, another Spartan ally, regularly employed Peloponnesian hoplites throughout his career (Diod. 14.44.1–2, 58.1, 62.1; cf. Polyaen. 5.8.2).[58]

The Spartans themselves probably played a role in the growing demand for Peloponnesian mercenaries.[59] Sparta had long possessed the only truly 'professional' army in Greece and the reputation for excellence in hoplite warfare. The Lacedaemonians' domination of the Aegean after the fall of Athens only increased their prestige and exposure, both of which would have redounded to the credit of their Peloponnesian allies.[60] The circumstances suggest that the Spartans, realizing the potential benefits to be gained from controlling this highly demanded military resource, began to serve as 'middlemen' regulating the employment of mercenaries from the peninsula and essentially turned the Peloponnesus into a huge mercenary recruiting center for themselves and their allies.[61] As noted above, the Spartans themselves had employed Peloponnesian mercenaries in connection with the campaigns of Brasidas, Pedaritus, Lysander, and Cyrus.[62] The Spartan authorities may also have given Cyrus permission – if not actual assistance – to recruit the thousands of Peloponnesian mercenaries that formed the bulk of his force.[63] The Cyreians, in turn, participated in a number of the Spartans' campaigns against the Persians under Thibron, Dercylidas, Agesilaus, and Herippidas.[64]

Diodorus, in addition, notes that Dionysius I hired mercenaries from the Lacedaemonians in 398 and 397 (14.44.2, 58.1), and he goes so far as to suggest that such employers could only hire their forces with Spartan permission and assistance (14.44.1–2):[65]

> Dionysius, the tyrant of the Syracusans, as soon as he had completed the major part of the task of making arms and building a fleet, began at once to assemble his army. He enrolled those Syracusans who were fit for military service in companies and summoned the able-bodied men from the cities subject to him. He also gathered mercenaries from Greece and especially from the Lacedaemonians, for they assisted in increasing his power by giving him permission to enlist as many mercenaries from them as he might wish.

The Spartans' policy of aiding Dionysius' employment of Peloponnesian mercenaries not only fostered the Sicilian tyrant's goodwill but also put him in their debt – as they had hoped (cf. Diod. 14.10.2–3). Dionysius later repaid his Spartan allies by supplying them with his own mercenary armies in the summers of 369 and 368, when their loss of hegemony and weakened ties with their Peloponnesian allies forced them to find new ways to recruit badly needed manpower (Xen. *Hell.* 7.1.20–2, 28–32).

Although the Spartans occasionally took advantage of the growing pool of Peloponnesian mercenaries, they also employed foreign soldiers, especially in their campaigns in Asia in the early fourth century. Xenophon, for example, notes the Spartans' use of mercenary peltasts from Thrace (*Hell.* 3.2.2; cf. 3.2.16; 3.4.16, 23–4) and Paphlagonia (4.1.3).[66] In his account of the Spartan commander Dercylidas' seizure of the cities of Scepsis and Gergis from the 'under-satrap' Meidias in 399, Xenophon further records that the Spartan commander took over Meidias' bodyguards and added them to his already extensive mercenary force (*Hell.* 3.1.23). When Agesilaus was forced to return to Sparta to deal with the Corinthian War in the early spring of 394, he brought back light-armed soldiers with him (Xen. *Hell.* 4.2.5–8), and it is likely that the peltasts he collected in Asia fought – together with the Cyreians – under the Spartan king at the battle of Coroneia later that year (Xen. *Hell.* 4.3.15; cf. *Ages.* 2.10).[67]

As Parke has pointed out, there is little evidence of further Spartan employment of either Peloponnesian or foreign mercenaries in their campaigns on the Greek mainland during the later 390s and early 380s (cf. Xen. *Hell.* 4.5.13). Xenophon makes a generalized statement about the Greeks' use of hired soldiers during the Corinthian War (*Hell.* 4.4.14), and Polyaenus mentions the Spartans' dispatch of a mercenary force to Corinth – probably in 393 (3.9.45) – without providing any details.[68] However, the Spartan commander Diphridas' hiring of mercenaries in Asia in 391 (Xen. *Hell.* 4.8.21) and the governor Anaxibius' employment of mercenaries at Abydus in 389 (Xen. *Hell.* 4.8.32–9; cf. Polyaen. 3.9.44; Frontin. *Str.* 1.4.7; 2.5.42) suggest that the Spartans continued to use such forces, at least in extended expeditions far from home.

4. The Peloponnesian League and Spartan hegemony in the late 380s and 370s

The Lacedaemonians' employment of mercenaries in their campaigns at home seems to have sharply increased in the late 380s and 370s, likely in response to the fundamental change in the organization of the Peloponnesian League that occurred in 382. According to Xenophon, Sparta's allies successfully proposed to convert their military obligations to the Peloponnesian League from contingents of soldiers to cash payments, which were likely to be used to hire mercenary substitutes for allied troops.[69] The League now allowed any state that so desired to contribute three Aeginetan obols for each hoplite and four times that amount for each horseman. The Spartans, in turn, were permitted to fine any state that failed to contribute its contingent or cash equivalent (Xen. *Hell.* 5.2.21–2). Xenophon, unfortunately, reveals nothing concerning the Spartans' part (if any) in this important change in the Peloponnesian League. Following his lead, scholars have generally argued that Sparta's war-weary allies, who were increasingly unwilling to shoulder so much of the military burden of the Spartans' hegemonic agenda, finally balked at the prospect of a new expedition against Olynthus and the Chalcidian Confederacy.[70]

It is unlikely, however, that the Spartans were compelled to accept this change, given their renewed imperial strength in the late 380s and their consequently strong position vis-à-vis their allies in the Peloponnesian League.[71] It seems entirely possible that the Spartans actively supported this change in the 'constitution' of the Peloponnesian League. Under the guidance of the Eurypontid king, Agesilaus II, the Lacedaemonians pursued policies in the later 380s that signaled an interest in greater autonomy from the League in terms of foreign policy. Following their diplomatic success with the Peace of Antalcidas in 386, the Spartans adopted an openly self-interested stance toward their allies that involved the forced dissolution of the Corinthian–Argive 'union' in 386 (Xen. *Hell.* 5.1.34, 36), the dioecism of Mantineia and overthrow of its democracy in 385 (Xen. *Hell.* 5.2.1–7; Diod. 15.5, 12), and the restoration of oligarchic exiles to Phleius in 384 (Xen. *Hell.* 5.2.8–10; *Ages.* 2.21). The Spartans may have seen in this proposal a golden opportunity to pursue their own rather than League interests without forgoing the manpower needed to realize their ambitions. One must wonder whether this weakening of the Peloponnesian League and the likely increased presence of mercenaries in their armies encouraged – and enabled – the Spartans to implement self-interested and unpopular policies (cf. Xen. *Hell.* 5.3.16; Diod. 15.19.4), such as their imposition of an oligarchy on formerly democratic Phleius in 379.[72]

The sources do not always delineate the exact composition of the armies that the Lacedaemonians led against various enemies from 382 onwards and only twice mention allies contributing cash payments instead of contingents. Xenophon reports that the people of Phleius gave money to the Agiad King Agesipolis I, who assumed command in the Olynthian campaign in the summer of 381 (*Hell.* 5.3.10). He also records the contributions made by a majority of allies in 373 before the Spartans' Corcyraean campaign (Xen. *Hell.* 6.2.16). Only one source, moreover, explicitly links such payments to the Spartans' employment of mercenaries in their post-382 campaigns (Xen. *Hell.* 6.2.16). The sources' repeated notice of mercenaries, however, shows that mercenaries – mostly in the form of peltasts – came to play the same role in Spartan campaigns on the Greek mainland that they had played in Spartan expeditions against the Persians early in the fourth century.[73] The Spartans' employment of mercenaries in Greece may have been a natural extension of their use of hired soldiers in Asia. Nevertheless, the increasing appearance of hired soldiers in Spartan campaigns in the late 380s and early 370s must be more than a coincidence, given the change in the Peloponnesian 'constitution' in 382. More importantly, such mercenaries repeatedly figure in the Spartans' imperialist strategy of controlling mainland Greece under the guise of observing the conditions of the Peace of Antalcidas of 386. They participated not only in the Spartans' expedition in 382 to break up the Chalcidian League and thereby curb Olynthus' expansion but also in the Spartans' successive forays against the Boeotians in the early 370s.

In their campaign against Olynthus, which precipitated the change in the obligations of the Peloponnesian League members, the Spartans employed mercenaries hired on their behalf by Amyntas of Macedon (Xen. *Hell.* 5.2.37–8). These mercenaries were likely the peltasts that fought under Agesilaus' half-brother, Teleutias, who was sent out to assume command of the army in the north in 382, and another Spartan commander, Tlemonides (Xen. *Hell.* 5.3.3–6). The sources do not mention mercenaries in their accounts of the later stages of the campaign against Olynthus, which dragged on until the summer of 379. However, the Phliasians' aforementioned payments in 381 to King Agesipolis, Teleutias' successor as commander, suggest that the Spartans continued to employ mercenaries in their long and costly struggle with Olynthus (Xen. *Hell.* 5.3.8–10).

Mercenaries figured more prominently in the Spartans' various campaigns in the Peloponnesus in the early 370s, especially in their establishment of garrisons and their repeated attempts to regain the control over Thebes that they had lost in 379. Agesilaus might have employed mercenaries in the garrison that he left in Phleius in 379, along with six months' pay (μισθός) for those who manned it (Xen. *Hell.* 5.3.25). The Agiad Cleombrotus, who succeeded Agesipolis in the summer of 380 and commenced an expedition against Thebes in winter 379/8 that employed peltasts (Xen. *Hell.* 5.4.14), likewise stationed a force at Thespiae that was largely composed of mercenaries. According to Xenophon, Cleombrotus left Sphodrias as governor at Thespiae and gave him all of the money that he had chanced to have brought from home and directed him to hire a force of mercenaries (*Hell.* 5.4.15; cf. Isoc. 14.13; Plut. *Pel.* 14.3).[74] In advance of his own expedition against Thebes later in 378, Agesilaus 'borrowed' light-armed mercenaries employed by Clitor, a small Arcadian city, and used them to occupy Mount Cithaeron (Xen. *Hell.* 5.4.36–7). Agesilaus later employed these mercenaries in his raids on Theban territory (Xen. *Hell.* 5.4.39; Diod. 15.32.4; cf. Polyaen. 2.1.2).[75] On his return to Sparta, he left Phoibidas, Sphodrias' successor, as governor in Thespiae, along with a force that included peltasts (Xen. *Hell.* 5.4.42–5; cf. Polyaen. 2.5.2).

The Spartans' increasing need and use of light-armed soldiers is reflected in the further change in Peloponnesian League members' obligations that occurred in 378 in response to growing allied disaffection (Diod. 15.31.1–3). In preparation for one of their many campaigns against Thebes, the Spartans included light-armed soldiers (at a ratio of two ψιλοί to one hoplite) in their calculation of the cash equivalents paid by states that chose not to send their normal contingents to the League force (Diod. 15.31.2).[76] As Xenophon notes, the allies took advantage of their right to contribute money rather than men a number of years later, when the Spartans sent a force against Corcyra under Mnasippus in 373 (*Hell.* 6.2.16). It is less clear, however, what funds enabled the Spartans to hire those mercenaries that served under Cleombrotus both at Mount Cithaeron in 376 (Xen. *Hell.* 5.4.59) and at Leuctra in 371 (Xen. *Hell.* 6.4.9), those employed by Polytropus and Agesilaus in Arcadia in 370 (Xen. *Hell.* 6.5.13–15, 17), those from Arcadian Orchomenus that aided the defense of Sparta town in midwinter 370/69 (Xen. *Hell.* 6.5.29), and those that Agesilaus commanded at the battle of Mantineia in 362 (Xen. *Hell.* 7.5.10). Whatever the case may be, the Spartans had certainly become accustomed to employing mercenary forces, as Xenophon suggests in his *Lacedaemonion Politeia*, likely composed after the Spartans' defeat at Leuctra (12.3, 13.4).[77]

While it is clear that mercenary power played a number of important roles in Sparta's bid for hegemony both at home and abroad, it remains true that many other Greek *poleis* made far greater use of mercenaries, especially Athens.[78] We also know that certain policies, such as the export of military expertise and mercenary armies in exchange for alliance and its concomitant benefits, were not specific to Sparta but also served the interests of *poleis* such as Thebes and Argos.[79] The Spartans, moreover, were not the only Greeks who gained added manpower and expertise (especially in terms of light-armed tactics) through their employment of mercenaries. The Spartans' mercenary activities were thus not all that unique, except for their exploitation of the Peloponnesus as a mercenary market.

What is so striking about the Spartans' involvement in mercenary warfare – as military advisers, commanders, and overseers of Peloponnesian mercenary forces sent abroad – was their direct and indirect exploitation of hired soldiers to spread their influence further than their own limited manpower would have allowed. Likewise, the Greek and non-Greek mercenaries that the Spartiates employed allowed the Spartans to expand the scope of their military activity. Such mercenaries not only helped to address Sparta's chronic shortage of manpower (*oliganthrōpia*), but they also enabled the Spartans to become less dependent on their increasingly disenchanted Peloponnesian allies. Sparta's manpower problems became manifest during the Peloponnesian War, especially after the Athenians captured 420 Lacedae-monian troops on Sphacteria in 425. The Spartans' horrified reaction to the news (Thuc. 4.14.2), concern with recovering what would seem to be a small number of citizens (*c.* 120: Thuc. 4.38.5), and willingness to make peace with Athens to effect this recovery reveal the severity of the problem.[80] Thucy-dides' account of Spartiate numbers at the battle of Mantineia (5.64.3, 68.3) further attests to the demographic crisis that had drastically reduced the total number of Spartiates of military age from 8000 in 480 (Hdt. 7.234.2) to roughly half that number in 418.[81] The Spartans' shrinking pool of available manpower inevitably forced them to make the important military reform of combining Spartiates and *perioikoi* in the same contingents, which was in effect by at least 425 (Thuc. 4.38.5) and was geared to place more of the Lacedaemonians' military responsibilities on perioikic shoulders.[82]

Even more indicative of Spartan *oliganthrōpia* is the Spartans' decision to exploit militarily their vast servile population. As we have seen above, the Spartans enrolled 700 helots as hoplites for Brasidas' campaign in 424 (Thuc. 4.80.5), and they also created a new force of emancipated helots, known as *neodamōdeis*, sometime between 424 and 421 (Thuc. 5.34.1).[83] In 421 the Spartans employed the emancipated remnants of Brasidas' helot force together with the *neodamōdeis* as a garrison in Lepreum, which the Spartans had occupied earlier in the year and wished to protect from the Eleans (Thuc. 5.34.1; cf. 31.1–5). According to Thucydides, special forces of helots served in the Spartans' invasion of Argos and expedition to Tegea in 418 (5.57.1, 64.2),[84] and the emancipated 'Brasideioi' again teamed up with *neodamōdeis* to fight soon thereafter at Mantineia (5.67.1; cf. 71.3, 72.3). A picked force of helots and *neodamōdeis* later served under the Spartiate Eccritus in Sicily in 413 (Thuc. 7.19.3; cf. 7.58.3), and we also hear of *neodamōdeis* participating in a Spartan campaign in Euboea in the winter of 413/12 (Thuc. 8.5.1).

The Spartans made increasing use of *neodamōdeis* in their attempt to forge their Aegean empire. Both Thibron and Agesilaus utilized thousands of *neodamōdeis* in their campaigns against Artaxerxes (*Hell.* 3.1.4, 4.2), and the *neodamōdeis* continued to figure in Spartan campaigns down to 370/69 (Xen. *Hell.* 6.5.24).

Spartan *oliganthrōpia* appears to have reached a critical stage in 381, when King Agesipolis marched to Olynthus with an array of volunteers, including high-ranking *perioikoi*, foreigners raised at Sparta (ξένοι τῶν τροφίμων), and the offspring of unions between Spartiates and helot women (νόθοι τῶν Σπαρτιατῶν) (Xen. *Hell.* 5.3.9; cf. Diod. 15.21.2). The damaging effects of this demographic crisis on Sparta's prestige and political clout became particularly clear in the summer of 375, when Polydamas of Pharsalus asked for Lacedaemonian aid against Jason of Pherae in 374. Polydamas specified that he needed a force of 'real' Lacedaemonians rather than *neodamōdeis* in order to overcome Jason's brilliance as a commander. The Spartans, who had obviously become dependent upon *neodamōdeis* for such distant expeditions, simply did not have enough Spartiate manpower available to meet this demand and informed Polydamas that they could not send him an adequate supporting force (Xen. *Hell.* 6.1.14–17).[85] By failing to support Polydamas, the Spartans lost a precious opportunity to intervene in Thessaly and allowed Jason of Pherae to assume control over a united Thessaly that soon concluded an important alliance with the Spartans' Theban enemies.

Given the severity of the Spartans' manpower shortage, it is no wonder that they increasingly employed mercenaries during the late fifth and early fourth centuries. Hired soldiers stretched the range of Spartan activity considerably during the Peloponnesian War, enabling the Spartans to undermine Athenian hegemony in the Thraceward region in the 420s, to challenge the Athenians at sea during the later stages of the Peloponnesian War, and to gain footholds in the eastern Aegean, especially at Byzantium in 408 (cf. Diod. 13.66.5). The availability of mercenaries later facilitated Lysander's intervention at Athens in 403, the Spartans' support for Cyrus' expedition in 401, and Lacedaemonian operations against Artaxerxes in the 390s.[86] If Lysander had succeeded in his plan to establish a new Aegean empire or Agesilaus' Persian expedition had not been forestalled by the Corinthian War, it seems probable that mercenaries would have continued to play a central role in the Spartans' plans in the East.[87] Like the *neodamōdeis* who, notably, often accompanied them on these extended and far-flung operations (Xen. *Hell.* 3.1.4, 4.2; cf. Thuc. 4.80.5), hired soldiers allowed their commanders to expand their plans and likely proved more amenable to such missions than the Spartans' Peloponnesian allies. Such considerations, along with the increasing unpopularity of Spartan foreign policy, may also help to account for the Spartans' repeated use of mercenaries to man garrisons in their campaigns against their fellow Greeks, especially the Thebans (cf. Xen. *Hell.* 5.3.25; 5.4.15, 42–5).

The development of what we may justly call a 'mercenary industry', in addition, allowed the Spartans to capitalize on both their reputation as Greece's only truly 'professional' soldiers and their political and military stranglehold on most of the Peloponnesus. By exporting their military expertise, in the form of mercenary commanders and military advisors, and by controlling the flow of mercenaries from the peninsula, they were able to forge and maintain important alliances – especially with Dionysius I – without having to risk their ever-shrinking citizen population.[88] In this way the Spartans managed to create the illusion of continued military predominance at a time when their own military force was often no longer adequate to meet the most basic demands created by their ambitious foreign policy. Such deficiencies were manifest in 382, when the Lacedaemonians sent Eudamidas against Olynthus with a force composed of *neodamōdeis*, *perioikoi*, and Sciritans (Xen. *Hell.* 5.2.24), and in 381, when they resorted to the motley array of volunteers described above (Xen. *Hell.* 5.3.9).

II. MERCENARIES AND THE SPARTAN CRISIS

The illusion of power that Sparta's exploitation of mercenaries created ultimately proved fatal to the Lacedaemonians. Mercenaries provided, at best, an external and temporary solution to the Spartans' *oliganthrōpia*. By looking beyond their traditional allies in the Peloponnesian League and their ever-growing subject population for the manpower needed to effect their policies at home and abroad, the Spartans ignored the web of economic and social problems that underpinned their demographic difficulties. Their employment of mercenaries also contributed in a number of ways to the political difficulties that facilitated Sparta's decline into a second-rate power after 371. The availability of mercenaries gave the Spartans what turned out to be a two-edged independence from their allies in the Peloponnesian League. By allowing the Spartans' allies to abstain – at least physically – from distant and extended expeditions and by enabling the Spartans to realize their imperialistic ambitions with a slightly freer hand, the change in Peloponnesian League obligations in 382 seriously weakened the bonds that had made this League such a successful instrument of Spartan foreign policy since the late sixth century. The Spartans' employment of mercenaries to pursue widely unpopular policies, such as their repeated campaigns against the Thebans, following the liberation of Thebes from Spartan control in 379, only further attenuated Sparta's relationship with its Peloponnesian allies. Their growing dissatisfaction with the Spartans' Boeotian policy (Xen. Plut. *Ages.* 26.6–9; cf. Xen. *Hell.* 5.4.60), in turn, seems to have resulted in the second restructuring of the Peloponnesian League in 378 that gave Sparta an even freer hand to pursue such dangerous policies (Diod. 15.31.1–3).[89]

Allied resentment and low morale may also have been fed by the Spartans' generally lackluster performance as leaders of mercenaries in the 380s and 370s. While Agesilaus II and other Spartans may have successfully commanded forces that included mercenary hoplites and light-armed soldiers, Sparta's generals repeatedly demonstrated an inability to employ light-armed troops effectively.[90] Agesilaus' half-brother Teleutias sent Tlemonides and many of his peltasts to their deaths when he ordered them to pursue Olynthian cavalry, and his failure to control this force eventually led to the defeat of his army and to his own death in the summer of 381 (Xen. *Hell.* 5.3.3–6). Phoibidas' similar failure to support his light-armed mercenaries with hoplites as they attempted to drive the Thebans out of the Thespian χώρα led to his death and the defeat of his peltasts at the hands of Theban cavalry in 378.[91] In response to this disaster, the Spartans abandoned their practice of manning garrisons with mercenaries and sent a polemarch with a regiment (μόρα) to Thespiae (Xen. *Hell.* 5.4.46; cf. Plut. *Pel.* 17 on Orchomenus).[92]

The list of Spartan failures continues with the Agiad king Cleombrotus' later attempt to occupy Cithaeron in advance of his expedition against Thebes in the summer of 376. Cleombrotus failed to secure the summit, having sent his peltasts ahead into a trap set by the Athenians and the Thebans, and he was forced to return home and disband his army (Xen. *Hell.* 5.4.59; 6.4.5). The Spartan commander Mnasippus' fatal abuse of his 1,500 mercenaries (Xen. *Hell.* 6.2.5) during his expedition to Corcyra in 373, in turn, put an end to Spartan adventures abroad. After keeping his mercenaries poorly supplied and attempting to defraud them of their pay, the greedy *nauarch* responded to the complaints of their captains with violence (Xen. *Hell.* 6.2.16–19). Not surprisingly, Mnasippus' demoralized mercenaries were routed by the Corcyraeans, and their Spartan taskmaster fell in battle (Xen. *Hell.* 6.2.20–24).[93] Xenophon further suggests that the Spartans' mercenaries unwittingly contributed to the worst defeat of all – at Leuctra in 371, by driving enemy deserters back into the Boeotians' camp and thereby making the Boeotian army both larger and denser (*Hell.* 6.4.9). Finally, the commander Polytropus' misuse of his mercenaries against the Mantineians ultimately undermined Agesilaus' expedition against Arcadia in 370 (Xen. *Hell.* 6.5.13–15; cf. Diod. 15.62.1–2). It is no wonder that the Spartans, the erstwhile military experts, turned to professional help – in the guise of the mercenary commander Symmachus of Thasos – when they found themselves forced to defend Sparta town in the winter of 370/69 (Polyaen. 2.1.27).[94]

After their defeat in 371 and the Thebans' subsequent invasion of Laconia, the Spartans found it difficult to get support from their increasingly lukewarm allies, who eventually concluded a separate peace with the Boeotians in 365 (Xen. *Hell.* 7.4.6–11).[95] Faced with this obstacle at home, the Spartans were forced to look abroad for the manpower that they needed to recapture Messenia and to restore their hegemony in the Peloponnesus. Loyal allies such as Dionysius I of Syracuse and Ariobarzanes, the satrap of Phrygia, directly lent mercenary armies to Sparta in 369 and 368.[96] Without Dionysius' mercenaries, the Eurypontid prince, Archidamus, could not have won the famous 'Tearless Battle' against a force of Arcadians, Messenians and Argives in the summer of 368 – the Spartans' first successful venture in a number of years.[97] The aid sent by the Sicilian tyrant's successor, Dionysius II, in 365, likewise helped the Spartans recapture Sellasia, the closest perioikic town to Sparta (Xen. *Hell.* 7.4.12).

The Spartans, however, also needed to raise money to hire mercenaries, as Plutarch emphasizes in his scathing portrait of Agesilaus after the battle of Mantineia in 362. According to Plutarch, the Spartans' desperate shortage of funds compelled the Eurypontid king to extort loans (δανείζεσθαι) and contributions (συνερανίζεσθαι) from his Spartiate friends in order to finance his dream of reconquering Messenia (*Ages.* 35.4–6). The Spartans' financial difficulties, together with their unrelenting and unrealistic hope of regaining their hegemony, ultimately forced them to place their commanders in the service of leaders abroad in order to finance mercenaries at home. Thus began a vicious cycle that ultimately resulted in the aged Eurypontid king Agesilaus II's service as a sort of state-sponsored *condottiere* in both Persia and Egypt to raise the funds needed to procure yet more mercenaries.[98] The king who had inherited the remaining Cyreians from Dercylidas in 396 found himself about thirty years later fighting – although he had ostensibly been sent out as an ambassador – on behalf of Ariobarzanes, who had sent aid to Sparta a few years earlier and now rewarded Agesilaus generously for his services (Xen. *Ages.* 2.25–7).[99] In his account of Agesilaus' successful 'work' for Ariobarzanes, Xenophon claims that the Spartan king received gifts of money from both those he helped and the opponents he scared off, including Mausolus of Caria (whom he labels as a *xenos* of Agesilaus) and the Egyptian pharaoh, Tachos (*Ages.* 2.27; cf. 29).[100]

In 360, when he was approximately eighty-four years old, Agesilaus sailed to Egypt with a thousand hoplites (Diod. 15.92.2), most likely mercenaries (cf. Plut. *Ages.* 36.6; *Mor.* 214d),[101] and thirty Spartiate advisers (σύμβουλοι: Plut. *Ages.* 36.6) to enter the service of Tachos, who was at war with Artaxerxes.[102] Plutarch, who provides a particularly negative treatment of this expedition, portrays the elderly king as nothing more than an Egyptian hireling (*Ages.* 36.1–2; cf. *Mor.* 214d):

> His reputation declined even further when he offered himself as commander
> under Tachos the Egyptian. For it was thought unworthy that a man, who had
> been judged noblest in Hellas and who had filled the world with his renown,
> should let his person, his name, and his reputation out to hire to a rebel against
> the Great King, a mere barbarian, rendering the service of a hired commander
> of mercenaries (ἔργα μισθοφόρου καὶ ξεναγοῦ διαπραττόμενον).

The presence of the Spartiate counselors on this campaign, however, makes it
clear that the Spartan authorities sent Agesilaus as a commander to Egypt.[103]
Even Plutarch, who treats the king as an independent contractor (*Ages.*
36.1), admits that Agesilaus was a representative of the Spartan state (*Ages.*
37.5–9). Diodorus also claims that the Spartans had become allies of Tachos
(15.90.2, 92.2).[104] Nevertheless, Agesilaus was not just another commander
sent out to aid an ally, like Gylippus, Cheirisophus, or the host of Spartans
sent to Dionysius I.[105] The sources emphasize Agesilaus' focus on procuring
payment for his services (cf. Xen. *Ages.* 2.28, 31; Plut. *Ages.* 36.2; *Mor.* 214d).
Any interest in repaying his debt to Tachos or in continuing the fight against
the Persians was secondary.[106]

After suffering the humiliation of being put in command of Tachos'
mercenaries rather than the whole force, Agesilaus switched his allegiance
to Nectanebo II and defended him against another Egyptian pretender.[107] In
return for these services, the elderly king received gifts for himself and 230
silver talents for the Spartans' financing of mercenaries.[108] On his way home
Agesilaus died in a spot known as the Harbor of Menelaus (Plut. *Ages.* 40.3;
cf. *Mor.* 215a). One cannot help but be struck by this twist of fate. The great
Eurypontid king, whom Theopompus described as 'the greatest and most
illustrious man of his time' (*FGrH* 115 F 321) and who had styled himself
as a second Agamemnon before his crusade against the Persians in 396,[109]
was reduced in his old age to serving Egyptian paymasters in order to feed
the endless need for mercenaries created by the imperialistic agenda that he
himself had fostered (cf. Plut. *Ages.* 35.5–6). Even more ironic, perhaps, is the
close relationship between Agesilaus' foreign service and the dissolution of
the Peloponnesian League. Agesilaus had become so obsessed with amassing
the wealth he needed to acquire mercenaries that he was very likely far away
from Sparta, serving as a mercenary commander under Ariobarzanes, when
Sparta's disaffected allies effectively dissolved the Peloponnesian League
in 365 by seeking rapprochement with the Thebans.[110] Politically isolated,
financially strapped, and reduced to sending their king to serve foreign
masters, the Spartans had lost sight of those policies and forfeited the allied
manpower that had sustained their hegemony in the Peloponnesus since the
late sixth century.

Notes

[1] All dates are BCE. On the Ionian mercenaries, see Hdt. 2.152.4–5, 154; cf. 2.163; 3.11; Pl. *Lach.* 187b; Diod. 1.66.12; Polyaen. 7.3. Bettalli 1995, 53–73, provides a full discussion of the literary, epigraphical, and archaeological evidence concerning the Egyptians' use of Greek and Carian mercenaries in the archaic period. See also Kaplan 2002, 237–40.

[2] See, however, Kaplan 2002, 233, who argues that the term ἐπίκουρος in this fragment does not yet clearly mean 'mercenary' but is rather 'in a transitional state where it is a euphemism for a disagreeable condition'. Kaplan, however, admits that the context of this fragment, a scholion to Plato, *Laws* 187b, suggests that we should interpret ἐπίκουρος as 'mercenary' and does not fully account for the ambiguity that he sees in the Archilochean line. On Archilochus' meaning in this fragment, see also Burnett 1983, 41 n. 22.

[3] On this 'explosion' of mercenaries in the late classical period, see, esp., Miller 1984; Trundle 2004. For more general studies of mercenaries in ancient Greece, see Parke 1933; Griffith 1935; Aymard 1959; Roy 1967; Marinovich 1988; Krasilnikoff 1992 and 1993; Bettalli 1995.

[4] Parke 1933, 15–19, 43–8, 83–90, 109–12, and Cartledge 1987, 314–30, offer the most detailed treatments of Spartan involvement in mercenary warfare.

[5] Parke 1933, 16, argues that Thucydides collectively alludes to the rest of Eurylochus' infantry as τὸν μισθοφόρον ὄχλον. See also Bettalli 1995, 132–3. See, however, Gomme in Gomme et al. 1945–81, 2.422. Parke has also suggested (15) that the Peloponnesians might have found it useful to employ mercenaries for such expeditions, since 'their citizen soldiers were not much accustomed to face the discomforts and perils of long campaigns'.

[6] Thuc. 4.78–88, 102–16, 120–32, 135; 5.6.3–10.

[7] See Parke 1933, 16; Cartledge 1979, 246; Hodkinson 2000, 168; Trundle 2004, 51.

[8] For examples of insularity and hesitancy to commit troops, see Hdt. 1.152; 3.148; 5.49–51; 6.106; 7.206–7; 8.4–5, 40, 49, 56–63, 70.2–72, 74–5, 108, 132, 144.4–5; 9.6–11, 77, 106, 114.2; cf. 1.83. See Millender 2002, 41–3.

[9] See Bettalli 1985, 135. Trundle 2004, 13, 30 identifies the ἐπίκουροι serving under the Peloponnesian commander Polydamidas at Mende (Thuc. 4.129.3, 130.3, 131.3) as 'mercenaries' but later (17–18) suggests that Thucydides also used the term ἐπίκουροι to designate 'allies.' As he rightly notes (21), 'the obscure terminology employed by the Greeks for mercenaries does not help the historian identifying them'. See also Lavelle 1989 and 1997.

[10] On Brasidas' use of peltasts, see Best 1969, 29–35.

[11] Parke 1933, 16 discusses the disadvantages and advantages of Brasidas' dependence on this mercenary force. On Brasidas' unusual degree of independence and power, see also Cartledge 1987, 322; Trundle 2004, 63.

[12] Payment of rowers: Thuc. 8.29, 36, 45.2 and 6, 57–8, 78, 80.1–3, 83.2–85; Xen. *Hell.* 1.5.3–7; 2.1.12–15.

[13] See Parke 1933, 17.

[14] On Gylippus' position in Syracuse, see Parke 1930, 43–4, who views him as 'a commander on loan to a foreign Power (not an ally on the ordinary terms of the Peloponnesian league)'.

[15] Cartledge 1987, 318–20. Parke 1933, 64–5 rather views Dexippus as an adventurer operating without state support. See also Caven 1990, 47.

[16] Meiggs and Lewis 1988, 280–1.

[17] On Aretas, see Sansone 1981; Caven 1990, 82.

[18] For Lysander's influence on the Spartans' decision, see Hamilton 1979, 105–6; and Cartledge 1987, 191, 352, who argues that Lysander would have seen opportunities for personal power in western Asia Minor (Cyrus' satrapal seat). See also Hodkinson 2000, 349. On Lysander's *xenia* with Cyrus, see Cartledge 1987, 79–81, 89, 184, 187, 190–1, 348, 352; Mitchell 1997, 87, 118–19, 152; Hodkinson 2000, 345.

[19] See Cartledge 1987, 191, 320–1.

[20] See Lewis 1977, 138. Westlake 1987, 242 examines the differences between Xenophon's and Diodorus' treatments of the relationship between the Spartan government and Cyrus.

[21] Xenophon refers to this admiral as Pythagoras in his *Anabasis* (1.4.2), while Diodorus calls him Samus (14.19.4–5). See also Xen. *Anab.* 1.2.21; Diod. 14.21.1.

[22] For the view that these hoplites were Peloponnesian mercenaries, see Roy 1967, 300; Cartledge 1979, 272; Herman 1987, 100.

[23] Herman 1987, 45, 99–100; Hodkinson 2000, 349.

[24] Xen. *Anab.* 2.6.4–5; cf. Diod. 14.12.7–9; Polyaen. 2.2.2–3. On Clearchus' exile, see Xen. *Anab.* 2.6.2–4; Diod. 14.12.2–7; Polyaen. 2.2.6–10. For the various theories concerning his exile, see Best 1969, 51–2; Mitchell 1997, 83; Laforse 2000, 75–6; Bassett 2001. Bassett, who offers sound reasons for privileging Diodorus over Xenophon, argues (9; cf. 13) that 'Xenophon has not merely omitted significant detail here, which is his most common method of dealing with unpleasant realities, but has actively attempted to re-write the portrait to cover unpalatable aspects of Clearchus' career.' See also Parke 1930, 57–8; Westlake 1987.

[25] Xen. *Anab.* 1.1.9, 2.6.4–5; cf. 1.6.5; Diod. 14.12.9.

[26] On Clearchus' *xenia* with Cyrus, see Herman 1987, 17–18, 45, 91, 99, 100, 119–21, 126.

[27] *Proxenos* at Byzantium: Xen. *Hell.* 1.1.35. Commands in the Hellespont: Thuc. 8.8.2, 39.2, 80.1–4; Xen. *Hell.* 1.1.35–6; Diod. 13.40.6, 51.1–8. Harmost of Byzantium: Xen. *Hell.* 1.3.15–19; Diod. 13.66.5–6. Later activity in the Hellespont: Diod. 14.12.2–9; cf. Xen. *Anab.* 2.6.2–5; Polyaen. 2.2.6–10. See Bassett 2001, 1–3.

[28] See Hamilton 1979, 106; Cartledge 1987, 191, 320–1; Bassett 2001, 10–12. See also Cartledge 1987, 352, who argues that Lysander would likely have been pleased by Cyrus' appointment of Clearchus, a 'man in the Lysandreian mould'. Roy 1967, 300 argues that the Spartans 'may have connived at Clearchus' recruiting and campaign in the Chersonese,' but he later (308) suggests that Clearchus operated without Spartan authority.

[29] See Roy 1967, 299–300.

[30] Bassett 2001, 12. See also Roisman 1985–8, 38 n. 22. Westlake 1987, 242–3 finds Diodorus' claim that all of the Greek *stratēgoi* knew Cyrus' real intention to fight Artaxerxes (14.19.9) 'more consistent and convincing than that of Xenophon'.

[31] For a detailed treatment of Clearchus' relationship with Cyrus and the gradual development of his leadership in Cyrus' army, see Roisman 1985–8, who argues (33–8) that Clearchus came to occupy the leading position in the force after quelling the revolt at Tarsus (Xen. *Anab.* 1.3). See also Westlake 1987, 246.

32   See Xen. *Anab.* 1.7.1; 1.8.4–5, 12–13; 1.10.14; cf. Diod. 14.22.5, 23.1, 24.2–5. On Cyrus' preferential treatment of Clearchus, see, esp., Roisman 1985–8, 31–41, who (33, 41) points out the inferior position that Clearchus occupied earlier in the expedition (Xen. *Anab.* 1.2.15). See also Roy 1967, 292–3; Herman 1987, 100; Trundle 2004, 139.

33   Xen. *Anab.* 2.5.31–6.1; Diod. 14.26.6–7. Roisman 1985–8, 41–52 discusses Clearchus' leadership of the force after Cunaxa.

34   For Cheirisophus' informal command, see Xen. *Anab.* 3.1.45–3.2.3; 3.2.33, 37; 3.3.3. As Roy 1967, 293–4 rightly points out, Diodorus' claim that Cheirisophus formally took command of the army right after Clearchus' death (14.27.1) passes over the period when Cheirisophus informally became 'primus inter pares' and may have been influenced by Xenophon's account of the Spartan's election as commander-in-chief (*Anab.* 6.1.32; cf. 6.1.17–18). On these sources' different accounts of Cheirisophus' status, see also Westlake 1987, 246.

35   On Neon's assumption of Cheirisophus' place, see Roy 1967, 289.

36   Cartledge 1987, 320. Parke 1933, 29 rather views Dexippus as a 'professional mercenary'.

37   See, e.g., Roy 1967, 298 n. 58, who notes the lack of evidence of co-operation between Neon and the Spartan authorities and who argues (308) that 'the apparent importance of Spartans on the anabasis is accidental'.

38   Cartledge 1987, 320–1 views both Dracontius and Cleonymus as 'soldiers of fortune'.

39   I would like to thank Anton Powell for this alternate interpretation of Dracontius' role in the expedition.

40   See Hodkinson 2000, 349.

41   This inconsistency might account for the divergence in Xenophon's and Diodorus' treatments of the Spartans' response to Cyrus' request, which Westlake 1987, 242 seems to overstate.

42   Cartledge 1987, 321 (cf. 191, 352): 'Sparta was eating her cake and having it: while posing as the liberator of the Greeks from Athenian tyranny she had been constrained to take much money from Persia, herself no stranger to despotism over Greeks, and now she was both repaying a debt to the man most responsible for channelling that decisive Persian money, at minimum cost in terms of cash and citizen manpower, and at the same time notionally pursuing a consistent policy of liberating the Greeks... Besides, by conducting a war against Artaxerxes in effect by proxy, Sparta was obviating the danger of the mercenaries being turned against Spartan power in the Aegean by their immediate commanders.'

43   Xen. *Hell.* 3.1.1; cf. Xen. *Anab.* 1.2.21, 4.2–3; Diod. 14.19.4–5, 21.1.

44   Xen. *Anab.* 7.2.6–15; 7.3.3; 7.6.13–14, 24–7.

45   Cf. Xen. *Anab.* 6.6.9, 12–14; 7.1.28.

46   See, e.g., Xen. *Anab.* 7.1.2–4; 7.2.4, 7, 12–14. Mitchell 1997, 120 examines Anaxibius' relationship with Pharnabazus.

47   Xen. *Anab.* 7.2.15–17; 7.3.3–6; 7.6.13–14, 24–7.

48   Thibron's appointment of the Cyreians: Xen. *Hell.* 3.1.6; *Anab.* 7.6.1–40; 7.7.10–19, 31, 56–7; 7.8.6, 24; Diod. 14.37.1–4. *Neodamōdeis*: Xen. *Hell.* 3.1.4; cf. Diod. 14.36.1, who identifies them as Spartiates. Allies: Xen. *Hell.* 3.1.4–5; Diod. 14.36.2. Parke 1933, 43 compares Brasidas' and Thibron's forces.

[49] Scholars do not agree on the identification of the Dercylideioi with the Cyreians. Parke 1933, 44, for example, views 'Dercylideioi' as another name for the Cyreians. See, however, Bruce 1967, 136. On the special relationship between Dercylidas and his soldiers, see Cartledge 1987, 322–3. On both Dercylidas' and Agesilaus' use of these mercenaries, see Marinovic 1988, 36–43; Krasilnikoff 1992, 30–3.

[50] Cf. Trundle 2004, 137, 156.

[51] Diod. 14.63.4; cf. 14.68.5, 69.4; Polyaen. 2.11. Poralla/Bradford 1985, nos. 717, 19, and Cartledge 1987, 322 identify Pharacidas with the Pharax who was *nauarch* in the Aegean in the early summer of 397 (cf. Xen. *Hell.* 3.2.12).

[52] On the Peloponnesians' – and particularly the Arcadians' – dominant position among Greek mercenaries operating around the Mediterranean, see Griffith 1935, 237–8; Roy 1967; Cartledge 1987, 316; Trundle 2004, 53, 72, 74–5, 122–3.

[53] For examples of the Greeks' interest in Peloponnesian mercenaries, see, e.g., Thuc. 1.60.1; 4.52.2, 76.3; 7.19.4, 57.9, 58.3.

[54] For the Persians' use of Greek hoplites to man their garrisons, see Tuplin 1992, 67–70; Trundle 2004, 51, cf. 72–4.

[55] Roy 1967, 298, 307–9, 320; Nielsen 1999, 40–3; Trundle 2004, 53–4.

[56] Roy 1967, 298, 301–6; Trundle 2004, 53.

[57] Trundle 2004, 136–7. For evidence of Spartans commanding Peloponnesian troops, see, e.g., Thuc. 2.75.3 and Xen. *Hell.* 4.2.19. Such evidence suggests that Peloponnesian allies at least occasionally were led by Spartan *xenagoi* rather than by their own commanders. While such leadership does not necessarily imply the Peloponnesians' familiarity with Spartan military organization when they were not actually involved in joint allied expeditions, it is strongly suggestive of some familiarity. I would like to thank Paul Cartledge for pointing out these references to me.

[58] For Dionysius' use of Peloponnesian mercenaries, see Parke 1933, 68, 71; Trundle 2004, 53.

[59] The Spartans also likely contributed to the availability of Peloponnesian mercenaries. Diodorus, for example, makes it clear that Messenian rebels had been driven to join Dionysius I or to Cyrene in 401 or 400 (14.34.2–5). Trundle 2004, 75 also suggests that Spartan hegemony in the Peloponnesus induced Peloponnesians, who had no 'option to fight for their own states' causes,' to enter mercenary service. As he points out, the Arcadian supply of mercenaries appears to have dried up after the establishment of Arcadian autonomy in 369.

[60] See Trundle 2004, 75; cf. 137.

[61] See Cartledge 1987, 322; Trundle 2004, 43, 106–7, 157.

[62] Brasidas: Thuc. 4.80.5. Pedaritus: Thuc. 8.28.4–5, 38.3, 55.3. Lysander: Xen. *Hell.* 2.4.29–30; cf. Lys. 12.59–60; Diod. 14.33.5. Cyrus: Xen. *Anab.* 1.4.3.

[63] See Roy 1967, 297; Hamilton 1979, 104 n. 15.

[64] Thibron: Xen. *Hell.* 3.1.6; *Anab.* 7.6.1–40; 7.7.10–19, 31, 56–7; 7.8.6, 24; Diod. 14.37.1–4. Dercylidas: Xen. *Hell.* 3.1.8; 3.2.6–7; Agesilaus and Herippidas: Xen. *Hell.* 3.4.20; 4.3.15–17; *Ages.* 2.10–11; Isoc. 4.144.

[65] Cartledge 1987, 356 suggests that Sparta might have granted permission to Dionysius I to recruit mercenaries in 398 and 397 in order to rid Sparta of malcontents following Cinadon's abortive conspiracy.

[66] See also Xen. *Hell.* 4.1.21; *Ages.* 1.25, 31–2, where the provenance of the peltasts is less clear. Cf. Plut. *Ages.* 10.3; Isoc. 4.144, along with Best 1969, 79–82; Anderson 1970,

303 n. 33. On the provenance of peltasts, see Best 1969; Trundle 2004, 47–54.

[67] See Best 1969, 83–5. *Contra* Anderson 1970, 120.

[68] Parke 1933, 47–8, 83. See also Best 1969, 85.

[69] For the view that the cash equivalents would have been used to hire mercenaries, see Cartledge 1987, 271, 323, 373–4; Hamilton 1991, 138–9; Krasilnikoff 1993, 90–1; Trundle 2004, 71. Trundle 2004, 94, however, later argues that 'the money is not necessarily related to the pay of mercenaries', and his suggestion that the money would be used to support more Spartan citizens fails to take into account Sparta's chronic *oliganthrōpia*.

[70] Cartledge 1987, 374, for example, argues that 'this is an important surface indication of deeper economic and political malaise within the Peloponnesian League'. See also Parke 1933, 86; and Hamilton 1991, 138–9, who however also considers the possible benefits the Spartans might have seen in the allies' proposal.

[71] See also Trundle 2004, 94; *contra* Cartledge 1987, 271, 323.

[72] Xen. *Hell.* 5.3.10–17, 21–5; Diod. 15.19.3. See Cartledge 1987, 226–9, 256, 262–6, 372–3.

[73] On the Spartans' use of mercenaries after 383, see Parke 1933, 84–90; Best 1969, 97–101. See also Anderson 1970, 132; Trundle 2004, 71.

[74] Best 1969, 98 argues that Sphodrias' mercenaries were likely peltasts.

[75] See Best 1969, 98–9; Cartledge 1987, 231.

[76] For this further change to the Peloponnesian League 'constitution,' see Parke 1933, 86; Cartledge 1987, 230–1, 272–3; Hamilton 1991, 174–5.

[77] Cartledge 1987, 314. Scholars have suggested dates for the *Lac. Pol.*'s composition ranging from *c.* 395 (cf. Chrimes 1948, 17–22) to the period of Cleomenes III, *c.* 260–219 (Wüst 1959, 53–60). Cartledge 1987, 57 offers cogent arguments for dating the *Lac. Pol.* after 371. On this work's authorship, see, most recently, Proietti 1987, 44 n.1; Flower 1991, 90 n.68.

[78] Thucydides, for example, makes it clear that the Athenians regularly employed mercenaries to serve as rowers and hoplites during the Sicilian Expedition. See, e.g., Thuc. 6.43; 7.57.3, 9–10. Demosthenes (4.19–24) later revealed concern about the Athenians' dependence on mercenaries.

[79] Thebes: Diod. 16.34.1, 44.2; Dem. 23.183. Argos: Diod. 16.44.2. See Trundle 2004, 107.

[80] For the Spartans' continued concern to recover these men, see Thuc. 4.15, 19.1, 41.3, 108.7, 117.1–2; 5.15. On Spartan *oliganthrōpia*, see, esp., Cartledge 1979, 257, 307–18; 1987, 37–43; Cawkwell 1983; Lazenby 1985, 57–61; Figueira 1986; Hodkinson 2000, 399–445; Millender 2001, 146–7.

[81] Cartledge (1979, 308; cf. 257) puts the number at 3500, while Hodkinson (2000, 399–400, 421) posits either 2400 or 4200, depending on one's view of Thucydides' treatment of Spartiate military divisions and numbers. For the debate concerning Thucydides' numbers, see, esp., Andrewes in Gomme et al. 1945–81, 4.110–17; Anderson 1970, 228–51; Cartledge 1979, 254–7; 1987, 429–31; Lazenby 1985, 8, 41–4.

[82] Herodotus suggests that the *perioikoi* formed separate contingents during the Persian War (9.11.3). On this reform of the Spartan army, see Cartledge 1979, 208, 256–7; 1987, 40–3; Hodkinson 2000, 421. See also Lazenby 1985, 14–16, 45–6, 48.

[83] On the Spartans' creation of the *neodamōdeis* and the important role that they played in Spartan campaigns abroad, see Andrewes in Gomme et al. 1945–81, 4.35–6.

See also Oliva 1971, 166–70; Cartledge 1979, 251; 1987, 39, 175, 213; Hamilton 1991, 76–8. On the Spartans' need to recruit soldiers from their servile population, see Lazenby 1985, 47; Cartledge 1987, 40, 290.

[84] See Andrewes in Gomme et al. 1945–81, 4.79; Cartledge 1979, 253–4.

[85] See Parke 1930, 74–5.

[86] Hodkinson 2000, 425–6 rightly notes that 'throughout most of the period of war and empire, from the 420s down to the 370s, Sparta conducted all her overseas campaigns and many of those in distant parts of the Greek mainland in such a way as to commit abroad only a minority of Spartiates, who acted as commanders or staff officers'. See also Bettalli 1995, 141–3.

[87] As Cartledge 1987, 93 notes, the harmosts installed by Lysander invariably commanded forces that included mercenaries and *neodamōdeis*. See, e.g, Xen. *Hell.* 2.4.28–30, 43.

[88] See Trundle 2004, 149, who rightly argues that 'mercenary service, if indeed it can be called such, served the Greek *poleis* as an important branch of international diplomacy and policy'. See also Herman 1987, 97–101; Mitchell 1997, 119, 131.

[89] Cartledge 1987, 231–2; Hamilton 1991, 174.

[90] For Agesilaus' successful command of mercenaries, see, e.g., Xen. *Hell.* 3.4.23, 4.3.17; *Ages.* 1.31; Plut. *Ages.* 10.3, along with Best 1969, 81–5, 114; Hamilton 1991, 60–4. On the Spartans' inability to command mercenaries effectively, see, esp., Parke 1933, 84–7; Cartledge 1987, 232, 323. Although Anderson 1970, 123–8 points out that the Spartans' problem lay in their failure to support their light-armed troops with sufficient hoplites, he less cogently argues that Spartan commanders like Teleutias and Phoibidas understood how to utilize peltasts. See also Best 1969, 113–15.

[91] Xen. *Hell.* 5.4.42–5; Diod. 15.33.6; Plut *Pel.* 15.6; Polyaen. 2.5.2. See Best 1969, 99–100; Anderson 1970, 126–7.

[92] Parke 1930, 74; 1933, 85.

[93] On the extent of this disaster, see Parke 1933, 86–7; Anderson 1970, 55–7; Lazenby 1985, 39–40, 148–50; Cartledge 1987, 323–4.

[94] Cartledge 1987, 324.

[95] See also Xen. *Hell.* 7.2.2; Diod. 15.89.1–2; Plut. *Ages.* 35.3–4.

[96] Xen. *Hell.* 7.1.20–2, 27–32; cf. 7.1.41; Diod. 15.70.1–2.

[97] Xen. *Hell.* 7.1.28–32; cf. Diod. 15.72.3; Plut. *Ages.* 33.5–8. See Cartledge 1987, 387.

[98] See Parke 1933, 90, 111; Pritchett 1974, 89–90; Cartledge 1987, 314, 325–9, 392; Trundle 2004, 65, 78, 156, 163.

[99] See Cartledge 1987, 325, 389, who argues (325) that 'in reality he had gone to Ariobarzanes with an eye to the main chance, and even Xenophon could not resist pointing out that the success of his mission took a military, not a diplomatic, form. Whatever exactly it was that Agesilaos did for Ariobarzanes (Xenophon, our only source, does not elaborate), he did it virtually as a hired agent, and Ariobarzanes rewarded him handsomely.' See also Parke 1933, 109.

[100] See Parke 1933, 109–10. Cartledge 1987, 327 argues that the money that Agesilaus received from Ariobarzanes, Tachos, and Mausolus later paid for the mercenary force that Sparta sent to fight at Mantineia in 362. On Mausolus' relationship with Agesilaus, see Hornblower 1982, 174, 201–2; Cartledge 1987, 326–7.

[101] *Contra* Trundle 2004, 156.

[102] Xen. *Ages.* 2.28–31; Diod. 15.92.2; Plut. *Ages.* 36–7; *Mor.* 214d; Nep. *Ages.* 7.2. On the date of this expedition, see Kienitz 1953, 175–7; Cartledge 1987, 328.

[103] Pritchett 1974, 36–8 examines the Spartan practice of sending such counsellors.

[104] Pritchett (1974, 44–5, 90), Cartledge (1987, 328), and Trundle (2004, 156, 163) emphasize the state support behind Agesilaus' campaign. Although Trundle 2004, 156 cites Xen. *Ages.* 2.28–31 as evidence for Spartan alliances with Egypt, Xenophon never precisely refers to their relationship in such terms.

[105] As Anton Powell has rightly reminded me, Cyrus had been a generous paymaster to Lysander, and one can only speculate how vast a treasure Cyrus must have promised the Spartans if the 10,000 had won the Persian throne for him. Xenophon, however, never mentions the financial inducements that tempted the Spartans to send Cheirisophus and other Lacedaemonians to aid Cyrus.

[106] See Cartledge 1987, 328. *Contra* Trundle 2004, 156.

[107] On Agesilaus' humiliating position, see Xen, *Ages.* 2.30; Diod. 15.92.2; Plut. *Ages.* 37.1–2.

[108] Plut. *Ages.* 37.3–40.2; Xen. *Ages.* 2.31; cf. Plut. *Mor.* 214f.

[109] Xen. *Hell.* 3.4.3–4; 3.5.5; 7.1.34; Plut. *Ages.* 6.6–11.

[110] Cartledge 1987, 388; Hamilton 1991, 241.

Bibliography

Anderson, J.K.
    1970   *Military Theory and Practice in the Age of Xenophon*, Berkeley and Los Angeles.

Aymard, A.
    1959   'Mercenariat et histoire grecque', *Etudes d'archéologie classique* 2, 16–27.

Bassett, S.R.
    2001   'The enigma of Clearchus the Spartan', *AHB* 15, 1–13.

Best, J.G.P.
    1969   *Thracian Peltasts and their Influence on Greek Warfare*, Groningen.

Bettalli, M.
    1995   *I mercenari nel mondo Greco*, Pisa.

Bruce, I.A.F.
    1967   *An Historical Commentary on the 'Hellenica Oxyrhynchia'*, Cambridge.

Buckler, J.
    1980   *The Theban Hegemony 371–362 BC*, Cambridge, Mass., and London.

Burnett, A.P.
    1983   *Three Archaic Poets: Archilochus, Alcaeus, Sappho*, Cambridge, Mass.

Cartledge, P.
    1979   *Sparta and Lakonia: A regional history 1300–362 BC*, London.
    1987   *Agesilaos and the Crisis of Sparta*, London and Baltimore.

Caven, B.
    1990   *Dionysius I: War-Lord of Sicily*, New Haven and London.

Cawkwell, G.L.
    1976   'Agesilaus and Sparta', *CQ* n.s. 26, 62–84.
    1983   'The Decline of Sparta', *CQ* n.s. 33, 385–400.

Chrimes, K.M.T.
  1948   *The* Respublica Lacedaemoniorum *Ascribed to Xenophon*, Manchester.
Figueira, T.
  1986   'Population patterns in late archaic and classical Sparta', *TAPA* 116, 165–213.
Flower, M.A.
  1991   'Revolutionary agitation and social change in classical Sparta', in M.A. Flower and M. Toher (eds.) *Georgica: Greek studies in honor of George Cawkwell*, *BICS* Suppl. 58, London, 78–97.
Gomme, A.W., Andrewes, A., and Dover, K.J.
  1945–81   *A Historical Commentary on Thucydides*, 5 vols., Oxford.
Griffith, G.T.
  1935   *The Mercenaries of the Hellenistic World*, Cambridge.
Hamilton, C.D.
  1979   *Sparta's Bitter Victories: Politics and diplomacy in the Corinthian war*, Ithaca and London.
  1991   *Agesilaus and the Failure of Spartan Hegemony*, Ithaca and London.
Herman, G.
  1987   *Ritualised Friendship and the Greek City*, London and New York.
Hodkinson, S.
  2000   *Property and Wealth in Classical Sparta*, London.
Hornblower, S.
  1982   *Mausolus*, Oxford.
Kaplan, P.
  2002   'The social status of the mercenary in archaic Greece', in V.B. Gorman and E. W. Robinson (eds.) *Oikistes: Studies in constitutions, colonies, and military power in the ancient world offered in honor of A.J. Graham*, Leiden, 229–43.
Kienitz, F.K.
  1953   *Die politische Geschichte Ägyptens vom 7. bis zum 4. Jahrhundert vor der Zeitwende*, Berlin.
Krasilnikoff, J.
  1992   'Aegean mercenaries in the fourth to second centuries BC: A study in payment, plunder, and logistics of ancient Greek armies', *C&M* 43, 23–36.
  1993   'The regular payment of Aegean mercenaries in the classical period', *C&M* 44, 77–95.
Laforse, B.
  2000   'Xenophon's Clearchus', *Syll. Class.* 11, 74–88.
Lavelle, B.
  1989   '*Epikouroi* in Thucydides,' *AJP* 110, 36–9.
  1997   '*Epikouros* and *Epikouroi* in early Greek literature and history' *GRBS* 38, 229–62.
Lazenby, J.F.
  1985   *The Spartan Army*, Warminster.
Lewis, D.M.
  1977   *Sparta and Persia: Lectures delivered at the University of Cincinnati, Autumn 1976 in memory of Donald W. Bradeen*, Leiden.

Marinovich, L.

1988   *Le mercenariat grec au IVe siècle avant notre ère et la crise de la polis*, Paris.

Meiggs, R. and Lewis, D.M. (eds).

1988   *A Selection of Greek Historical Inscriptions to the End of the Fifth Century BC*, rev. edn, Oxford.

Millender, E.G.

2001   'Spartan literacy revisited', *Cl. Ant.* 20, 121–64.

2002   'Νόμος Δεσπότος': Spartan obedience and Athenian lawfulness in fifth-century thought', in V.B. Gorman and E.W. Robinson (eds.) *Oikistes: Studies in constitutions, colonies, and military power in the ancient world offered in honor of A.J. Graham*, Leiden, 33–59.

Miller, H.F.

1984   'The practical and economic background to the Greek mercenary explosion', *G&R* 31, 153–60.

Mitchell, L.

1997   *Greeks Bearing Gifts: The public use of private relationships in the Greek world*, Cambridge.

Nielsen, T.H.

1999   'The concept of Arkadia – the people, the land, and their organisation', in T.H. Nielsen and J. Roy (eds.) *Defining Ancient Arkadia: Acts of the Copenhagen polis centre*, vol. 6, Copenhagen, 16–79.

Oliva, P.

1971   *Sparta and Her Social Problems*, Amsterdam and Prague.

Parke, H.W.

1930   'The development of the second Spartan empire (405–371 BC)', *JHS* 50, 37–79.

1933   *Greek Mercenary Soldiers: From the earliest times to the battle of Ipsus*, Oxford.

Poralla, P.

1985   *Prosopographie der Lakedaimonier bis auf die Zeit Alexanders des Grossen*, Breslau, 1913. Rev. edn, A.S. Bradford, Chicago.

Pritchett, W.K.

1974   *The Greek State at War*, vol. 2, Berkeley and Los Angeles.

Proietti, G.

1987   *Xenophon's Sparta: An introduction*, Leiden and New York.

Roisman, J.R.

1985–8 'Klearchos in Xenophon's *Anabasis*', *Scripta Classica Israelica* 8–9, 30–52.

Roy, J.

1967   'The mercenaries of Cyrus', *Historia* 16, 287–323.

Sansone, D.

1981   'Lysander and Dionysius (Plut. *Lys.* 2)', *CP* 76, 202–6.

Trundle, M.

2004   *Greek Mercenaries: From the late archaic period to Alexander*, London and New York.

Tuplin, C.

1992   'Persian garrisons in Xenophon and other sources', in A. Kuhrt and H. Sancisi-Weerdenburg (eds.) *Achaemenid History III: Method and Theory:*

Proceedings of the London 1985 Achaemenid History Workshop, Leiden, 67–70.

West, M.L. (ed.)

1971   *Iambi et Elegi Graeci: Ante Alexandrum Cantati,* vol. I, Oxford.

Westlake, H.D.

1987   'Diodorus and the expedition of Cyrus', *Phoenix* 41, 241–54.

Wüst, F.R.

1959   'Laconica', *Klio* 37, 53–62.

9

SPARTANS AND THE USE OF TREACHERY AMONG THEIR ENEMIES

Françoise Ruzé

Our ancient sources make clear that major tensions existed in classical Greek city-states, involving attitudes towards Sparta. In this period, there was a settled hatred between men who hoped for, or requested, a Spartan intervention in their own city, and men who feared and strongly resisted such a prospect. However, for a long period Sparta was not an imperialistic state;[1] so, why such antagonism ? It is hard to believe that the opposition between Dorians and Ionians was sufficient to provoke such confrontations, although allusion to it is frequent in ancient rhetoric.[2] Rather, Sparta is a political reference: it stands for oligarchy against democracy.[3]

Since antiquity, confrontations between philo-Laconian oligarchs and philo-Athenian democrats have caused many historians to see partisan or financial interests as more influential than patriotism. Indeed, treachery relies generally on internal and socio-political discords, and also on a state of *stasis*. Thucydides, in his commentary on the Corcyraean *stasis* of 427–425, says that it seemed awful because it was the first to reach such a degree; but he adds :

> for afterwards, practically all the Greek world was convulsed, everywhere disagreements (*diaphorai*) occurred, since in each state the leaders of the democratic party sought to bring in the Athenians, the *oligoi* to bring in the Lacedaemonians. (3.82.1)

There is a systematic contrast between the small number of *oligoi*, who are also men of merit, *agathoi*, and the many, the *polloi*, or *plēthos*, or even *dēmos*, low-born people, hence bad, *kakoi*.

Such a schematic opposition does not fit the complicated reality. The supporters of a more oligarchic form of government may feel reluctant to promote the loss of their city's autonomy, in favour of Sparta. This is the case with the moderate Athenians in 411 and 405, with many Corinthians during the 390s,[4] and again with the Thebans when the Kadmeia was lost in 382. On the other hand, during the fifth century, some true democrats hoped to get rid of the excessive burden of the Athenian empire.[5] But those temperate citizens from both parties were quickly compelled to more radical choices, firstly because of the confrontation between the two cities, then because of the growth of Lacedaemonian imperialism; the latter, because it could not rely on a majority within the cities, traded systematically upon the oligarchs' feelings and induced them to commit treachery. Then their enemies became so suspicious that at times we find outbursts of slaughter, in Corinth or Argos for instance; these abruptly ceased as soon as the risk of treachery was perceived to have passed. Should we agree with A.H. Chroust, that belonging to a small group of supporters outweighed patriotism?[6] That would be to forget that many people we call traitors thought that the form of government they dreamed of was the only correct one for their city. Private relationships, such as *hetaireia, philia* or *xenia,* were in conflict with formal, public, relationships in the cities.[7]

In this chapter we are not concerned with the general political psychology of philo-Laconians, but we shall try to answer three questions: how did the Spartans make use of their supporters in the city-states, what did they expect from them and how did they help them? Before we examine cases in detail, we must remember that the Lacedaemonians had certain commonplace reasons for inducing treachery: after they chose to spread their rule over most of the Peloponnese and then beyond, they met important difficulties arising from their ignorance about the people they were trying to control; so they needed friends in the field, who would give them intelligence and advice. Besides, for a long period the Greeks were unable to take by force a well-protected town; lacking good siege engines,[8] and short of soldiers and financial means, they had to improvise. Treachery had the advantage of being relatively swift and economical. It became so common that Aineias the Tactician, in the first chapters of his *Siegecraft,* wrote at length about the ways to avoid such a threat. More than any other power, Sparta because of its shortage of warriors and money might indeed be expected to resort to treachery. Otherwise, failing a rapid victory, a war might last indefinitely, unless the Spartans could find a ruse to break down their enemy's defences.[9]

Treachery took various forms, from the traitors' point of view. One could surrender the city to the besieging enemy by giving him intelligence, by opening the gates, by getting rid of the guards. Such action might arise from fear, from private interest or from political fellow-feeling; but there are only a few documented instances of such grounds – less than a third of all cases. More often than not, it seems that a group called in the Lacedaemonians in order to modify the policy of a city in which they were a minority. Such a group might be concerned about foreign policy, might wish to leave an inconvenient alliance or to be rid of war, but treachery appears more frequently when linked with domestic policy. In such cases, a small group looks for Sparta's support so as to take political office and to alter the form of government. For its part, Sparta could hope that such a city would prove submissive: a faithful ally should be at the same time a politically congruent ally.

In addition, the Spartans did not allow an allied city or political group to gain influence of its own in the Peloponnese or even in Central Greece, still less to escape their supervision. Accordingly, they expected intelligence from their supporters and their active assistance in order to suppress any such tendency. Any pretext for intervention would suffice; they acceded with especial rapidity to the requests of those who come crying for their help. Thus, they forbade the unification of its area by Elis in 399; they dissolved the union between Corinth and Argos in 394/3, and they set the members of the Arcadian League against each other in 370/69.

In some cases the Spartans experienced severe failure when trusting 'friends' and intervening with military force against a people, as for instance at Athens in the late sixth century. In 510, they had been lucky against the Peisistratids who apparently no longer enjoyed the support of the Athenian people. But in 508 the Spartans came up against fierce and spontaneous opposition when they tried to stop the Kleisthenic reforms and to give autocratic power to Isagoras who had called for the aid of king Kleomenes, his guest-friend. The two next attempts to give the Athenians a tyrant – Isagoras for a second time, then Hippias who had been driven away with Spartan help some years before – met resistance from Sparta's own allies, particularly the Corinthians, who refused, as they claimed, to have a share in so unjust an intervention. The Spartans would need to learn to manipulate their supporters with more skill.[10]

For understanding the aims and increasing sophistication of Spartan policy, three sets of actions are especially helpful, ranging from the 490s to the 360s. They concern respectively Argos, the eternal enemy and rival; the cities of Khalkidike which seceded from Athens and went over to Brasidas; and Phleious, an absolutely faithful ally yet one over which some Spartans aspired to an absolute political control.

How to weaken an enemy by treason: the case of Argos
The case has a certain simplicity. Always an enemy, Dorian Argos was for long a rival which might have outdone Sparta in the Peloponnese, had it been more interested in events abroad, and less hampered by its internal differences. Within this aristocratic society, the government tended to democracy, as early as the 490s. At that stage, it was not very difficult for Sparta to use frustrated oligarchs in order to help its offensives against the city.[11]

Immediately after the battle of Sepeia (494?), king Kleomenes seems to have informers amongst the Argives. Soldiers from Argos had taken refuge in a sacred grove and

> Kleomenes had with him certain deserters (*automoloi*) and, informed by them, he sent a herald, calling by name the Argives who were shut up in the sacred precinct and inviting them to come out... About fifty Argives came out, called one after the other, and he slew them. (Hdt. 6.79)

Subsequently Argos was for long weakened by having lost the majority of its citizen-soldiers, even though, incidentally, the democracy became stronger.

In 418/7, this city which so long stood for democracy in the Peloponnese veered towards the side of philo-Laconian oligarchy. An early incident suggests a complicity between two Argive leaders – Thrasyllos the commander-in-chief, and Alkiphron, proxenos of the Lacedaemonians – and Agis, king of Sparta: they agree to put an end to a battle. Such an agreement circumvented the law of both cities, and these men would meet legal challenges as a result; Thrasyllos was even threatened with a spontaneous stoning (Thuc. 5.57–63).

Shortly afterwards came the battle of Mantineia (Thuc.5.67–73); according to Thucydides, the Spartans tried on that occasion to prevent the Arcadians from siding with Argos; Agis again is in command of the army and we are told that he hoped to atone for his recent fault. Here, we are informed that the democratic Argives had created a picked regiment of one thousand professional soldiers, supported by the city. They fought quite well on the right wing of the alliance, and they shared the victory in their part of the battlefield, but that victory was reversed by king Agis and his Lacedaemonians who fought in the centre. Now, although the victors did not pursue far, most of the Mantineians were killed while those who had fought beside them, the Thousand from Argos, were saved; the other Argives suffered heavy losses. Did the Thousand run faster? Or may Agis have ordered that these young men be spared? The following story may suggest a reason for such restraint.

Next winter (418/7), the Lacedaemonians again took the field, and proposed peace and alliance to the Argives. A party of philo-Laconians now exploited the defeat at Mantineia and secured the abandonment of former alliances, but it seems that they still adhered to the laws of the city (Thuc. 5.76–77).[12] However, it was a contingent of a thousand Argives which shared certain operations with the Spartans, with what aims we do not know. With their help, the Spartans dissolved the Argive *dēmos,* in place of which they established an 'oligarchy favourable to the Lacedaemonians' (Thuc. 5.81.2). Diodorus adds that

> the men who had been accustomed to be the leaders of the *dēmos* (τοὺς δημαγωγεῖν εἰωθότας) were put to death; then, by terrorizing the other citizens,

they abolished the laws and managed the state by themselves (κατέλυσαν τοὺς νόμους καὶ δι' ἑαυτῶν τὰ δημόσια διῴκουν)'. (12. 80.3)

Thucydides has no doubt: all this had been planned before the battle of Mantineia, but the victory helped to promote the project:

> They wished to make first a truce (*spondai*) with the Lacedaemonians, then, just after, to conclude an alliance (*symmakhia*) and, having done so, to attack the democracy. (5.76.2)

So, it would have made sense for Agis and the Spartans to save the Thousand, just as it was advisable also to have them defeated.

Afterwards, the Lacedaemonians might have been expected to support those who had perpetrated treachery and assumed power, and to exploit their chance to put an end to a century of struggles, damaging for both cities. However, in summer 417, when events turned against the *oligoi,* the Lacedaemonians were so long in coming to help that, while their Argive supporters were killed or forced into flight, they did nothing:

> Hearing at Tegea that the oligarchs had been defeated, they refused to go further in spite of the requests of the fugitives, and, returning home, they proceeded with the celebration of the Gymnopaidiai. (Thuc. 5.82.3)

At the congress of their allies, those Argives who had restored democracy were declared guilty (of what?). However, neither the Spartiates nor their allies made any further move, so that, seeing them wavering, the Argive *dēmos* now left the Spartan alliance and, once again, turned towards Athens whose alliance seemed more favourable. Then, they fortified their town, with a great common impulse and some help from outside (Thuc. 5.82.2–6).

Should we reckon that the Lacedaemonians did not understand the urgency of helping their Argive supporters, but supposed that, although abandoned, they would remain completely faithful and even able to gain additional followers in their city? The opposite was to occur (Thuc. 5.83.1–2). When, in winter 417/6, the Spartans decided to return to the Argolid, they received no help from the traitors. So, they devastated the country and pulled down walls. Twice again they would return, in spring 414, only the true victims would not be the Argives, but the Phliasians on whom the Argives took revenge for their own incapacity to check the Lacedaemonians and from anger that their oligarchic exiles had found shelter close at hand, at Phleious.

In the case of Argos, so grave were the matters in dispute that any hope for peace supposed a different form of government. Probably, the Lacedaemonians themselves had no confidence in such a solution, and so did not play fair with their friends. For them, the main point was won: thanks to these attacks, Argos was weakened for a long time by its domestic problems and, perhaps, by the death of a number of good warriors. Lasting trust between the two cities was impossible, whatever the form of government; Argos would make a very awkward ally, one which would demand a certain share of power. Accordingly, the Spartiates did not move when two crises involving oligarchs at Argos occurred in the fourth century. On the first occasion, some time between 386 and 371,[13] the oligarchs attempted a coup d'état, helped by mercenaries, but it was stopped in time by the *prostatēs tou dēmou,* thanks to a skilful scheme. On the second, in 370, according to Aineias the Tactician (11.7.10) and Diodorus, the process named *skytalismos* (bastinado) produced a terrible slaughter of oligarchs.[14] These men received not the slightest support from the Spartans, and perhaps did not even look for it; remembering what had happened in the past, they could rely only upon themselves. It was in Sparta's interest to leave the Argives to slaughter each other.

On the whole, then, the treachery of the Thousand did some good to Sparta, but not what we might have expected. The main thing was the weakening of the city, due to conflicts between the *oligoi* and the *dēmos.* Argos is not the only example: any city, once it had a position of power, would not rejoin the Spartans permanently without the agreement of a majority of its citizens, and would not be easy to destroy. Such was the case with Thebes, unlike Plataia which was weaker, with Corinth and even with Athens. Already in 411, Agis did not believe in the possibility of a true oligarchic revolution in Athens.[15] For him, as for Pausanias, a democracy would be better, provided internal opposition to it would never cease. In 404/3, the dreams of a Lysander come up against Pausanias' common sense. True, the king was especially happy to deal with democrats, a fact which was to prove costly for him. In the case of Mantineia, king Agesipolis took the town in 386 after sapping its fortifications; the people were scattered into the *kōmai* and power was dispersed among the *oligoi,* masters of the *kōmai.* This arrangement was destined not to last long, both for external reasons (the defeat at Leuktra), and probably because the Spartan king had spared the defeated democrats (at the request of his exiled father, Pausanias).

Quite another strategy: Brasidas and the Khalkidian cities.

Thucydides (4.79–80) says that Brasidas' expedition to Thrace, in 424, served several purposes: to bear hard on the Athenians who threatened Sparta in the Peloponnese, especially with the occupation of Pylos; to remove to a distance some outstanding helots, and to respond to Perdikkas, the Macedonian king, and to the Khalkidian cities 'inviting the Peloponnesians to intervene'. The historian, who was also the unsuccessful commander-in-chief against

Brasidas, describes the latter's dual approach:

> For the present, by showing himself just and moderate (δίκαιον καὶ μέτριον) towards the cities, he caused most of them to revolt and secured possession of others through treachery on the part of their inhabitants. (4.81.2)

Thucydides' account also shows various ways in which the traitors themselves acted. Brasidas had been invited by a small party of Akanthians, but the *dēmos* resisted and the Spartan was not allowed into the town. He then threatened the harvest and gave a promise that the city would preserve its autonomy. So, after many speeches had been delivered in the assembly, a secret vote was taken and the majority gave way; Brasidas' army was received into the town (Thuc. 4.88). The case of Amphipolis was rather similar (4.103.2–106). There too Brasidas held the country but not the town, in spite of some few traitors acting in secret. The latter had no need to reveal themselves, for the Amphipolitans knew that Brasidas had hostages: he might threaten the prisoners he had already made. In addition, his demands were moderate. Also reinforcements from Athens, of which Thucydides himself was in command, were late. So the Amphipolitans gave up and accepted an agreement (*homologia*). In both cases, traitors were useful, but only for drawing Brasidas' attention to their city. Also, it seems that, although the Spartan's behaviour was so moderate as to induce other cities to revolt from the Athenians, they were in no hurry to do so, so long as Brasidas and his men did not come to help them.

On the other hand, at Torone later on, there was no question of a voluntary surrender. The Athenians held the town and the *polis* was still on their side. Secretly, some *oligoi* contrived for seven *psiloi* from Brasidas' army to enter the town; the latter killed the sentries and opened the gate so that a hundred peltasts were able to enter. The mass of citizens (τὸ πολύ), panic-stricken, gave way in the face of the common action of traitors and invaders. Again, Brasidas soothed them, using the same words as in Akanthos. Some Toronaians did try to resist, with the help of the Athenians, but they failed (4.110–15).

Finally, the capture of Mende provides an interesting tale but one that is not always clear (Thuc. 4.123). The truce which led to the so-called Peace of Nikias had already been sworn; this city should not therefore have been taken. Here, surrender was due to the *oligoi* who were so advanced in their action that it was too late for them to desist, in spite of the truce: 'The *oligoi*…went in terror for their lives if their plot was divulged, so they coerced the *polloi* against their will.'[16] Probably neither the assembly nor the authorities were informed, but we do not know how the traitors managed to introduce their new friends into the town. Perhaps, as the truce had been published, they could more easily act by surprise. The agreement proved fragile; because of the maladroitness of Polydamidas, the Peloponnesian commander left in place, the *dēmos* became so angry that it attacked the Peloponnesians and their supporters and routed them. The Athenians recovered the city but allowed the Mendaians to govern themselves and to bring to trial those who were responsible for the defection.

What is so important for us in these stories ? It seems clear that the request for help came from parties which, though opposed to Athens, were a minority in their city. However, the Spartan commander-in-chief was a good one: on his own initiative or on orders from his city, he issued promises of autonomy which seemed serious and thereby strengthened the wish to get rid of the Delian League (cf. Thuc. 4.88). Brasidas' conduct and good propaganda were more important for his success than the battles he fought or the help given by traitors. Most of all, he knew how to make treachery appear noble, as we learn in his speech to the soldiers before they met the troops of Kleon, at Amphipolis:

> You, Klearidas, show yourself a valiant man (*agathos*), as can be expected of a Spartan, and you, allies, follow him bravely; bear in mind that a good fight needs three conditions: zeal, sense of honour and obedience to the leader; that, on this day, you will get, if you are brave, freedom and the right to be called allies of the Lacedaemonians, or else, you will come to be vassals of the Athenians (if you are so fortunate as to escape death or being sold into slavery) and then to be in a harsher bondage than before; further, you would prevent the liberation of the rest of the Greeks.   (Thuc. 5.9.9)

Such a speech turns the traitors into loyal citizens once a majority of the assembly has been convinced.

Nevertheless, the agreements between the cities and Brasidas did not prescribe a new form of government; so, were the traitors who called for him simple dupes? Perhaps, but in any case the promises were not kept: young Spartans were sent to be 'archons' in the cities; 'proto-harmosts' says Cartledge.[17] Who were these men ? For the Spartans, the main point was: not just anybody (μὴ τοῖς εὐτυχοῦσιν). But they knew nothing about local realities and about local people; moreover, their presence was a breach of the autonomy promised by Brasidas, who had said to the citizens of Torone and Amphipolis that all of them would preserve all their citizens rights, should they cease to fight (Thuc. 4.106.1 and 114.3). It is said that these young Spartan citizens had been sent παρανόμως, that is to say in breach of custom. We may infer that the Spartans no longer trusted the agreements made but required other measures to protect their position, neglecting the expectations of the cities in question and not rewarding their supporters.

Autonomy forbidden : Phleious or fidelity ill-rewarded

With Phleious, Sparta went still further, but by now Agesilaos was king. There was no such ground for intervention as in the cases of Argos or Khalkidike, but here, too, a small faction invited in the Lacedaemonians to resolve an internal conflict among the citizens. Neither Sparta nor the Peloponnesian League was threatened by Phleious. On the contrary, Phleious had proved absolutely trustworthy. Among the reasons for this fidelity was the city's excellent position on the road leading from Arcadia to Corinth or Argos; the Phliasians dreaded the claims, first of the Argives, and later of the Arcadians, to have control over their city. Sparta seemed the best guarantor of their autonomy. Additionally, the strategic position of the city and its traditional fidelity made it a very good place to muster troops of the Spartan alliance especially when they were heading for the Argolid.[18] Phleious was thus exposed to vengeance, above all from Argos. In the light of all this, it is an interesting question why the Spartans thought it worthwhile to subject so loyal a city to a siege of eighteen months.

For what happened, Xenophon is almost our only source.[19] It is possible that some tension had existed as early as 394; perhaps the sacred truce (*ekekheiria*) which the Phliasians used to justify their non-participation in the battle of Nemea was a pretext. We know that the Phliasians had banished some men for 'philo-Laconism' (*HG* 4.4.15); it is not clear where these exiles went. Xenophon's reference to an assembly of five thousand citizens implies that the city was democratic.[20] So, the exiles may have been ready to surrender their city's autonomy in order to achieve dominance at home, but they were only one group among the oligarchs; normally the oligarchs seem to come to terms with a local regime which defends the city's autonomy.

In 391, Phleious suffered from the action of Sparta's adversaries, led by Iphikrates. The consequences are important :

> The Phliasians, although they had refused previously to receive the Lacedaemonians within their walls, for fear that they would bring back the people who said that they were in exile on account of their Lacedaemonian sympathies, were then seized with such panic fear of the men from Corinth, that they sent for the Lacedaemonians and put the town and the citadel in their hands to guard.
>
> (Xen. *HG* 4.4.15)

The Spartans on this occasion behaved with moderation; they did not attempt to restore the exiles or to change the city's laws. Again, after the Peace of Antalkidas, when they reviewed and judged the past behaviour of their allies, they attacked Mantineia (385) but apparently said nothing of Phleious (*HG* 5.2.1–2). But the Spartan action against Mantineia gave ideas to the Phliasian exiles; in 384 they made an approach to Sparta, and there represented Phleious as having been a bad ally since the time of their own exile. The ephors were convinced and asked Phleious to restore the exiles as 'the Lacedaemonians' friends' who had been unjustly condemned, 'having done nothing wrong' (ἀδικοῦντες οὐδέν; Xen. *HG* 5.2.9). Behind the superficial politeness ('They said that they deemed it proper to effect their return not by compulsion but by voluntary consent of the Phliasians'), the threat was well understood by the Phliasians. The latter decided to yield, from fear of a possible combination of a Spartan offensive from outside and of treachery from within, by exiles, their families and friends, and also by the supporters of a new regime.[21] So

> the Phliasians voted to take back the exiles and to restore them to their indisputable properties (ἐμφανῆ κτήματα)...and if any dispute should arise between them (i.e. the exiles and those who had purchased their properties), it was to be settled by legal process. (Xen. *HG* 5.2.8–10)

Predictably the restitutions did not go smoothly, as ever when there is a need to give satisfaction both to former owners and to those who have purchased their estates.[22] According to Xenophon,

> The people of Phleious...boldly refused to grant any of their rights to the restored exiles, for, while the exiles demanded that questions in dispute should be brought to trial before an impartial court, the Phliasians wanted to compel them to plead their cases in the city itself. (*HG* 5.3.10)[23]

But Xenophon here has a strange concept of good justice. When he speaks about the oligarchs, he seems to accept their words, saying that they had done no wrong at all and that they rejected the city's court in favour of an impartial one (that is to say a Spartan one?). On the other hand, when later the Phliasians were defeated, Agesilaos imposed an agreement by which the same oligarchs had the power of life and death over their fellow-citizens; then, Xenophon does not find anything wrong... Now, on the rights of the exiles allowed back into Phleious, Xenophon gives the important information that, when they went to Sparta, they were backed by their friends and by 'many even among the citizens' (*HG* 5.3.11). But, since the Phliasian authorities 'fined all who had gone to Lacedaemon without being sent by the state', we can infer that these men asked for judicial arbitration in Sparta on their own initiative. This may seem to have been a normal resort to the *hegemōn*, inasmuch as the matter did concern obedience to Sparta's authority. And it would not be the only instance of a Spartan decision about a law-court for settling *stasis* within a city. There is the case of the leader of the Thebans democrats, Ismenias, who was judged by the Spartans in 382. But the Phliasian case now had nothing directly to do with strategy, and had not been brought to Sparta by the Phliasian authorities. The Phliasians who took it upon themselves to ask another city to intervene at Phleious were committing treachery. Normally, private citizens were concerned at most with the internal policy of their city: any invitation to foreign judges had to proceed from the civic authorities.

In the present case, on Sparta's side, the ephors likewise decided alone: 'since it seemed that the Phliasians were really acting with arrogant malice (ὑβρίζειν), the ephors called out the ban against them' (*HG* 5.3.13).[24] Xenophon says that Agesilaos approved of this decision, and it is noteworthy that one of the exiles who complained was Podanemos, a guest-friend of Agesilaos' father, and that one of the opposition's leaders was Procles, his own guest-friend.[25] Now, many authors emphasize this trait of Agesilaos' character: personal relations, love, friendship, guest-friendship are of prime importance for him and his political choices.

So, these men who, in the eyes of Agesilaos, were victims because they were pro-Spartan, but who were traitors in the eyes of the Phliasians, these men will allow Sparta to launch a war against their own city.[26] But, during the war, 'many Lacedaemonians said that merely for the sake of a few individuals they were making themselves hated by a state of more than five thousand men' (*HG* 5.3.16). So, the Spartans disagreed about the way to behave when some *oligoi* betrayed their city. The eighteen months of the siege were from 381 to 379. In the town, watchfulness was the rule. The conduct of affairs was steadfast, and there was no betrayal from within; the Phliasians were reduced by starvation. But some left the town, and then another form of treachery took place, as Agesilaos responded to the grumblings on his own side: 'when friends or kin of the exiles came out the town, he instructed them to form common messes and...to undertake army-training' (*HG* 5.3.17).[27] These men, when they re-entered the city after Sparta's victory, would be brothers-in-arms of the Spartans.

We come now to the final, harsh, settlement imposed by Agesilaos: 'fifty men from the restored exiles and fifty from the people at home should, in the first place, make inquiry to determine who, in the city, ought justly to be left alive and who ought to be put to death, and, secondly, they should establish the laws by which the city should be conducted' (*HG* 5.3.25). It is plain that the majority of the Phliasians had no say in the matter, and that an oligarchic government was established which endured for some time, with the help of a garrison composed of outsiders. In 369, the city headed off an attack from exiled democrats helped by Argos, and Xenophon would have us believe that the defence was a popular one, supported by the whole *dēmos*.[28] But the soldiers, he says, were horsemen and some picked troops (*epilektoi*); evidently they were not popular troops.[29] Not long afterwards, in 366, the Phliasians were to rejoin the Athenian alliance,[30] but by then Sparta had other concerns.

So, we have an autonomous and trustworthy city which has fallen under Spartan domination, with its allegiance consequently dependent on the power of a small faction. Politically, this makes little apparent sense for Sparta, and it arose from real treachery, that is to say the calling in of an external power without the agreement of the government and the majority of the citizens, and indeed against their interest. Why did the Lacedaemonians enact such a policy? Obviously, Agesilaos imposed his own views: for him, such a city with its good position could not escape from his oligarchic friends, and that justified the war as well as the final settlement. Did he go too far, even for much Spartan opinion? We may detect an echo to the complaints from within Sparta's army at Phleious when Agesilaos refused to command the expedition against the Thebans in 382: 'He well knew that, if he was in command, the citizens would say that, in order to give assistance to tyrants, Agesilaos was making trouble for the state' (*HG* 5.4.13). Some Spartans apparently disapproved of the means by which cities were being brought into subjection – disapproved not out of any anti-imperialist principle, but because this particular method of imperialism was unsound. Nevertheless, Agesilaos' political acumen prevailed over such complaints.[31]

Conclusions

We have attempted to analyse three instances of Sparta's use of treachery, all different in time and method. Is it possible to detect anything distinctively Spartan in this form of exploiting enemy weakness, or any development therein? Lacedaemonian policy never aimed to take more and more towns; only as a last resort did Sparta try to capture a town, but in such cases it often needed to use plain treachery.[32] The Spartans preferred to conquer cities from within, in order to have in charge local people who would obey their orders, at least in foreign affairs. Accordingly, the traitors we know of were not so much concerned to bring an enemy into the town permanently; rather, they invited in Spartan power in order to get rid of the local regime and to take all powers themselves within the city.[33] We may add that, when using treachery, Sparta did not try to preserve and exploit existing leagues, but tried always to dissolve them.

When Xenophon emphasizes that, as at Phleious, it had become customary to bring the exiles back, with foreign help if necessary, in order to revolutionize a city,[34] he reveals the confusion that existed between oligarchy, philo-Lakonism and treachery. Indeed, when a Greek endeavoured to overthrow the political institutions of his city for the benefit of a small faction, he behaved as a traitor, but not exactly in the way which ordinarily afflicted cities at war. Traditional values were reversed: usually, the traitor was scorned by those he served as well as by his victims. But, if a traitor was the 'friend' of the enemy power,[35] if he acted for a good cause as the enemy saw it, then he was called an *agathos* acting against *kakoi,* he was not scorned by the enemy but trusted.[36] On principle, the Lacedaemonians supported the oligarchic faction (Thuc. 1.19), among which they found their friends, and so they maintained the best relations with men who continued to behave as traitors. Bonds between traitors and Spartan leaders became firmly established.[37] In Phleious, in 379, Agesilaos went further by arranging for dissident Phliasians to become, collectively, fellows of the Spartan soldiers. Such friends were always justified in their actions and would always know which policy was best for their city.

Nevertheless, there was no typical 'friend of Sparta'. Some became such because they were realists and recognized Spartan superiority; some were friends of Sparta through tradition, especially the kings' guest-friends or the *proxenoi*; some were so through shared ideology; others, more numerous, through hunger for power.[38] Now, from the point of view of Sparta's interest, dependence on the small friendly groups who opposed the *dēmos* or *plēthos* could be very hazardous, and might lead during a war to those cities' failing Sparta. In addition, according to the *Hellenica Oxyrhynchia*, the cities engaged in the Corinthian war had long been ill-disposed towards the Spartans; among them 'the Argives and the Boeotians hated the Spartans because they treated as friends their enemies among the citizens (ὅτι τοῖς ἐναντίοις τῶν πολιτῶν αὐτοῖς ἐχρῶντο φίλοις)'; Sparta's support for traitors could lead to violent resentment within the cities concerned.[39]

Sparta had its reasons for preferring an insecure oligarchy even to a moderate democracy. It was easier and more discreet to negotiate with a few friends than openly with the representatives of all the citizens. In other respects, the troops that oligarchs might supply were few but of high quality and reliable, often picked soldiers. But I believe that in general the insecurity of an oligarchy was not a major negative consideration for Sparta; rather, it may have been a *positive* consideration: the *stasis* which such oligarchies might induce made their cities powerless, and to create that weakness was Sparta's purpose. Sometimes even, Spartans induced their friends to spare their opponents, surely because as long as the latter stayed in the city, the oligarchs would be faithful to Sparta and the city would be weakened. Such was the case in Thespiae in 377 when Agesilaos 'did not allow' the supporters of Lacedaemon to put their opponents to death but 'reconciled them and compelled them to give oaths to one another' (*HG* 5.4.55). Similarly in the opposite case: Sparta could behave moderately towards democracies if she was sure that the oligarchs in the relevant cities could weaken those democracies. That perhaps was the policy of Brasidas in the cities of Thrace, of Pausanias in Athens in 403, of the Lacedaemonians in Phleious in 391.

Nevertheless, the traitors were not to delude themselves: a single criterion ruled Sparta's policy, the interests of Sparta.[40] The Spartans' aim was obvious, as we read in a speech attributed to the Thebans when, in 395, they sought alliance with Athens:

> No, it is their helots they deem it proper to appoint as harmosts, while toward their allies, who are free men, they have behaved themselves like masters since they have achieved success. Furthermore, it is plain that they have deceived in like manner the peoples whom they won away from you; for, instead of freedom, they gave them a double servitude: they are tyrannized both by harmosts and by the ten which Lysander established in each city. (*HG* 3.5.12–13)

Spartans would not maintain help for their partisans elsewhere who met a reverse,[41] as we saw in the case of the Argives,[42] nor would they help those who began an action without their consent, as they made clear in the case of the Athenian oligarchs in 411.[43]

Such was general Spartan policy; we must not judge Agesilaos too severely. The king wanted to have his supporters as leaders in the cities, and his policy was more self-assertive and ruthless than his predecessors had achieved, with the significant exception of Lysander, his former lover and political patron. Nevertheless, this was not a strikingly new policy; it is just that Agesilaos took it to its extreme. Traitors had no right to fail and they were friends only if they forgot their city's interests in favour of Sparta's. This is indeed imperialism. It took no account of the sufferings of cities whose citizens allowed themselves to get involved in struggles promoted from outside. Men who, through ambition or folly, imported struggles into their own city, contributed to the important process of weakening that city. By exploiting this process Sparta succeeded for long, but not for ever.

Notes

[1] It is true that, at the beginning, the cities were not bound to Sparta by strict obligations in foreign policy, but according to Yates 2005, 65, 'the early Spartan alliance was bound by treaties that focused on the preservation of pro-Spartan factions'.

[2] Hdt. 1.56; 5.76 ('Dorians' arrive in Attica); Thuc. 6: in 415, Hermocrates, the Syracusan, contrasts the free Dorians with the Ionians, always slaves (77.1); Euphemos, the Athenian, retorts: 'Always, Ionians have been enemies of Dorians. It is even so. Accordingly, we, being Ionians, have considered in what way we should be least subject to Peloponnesians who are Dorians and who are not only more numerous but our neighbours' (82.2).

[3] Those who praise oligarchy would surely find unacceptable the way of life ascribed to the Spartans. We must also remember that Aristotle seems right in not classifying the Spartan form of government among true oligarchies. Cf. Ruzé 1997, 128–240.

[4] Xen. *HG* 4.4.1–2: in 394/3, many Corinthians were tired of war and the allies

understood that such weariness might cause the city to 'laconize'.

⁵ See the criticisms of de Ste Croix 1954, by Bradeen 1960 and Quinn 1964. Compare Thuc. 2.8.4–5 (or 1.75.1–3) with the words of Cleon (3.39.6) and those of Diodotos (3.47.2): *pace* Diodotos, Thucydides, Pericles and Cleon – a strange trio – agree that the Empire created universal opposition in the cities. Likewise, although the revolts of the Thracian Khalkidians are in some ways obscure, Thucydides suggests in 4.108.1–3 that the liberty promised by Brasidas incited them, and in 5.21.1–3 and 35.3 and 5, all the Amphipolitans would resist with the Spartans against being handed back to the Athenians.

⁶ Chroust 1954.

⁷ Mitchell 1997 and G. Herman, 1981, (*non vidi*).

⁸ Catapults did not become widespread before 370.

⁹ Such was the procedure of Agesipolis at Mantineia in 385 : when the river was high, he blocked its bed, so that the water overflowed and undermined the walls of the town, which collapsed.

¹⁰ Another example is found in the case of Pedaritos at Chios (Thuc. 8.38.3; 40.1; 55.3) whose policy provoked troubles; cf. Piérart 1995, 266, 268, 273.

¹¹ On the political crises in Argos, Ruzé 1997, 245–61, 285–7, with bibliography.

¹² David 1986a.

¹³ This is the date that David 1986b has proposed with impressive arguments; Whitehead 1990, 130, agrees.

¹⁴ Diodorus 15.58, says that the violence fell away as quickly as it had started, but the city had been weakened.

¹⁵ Cf. Thuc. 8.71.1: 'But, thinking that the city would not become quiet and that the *dēmos* would not give up its old freedom, and also that, if they saw a great Peloponnesian army they would not keep quiet, and being absolutely convinced that present disturbances would not cease, Agis did not come to any agreement with the delegates of the Four Hundred'.

¹⁶ The translation – and the understanding – of καταβιασαμένων παρὰ γνώμην τοὺς πολλούς are uncertain: some understand 'contrary to all expectations'; others 'contrary to common sense'. It seems that we must understand that everything had to be done secretly because it was contrary to the advice of the majority.

¹⁷ Cartledge 1987, 269. Cf. Thuc. 4.132.3 : 'Iskhagoras, however, Ameinias and Aristeus came by themselves to Brasidas, commissioned by the Lacedaemonians to oversee the situation, and, quite illegally, they brought with them from Sparta some of their young citizens who were to be placed as governors (*arkhontes*) of the cities instead of entrusting them to just anybody. They placed Klearidas son of Kleonymos at Amphipolis and Pasetilidas son of Hegesandros at Torone.'

¹⁸ Thuc. 5.57.2; Xen. *HG* 4.7.3, concerning Agesipolis in 388. When this king took the field for Olynthos, he received much money from the Phliasians, and thanked them.

¹⁹ See, for instance, Rice 1974, 171–5.

²⁰ Piccirilli 1974, 60–4 argued in favour of a moderate oligarchic regime, but the scant information we have points to a democracy with few oligarchic elements.

²¹ Cf. Aineias the Tactician who describes useful steps in such a situation: 1.3, 4, 6; 5.1; 11; 22.7. For the aims of the Spartans, Diodorus 15.19.3–4: the same year as Phoibidas was sent to help Amyntas against the Olynthians, the Lacedaemonians 'also sent out another army against the Phliasians and, victorious in the battle, they compelled them to

submit to their rule (ἠνάγκασαν ὑποταγῆναι τοὺς Φλιουντίους τοῖς Λακεδαιμονίοις)'. Sparta's kings disagreed on policy: Agesipolis wished to have the peace settlements respected because Sparta was in ill repute; but 'Agesilaos, by nature a man of action and fond of war, yearned for full powers over the Greeks (τῆς τῶν Ἑλλήνων δυναστείας)'. Note that, for Diodorus, *dynasteia* was the same as tyranny, that is to say a power without laws.

²² We know of such cases elsewhere, for instance at Halikarnassos some time between 475 and 450 (ML 32; *Nomima* I, 19; cf. Ruzé 1988); at Athens in 403 (cf. Loening 1987, ch. II); in Tegea after the edict from Alexander (cf. Heisserer, 1980, ch. 8).

²³ See Loraux 1997, 252–4.

²⁴ The fact that no advice had been taken from the Assembly or the League shows how the Spartan institutions worked at that time; it was very different during the Peloponnesian War; cf. Ruzé 1997, 187–202.

²⁵ This Procles will plead at Athens in favour of the Lacedaemonians when they are at war with the Arcadians in 369 (*HG* 6.5.38), and again the same year, in favour of an alliance between Athens and Sparta (*HG* 7.1.11).

²⁶ Unfortunately, Phleious had relied on its friendship with the other king, Agesipolis, but he was now at Olynthos. See Smith 1953/4, 279–80.

²⁷ It was very difficult to make a siege absolutely complete, and Xenophon makes it clear that these men went out in very small groups, maybe one by one, and that they were integrated into Sparta's force as they came (ὁπότε γὰρ ἐξίοιεν), *HG* 5.3.17.

²⁸ *HG* 7.2.1–23. Other attacks were repelled in 368 and 366.

²⁹ de Ste Croix 1981, 608 n. 49, rightly challenged Legon's assertion (1967, 335–7) that it was a democratic army; only the oligarchs are then 'citizens' in the full sense and their number, over 1,000, is sufficient against their adversaries (cf. *HG* 5.3.17).

³⁰ Tod 144 = *SEG* XXIX, 90, ll. 29–30.

³¹ I agree with Hodkinson, 2000, 151–2, who thinks that it was necessary for a political leader such as Agesilaos to use some *xenoi* as suppliants in the Spartan assembly, in order to seem to leave the decision to the Spartans themselves, 'without appearing over-mighty'.

³² Pausanias 4.17.2: 'The Peloponnesians were the first of whom we know to give bribes to an enemy, and the first who made victory in war a matter of purchase.'

³³ In Phleious, but also in Thebes in 382 (Xen. *HG* 5.2.25–36). Xenophon suggests in 5.4.1 that the misfortunes of the Spartans in Boeotia were their punishment for having violated the Thebans' autonomy – a strange way of thinking for one who had approved of many other violations.

³⁴ Cf. Xen. *HG* 5.2.9: 'For not only were there in the city many kinsmen of the exiles and other people who were friendly to them, but also, as is indeed usual in most cities, some who desired a change of government and therefore wanted to bring back the exiles.'

³⁵ The external policy of the Spartans, even inside the League, rested often on 'friends' in the cities: Cartledge 1987, 242 f., insists on the confusion between foreign affairs and private bonds. For Xenophon, *philetaireia* is an important matter.

³⁶ That combined with a political ideology founded on a strong class consciousness: for the rich, merit and power. But we must remember that the oligarchs thought the best regime for any city was the government of the few, as is argued, for instance, by Cawkwell 1976, 73–7.

[37] For instance, Athens in 507: Kleomenes and Isagoras, his guest-friend (Hdt. 5.70); Corinth in 394/3, when the Corinthians Pasimelos and Alkimenes conspired with the Spartan polemarch, Praxitas (*HG* 4.4.7–8); Thebes in 382: the Theban Leontiades and the Spartan Phoibidas (*HG* 5.2.25 f.). Yet some Spartan leaders , like king Pausanias, were well connected with leading democrats.

[38] Some authors, as Chroust 1954, think that partisan ideology prevailed over patriotism; but this is no more than the ordinary cowardice of men threatened by a stronger enemy.

[39] *HO* 7.2.

[40] Thuc. 5.105.4; Plut., *Alc.* 31.8.

[41] Some subversive attempts failed because Sparta refused the adventure, or because of the traitors' clumsiness (so Elis in 399, *HG* 2.2.27–9), or because of Sparta's enemies inside the city (so Athens in 457, Thuc 1.107.4–6). On the other hand, during wars, the Lacedaemonians made mistakes because they ignored the mentality and feelings of local people: Polydamas in Mende, Klearkhos at Byzantion in 408 (*HG* 1.3.14–20), or Salaithos at Mytilene in 428/7 (Thuc. 3.27–28). It was better to have a manageable local power.

[42] An example: people exiled for taking the Athenian side were welcomed in Athens (cf. Cartledge 1987, 296), but Sparta did not do the same for its supporters, unless it had at its disposal an abandoned site (for instance at Plataia, Thuc. 3.68) or a small fort, as for the Eleians (*HG* 3.2.29).

[43] There was no help for the Four Hundred in 411; and so the pursuit of the war, combined with the suspicion provoked by the construction of the fort of Eetioneia, led to the downfall of the oligarchs: Thuc. 8.71 and 90–2; Xen., *HG* 2.3.45. Again in 404/3, Pausanias understood that the Thirty were not an effective instrument for Sparta; they were abandoned to the Athenians (*HG* 2.3.35–41).

Bibliography

ML	R. Meiggs and D. Lewis, *A Selection of Greek Historical Inscriptions to the End of the Fifth Century* BC, Oxford, 1998.
Nomima	H. van Effenterre and F. Ruzé, *Nomima. Recueil d'inscriptions politiques et juridiques de l'archaïsme grec,* I et II, École Française de Rome, 1994–1995.
SEG	*Supplementum Epigraphicum Graecum,* Leiden and Amsterdam, in progress.
Tod	M.N. Tod, *A Selection of Greek Historical Inscriptions, II,* Oxford, 1948.

Bradeen, D.W.
1960   'The popularity of the Athenian Empire', *Historia* 9, 256–69.
Cartledge, P.
1979   *Sparta and Lakonia. A regional history; 1300–362 BC,* London.
1987   *Agesilaos and the Crisis of Sparta,* London.
Cawkwell, G.L.
1976   'Agesilaus and Sparta', *CQ* 26, 62–84.
Chroust, A.H.
1954   'Treason and patriotism in ancient Greece', *Journal of the History of Ideas,* 15.

David, E.

    1986a 'The oligarchic revolution in Argos, 417 BC', *AC* 55, 113–24.

    1986b 'Aeneas Tacticus, 11.7–10 and the Argive revolution of 370 BC', *AJP* 107, 343–9.

de Ste Croix G.E.M.

    1954 'The character of the Athenian Empire', *Historia* 3, 1–41.

    1981 *The Class Struggle in the Ancient Greek War*, London.

Heisserer, A.J.

    1980 *Alexander and the Greeks. The epigraphic evidence*, Norman, Okla.

Herman, G.

    1987 *Ritualised Friendship and the Greek City*, Cambridge.

Hodkinson, S.

    2000 *Property and Wealth in Classical Sparta*, London and Swansea.

Legon, R.P.

    1967 'Phliasian politics and policy in the early fourth century', *Historia* 16, 324–37.

Loening, T.C.

    1987 *The reconciliation agreement of 403/2 BC in Athens*, Hermes Einz., 53.

Loraux, N.

    1997 *La cité divisée*, Paris.

Losada, L.A.

    1972 *The Fifth Column in the Peloponnesian War*, Suppl. Mnemosyne, Leiden.

Mitchell, L.G.

    1997 *Greeks Bearing Gifts. The public use of private relationships in the Greek world, 435–323 BC,* Cambridge.

Piccirilli, L.

    1974 'Fliunte e il presunto colpo di stato democratico', *ASNSP*, III, iv 1, 57–70.

Piérart, M.

    1995 'Chios entre Athènes et Sparte. La contribution des exilés de Chios à l'effort de guerre lacédémonien pendant la guerre du Péloponnèse: *IG* V 1, 1+ (*SEG* XXXIX 370)', *BCH* 119, 253–82.

Quinn, T.J.

    1964 'Thucydides and the unpopularity of the Athenian Empire', *Historia* 13, 257–66.

Rice, D.G.

    1974 'Agesilaus, Agesipolis and Spartan politics, 386–379 BC', *Historia* 23, 164–82.

Ruzé, F.

    1988 'La cité, les particuliers et les terres: installations ou retours de citoyens en Grèce archaïque', *Ktema* 23, 181–9.

    1997 *Délibération et pouvoir dans la cité grecque, de Nestor à Socrate*, Paris.

Seager, R.

    1994 'The Corinthian War' and 'The King's Peace and the Second Athenian Confederacy', in D.M. Lewis et al. (eds.) *The Cambridge Ancient History,* VI, Cambridge, chs. 4 and 6.

Smith, R.E.

    1953/4 'The opposition to Agesilaus' foreign policy', *Historia* 2, 274–88.

Starr, C.G.
   1974   *Political Intelligence in Classical Greece*, Leiden.
Whitehead, D.
   1990   *Aineias the Tactician: How to survive under siege. Translated with introduction and commentary*, Oxford.
Yates, D.C.
   2005   'The archaic treaties between the Spartans and their allies', *Classical Quarterly* 55, 65–76.

10

WHY DID SPARTA NOT DESTROY
ATHENS IN 404, OR IN 403 BC?

Anton Powell

Athens in 404 was utterly defeated, starved out and at Sparta's mercy. Again, in 403, Sparta stood in control over the city. Why did the Spartans on both occasions decide not to destroy their great enemy? This is something which has interested scholars too rarely.[1] Perhaps most historians see Athens' survival as unsurprising and easily explicable in the circumstances. I believe that such a view would be wrong. Athens, as I shall argue, in 404–3 was very close to complete destruction. The Athenians were being reasonable when, in Xenophon's words, 'they thought they would be sold as slaves' (ᾤοντο...ἀνδραποδισθήσεσθαι, *Hell.* 2.2.14) or put to death (ibid. 2.2.3, 10).

Perhaps our sources have been misleading. The two main authorities for the way Athens survived are Xenophon's *Hellenica* and Plutarch's *Life of Lysandros*. I shall argue that the man most likely to have erased Athens from the map was Lysandros. If so, we can think of reasons why neither Xenophon nor Plutarch might want to say much on that subject. Both writers were embarrassed. Xenophon is notorious for how little he mentions Lysandros. Xenophon himself was compromised, in the eyes of his fellow Athenians. Exiled for taking the Spartan side against his own city, Xenophon was a friend of king Agesilaos. And Agesilaos had been Lysandros' protégé. Lysandros' influence had done much to help the irregular process by which Agesilaos became king; Xenophon makes this clear in the *Hellenica* (3.3.3; cf. Plut. *Lys.* 22.6, 10–13). But when writing a different text, the laudatory biography *Agesilaos*, he chose not to name Lysandros (note especially the silence at 1.5). If Lysandros, the patron of Agesilaos, had been remembered as wanting to destroy Athens, Xenophon might well prefer not to advertise that. It suited Xenophon to emphasize that it was other Greeks, Corinthians and Thebans especially, who had argued for Athens to be demolished and its people to be sold as slaves (*Hell.* 2.2.19–20). Sparta, in contrast, had decided to save Athens. In later decades that memory, simplified, became more and more valuable for Spartan diplomacy, as a declining Sparta increasingly needed Athenian help (e.g. Xen. *Hell*. 6.5.35–6).

And Plutarch? He handles Lysandros with horror – a fitting parallel for an embarrassing Roman, Sulla. Plutarch shows us with emphasis that Lysandros at the fall of the Athenian empire carried out 'an uncounted slaughter of democrats' in cities which had belonged to that empire (ἦν δὲ καὶ τῶν ἄλλων ἐν ταῖς πόλεσι δημοτικῶν φόνος οὐκ ἀριθμητός, *Lys*.19.4). He presided over many of these throat-cuttings in person (*Lys*. 13.7; 19.4), and was helped in doing so by the deceptive use of religious oaths (*Lys*. 8.5; 19.3; cf. Nepos *Lys*. 2 and Polyain. 1.45.4). Why was there no such massacre at Athens, the source of this widespread *dēmokratia*? If, as I believe, Lysandros at first wanted to destroy Athens – before he was overruled by other Spartans – the pressure on Sparta from Thebans, Corinthians and others to destroy Athens would have been, in retrospect, all the more disturbing for Plutarch, because closer to having succeeded. Plutarch was a Boiotian, but also under the Roman Principate a singer of the glories of Greece generally. It was bad enough for him that his Boiotia had taken the wrong side, the barbarians' side, in the Persian Wars of 480–79. Here was Boiotia again taking the wrong side *sub specie aeternitatis*. Plutarch's emotional investment in this question, of whether his Boiotia had threatened the survival of glorious Athens, is obvious – as we shall shortly see. A few months after Thebes had pressed for Athens to be destroyed, the Thebans changed policy (cf. D.S. 14.6.3). Now, in 403, they helped the Athenian democrats against Sparta's interest. And Plutarch is much happier. After reporting sentimental praises of Athens in an earlier chapter (15.4), he excitedly eulogizes the pro-Athenian actions of Thebes. Thebes was now doing thoroughly Greek and philanthropic things (Ἑλληνικὰ καὶ φιλάνθρωπα), things 'worthy of, indeed closely akin to, the actions of Herakles and Dionysos' (πρεποντὰ καὶ ἀδελφὰ ταῖς Ἡρακλέους καὶ Διονύσου πράξεσιν, *Lys*. 27.6–7) – two supernatural figures carefully chosen, each for his close link with Boiotia.

So, on the process by which Sparta decided to spare Athens, both our main sources are seriously disappointing. This was perhaps the most important decision that Sparta would ever make. Thucydides spent much of his first book trying to explain why Sparta had gone to war with Athens; modern scholarship has followed with its own abundant literature on that question. Yet the strangely serene conclusion of the war is passed over relatively briefly, in ancient times and in our own. To be sure, we know – from Xenophon – of how the Spartans destroyed Athens' Long Walls to the music of flute girls (*Hell*. 2.2.23, cf. 20, and Plut. *Lys*. 15.5). That piece of knowledge reflects values which from the start have shaped accounts of the period 404–3. The psychology known now as journalistic is evidently far older than journalism.

Not only do the flute-girls suggest glamorous sex, in the way beloved of journalists; more importantly, like journalists, our historians from Xenophon onwards privilege change (especially violent change) over continuity. The Long Walls are mentioned now, because abruptly destroyed. On the other hand, Athens' surrounding wall, the *peribolos*, is not mentioned (Xen. *Hell.* 2.2.20, cf. Plut. *Lys.* 14.8).² It evidently survived (cf. Xen. *Hell.* 2.4.37). Yet that survival, I suggest, is worthy of note. Shortly after the Persian Wars, the Spartan authorities had schemed to prevent the construction of the *peribolos*, and had been duped, and aggrieved, as the wall was raised in their despite (Thuc. 1.89.3–92). There might, then, be a special and symbolic motive for choosing to do what Sparta was to do after other successful invasions of Greek territories (Elis shortly after the Peloponnesian War, Mantineia in 385): to consolidate (and advertise) success by removing the walls of conquered towns.³ Again, the survival of the Athenian wall in 404 meant that Sparta was deciding against the dispersal into villages which was to be used some twenty years later in the case of Mantineia. We should, therefore, resist any temptation to think that the non-destruction of Athens' wall is a non-event, and that to discuss it is to perform a sort of *histoire non-événementielle*. Unless we think journalistically, the survival of the *peribolos* was an event, the result almost certainly of deliberation. And so was the non-destruction, the survival, of Athens itself.

In 404 Sparta, we are told, even passed a resounding public compliment to its defeated enemy. Xenophon records that, when Sparta's allies, Corinthians, Thebans 'and many others of the Greeks' gathered in Lakonia and clamoured for the utter destruction (ἐξαιρεῖν) of Athens, the Spartans answered by saying that they 'would not sell into slavery a Greek city which had done a great good service at the time of Greece's greatest danger' – during the Persian Wars, that is (*Hell.* 2.2.20). In Xenophon, Sparta's position on this appears monolithic. In reality the decision on how to treat Athens in 404 had surely been controversial within Sparta; a single, agreed, position would have been worked out in advance to present to the visiting allied delegations. The latter were hardly to be allowed to open a visible division within the hegemonic power, at Sparta. In 403, how to treat Athens was again to be deeply controversial within Sparta, but this time more obviously. Spartan imperial policy in this period was, as we shall see, viciously divided.

We do get some precise hints on controversy, within the Sparta of 404. Plutarch in his *Lysandros* suggests tantalizingly that 'some' (ἔνιοι) report that *andrapodismos*, literal slavery, for Athens was proposed to a meeting of the Spartan alliance. The logic of the passage suggests that the proposal may have come from the Spartan side, as part of Lysandros' reaction – which is mentioned just previously – to Athens' alleged slowness in carrying out the

terms of surrender. This meeting of the alliance was the one at which the
Theban Erianthos asked for Athens to be rased to the ground (κατασκάψαι),
and Attica converted into a sheep-farm (*Lys.* 15.3, cf. Isok. 14.31). But
Plutarch does not pursue this embarrassing matter. Instead he continues the
report with a tale of how the leaders of the victorious allies had a party with
wine, at which someone sang some lines of Euripides and everyone cheerfully
agreed that it would be a terrible thing to destroy the glorious city which had
produced such fine fellows (ibid.). One sees the difference between writing
history and writing heritage. There is another brief report, which Plutarch
gives but dismisses as a cosmetic fraud (εὐπρεπείας χάριν οὗτος ὁ λόγος
πέπλασται, *Lys.* 14.6–7): Lysandros sent a message to the ephors as follows:

'Athens is captured' (ἁλώκαντι ταὶ Ἀθᾶναι),

and they replied,

'Right. But having captured it is enough' (ἀρκεῖ τό γε ἑαλώκειν).

We do not know why Plutarch dismissed this as a forgery. But, even if
a forgery, it may preserve a valid tradition. It was one which, according
to Plutarch, was current among the Spartans themselves (Λακεδαιμονίων
ἐστὶν ἀκοῦσαι λεγόντων). Some of the latter seemingly believed that, in
his treatment of Athens, Lysandros had needed to be restrained by fellow
citizens.

Then there is the report of Pausanias the Periegete. He writes (3.8.6) that
after the battle of Aigospotamoi Lysandros, and king Agis, on their own
initiative and against the sworn agreement of the Spartan state, proposed
to Sparta's allies to 'cut out Athens from the root' (ἐκκόψαι προρρίζους τὰς
Ἀθήνας). In context, the primary focus is on Agis, of whom Pausanias is
giving a brief biography. So it is interesting that here the name of Lysandros
is mentioned first.[4]

In these three reports there are some significant points of agreement.
Pausanias' story shares with Plutarch both the idea of physical eradica-
tion ('cutting out from the root', 'rasing to the ground') and the setting,
a meeting of the Spartan alliance *after* the agreement of surrender terms. And
Pausanias' account agrees with the implication of the Spartans' tale which
Plutarch reports, in that both distinguish – explicitly in the case of Pausanias,
implicitly in the case of the story told by Plutarch's Spartans – the aggression
of Lysandros from the relative moderation of other Spartan authorities.

Division between Spartans, on the question how to treat Athens, is even
clearer at the time when the Thirty fell, in 403. Lysandros moved against
Athens. He had secured a large sum of money from the Spartan authorities, 100 talents, to hire mercenaries to support the Thirty (Lys. 12.59, Xen.

Hell. 2.4.28). The Thirty were Sparta's chosen regime, appointed in 404 with Lysandros' approval (Xen. *Hell.* 2.3.13–14, Plut. *Lys.* 15.6). Now, in 403, he himself was appointed harmost for the area, and his brother Libys held, in name, the mighty command of *nauarkhos*. Firm action was planned, by Lysandros, against the Athenian democrats. But then king Pausanias of Sparta appeared with the regular Spartan army, overruled Lysandros, and agreed to the exclusion from Athens of the Thirty (Xen. *Hell.* 2.4.29–43). The lamentable Athenian democrats, Sparta's ancestral enemies, were repaid for their violent resistance to Sparta's agents, the Thirty. How was their action requited, these uncontrollables who had refused to obey Sparta even after Aigospotamoi and after the formal peace treaty? By being allowed, by king Pausanias and the Spartan authorities, to resume governing Athens. We read, without surprise, that Pausanias was subsequently put on trial at Sparta (Paus. 3.5.2, cf. Plut. *Lys.* 21.7); the court decided for Pausanias, by a *small* majority.[5] We could guess what position Lysandros himself took, Lysandros, the author of 'uncounted slaughter of democrats'. But we do not have to guess. After Lysandros' death in 395, king Pausanias was put on trial again, blamed by Lysandros' faction for their man's death; this time we are told of the further accusation – no doubt coming also from Lysandros' angry partisans – that Pausanias had freed the democrats of Athens after capturing them (in 403) in the Peiraieus (Xen. *Hell.* 3.5.25). There is little doubt: if Lysandros had had his wish, those democrats would have been treated very differently.

History has remembered Sparta's generous words, about sparing Athens out of respect for its former services against Persia. But public words from the Spartans, especially when addressed to non-Spartans, were above all instruments of diplomacy. We remember how Xenophon praises king Agesilaos for completely outdoing Tissaphernes in deception, once war existed (*Ages.* 1.17). Agesilaos' old lover, Lysandros, was famously supposed to have said that one should deceive children with toys, and adults with religious oaths (Plut. *Lys.* 8.4–5). In understanding Spartans, it is especially important to study what they *do*, even more than what they – reportedly – say. And there is one episode in 405–4 which may show us, from Lysandros' actions, what he was planning to do to Athens. After Aigospotamoi and before Athens' surrender, there was no time for Lysandros to waste. With the illness, then death, of the Great King Darius II (early in 404), there was now a question whether Lysandros would be in a position to continue to exploit his vital partnership with the Persian prince Kyros. Consequently Lysandros' personal position among Spartans was less strong than before. He needed to get to Athens as soon as possible, not just to make his strategic contribution, but to have his name inscribed for ever on Athens' surrender. It would have been a tragedy for Lysandros personally if he had been replaced as commander before the surrender, or if for any reason Athens had surrendered to other Spartans, in his absence. And yet he delayed in moving to Athens. What did he do? (Chronology is usually a problem in this period, without Thucydides; but we have here perhaps our least bad guide, Xenophon.) Lysandros went to the isle of Aigina – en route and close to Athens, and there 'gathered together as many [sc. of the former population of the island] as he could' and formally gave back to them the territory from which Athens had earlier evicted them, a process perhaps requiring a little time. Xenophon says in this connection that Lysandros also gave back their former territory to the people of Melos 'and to the others who had been deprived of their land' – by the Athenians (*Hell.* 2.2.9). Why spend any time doing this now, rather than a little later? These actions were widely popular, but after Aigospotamoi Lysandros was not short of acclaim. Indeed, he was hailed as a god (Douris, at Plut. *Lys.* 18.5). Was Lysandros preparing, in advance, justification for an action somewhat unusual, if only in its scale? By advertising the cases of Aigina, Melos and the rest, at a busy time and with Athens still resisting, the Spartan admiral was making sure that Greece generally remembered why Athenians themselves deserved to lose their territory, their freedom – or their lives.

Athens, even in 404, will still have contained many tens of thousands of people, of various statuses. Destroying it would make a piteous spectacle. Spartans knew how to manipulate a spectacle for political purposes (Powell 1989), and were familiar with charges that they themselves on occasion had treated other Greeks cruelly (Thuc. 3.32.2). If the fate of Athens was not itself to become, as a negative spectacle, a moral wound for Sparta, it was worth preparing public opinion by recalling Athens' sins. The connection between Athens' past treatment of Melos, Aigina, Skione and the rest, and the Athenians' fate now, was in the forefront of minds, according to Xenophon. He tells, with some repetition, that when the news of Aigospotamoi reached Athens, Athenians expected to suffer what they had made those others suffer (*Hell.* 2.2.3, 10): that is, expulsion, or enslavement, or massacre.

So, why did Sparta – in spite of Lysandros – spare Athens, and treat her so gently? First, to Sparta's public explanation – Athens' good war-service in defence of the Greeks against the Persians: did Sparta feel strongly about this?[6] We should look at what Sparta did in 427, when she had captured Plataia after a siege. The Plataians argued that they should be spared because of their excellent war-service against the Persians (Thuc. 3.54.3–4). And the Spartans refused to accept that defence. Sparta insisted on asking the Plataian captives just one question: 'Have you done any service to the Spartans and their allies in *this* war?' (Thuc. 3.52.4; 68.1). The Plataians, of course, had no answer: the Spartans then killed them; all the men, without exception, says Thucydides (3.68.1). The women were enslaved (3.68.2). Thucydides writes that Sparta's negative attitude towards Plataia existed almost entirely because of Thebes; Sparta thought Thebes would be useful to Sparta in the war (3.68.4) – and Thebes hated Plataia. Sparta massacred from *Realpolitik*, therefore.

The Spartan procedure here, before execution, of asking an unanswerable question may be important for us. The procedure seems to have been carefully thought out: the prisoners from Plataia were kept alive while five judges were brought from Sparta to deal with them (Thuc. 3.52.3). The Spartans wanted the condemned men in effect to condemn themselves. Sparta loved the moral spectacle, and loved exemplary death. Spartan anecdotes are an analogue of Athenian tragedy: both genres privilege instructive death in the cause of official morality. *La belle mort spartiate* could be negative as well as positive. Not just virtuous soldiers but also condemned offenders had their part to play, in dying as fine moral examples. Stories flourished about the end of regent Pausanias as well as that of king Leonidas. And Lysandros in particular thought like this. After Aigospotamoi, faced with a host of prisoners of war from the Athenian fleet, Lysandros called together his allies and 'ordered them to consider the fate of the prisoners'. 'Many accusations' were made against the Athenians. Into this theatre of condemnation Lysandros introduced the Athenian commander, Philokles, and (before cutting his throat) asked him a question which may have deliberately played on Athens' own judicial procedure of requiring a convicted person to propose his own penalty: 'What punishment do you deserve, you who have introduced illegal behaviour towards the Greeks?' (Xen. *Hell.* 2.1.31–2). Plutarch, citing a promising source, Theophrastos, shows Philokles bravely doing some counter-theatre and (as we may see) himself in turn adopting Spartan method. Philokles refused to respond to Lysandros' question, and, as a good Athenian, said, 'Don't play the prosecutor where there is no jury' (μὴ κατηγορεῖν ὧν οὐδείς ἐστι δικαστής). But then Philokles (like the Spartans combing their hair at Thermopylai) made himself look his best: he washed, put on a shining garment and walked 'at the head of his fellow citizens, first to the slaughter' (*Lys.* 13.1–2). He understood, and resisted to the last, Sparta's desire to advertise Athenian guilt. And he played Sparta's own game of *la belle mort* against her. There evidently followed a general massacre, on which neither Xenophon nor Plutarch is quite explicit (though cf. Xen. *Hell.* 2.2.3); contrast the stark notices of massacre with which Thucydides concludes certain episodes. According to Plutarch, the number of Athenians condemned (and, he leaves us to infer, executed) was 3000 (*Lys.*13.1). These two cases of victors' justice, at Plataia and after Aigospotamoi, may confirm what Lysandros was trying to do later on Aigina. There, in a similar but even more ambitious procedure, he publicized the interstate crimes of the Athenians as a community, over a far longer period, several decades – preparing the way, perhaps, for a far greater massacre, of the Athenian male citizen community.

What reasons do modern scholars most often give for Sparta's decision to spare Athens? They are of two kinds, and – as with the massacre at Plataia – they both concern Thebes. Sparta, it is suggested, in 404 feared the rise of Thebes and thought an empty Attica might fall under Theban control. Paul Cartledge and Donald Kagan[7] have each collected cases where Thebes and Sparta in recent decades had had conflicting interests. Spartans might, perhaps, have wished to avoid giving this menacing Thebes a chance – as Cartledge puts it (1987, 275–6) – to 'step into Athens' shoes in central Greece'. Better to leave Athens a middle-sized power, what Cartledge describes as 'etiolated', as a rival to check the growth of Thebes (1987, 275–80). Indeed, Sparta might hope to control a weakened Athens, to gain an obedient ally (cf. Xen. *Hell.* 2.4.30). This explanation might work for 404, when Athens and Thebes were bitterly opposed, as usual. But events in 403, as we shall see, offer an interesting control.

Hindsight, as ever, is seductive. Unlike the Spartans, we know and cannot forget that Thebes would *one day* crush Sparta for ever. Just possibly, in reconstructing Sparta's predictions in 404, we may be too liable to what Diodorus, in another connection, called *Leuktrika phronēmata*. Yes, Thebes might step into Athens' shoes, might repopulate Attica. As for those twin evils, *dēmokratia* and naval power: Thebes might *just* become pro-democratic and unleash the force of *dēmokratia* in the Greek cities, might even – against precedent – become a naval power. But such developments were unlikely. Athens, on the other hand, was still to an important degree in her own old shoes, already populating Attica, already with pre-eminent and ingrained experience of democratic and naval methods. We should ask, which was more impressive *at the time*: recent friction between Sparta and Thebes, never amounting to war, or memories of sixty years of intermittent war between Sparta and Athens – war which, some twenty years earlier, had brought upon Sparta near-panic (Thuc. 4.55.3 f.) and then the qualified defeat of 421? Athens might be a useful check on Thebes; but she might instead combine with Thebes against Sparta. Indeed, in 403, when Pausanias made his mild settlement of Athens and put the democrats back in charge, Thebes was already combining with those democrats against Sparta – and Pausanias probably knew it (cf. Lys. 12.58). If the threat of Thebes had loomed so large in Spartan minds, why leave Athens available as an ally for the Thebans? The question why Sparta let Athens survive in 404 is similar to the question why Sparta let Athens survive again in 403. But there is the important difference, that in 403 Athens' democrats had been defiant, against the Spartan interest and in collaboration with Thebes. And yet Sparta persisted in her gentleness, and even abandoned the idea of controlling Athens with a garrison. Sparta's grounds for predicting the utility of Athens against Thebes are not the same, not common, to the two decisions to spare Athens. We should perhaps look instead for a prominent consideration which *was* common to both occasions, to 404 and 403.

A proper explanation of the survival of Athens is unlikely to be simple. No doubt Spartan worries about Thebes counted for something. So did anti-Persian sentiment in some Spartans. While Lysandros was willing to work closely with prince Kyros of Persia, his rival navarch, the Spartan Kallikratidas, had shown angry hostility towards the barbarian (Xen. *Hell.* 1.6.6–11, Plut. *Lys.* 6). That anger fitted with Spartan pride in their own history. A late source, Justin (5.8.4), reports that Sparta refused to destroy Athens now because that would 'tear out one of Greece's two eyes'. The optical metaphor may help. In looking at Athenian achievements against Persia, Sparta saw her own glorious past reflected. She could admire herself in the glass of Athenian opinion. The literary works of Athenian (qualified) lakonophilia which now survive, Xenophon's *Constitution of the Spartans*, Plato's *Republic* and *Laws*, were in the future. But Kritias' praise of Sparta may already have been known. Perikles in the Funeral Speech had played to a high image that Athenians evidently had of Sparta.[8] Kimon, in naming his son 'Lakedaimonios' (Thuc. 1.45.2), presumably expected not to provoke Athenian opinion, but to an extent to reflect it. So when in 404 Athenian diplomats, such as Theramenes, pleaded with Sparta for the life of their community, they could deploy sincere flattery expressed collectively over generations, effective flattery, since a compliment from long-mighty Athens was a compliment indeed. Thucydides conceived of the idea, which he attributes to Athenian speakers in the Melian Dialogue, that Spartan vindictiveness towards a defeated Athens might be limited by a certain shared attitude (if not fellow feeling):

> We are not alarmed at the thought of what might happen if our empire should come to an end. It is not imperial powers, which is what the Spartans are too, who are so severe on their defeated opponents...; rather, it is former subjects if they revolt and overpower their former rulers...   (5.91.1)

Now, whether this could have been written before the fall of Athens in 404, is uncertain (Gomme ad loc. suggested that the remarks were intrusive in their context and therefore possibly an anachronistic reflection of Thucydides' own, inspired by thoughts of Sparta's restraint in 404. Gomme's continuator, Andrewes, disagreed.) But for those who, like the present writer (2001, 182–6), consider the Melian Dialogue to be meant to show the Athenian

speakers as being fundamentally right in their generalizations and predictions, the present passage might suggest that, in Thucydides' view, behind
Sparta's advertised hostility to Athens there operated some complaisance.

The personal politics of king Pausanias may have had a certain influence
in producing settlement without massacre. When in exile, in 385, he exerted
himself with success to protect the lives of defeated democratic leaders in
Mantineia with whom, in Xenophon's pointed phrase, he had 'very friendly
relations indeed' (*Hell.* 5.2.3, 6). On that occasion, he was able to work
through the power of his son, king Agesipolis. Pausanias' own power as king
and thus as supreme general in 403 would have been great. But his policies
had to be chosen with an eye to their acceptability at home. His judgment
in that area ultimately proved defective, whence his exile (in 395). But in the
jealous climate of Spartan politics he would know that his public decisions
could not be eccentric; in the event his settlement of Athenian affairs in
403, though subsequently challenged at Sparta, did prove (by a narrow
margin) acceptable.

There remains the possibility of religious restraint. The main oracular
centres had sufficient influence over Spartans for Lysandros apparently to
have found them worth seeking to bribe (see below). And it may have been in
part religious scruples which Lysandros, and other Spartans, were addressing
when they carefully advertised the guilt of those they were about to kill. The
formal declarations of war each year against the helots, for which it seems
Aristotle was Plutarch's informant, were reportedly conducted so that the
killing of helots should be *euages*, should not incur religious pollution (*Lyk.*
28.7). There is some ancient testimony to the effect that Delphoi issued
a prophecy to indicate that Athens in 404 should be spared. A scholion
on Aristides (s.341) and a passage of Aelian's *Varia Historia* (4.6) refer to
Delphic advice 'not to destroy (or 'move') the common hearth of Hellas'.
However, this tradition is suggestively late and faint. It comes, so far as we
can trace it, from the Roman Imperial period, by which time Athens had
become the capital of Greek heritage and its destruction (especially by other
Greeks) an almost inconceivable offence against civilization. In this matter
the silence of Plutarch has some importance. As himself an evoker of Greek
bygone glories, with a special interest in Delphoi (of which he became
a priest), and an intrusive enthusiasm for the idea of *praotēs* (gentleness, self-
control) as imputed to leading figures of the hellenic past,[9] he would quite
likely have exploited prominently any credible account known to him of
Delphoi's having used its influence in 404 to secure the salvation of Athens.
That he does nothing of the kind when he treats – with intense interest, as
we have seen – the crucial decision of 404, suggests that he knew of nothing
in this episode which was significantly to the credit of his revered Delphoi.

The idea that there might once have been a serious case for destroying Athens was, by the Imperial period, sufficiently exotic to appeal to the contemporary taste for paradoxical exercises in rhetoric. With this engaging scenario would readily arise the question of how Greece's most famous shrine had reacted. It is of interest that the tradition about Athens' peril in 404 persisted for centuries. But that Delphic intervention had been real, let alone highly influential, cannot be assumed. Not only would the idea of religiously-inspired restraint conflict with the fact of massacres which Sparta did carry out during the Peloponnesian War; such restraint would also not explain why Sparta in 404 (as in 403) refrained from taking other, less drastic and perfectly familiar, measures against Athens which could hardly have been criticized on religious grounds. We need a hypothesis which can cover the full, remarkable, scope of Spartan restraint at this period.

Sparta in 404 had a grave financial problem. The city was threatened, as many Spartans saw it, with having far too much money. Our understanding of Sparta's crisis now, concerning money, has been advanced by the work of contemporary scholars – Jacqueline Christien (2002), Thomas Figueira (2002), and most fully Stephen Hodkinson (2000).[10] From their work it emerges that now was the time when Sparta invented, or adjusted, the tradition that Lykourgos had banned the use of coinage (Xen. *Lak. Pol.* 7.5–6, 14.1, 3; D.S. 7.12.8; Plut. *Lys.* 17). Plutarch (ibid.) has unusually full information on a debate at Sparta, in this period: Lysandros was severely criticized for all the money he brought back. Theopompos and Ephoros, as recorded here by Plutarch, each names a different Spartan, Skiraphidas and Phlogidas respectively, as proposing a ban on the bringing of gold and silver coin into Sparta. On the other hand, 'friends of Lysandros' pressed for money to remain legal at Sparta. A compromise is reported: a ban on private ownership of gold and silver coin but permission for the state to use it. In Plutarch's narrative, the debate followed a scandal: Lysandros had sent back sacks of cash and other treasure to Sparta, and Gylippos, strategic hero of the war at Syracuse against Athens, had been caught stealing from it (*Lys.* 16–17.1; cf. D.S. 13.106.8–9). He exiled himself, a good man lost to Sparta.

Worse seems to have followed, though the timing is unclear. One of Lysandros' 'friends and fellow generals' (Plut. *Lys.* 19.7), perhaps his right-hand man, was Thorax. Thorax had commanded victoriously under Lysandros in the Hellespont (Xen. *Hell.* 2.1.18, 28), and, when Lysandros had conquered the most powerful of Athens' allies in the Aegean, Samos, it was Thorax whom he put in charge of it, as harmost (D.S. 14.3.5). When Thorax, this illustrious agent of Spartan victory, came to Sparta, he was put to death, for being caught in possession of silver (Plut. *Lys.* 19.7). The political climate at Sparta just after victory was clearly not one of solidarity and of mutual generosity. How Thorax's death reflected on the position of his chief, Lysandros![11] It is clear that many influential Spartans feared or hated Lysandros, and that in some matters of the highest importance to himself he could not get his own way. The case of an earlier grand victor, Pausanias the regent, comes to mind, as it no doubt did also for Lysandros' Spartan contemporaries (cf. Athen. 543bc).

Here was ferocious faction, intense from personal jealousy (e.g. Xen. *Hell.* 2.4.29) and licensed by public principle, fear for the constitution. In oligarchic Rome there were to be problems when Pompey the Great, using government troops, had made himself the private owner of client kingdoms in the East. In oligarchic England of the eighteenth century, there was fear and jealousy in the establishment when Robert Clive had used the army of the East India Company to enrich himself and other Englishmen, the 'nabobs'. Cross-cultural examples do not yield neatly mathematical *a fortiori* arguments. But, at Sparta, where moderate uniformity was the rule in many areas, it was customary even for the wealthy among the *homoioi* to wear 'clothes such as even any poor man could afford' (Ar. *Pol.* 1294b). Indeed, as Hodkinson's book shows, Spartan society was largely structured to resist the power of private wealth. One can see the extremity of the threat posed by the fortunes now arriving from Lysandros. Shortly after the war's end, more than 470 talents arrived in one consignment (Xen. *Hell.* 2.3.8–9); in another had come 1000 talents (Plut. *Nik.* 28.4), or indeed 1500 (D.S. 13.106.8–9). One could run imperial armies for years with money of that order. And Sparta simply was not used to handling such vast sums. For example, Sparta's day-to-day authorities, the ephors, Aristotle later described as men of little wealth and consequently 'for sale' (ὤνιοι, *Pol.* 1270b); could Lysandros be trusted not to use bribery to control them? He was thought to be willing to bribe religious shrines; the authorities of Zeus Ammon sent formally to Sparta to accuse him of that (D.S. 14.13.3–7, on Delphoi, Dodone and Ammon; Plut. *Lys.*25.3–4, citing Ephoros). And Bommelaer (1981, 205) has rightly suggested that the large deposit left by Lysandros at Delphoi, of nearly 2 talents (Plut. *Lys.* 18.3), was part of a fund, private and personal, for potential bribery of that shrine. Theopompos (ap. Athen. 543bc; Plut. *Lys.* 30.2) indeed wrote that Lysandros was not personally corrupted, not a person given to luxury. But here we should use a distinction provided by the French language. Lysandros may not have been passively corrupt. But he was thought to be a master of active corruption.[12] And in any case the wealth he collected, for himself and others, put him and others in a position to corrupt Sparta. Now, what has this to do with the fate of Athens?

When, shortly before Aigospotamoi, Lysandros and his men captured and plundered Lampsakos in the Hellespont, the results were impressive.

Our tradition remembers the wealth of that town, which its conquerors, Lysandros, Thorax and their soldiers, 'tore apart' (Xen. *Hell.* 2.1.18–19; D.S. 13.104.8). Little Lampsakos at mid-fifth century had paid Athens a steady 12 talents a year in *phoros*. In contrast, what order of plunder would result if Athens were sold – the ancient mistress of an empire, to which Lampsakos had been just one of a host of satellites? No matter what was the state of Athens' *public* finances at the end of a ruinous war. It was private wealth, some of it in the form of treasure which could be hidden, which might do more to enrich a conqueror. Our own information is scant; we happen to know of treasure which survived in the family of the metic Lysias (e.g. Lys. 12.10–11, 19), and Sparta's appointees, the Thirty, certainly believed that extortion was worthwhile (e.g. Lys., ibid.; D.S. 14.5.5–7). But what matters most for present purposes is whether the Spartans, in their state of information, would have *feared* that defeated Athens still contained wealth, in various forms, large enough to pose a threat. And surely the wealth within Attica was enough to have that effect, especially since at the extreme it included a very large population – free and unfree – which might be sold. We think also of Sparta itself later, after Leuktra, its territory ravaged, plundered and drastically reduced by Thebes; and yet, as Hodkinson has shown, there were still individuals able to spend large amounts of wealth on horse-breeding and solid sums on religious offerings (2000, 437, 175, cf. Isok. 6.55). Athens, with more than ten times Sparta's citizen population, would have far more such individuals, whose knowledge of where the wealth lay would enable them to bargain with and corrupt a conqueror, the conqueror on the ground. The Spartans from the 390s had a lively, indeed an institutionalized, awareness of plunder and its significance; from that period, if not earlier, Sparta had officials to sell plunder on the state's behalf, the *laphyropōlai* (Xen. *Hell.* 4.1.26; *Lak.Pol.* 13.11; with Cartledge 1987, 323). Sparta alone, so far as we know, had such officials (Hodkinson 2000, 169). Sparta was perhaps uniquely sensitive to the fact that loot tended to evade public controls, that extortion and bribery from captured populations happened multifariously and in secret. Every Spartan surely knew that no Spartan knew, other than Lysandros, how he had profited from his conquests outside Athens. That he had secreted vast sums was assumed by those suitors for his daughters who notoriously abandoned them at Lysandros' death, when the girls turned out to have no big inheritance (Plut. *Lys.* 30.6). Did Sparta dare to sell Athens, when Lysandros and his faction might profit? Was the predicted fallout of Athenian wealth simply too big for little Sparta to digest? On both occasions when Sparta spared Athens, in 404 and 403, Lysandros was present as a commander. For both occasions we have some evidence that to spare Athenians was not his first wish. If Lysandros was known at Sparta to have wanted

Athens destroyed in 404, such – I suggest – was the fear of him in Sparta that his wishes *for* destruction would have been, for many Spartans, a strong argument *against* destruction. Similarly his desire in 403 to support the Thirty – a scaled-up dekarchy – would have been a reason in itself for other Spartans to prefer a regime for Athens, *dēmokratia*, which in spite of its great and obvious disadvantages from a Spartan viewpoint had one crucial merit: its very diffusion of power meant that *dēmokratia* could not be manipulated by Lysandros as could the dekarchies.[13]

Let us assume, for argument's sake, that some Spartans had moral or sentimental objections about selling Greek citizens, and especially citizens of anti-Persian Athens. Also let us assume that Spartans feared the impression that massacre and enslavement on a vast scale would make on Greek opinion. Nevertheless, Spartans had an established procedure, familiar to Lysandros and his senior colleagues, for avoiding such problems, while still getting large wealth from a captured community: to take its treasure and sell its existing slaves while letting free people stay in place, stay free. Thucydides notes of 412/1 that the Spartan Astyokhos, when dealing with Kos Meropis, preserved the free population while plundering their possessions (Thuc. 8.41.2); by implication the unfree, slaves, were taken. When the anti-Persian Kallikratidas captured Methymna of Lesbos in 406, his troops pillaged but he himself uttered noble words, we are told, about not enslaving Greeks. He let the free people of Methymna go free, while enslaving the Athenian garrison and, more significantly for us, selling for Sparta's benefit the existing slaves (Xen. *Hell.* 1.6.14–15; D.S. 13.76.5). Contrast Kedreiai where all were reportedly enslaved by Lysandros (Xen. *Hell.* 2.1.15), and Iasos, where men citizens are said to have been killed by Lysandros, the others enslaved and the city 'rased to the ground' (κατέσκαψε, D.S. 13.104.7). When Lysandros seized the wealth of Lampsakos, he – in Xenophon's words – 'let go all the free bodies' (Xen. *Hell.* 2.1.19; cf. D.S. 13.104.8). In other words, he sold the existing slaves. If Sparta wished to 'etiolate', rather than destroy, Athens, wished to preserve the decencies of anti-Persian solidarity (cf. Forrest 1968, 121), why not spare the citizens but sell Athens' slaves – and plunder other wealth? Many Athenian slaves had already been taken by king Agis and colleagues (esp. Thuc. 7.27.5). Yet large numbers, especially of female slaves, surely remained. The city's wealth, and its slaves, were evidently not systematically plundered by Spartan-led troops (although one might consider the depredations of the Thirty to be Spartan policy conducted through surrogates; D.S. 14.6.1). Contrast Sparta's action in Elis a few years later, when king Agis captured 'huge numbers of slaves' (ὑπέρπολλα…ἀνδράποδα); with other booty they were, in Xenophon's phrase, 'like a stocking-up for the Peloponnese' (Xen. *Hell.* 3.2.26, 30). And we might guess that this was a financial harvest for Sparta, above all; but by then Lysandros was in eclipse, and no doubt much of the cash mountain of 404 had already been used for imperial purposes such as running a fleet. Athens was an exception: in the immediate aftermath of surrender there was no massacre, no enslavement, no general plundering. In 404 and in 403, when Lysandros was at his height, the wealth of Athens was one harvest Sparta did not want. Indeed, Sparta wanted *not* to have it. The preservation of Sparta's internal harmony, her commitment to avoiding *stasis* at home, took precedence even over the temptation to destroy her greatest external enemy by exploiting, in the way she normally did,[14] – and as Lysandros had just done at Aigospotamoi – an exceptional opportunity to achieve a coup with minimal risk to the lives of her soldiers.

To speculate: in the long term Sparta's decision to spare Athens may have contributed to the sparing of Sparta herself. Thebes in 370 was in a position to attempt to wipe out Sparta, but did not. The Macedonians, after Sellasia (222), could have annihilated the city of Sparta with the utmost ease, but did not. Sparta's action in 404 had avoided fortifying a tradition of annihilating major states. The survival of these two cities, Athens and Sparta, to stimulate and pass on tradition about themselves, is very likely a necessary condition of Hellenic studies' surviving as they do. Living cities generated far more for posterity than the ghosts of Miletos and of Sybaris. There was one Spartan, a certain Eteokles, who reportedly claimed that 'For Greece, *two* Lysandroi would have been unbearable' (Plut. *Lys.* 19.5, Ael. *VH* 11.7). But perhaps it was the very fact of *one* terrifying Lysandros, combined with the village politics of Lakonia, which accidentally enabled the glories of Greece to survive to the present.

Acknowledgements
Versions of this paper were presented in 2004 at the Celtic Conference in Classics at the University of Rennes II, and in 2006 at the École Normale Supérieure, Paris, during my period as *professeur invité* of that institution. I am grateful for criticisms and suggestions made by colleagues on those and other occasions, and for further improvements made by Pierre Carlier and Jacqueline Christien. Especially I wish to thank Francis Prost, for generous and judicious help at ENS; my co-editor Stephen Hodkinson for valuable criticism; and Pierre Brulé, *animateur* at Rennes, for his friendship.

Notes
[1] Distinguished exceptions include Cartledge 1987, Kagan 1987, Lévy 1976.

[2] D.S. 14.3.2 is presumably a garbled abbreviation; compare the fuller 13.107.4.

[3] Elis agreed, under pressure from Sparta, to remove the town-walls of Phea (Xen. *Hell.* 3.2.30; cf. Paus.3.8.5). Sparta ensured that Mantineia in 385 had its wall demolished and was broken up into several, separate communities (Xen. *Hell.* 5.2.7).

⁴ On the other hand, Polyainos (1.45.5) wrote that Lysandros spoke against destroying Athens.

⁵ 15 *gerontes*, including Agis, voted 'guilty'; 14 *gerontes* and 5 ephors 'not guilty'.

⁶ Late in the Peloponnesian War the Spartans had formally accepted Persian control of the Greeks of Asia Minor; references at Cartledge 1987, 187–190.

⁷ Kagan 1987, 405–6.

⁸ Powell 2001, 157–9.

⁹ Martin 1960; Powell 1999, 398.

¹⁰ Hodkinson 2000, index under 'Currency, precious metal'.

¹¹ Plutarch relates the execution of Thorax and the recall of Lysandros to complaints made by the Persian satrap Pharnabazos, a subject on which he has much detail (*Lys.* 20.1–5).

¹² Cf. Plut. *Lyk.* 30.1, Athen. 543bc.

¹³ Hamilton (1979, 300) writes well (citing Xen. *Hell.* 2.4.29, D.S. 14.33.6, Plut. *Lys.* 21.3): 'The one motive on which all the sources agree is the desire of the Spartan government, expressed in the mission of Pausanias, to check Lysander and keep him from a new accretion of power and fame.'

¹⁴ On Sparta's policy of exploiting military *kairos*, Powell 1980.

Bibliography

Bommelaer, J.-F.
  1981   *Lysandre de Sparte: histoire et traditions*, Paris.
Cartledge, P.
  1987   *Agesilaos and the Crisis of Sparta*, London.
Christien, J.
  2002   'Iron money in Sparta: myth and history', in A.Powell and S.Hodkinson (eds.) *Sparta: Beyond the mirage*, London and Swansea, 171–90.
David, E.
  1979   'The pamphlet of Pausanias', *Parola del Passato* 185, 94–116.
  1979/80   'The influx of money into Sparta at the end of the fifth century BC', *Scripta Classica Israelica* 5, 30–45.
Figueira, T.
  2002   'Iron money and the ideology of consumption in Laconia', in Powell and Hodkinson (eds.) *Sparta: Beyond the mirage*, London and Swansea, 137–70.
Forrest, W.G.
  1968   *A History of Sparta c. 950–192 BC*, London.
Hamilton, C.D.
  1979   *Sparta's Bitter Victories. Politics and diplomacy in the Corinthian War*, Ithaca.
Hodkinson, S.
  2000   *Property and Wealth in Classical Sparta*, London and Swansea.
Kagan, D.
  1987   *The Fall of the Athenian Empire*, Ithaca.
Krentz, P.
  1982   *The Thirty at Athens*, Ithaca.

Lévy, E.
 1976   *Athènes devant la défaite de 404. Histoire d'une crise idéologique*, Paris.
Lotze, D.
 1964   *Lysandros und der Peloponnesische Krieg*, Berlin.
Martin, H.
 1960   'The concept of *praotes* in Plutarch's Lives', *GRBS* 3, 65–73.
Parke, H.W.
 1930   'The development of the Second Spartan Empire', *JHS* 50, 37–79.
Powell, A.
 1980   'Athens' difficulty, Sparta's opportunity: causation and the Peloponnesian War', *Antiquité Classique* 49, 87–114.
 1989   'Mendacity and Sparta's use of the visual' in id. (ed.) *Classical Sparta: Techniques behind her success*, London, 173–92.
 1999   'Spartan women assertive in politics? Plutarch's Lives of Agis and Kleomenes', in Hodkinson and Powell (eds.) *Sparta: New perspectives*, London and Swansea, 393–419.
 2001   *Athens and Sparta*, 2nd edn, London.

INDEX

Wherever possible, spellings have been hellenized. Thus 'Kerkyra' not 'Corcyra'.